INTRODUCTION TO COMPUTER ORGANIZATION: ARM

INTRODUCTION TO COMPUTER ORGANIZATION: ARM

An Under-the-Hood Look at Hardware and ARM A64 Assembly

by Robert G. Plantz

no starch press®

San Francisco

Printed in the United States of America

First printing

29 28 27 26 25   1 2 3 4 5

ISBN-13: 978-1-7185-0274-1 (print)
ISBN-13: 978-1-7185-0275-8 (ebook)

 Published by No Starch Press®, Inc.
245 8th Street, San Francisco, CA 94103
phone: +1.415.863.9900
www.nostarch.com; info@nostarch.com

Publisher: William Pollock
Managing Editor: Jill Franklin
Production Manager: Sabrina Plomitallo-González
Production Editor: Rachel Head
Developmental Editors: Annie Choi and Alex Pabàn Freed
Cover Illustrator: Gina Redman
Interior Design: Octopod Studios
Technical Reviewer: Mike Lyle
Copyeditor: Gary Daniel Smith
Proofreader: Debbie Greenberg

Library of Congress Control Number: 2024946402

For customer service inquiries, please contact info@nostarch.com. For information on distribution, bulk sales, corporate sales, or translations: sales@nostarch.com. For permission to translate this work: rights@nostarch.com. To report counterfeit copies or piracy: counterfeit@nostarch.com.

[S]

To my life partner, João Barretto,
who introduced me to the Raspberry Pi,
which led to my writing this book.

About the Author

Bob Plantz got his BS in electrical engineering from UC Berkeley, specializing in control systems and computers. His first job was designing analog electronics for the horizon scanners on the Gemini Space Capsule and the Lunar Entry Module. He then returned to further his education at UC Berkeley, obtaining his PhD in electrical engineering with a specialty in bioengineering. That led to a postdoctoral position at UC San Francisco, where he did research on the auditory brainstem response and wrote software for a Data General Nova 3 minicomputer. Following that, Bob spent several years in industry, where he wrote assembly language on half a dozen different architectures at the software/hardware interface level. He then transitioned into a 21-year university teaching career in computer science at Sonoma State University. He retired from teaching in 2004 and is now enjoying learning new things, not only in high tech, but also expanding his knowledge into other fields. He is a strong believer in finding ways to build a sustainable future here on Earth.

About the Technical Reviewer

Mike Lyle got his start in computer science at Hughes Aircraft, which, despite its name, mostly built military electronics. He designed logic circuits and wrote microcode and assembly programs for a variety of computers to control radar, avionics, and sonar systems. With that knowledge, he worked with a group designing a token ring network at UC Irvine. That led to positions as a professor at UC Berkeley teaching computer design and at Sonoma State University teaching programming, hardware design, networking, and operating systems. Mike is currently retired and enjoying travel and family.

BRIEF CONTENTS

CONTENTS IN DETAIL

3
COMPUTER ARITHMETIC   37

4
BOOLEAN ALGEBRA   53

11
INSIDE THE MAIN FUNCTION   207

12
INSTRUCTION DETAILS   227

13
CONTROL FLOW CONSTRUCTS   243

ACKNOWLEDGMENTS

My work is the result of the help of hundreds of people over the years. The people who've helped me most are the many students I've had in my classes during my two decades of teaching. They asked questions that showed where my explanations were lacking. You, the reader of this book, get to judge whether I've been successful at improving my explanations.

Next, I would like to specifically thank those who directly helped me in the writing of this book. Working with Bill Pollock, the owner of No Starch Press, has been a pleasure. I agree with his ideas of what makes up a good book, and he put together a fantastic team to work with me. I worked directly with Alex Pabàn Freed and Annie Choi as developmental editors, Gary Daniel Smith as copyeditor, Rachel Head as production editor, and Jill Franklin as managing editor. They all contributed significantly to improve the quality of this book. In addition, other people at No Starch Press were working behind the scenes to make this book a reality. I truly appreciate their help.

The technical reviewer from outside No Starch Press, Mike Lyle, did a great job of finding my errors and suggesting improvements to the book.

I would also like to thank my life partner, João Barretto, for his support and encouragement while I spent many hours on my computer.

INTRODUCTION

This book introduces the concepts of how computer hardware works from a programmer's point of view. The hardware is controlled by a set of *machine instructions*. The way these instructions control the hardware is called the *instruction set architecture (ISA)*. A programmer's job is to design a sequence of these instructions that causes the hardware to perform operations to solve a problem.

Nearly all computer programs are written in a high-level language. Some of these languages are general-purpose, and others are geared toward specific applications. But they are all intended to provide a programmer with a set of programming constructs more suitable for solving problems in human terms than working directly with the ISA and the details of the hardware.

Who This Book Is For

Have you ever wondered what's going on "under the hood" when you write a program in a high-level language? You know that computers can be programmed to make decisions, but how do they do that? You probably know that data is stored in bits, but what does that mean when storing a decimal number? My goal in this book is to answer these and many other questions about how computers work. We'll be looking at both the hardware components and the machine-level instructions used to control the hardware.

I'll assume that you know the basics of how to program in a high-level language, but you don't need to be an expert programmer. After discussing the hardware components, we'll look at and write lots of programs in *assembly language*, the language that translates directly into machine instructions.

Writing in assembly language is a tedious, error-prone, time-consuming process, so it should be avoided whenever possible. The best language for most programming projects on a Raspberry Pi is Python, which is included with Raspberry Pi OS and has excellent support for electronics projects. Python is very good at isolating us from the tedium of writing in assembly language. However, our goal here is to study programming concepts, not to create applications, so we'll mainly be using C as our high-level language.

About This Book

The guidelines I followed in creating this book are:

- Learning is easier if it builds on concepts you already know.

- Real-world hardware and software make a more interesting platform for learning theoretical concepts.

- The tools used for learning should be inexpensive and readily available.

The Programming in the Book

This book is based on the AArch64 architecture, which is the 64-bit version of the ARM architecture. It supports both the 64-bit A64 and 32-bit A32 instruction sets.

All the programming in the book was done using the GNU programming environment running under the 64-bit Raspberry Pi OS. All the programs have been tested on both my Raspberry Pi 3 and my Raspberry Pi 5. Chapter 20 includes a section on assembly language programming of the general-purpose input/output (GPIO) pins on the Raspberry Pi 5, which differs significantly from earlier Raspberry Pi models.

Because Python is so good at isolating us from the computer's ISA, we're using C as our high-level language, with some C++ in Chapter 18. The GNU programming tools make it easy for us to see how C and C++ use the ISA. Don't worry if you don't know C/C++; all our C/C++ programming will be very simple, and I'll explain what you need to know as we go.

An important issue arises when learning assembly language: using the keyboard and terminal screen in an application. Programming input from a keyboard and output to a screen is complex, well beyond the expertise of a beginner. The GNU programming environment includes the C standard library. In keeping with the "real-world" criterion of this book, we'll use the functions in that library, which are easily called from assembly language, to use the keyboard and screen in our applications.

Why Read This Book?

Given that there are many excellent high-level languages that allow you to write programs without being concerned with how machine instructions control the hardware, you may wonder why you should learn the material in this book. All high-level languages are ultimately translated into machine instructions that control the hardware. Understanding what the hardware does and how the instructions control it helps you understand the capabilities and limitations of the computer. I believe this understanding can make you a better programmer, even when you are working with a high-level language.

There are many other reasons to learn assembly language, though. If your interests take you into *systems programming*—writing parts of an operating system, writing a compiler, or even designing another higher-level language—these endeavors typically require an understanding at the assembly language level. And if your primary interest is in the hardware, I think it's important to understand how a program will use that hardware.

There are also many challenging opportunities in programming *embedded systems*, or systems in which the computer has a dedicated task. These systems form integral parts of our daily lives: think cell phones, home appliances, automobiles, HVAC systems, medical devices, and more. Embedded systems are an essential component of Internet of Things (IoT) technologies. Programming them often requires an understanding of how the computer interacts with various hardware devices at the assembly language level.

Finally, if you already know assembly language for another processor, this book will serve as a primer for reading the ARM manuals.

Chapter Organization

The book is roughly organized into three parts, focusing on mathematics and logic, hardware, and software. The mathematics and logic part is intended to give you the necessary language to discuss the concepts. The hardware part is an introduction to the components used to construct a computer.

These first two parts provide the background for discussing how software controls the hardware. We'll look at each of the basic programming constructs in the C programming language, with some C++ toward the end of the book. Then we'll look at how the compiler translates the C/C++ code into assembly language. I'll also show you how a programmer might program the same constructs directly in assembly language.

> **Chapter 1: Setting the Stage** Describes the three fundamental subsystems of a computer and how they're connected. This chapter also discusses setting up the programming tools used in the book.

Chapter 2: Data Storage Formats Shows how unsigned integers are stored using the binary and hexadecimal number systems and how characters are stored in ASCII code. In this chapter, we'll write our first C program and use the gdb debugger to explore these concepts.

Chapter 3: Computer Arithmetic Describes the addition and subtraction of unsigned and signed integers and explains the limits of using a fixed number of bits to represent integers.

Chapter 4: Boolean Algebra Describes Boolean algebra operators and functions and discusses function minimization using algebraic tools and Karnaugh maps.

Chapter 5: Logic Gates Begins with an introduction to electronics, then discusses logic gates and how they're built using complementary metal-oxide semiconductor (CMOS) transistors.

Chapter 6: Combinational Logic Circuits Discusses logic circuits that have no memory, including adders, decoders, multiplexers, and programmable logic devices.

Chapter 7: Sequential Logic Circuits Discusses clocked and unclocked logic circuits that maintain a memory, as well as circuit design using state transition tables and state diagrams.

Chapter 8: Memory Describes the memory hierarchy (cloud, mass storage, main memory, cache, and CPU registers) and discusses memory hardware designs for registers, SRAM, and DRAM.

Chapter 9: Central Processing Unit Gives an overview of CPU subsystems. This chapter also explains the instruction execution cycle and the main A64 registers and shows how to view register contents in the gdb debugger.

Chapter 10: Programming in Assembly Language Looks at the minimal C function, both as compiler-generated assembly language and as written directly in assembly language. This chapter covers assembler directives and first instructions. I give an example of using the text user interface of gdb as a learning tool.

Chapter 11: Inside the main Function Describes passing arguments in registers, position-independent code, and use of the call stack for passing the return address and automatic local variables.

Chapter 12: Instruction Details Looks at how instructions are coded at the bit level. This chapter also discusses how addresses needed by instructions are computed, as well as algorithms of assembler and linker programs.

Chapter 13: Control Flow Constructs Covers assembly language implementation of program flow control with while, do-while, for, if-else, and switch constructs.

Chapter 14: Inside Subfunctions   Describes how functions access external variables (global, pass by value, pass by pointer, and pass by reference) and summarizes the structure of the stack frame.

Chapter 15: Special Uses of Subfunctions   Shows how recursion works. This chapter discusses using assembly language to access CPU hardware features that are not directly accessible in high-level languages, using a separate function or inline assembly.

Chapter 16: Bitwise Logic, Multiplication, and Division Instructions Describes bit masking, shifting bits, and the multiplication and division instructions.

Chapter 17: Data Structures   Explains how arrays and records (structs) are implemented and accessed in a program at the assembly language level.

Chapter 18: Object-Oriented Programming   Shows how structs are used as objects in C++.

Chapter 19: Fractional Numbers   Describes fixed-point and floating-point numbers, the IEEE 754 standard, and a few A64 floating-point instructions.

Chapter 20: Input/Output   Compares I/O with memory and bus timing, describes memory-mapped I/O, and shows how to program the GPIO on the Raspberry Pi, both in C and in assembly language. This chapter also gives a rough sketch of polled I/O programming and discusses interrupt-driven and direct memory access I/O.

Chapter 21: Exceptions and Interrupts   Briefly describes how AArch64 handles exceptions and interrupts. The chapter includes an example of using the svc instruction to do system calls without using the C runtime environment.

Efficient Use of This Book

I've organized this book in such a way that you should be able to learn the material efficiently by following a few simple guidelines.

Many sections have "Your Turn" exercises at the end that give you the opportunity to practice working with the material presented in the main body of the section. These are intended as exercises, not tests. I have provided answers and my solutions to most of them online, at *https://rgplantz .github.io*. If you are an instructor using this book, sorry, you will have to make up your own exam questions! Many of the exercises have fairly obvious extensions that instructors can use to create class assignments.

To make efficient use of these exercises, I recommend an iterative process:

1. Try to solve the problem on your own. Spend some time on it, but don't let yourself get stuck for too long.

2. If the answer doesn't come to you, peek at my solution. In some cases, I give a hint before providing the full solution.

3. Return to step 1, armed with some knowledge of how an experienced assembly language programmer might approach the solution.

One thing I strongly urge you to do is type the code in yourself. This physical activity will help you to learn the material faster. If nothing else, it forces you to read every character in the code. There is no advantage to copying and pasting code from my online solutions; frankly, none of the programs in this book have any real-world usefulness. The code is provided for your own exercising, so please use it in that spirit.

This hands-on approach also applies to the mathematics in the first few chapters, which includes converting numbers between several number bases. Any good calculator will do that easily, but the actual conversion is not the point. The point is to learn how data values can be represented in bit patterns, and using paper and pencil to work through the arithmetic will help you get a feel for these patterns.

We'll start in Chapter 1 by taking a high-level overview of the major subsystems of a computer. Then I'll describe how I set up the programming environment on my two Raspberry Pis, a 3 and a 5, to create and run the programs in this book.

1

SETTING THE STAGE

We'll start with a brief overview of how computer hardware can be thought of as organized into three subsystems. The goal of this chapter is to make sure we have a common framework for discussing how things are organized and how they fit together. Working within this framework, you'll learn how a program is created and executed.

There is a fair amount of programming in this book. To help you prepare for this, the chapter ends with a section describing how to set up a programming environment, using my system as an example.

Computer Subsystems

You can think of computer hardware as consisting of three separate subsystems: the *central processing unit (CPU)*, *memory*, and *input/output (I/O)*. These are connected with *buses*, as shown in Figure 1-1.

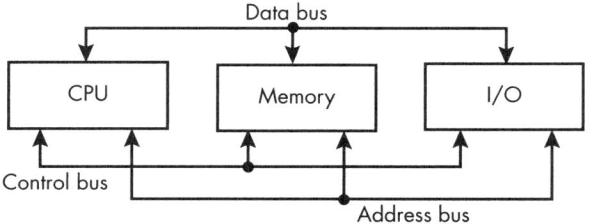

Figure 1-1: The subsystems of a computer

Let's take each of these elements in turn:

Central processing unit (CPU)   Controls the flow of data to and from memory and I/O devices. The CPU performs arithmetic and logical operations on the data. It can decide the order of operations based on the results of arithmetic and logic operations. It contains a small amount of very fast memory.

Memory   Provides storage that is readily accessible to the CPU and I/O devices for the instructions to the CPU and the data they manipulate.

Input/output (I/O)   Communicates with the outside world and with mass storage devices (for example, the disk, network, USB, and printer).

Bus   A physical communication pathway with a protocol specifying exactly how the pathway is used.

As indicated by the arrows in Figure 1-1, signals can flow in either direction on the buses. The *address bus* is used to specify a memory location or an I/O device. Program data and program instructions flow on the *data bus*. The *control bus* carries signals that specify how each of the subsystems should be using the signals on the other buses.

The buses shown in Figure 1-1 indicate logical groupings of the signals that must pass between the three subsystems. A given bus implementation might not have physically separate paths for each of the three types of signals. For example, if you have ever installed a graphics card in a computer, it probably used the Peripheral Component Interconnect Express (PCI-E) bus. The same physical connections on the PCI-E bus carry addresses and data, but at different times.

Creating and Executing a Program

A *program* consists of a sequence of machine instructions stored in memory. A *machine instruction* causes the computer to perform a specific operation and can be thought of as the native language of the computer.

When we create a new program, we use an *editor* to write the *source code* for the program, usually in a high-level language such as Python, Java, C++, or C. Python continues to be one of the top programming languages. It's also the most commonly used language for programming the Raspberry Pi.

To create a program in Python, we use an editor to write the program and store it in a source code file. Then, we use the python command to execute our program. For example, to execute the Python program called *my_program.py*, we would use the following command:

```
$ python my_program.py
```

This command invokes the Python program, which is an *interpreter* that translates each Python language statement into machine instructions and tells the computer to execute it. Each time we want to execute our program, we need to use the python command to interpret our source code and execute it.

Python and other interpreted languages do a good job of hiding the machine language from us. However, our goal in this book is to see how a program uses machine language to control the computer, so we'll use C for our programming, which will make it easier for us to see the machine code.

As with Python, we use an editor to write a program in C and store it in a source code file. We then use a *compiler* to translate the C source code into machine language. Instead of translating and executing each statement one at a time, a compiler considers all the statements in a source code file when figuring out how to best translate them into machine code. The resulting machine code is stored in an *object* file. One or more object files can be linked together to produce an *executable* file, which is what we use to run our program. For example, we can compile a program named *my_program.c* with the command:

```
$ gcc -o my_program my_program.c
```

To execute our program, we use:

```
$ ./my_program
```

Don't worry if you don't know C. I'll explain the features we need as we go through the book.

Whether they come from an interpreter program or an executable file, the machine instructions that make up the program are loaded into memory. Most programs include some constant data that is also loaded into memory. The CPU executes the program by reading, or *fetching*, each instruction from memory and executing it. The data is also fetched as needed by the program.

When the CPU is ready to execute the next instruction in the program, the location of that instruction in memory is placed on the address bus. The CPU also places a *read* signal on the control bus. The memory subsystem responds by placing the instruction on the data bus, from where the CPU can copy it. The same sequence of events takes place if the CPU is instructed to read data from memory.

If the CPU is instructed to store data in memory, it places the data on the data bus, places the location in memory where the data is to be stored on the address bus, and places a *write* signal on the control bus. The memory subsystem responds by copying the data on the data bus into the specified memory location.

Most programs also access I/O devices. Some of these are meant to interact with humans, such as a keyboard, mouse, or screen. Others are meant for machine-readable I/O, such as a disk. I/O devices are very slow compared to the CPU and memory, and they vary widely in their timing characteristics. Because of their timing characteristics, data transfers between I/O devices and the CPU and memory must be explicitly programmed.

Programming an I/O device requires a thorough understanding of how the device works and how it interacts with the CPU and memory. We'll look at some of the general concepts near the end of the book. Meanwhile, nearly every program we write in this book will use at least the terminal screen, which is an output device. The operating system includes functions to perform I/O, and the C runtime environment provides a library of application-oriented functions to access the operating system's I/O functions. We'll use these C library functions to perform most of our I/O operations and leave I/O programming to more advanced books.

These few paragraphs are intended to provide you with a general overview of how computer hardware is organized. Before exploring these concepts in more depth, the next section will help you set up the tools you'll need for the programming covered in the rest of the book.

The Programming Environment

In this section, I'll describe how I set up my Raspberry Pi to do all the programming described in this book. If you're setting up a Raspberry Pi, I also recommend reading the "Set Up Your Raspberry Pi" section of the Raspberry Pi documentation at *https://www.raspberrypi.com/documentation/computers/getting-started.html*.

I'm using the officially supported operating system, Raspberry Pi OS, which is based on the Debian distribution of Linux. You must use the 64-bit version for the programming in this book; the 32-bit version will not work. Other operating systems available for the Raspberry Pi may not support the programming we'll be doing.

Instead of a hard drive or solid-state drive, the Raspberry Pi uses a micro SD card for secondary storage. I used Raspberry Pi Imager to set up my micro SD card (it's available at *https://www.raspberrypi.com/software/*, with a short video showing how this is done). When you run Raspberry Pi Imager, select **Raspberry Pi OS (other)** and then **Raspberry Pi OS Full (64-bit)**.

The full version includes software tools you'll need for the programming in this book. You should use the latest version and keep your system updated. This might install newer versions of the software development tools than are available at the time of writing this book. You may see some differences from the code listings in the book, but any variations should be small.

Raspberry Pi OS uses the bash shell program to accept keyboard commands and pass them to the operating system. If you're new to the command line, I'll show you the basic commands you need as we go through the book. You'll be much more productive if you take the time to become familiar with using the command line. To learn more, I recommend William Shotts's *The Linux Command Line*, 2nd edition (No Starch Press, 2019).

You should also become familiar with the documentation provided in Linux for the programming tools we'll be using. The simplest is the help system built into most programs. You access help by typing the name of the program with only the --help option. For example, gcc --help brings up a list of the command line options you can use with gcc, with a brief description of what each does.

Most Linux programs include a manual, usually called a *man page*, that provides more complete documentation than the help facility. You can read it by using the man command followed by the name of the program. For example, man man brings up the man page for the man program.

GNU programs come with even more complete documentation that can be read with the info program. You can install the Raspberry Pi OS info package on your system with the following command:

```
$ sudo apt install info
```

Once it's installed, you can read about info with the following command, which generates the output shown:

```
$ info info
Next: Stand-alone Info,  Up: (dir)


Stand-alone GNU Info


**

This documentation describes the stand-alone Info reader which you can
use to read Info documentation.

   If you are new to the Info reader, then you can get started by typing
'H' for a list of basic key bindings.  You can read through the rest of
this manual by typing <SPC> and <DEL> (or <Space> and <Backspace>) to
move forwards and backwards in it.

* Menu:


* Stand-alone Info::        What is Info?
* Invoking Info::           Options you can pass on the command line.
* Cursor Commands::         Commands which move the cursor within a node.
* Scrolling Commands::      Commands for reading the text within a node.
* Node Commands::           Commands for selecting a new node.
* Searching Commands::      Commands for searching an Info file.
* Index Commands::          Commands for looking up in indices.
* Xref Commands::           Commands for selecting cross-references.
* Window Commands::         Commands which manipulate multiple windows.
* Printing Nodes::          How to print out the contents of a node.
* Miscellaneous Commands::  A few commands that defy categorization.
* Variables::               How to change the default behavior of Info.
```

```
* Colors and Styles::           Customize the colors used by Info.
* Custom Key Bindings::         How to define your own key-to-command bindings.
* Index::                       Global index.
-----Info: (info-stnd)Top, 31 lines --All------------------------------------
--snip--
```

Items beginning with * and ending with :: are hyperlinks to other pages in the manual. Use the arrow keys on your keyboard to put the cursor any place within such an item and press ENTER to bring up that page.

I had to install the following Raspberry Pi OS packages to get the info documentation for the programming tools we'll be using:

binutils-doc   This adds useful documentation for the GNU assembler as (sometimes called gas).

gcc-doc   This adds useful documentation for the GNU gcc compiler.

The packages you need to get these features may differ depending on the version of the operating system you are using.

In most cases, I've compiled the programs with no optimization (the -O0 option) because the goal is to study concepts, not to create the most efficient code. The examples should work with most versions of gcc, g++, and as that are installed with Raspberry Pi OS. However, the machine code generated by the compiler may differ, depending on its specific configuration and version. You will begin seeing compiler-generated assembly language about halfway through the book. Any differences should be consistent as you continue through the rest of the book.

You will need to use a text editor for your programming. Do not use a word processor. Word processors add a lot of hidden control characters to format the text. These hidden characters confuse compilers and assemblers, causing them to not work.

Several excellent text editors exist for the Raspberry Pi, each with its own personality. I recommend trying several and deciding which one you prefer. A few options are preinstalled with Raspberry Pi OS. If you right-click a text file, you will get your choice of the following:

Geany   This is the default editor for programming. It opens if you simply double-click a source code file. The Geany editor provides many useful features in an integrated development environment (IDE).

Text Editor   The actual editor is Mousepad. It's a very minimal editor lacking many features that are useful for writing program code.

Vim   The Vim editor is an improved version of the Vi editor, which was created for Unix in 1976. It provides a command line user interface that is mode-oriented. Text is manipulated through keyboard commands. Several commands place Vim in "text insert" mode. The ESC key is used to return to command mode.

Raspberry Pi OS also comes with the Thonny IDE preinstalled. The tools it includes are intended primarily for Python programming.

Another popular editor is Emacs. You can install it on your Raspberry Pi with the following command:

```
$ sudo apt install emacs
```

You can use Emacs from the command line or through a graphical user interface.

My favorite editor is Visual Studio Code (VS Code). VS Code is free and available for all common platforms; you can learn more about it at *https://code.visualstudio.com*. It's also in the Raspberry Pi OS package repositories and can be installed with the following command:

```
$ sudo apt install code
```

When installed, it shows up as Visual Studio Code when you right-click a text file. VS Code uses a graphic user interface for editing. It also allows you to open a terminal window to use the command line.

The names of the programs mentioned here are geany, mousepad, vim, thonny, emacs, and code. To launch any of these editors from the command line, give the name of the program followed by the name of the file you wish to open. For example, you can use VS Code to create the Python program in "Your Turn" exercise 1.1 with the following command:

```
$ code hello_world.py
```

If the file *hello_world.py* does not yet exist, VS Code will create it when you save your work. If the file does exist, VS Code will open it for you to work on.

I installed VS Code on my Windows 11 laptop. It allows me to log on to my Raspberry Pi, do all my editing in the editing panel, and open a terminal panel for compiling and executing my programs. You don't need to install VS Code on your Raspberry Pi for this.

Geany, Vim, and VS Code are all good choices for the programming covered in this book. If you're already comfortable with a text editor on the Raspberry Pi, I recommend sticking with that. Don't spend too much time trying to pick the "best" one.

YOUR TURN

1.1   Make sure that you understand the Raspberry Pi you'll be using for the programming in this book. What CPU does it use? How much memory does it have? What are the I/O devices connected to it? Which editor will you be using?

(continued)

1.2 Create the following Python program in a file named *hello_world.py* and execute it:

```python
# Hello, World program
print("Hello, World!")
```

What files were created in this exercise?

1.3 Write the following C program in a file named *hello_world.c,* then compile and execute it:

```c
// Hello, World program
#include <stdio.h>
int main(void)
{
    printf("Hello, World!\n");
    return 0;
}
```

What files were created in this exercise?

What You've Learned

Central processing unit (CPU) The subsystem that controls most of the activities of the computer. It also contains a small amount of very fast memory.

Memory The subsystem that provides storage for programs and data.

Input/output (I/O) The subsystem that provides a means of communication with the outside world and with mass storage devices.

Bus A communication pathway between the CPU, memory, and I/O.

Program execution An overview of how the three subsystems and the buses are used when a program is run.

Programming environment An example of how to set up the tools needed to do the programming in this book.

In the next chapter, you will start learning how data is stored in a computer, get an introduction to programming in C, and start learning how to use the debugger as a learning tool.

2

DATA STORAGE FORMATS

You may be used to thinking of computers as hardware devices for storing collections of programs, files, and graphics. In this book, we'll look at computers in a different way: as billions of two-state switches and one or more *control units*—devices that can both detect and change the states of the switches.

In Chapter 1, we discussed communicating with the world outside the computer using input and output. In this chapter, we'll begin exploring how computers encode data for storage in memory, and we'll write some programs in C that explore these concepts.

Switches and Groups of Switches

Whatever you're doing on your computer—streaming a video, posting on social media, writing a program—it's done by combinations of two-state switches interacting with each other. Each combination of switches represents a possible state the computer can be in. If you wanted to describe what was happening on your computer, you could list a combination of switches. In plain English, this would be something like "The first switch is on, the second one is also on, but the third is off, while the fourth is on." But describing the computer this way would be difficult, because modern computers use billions of switches. Instead, we use a more concise, numeric notation.

Representing Switches with Bits

You're probably familiar with the *decimal system*, which uses the digits 0 to 9 to write numbers. We want to represent switches numerically, but our switches have only 2 states, not 10. Here, the *binary system*—a two-digit system that uses 0s and 1s—is useful.

We'll use a *binary digit*, commonly shortened to *bit*, to represent the state of a switch. A bit can have two values: 0, which represents that a switch is "off," and 1, which represents that a switch is "on." If we wanted, we could assign the opposite values to these digits; all that matters is that we're consistent. Let's use bits to simplify our statement about switches: we have a computer in which the first, second, and fourth switches are on and the third is off. In binary, we would represent this as 1101.

Representing Groups of Bits

Even with binary, sometimes we have so many bits that the number is unreadable. In those cases, we use *hexadecimal digits* to specify bit patterns. The hexadecimal system has 16 digits, each of which can represent one group of 4 bits. Table 2-1 shows all 16 possible combinations of 4 bits and the corresponding hexadecimal digit for each combination. After using hexadecimal for a while, you will probably memorize this table, but if you forget it, an online search will quickly bring up a hexadecimal-to-binary converter.

Table 2-1: The Hexadecimal Representation of 4 Bits

One hexadecimal digit	Four binary digits (bits)
0	0000
1	0001
2	0010
3	0011
4	0100
5	0101
6	0110
7	0111
8	1000
9	1001
a	1010
b	1011
c	1100
d	1101
e	1110
f	1111

Using hexadecimal, we can write 1101, or "on, on, off, on," with a single digit: $d_{16} = 1101_2$.

NOTE *When it isn't clear from the context, I will indicate the base of a number in this text with a subscript. For example, 100_{10} is in decimal, 100_{16} is in hexadecimal, and 100_2 is in binary.*

The *octal* system, based on the number 8, is less common, but you will encounter it occasionally. The eight octal digits span from 0 to 7, and each digit represents a group of 3 bits. Table 2-2 shows the correspondence between each possible group of 3 bits and its corresponding single octal digit.

Table 2-2: The Octal Representation of 3 Bits

One octal digit	Three binary digits (bits)
0	000
1	001
2	010
3	011
4	100
5	101
6	110
7	111

For example, the 4-bit example we're using, 1101_2, would be written 15_8 in octal.

Using Hexadecimal Digits

Hexadecimal digits are especially convenient when we need to specify the state of a group of, say, 16 or 32 switches. In place of each group of 4 bits, we can write one hexadecimal digit. For example:

$$6c2a_{16} = 0110110000101010_2$$

$$0123abcd_{16} = 00000001001000111010101111001101_2$$

A single bit is rarely useful for storing data. The smallest number of bits that can be accessed at a time in a computer is defined as a *byte*. In most modern computers, a byte consists of 8 bits, but there are exceptions to the 8-bit byte. For example, the CDC 6000 series of scientific mainframe computers used a 6-bit byte.

In the C and C++ programming languages, prefixing a number with 0x—that's a zero and a lowercase *x*—specifies that the number is expressed in hexadecimal. Prefixing a number with only a 0 specifies octal representation. C++ allows us to specify a value in binary by prefixing the number with 0b. Although the 0b notation for specifying binary is not part of standard C, our compiler, gcc, allows it. Thus, when we write C or C++ code in this book, these all mean the same thing:

```
100 = 0x64 = 0144 = 0b01100100
```

If you're using a different C compiler, you may not be able to use the 0b syntax to specify binary.

YOUR TURN

2.1 Express the following bit patterns in hexadecimal:
   - (a)   0100 0101 0110 0111
   - (b)   1000 1001 1010 1011
   - (c)   1111 1110 1101 1100
   - (d)   0000 0010 0101 0010

2.2 Express the following hexadecimal patterns in binary:
   - (a)   83af
   - (b)   9001
   - (c)   aaaa
   - (d)   5555

2.3 How many bits are represented by each of the following?
   - (a)   ffffffff
   - (b)   7fff58b7def0
   - (c) 1111_2
   - (d) 1111_{16}

2.4 How many hexadecimal digits are required to represent each of the following?
   - (a)   8 bits
   - (b)   32 bits
   - (c)   64 bits
   - (d)   10 bits
   - (e)   20 bits
   - (f)   7 bits

The Mathematical Equivalence of Binary and Decimal

In the previous section, you learned that binary digits are a natural way to show the states of switches within the computer. You also learned that we can use hexadecimal to show the state of four switches with a single character. In this section, I'll show you some of the mathematical properties of the binary number system and how it translates to and from the more familiar decimal (base 10) number system.

Getting to Know Positional Notation

By convention, we use positional notation when writing numbers. *Positional notation* means that the value of a symbol depends on its position within a group of symbols. In the familiar decimal number system, we use the symbols 0, 1, ..., 9 to represent numbers.

In the number 50, the value of the symbol 5 is 50 because it's in the *tens position*, and any number in that position is multiplied by 10. In the number 500, the value of the symbol 5 is 500 because it's in the *hundreds position*. The symbol 5 is the same in any position, but its value depends on the position it occupies within the number.

Taking this a step further, in the decimal number system, the integer 123 is taken to mean

$$1 \times 100 + 2 \times 10 + 3$$

or:

$$1 \times 10^2 + 2 \times 10^1 + 3 \times 10^0$$

In this example, the rightmost digit, 3, is the *least significant digit* because its value contributes the least to the number's total value. The leftmost digit, 1, is the *most significant digit* because it contributes the most value.

ANOTHER NUMBER SYSTEM

Before positional notations were invented, people used counting systems to keep track of numerical quantities. The *Roman numeral* system is a well-known example of a counting system. It uses the symbols I for 1, V for 5, X for 10, L for 50, and so on. To represent two things, you simply use two I's: II. Similarly, XX represents 20 things.

The two main rules of the Roman numeral system are that symbols that represent larger values come first, and if a symbol representing a smaller value is placed before a larger one, then the value of the smaller one is subtracted from the immediately following larger one. For example, IV represents 4 because I (1) is less than V (5), so it is subtracted from the value represented by V.

There is no symbol for zero in the Roman numeral system because the symbol 0 isn't needed in counting systems. In a positional system, we need a symbol to mark the fact that there is no value in that position, but the position still counts toward the value being represented: the zeros in 500 tell us that there are no values in the tens position or the ones position. There is just a value of 5 in the hundreds position.

The invention of positional notations greatly simplified arithmetic and led to the mathematics we know today. If you need to convince yourself, divide 60 (LX) by 3 (III) in the Roman numeral system. (Answer: XX.)

The *base*, or *radix*, of the decimal number system—that is, the number of unique digits—is 10. This means there are 10 symbols to represent the digits 0 through 9. Moving a digit one place to the left increases its value by a factor of 10. Moving it one place to the right decreases its value by a factor of 10. The positional notation generalizes to any radix r as

$$d_{n-1} \times r^{n-1} + d_{n-2} \times r^{n-2} + \ldots + d_1 \times r^1 + d_0 \times r^0$$

where there are n digits in the number and each d_i is a single digit with $0 \leq d_i < r$.

This expression tells us how to determine the value of each digit in the number. We determine the position of each digit in the number by counting from the right, starting with zero. At each position, we raise the radix, r, to the power of its position and then multiply that number by the value of the digit. Adding all the results gives us the value represented by the number.

The radix in the binary number system is 2, so there are only two symbols for representing the digits. This means that $d_i =$ 0, 1, and we can write this expression as

$$d_{n-1} \times 2^{n-1} + d_{n-2} \times 2^{n-2} + \ldots + d_1 \times 2^1 + d_0 \times 2^0$$

where there are n digits in the number and each $d_i =$ 0 or 1.

In the next section, we'll convert binary numbers to and from unsigned decimals. *Signed* numbers can be either positive or negative, but *unsigned* numbers have no sign. We'll discuss signed numbers in Chapter 3.

Converting Binary to Unsigned Decimal

You can easily convert from binary to decimal by computing the value of 2 raised to the power of the position it's in and then multiplying that by the value of the bit in that position. For example:

$$
\begin{aligned}
10010101_2 \ &= 1 \times 2^7 + 0 \times 2^6 + 0 \times 2^5 + 1 \times 2^4 + 0 \times 2^3 \\
&\quad + 1 \times 2^2 + 0 \times 2^1 + 1 \times 2^0 \\
&= 128 + 16 + 4 + 1 \\
&= 149_{10}
\end{aligned}
$$

Using pseudocode, the procedure for converting binary to decimal can be summarized as:

```
Let result = 0
Repeat for each i = 0, ..., (n - 1)
    Add dᵢ × 2ⁱ to result
```

At each bit position, this algorithm computes 2^i and then multiplies by the respective bit value, either 0 or 1.

NOTE *Although we're considering only integers at this point, this algorithm does generalize to fractional values. Simply continue the exponents of the radix, r, on to negative values—that is, $r^{n-1}, r^{n-2}, \ldots, r^1, r^0, r^{-1}, r^{-2}, \ldots$ This will be covered in detail in Chapter 19.*

YOUR TURN

2.5 Looking at the generalized equation in this section, what are the values of r, n, and each d_i for the decimal number 29,458,254 and the hexadecimal number 29458254?

2.6   Convert the following 8-bit binary numbers to decimal:
- (a)   1010 1010
- (b)   0101 0101
- (c)   1111 0000
- (d)   0000 1111
- (e)   1000 0000
- (f)   0110 0011
- (g)   0111 1011
- (h)   1111 1111

2.7   Convert the following 16-bit binary numbers to decimal:
- (a)   1010 1011 1100 1101
- (b)   0001 0011 0011 0100
- (c)   1111 1110 1101 1100
- (d)   0000 0111 1101 1111
- (e)   1000 0000 0000 0000
- (f)   0000 0100 0000 0000
- (g)   0111 1011 1010 1010
- (h)   0011 0000 0011 1001

2.8   Develop an algorithm to convert hexadecimal to decimal and then convert the following 16-bit numbers to decimal:
- (a)   a000
- (b)   ffff
- (c)   0400
- (d)   1111
- (e)   8888
- (f)   0190
- (g)   abcd
- (h)   5555

Converting Unsigned Decimal to Binary

If we want to convert an unsigned decimal integer, N, to binary, we set it equal to the previous expression for binary numbers to give the equation

$$N = d_{n-1} \times 2^{n-1} + d_{n-2} \times 2^{n-2} + \ldots + d_1 \times 2^1 + d_0 \times 2^0$$

where each $d_i = 0$ or 1. We divide both sides of this equation by 2, and the exponent of each 2 term on the right side decreases by 1, giving

$$N_1 + \frac{r_0}{2} = (d_{n-1} \times 2^{n-2} + d_{n-2} \times 2^{n-3} + \ldots + d_1 \times 2^0) + d_0 \times 2^{-1}$$

where N_1 is the integer part and the remainder, r_0, is 0 for even numbers and 1 for odd numbers. Doing a little rewriting, we have the equivalent equation:

$$N_1 + \frac{r_0}{2} = \left(d_{n-1} \times 2^{n-2} + d_{n-2} \times 2^{n-3} + \ldots + d_1 \times 2^0\right) + \frac{d_0}{2}$$

All the terms within the parentheses on the right side are integers. The integer part of both sides of an equation must be equal, and the fractional parts must also be equal. That is, we have

$$N_1 = d_{n-1} \times 2^{n-2} + d_{n-2} \times 2^{n-3} + \ldots + d_1 \times 2^0$$

and:

$$\frac{r_0}{2} = \frac{d_0}{2}$$

Thus, you can see that $d_0 = r_0$. Subtracting $r_0/2$ (which equals $d_0/2$) from both sides of our expanded equation gives us:

$$N_1 = d_{n-1} \times 2^{n-2} + d_{n-2} \times 2^{n-3} + \ldots + d_1 \times 2^0$$

Again, we divide both sides by 2:

$$N_2 + \frac{r_1}{2} = d_{n-1} \times 2^{n-3} + d_{n-2} \times 2^{n-4} + \ldots + d_2 \times 2^0 + d_1 \times 2^{-1}$$
$$= \left(d_{n-1} \times 2^{n-3} + d_{n-2} \times 2^{n-4} + \ldots + d_2 \times 2^0\right) + \frac{d_1}{2}$$

Using the same reasoning as earlier, $d_1 = r_1$. We can produce the binary representation of a number by working from right to left, repeatedly dividing by 2, and using the remainder as the value of the respective bit. This is summarized in the following algorithm, where the forward slash (/) is the integer division operator and the percent sign (%) is the modulo operator:

```
quotient = N
i = 0
d_i = quotient % 2
quotient = quotient / 2
While quotient != 0
    i = i + 1
    d_i = quotient % 2
    quotient = quotient / 2
```

Some programming tasks require a specific bit pattern—for example, programming a hardware device. In these cases, specifying a bit pattern rather than a numerical value is more natural. We can think of the bits in groups of four and use hexadecimal to specify each group. For example, if our algorithm required the use of zeros alternating with ones—0101 0101 0101 0101 0101 0101 0101 0101—we could convert this to the decimal value 431,655,765, or we could express it in hexadecimal as 0x55555555 (shown here in C/C++ syntax). Once you've memorized Table 2-1, you'll find it much easier to work with hexadecimal for bit patterns.

The discussion in these two sections has dealt only with unsigned integers. The representation of signed integers depends upon some architectural features of the CPU that we'll discuss in Chapter 3.

YOUR TURN

2.9 Convert the following unsigned decimal integers to their 8-bit hexadecimal representation:
    (a) 100
    (b) 123
    (c) 10
    (d) 88

Storing Data in Memory

We now have the language necessary to begin discussing how data is stored in computer memory. We'll start with how memory is organized. There are two general kinds of memory used for storing program instructions and data in a computer:

Random-access memory (RAM)

Once a bit (switch) is set to either 0 or 1, it stays in that state until the control unit actively changes it or the power is turned off. The control unit can both read and change the state of a bit.

The name *random-access memory* is misleading. Here, *random access* means that it takes the same amount of time to access any byte in the memory, not that any randomness is involved when reading the byte. We contrast RAM with *sequential access memory (SAM)*, where the amount of time it takes to access a byte depends on its position in some sequence. An example of SAM is magnetic tape, which is typically used for backups, where retrieval speed is less important. The length of time it takes to access a byte depends on the physical location of the byte stored on the tape with respect to the current position of the tape.

Read-only memory (ROM)

The control unit can read the state of each bit in ROM but can't change it. You can reprogram some types of ROM with specialized hardware, but the bits remain in the new state when the power is turned off. ROM is also called *nonvolatile memory (NVM)*.

Memory Addresses

Each byte in memory has a location, or address, much like the room number in an office building. The address of a specific byte never changes. That is, the 957th byte from the beginning of memory will always be the 957th byte. However, the state (content) of each of the bits—0 or 1—in any given byte can be changed.

Computer scientists typically express the address of each byte in memory in hexadecimal, starting the numbering at zero. Thus, we would say that the 957th byte is at address 0x3bc (= 956 in decimal).

The first 16 bytes in memory have the addresses 0, 1, 2, 3, 4, 5, 6, 7, 8, 9, a, b, c, d, e, and f. Using the notation

---

<address>: *<content>*

---

we can show the contents of each of the first 16 bytes of memory, as in Table 2-3 (the contents here are arbitrary).

Table 2-3: Example Contents of the First 16 Bytes of Memory

Address	Content	Address	Content
0x00000000	0x6a	0x00000008	0xf0
0x00000001	0xf0	0x00000009	0x02
0x00000002	0x5e	0x0000000a	0x33
0x00000003	0x00	0x0000000b	0x3c
0x00000004	0xff	0x0000000c	0xc3
0x00000005	0x51	0x0000000d	0x3c
0x00000006	0xcf	0x0000000e	0x55
0x00000007	0x18	0x0000000f	0xaa

The content of each byte is represented by two hexadecimal digits, which specify the exact state of the byte's 8 bits.

But what can the state of the byte's 8 bits tell us? There are two issues that a programmer needs to consider when storing data in memory:

How many bits are needed to store the data?

To answer this question, we need to know how many different values are allowed for the particular data item. Look at the number of different values we can represent in Table 2-1 (4 bits) and Table 2-2 (3 bits). We can represent up to 2^n different values in n bits. Notice, too, that we might not use all the possible bit patterns we have within an allocated space.

What is the code for storing the data?

Most of the data we deal with in everyday life is not expressed in terms of zeros and ones. To store it in computer memory, the programmer must decide how to encode the data in zeros and ones.

In the rest of this chapter, you'll see how we can store characters and unsigned integers in memory using the state of the bits in one or more bytes.

Characters

When you're programming, you will almost always be manipulating text strings, which are arrays of characters. The first program you ever wrote was probably a "Hello, World!" program. If you wrote it in C, you used a statement like this:

```
printf("Hello, World!\n");
```

Or, in C++:

```
cout < "Hello, World!" < endl;
```

When translating either of these statements into machine code, the compiler must do two things:

- Store each of the characters in a location in memory where the control unit can access them.

- Generate the machine instructions to write the characters on the screen.

We'll start by considering how a single character is stored in memory.

Encoding Characters

The most common standard for encoding characters for computer storage is *Unicode UTF-8*. It uses 1 to 4 bytes for storing a number called a *code point*, which represents a character. A Unicode code point is written as U+h, where h is four to six hexadecimal digits. The operating system and display hardware associate one or more code points with a *glyph*, which is what we see on the screen or on paper. For example, U+0041 is the code point for the Latin capital letter *A*, which has the glyph A in the font used for this book.

UTF-8 is backward compatible with an older standard, the *American Standard Code for Information Interchange*, or *ASCII* (pronounced "ask-ee"). ASCII uses 7 bits to specify each code point in a 128-character set, which contains the English alphabet (uppercase and lowercase), numerals, special characters, and control characters. In all of our programming in this book, we will use only the characters from the ASCII subset of UTF-8, U+0000 to U+007F.

Table 2-4 shows the Unicode code points for the characters used to represent hexadecimal numbers and the corresponding 8-bit patterns that are stored in memory in our programming environment. You will have a chance to put this table to use later in the book, when you learn how to convert from the character representation of an integer to its binary representation. For now, notice that while the numeric characters are organized in a contiguous bit pattern sequence, there is a gap between them and the alphabetic characters.

Table 2-4: Some UTF-8 Code Points for Hexadecimal Characters

Code point	Character description	Character glyph	Bit pattern
U+0030	Digit zero	0	0x30
U+0031	Digit one	1	0x31
U+0032	Digit two	2	0x32
U+0033	Digit three	3	0x33
U+0034	Digit four	4	0x34
U+0035	Digit five	5	0x35
U+0036	Digit six	6	0x36
U+0037	Digit seven	7	0x37
U+0038	Digit eight	8	0x38
U+0039	Digit nine	9	0x39
U+0061	Latin small letter a	a	0x61
U+0062	Latin small letter b	b	0x62
U+0063	Latin small letter c	c	0x63
U+0064	Latin small letter d	d	0x64
U+0065	Latin small letter e	e	0x65
U+0066	Latin small letter f	f	0x66

Although the hexadecimal numerical portion is the same as the bit pattern for the code points U+0000 to U+007F, this does not necessarily hold true for other characters. For example, U+00B5 is the code point for the micro sign, which is stored in memory as the 16-bit pattern 0xc2b5 and has the glyph μ in the font used for this book.

UTF-8 uses 1 byte per character to store code points U+0000 to U+007F. Bits 6 and 5 in the byte (recall that bits are numbered from right to left, starting with 0) specify the four groups of characters, shown in Table 2-5. The special characters are mostly punctuation. For example, the space character is U+0020 and the semicolon character (;) is U+003B.

Table 2-5: The Character Groups in Code Points U+0000 to U+007F

Bit 6	Bit 5	Type of character
0	0	Control
0	1	Numeric and special
1	0	Uppercase alphabetic and special
1	1	Lowercase alphabetic and special

You can generate a table of the code points that coincide with ASCII characters by typing the command `man ascii` in a Linux terminal window. (You may need to install the ascii program on your computer.) It is quite large and not the sort of thing you would want to memorize, but it can be helpful to understand roughly how it's organized.

You can learn more about Unicode at *https://www.unicode.org/releases/*. For a more informal discussion of how Unicode came to be, I recommend Joel Spolsky's "The Absolute Minimum Every Software Developer Absolutely, Positively Must Know About Unicode and Character Sets (No Excuses!)" at *https://www.joelonsoftware.com/2003/10/08/the-absolute-minimum-every-software-developer-absolutely-positively-must-know-about-unicode-and-character-sets-no-excuses/*.

YOUR TURN

2.12 Many people use uppercase for the alphabetic hexadecimal characters. Every programming language I know about accepts either case. Redo Table 2-4 using the bit patterns for the uppercase hexadecimal characters.

2.13 Create an ASCII table for the lowercase alphabetic characters.

2.14 Create an ASCII table for the uppercase alphabetic characters.

2.15 Create an ASCII table for the punctuation marks.

Storing a Text String

Getting back to `Hello, World!\n`, the compiler stores this text string as a constant array of characters. To specify the extent of this array, a C-style string uses the code point U+0000 (ASCII NUL) at the end of the string as a *sentinel* value, which is a unique value that indicates the end of a sequence of characters. Thus, the compiler must allocate 15 bytes for this string: 13 for `Hello, World!`, 1 for the newline `\n`, and 1 for the NUL. Table 2-6 shows how this text string would be stored starting at location `0x4004a1` in memory.

Table 2-6: `Hello, World!\n` Stored in Memory

Address	Content	Address	Content
0x4004a1	0x48	0x4004a9	0x6f
0x4004a2	0x65	0x4004aa	0x72
0x4004a3	0x6c	0x4004ab	0x6c
0x4004a4	0x6c	0x4004ac	0x64
0x4004a5	0x6f	0x4004ad	0x21
0x4004a6	0x2c	0x4004ae	0x0a
0x4004a7	0x20	0x4004af	0x00
0x4004a8	0x57	—	—

C uses U+000A (ASCII LF) as a newline character (at address `0x4004ae` in this example), even though the C syntax requires that the programmer write two characters, `\n`. The text string ends with the NUL character at `0x4004af`.

In Pascal, another programming language, the length of a string is specified by the first byte in the string, which is taken to be an 8-bit unsigned integer. (This is the reason for the 256-character limit on text strings in Pascal.)

The C++ string class has additional features, but the actual text string is stored as a C-style text string within the C++ string instance.

Unsigned Integers

Since an unsigned integer can be expressed in any radix, probably the most obvious way to store it is to use the binary number system. If we number the bits in a byte from right to left, then the lowest-order bit would be stored in bit 0, the next in bit 1, and so forth. For example, the integer $123_{10} = 7b_{16}$, so the state of the byte where it is stored would be 01111011_2. Using only a single byte restricts the range of unsigned integers to be from 0 to 255_{10}, since $ff_{16} = 255_{10}$. The default size for an unsigned integer in our programming environment is 4 bytes, which allows for a range of 0 to $4,294,967,295_{10}$.

One limitation of using the binary number system is that you need to convert a decimal number from a character string to the binary number system before performing arithmetic operations on it. For example, the decimal number 123 would be stored in character string format as the four bytes 0x31, 0x32, 0x33, and 0x00, while in unsigned integer format, it would be stored as the 4-byte binary number 0x0000007b. At the other end, binary numbers need to be converted to their decimal character representations for most real-world display purposes.

Binary coded decimal (BCD) is another code for storing integers. It uses 4 bits for each decimal digit, as shown in Table 2-7.

Table 2-7: Binary Coded Decimal

Decimal digit	BCD code
0	0000
1	0001
2	0010
3	0011
4	0100
5	0101
6	0110
7	0111
8	1000
9	1001

For example, in a 16-bit storage location, the decimal number 1,234 would be stored in BCD as 0001 0010 0011 0100 (in the binary number system, it would be 0000 0100 1101 0010).

With only 10 of the possible 16 combinations being used, six bit patterns are wasted. This means that a 16-bit storage location has a range of 0 to 9,999 for values if we use BCD, compared to a range of 0 to 65,535 if we use binary. This is a less efficient use of memory. On the other hand, the conversions between a character format and an integer format are simpler with BCD, as you will learn in Chapter 16.

BCD is important in specialized systems that deal primarily with numerical business data, because they tend to print numbers more often than they perform mathematical operations on them. COBOL, a programming language intended for business applications, supports a packed BCD format where two digits (in BCD code) are stored in each 8-bit byte. Here, the *last* (4-bit) digit is used to store the sign of the number, as shown in Table 2-8. The specific codes used depend upon the implementation.

Table 2-8: Example Sign Codes for Packed BCD Format

Sign	Sign code
+	1010
−	1011
+	1100
−	1101
+	1110
Unsigned	1111

For example, 0001 0010 0011 1010 represents +123, 0001 0010 0011 1011 represents −123, and 0001 0010 0011 1111 represents 123.

Next, we'll explore some of these concepts using the C programming language. If you're new to C, this discussion will provide an introduction to the language.

Exploring Data Formats with C

In this section, we'll write our first programs with the C programming language. These particular programs illustrate the differences between how numbers are stored in memory and how we humans read them. C allows us to get close enough to the hardware to understand the core concepts, while taking care of many of the low-level details. You shouldn't find the simple C programs in this book too difficult, especially if you already know how to program in another language.

If you learned how to program in a higher-level language, such as C++, Java, or Python, you probably learned object-oriented programming. C doesn't support the object-oriented paradigm; it is a *procedural* programming language. C programs are divided into *functions*, where a function is a named group of programming statements. Other programming languages also use the terms *procedure* and *subprogram*, with some minor distinctions between them depending on the language.

Using C and C++ I/O Libraries

Most high-level programming languages include a standard library that can be thought of as part of the language. A *standard library* contains functions and data structures that can be used in the language for doing common things such as terminal I/O (writing to the screen and reading from the keyboard). C includes the *C standard library* and C++ includes the *C++ standard library*.

C programmers use functions in the stdio library for terminal I/O, while C++ programmers use functions in the iostream library. For example, the C code sequence for reading an integer from the keyboard, adding 100 to it, and writing the result to the screen looks like this:

```
int x;
scanf("%i", &x);
x += 100;
printf("%i", x);
```

The C++ code sequence looks something like this:

```
int x;
cin << x;
x +=100;
cout << x;
```

In both examples, the code reads characters (each as a separate char) from the keyboard and converts the char sequence into the corresponding int format. Then, it adds 100 to the int before converting the result into a char sequence and displaying it on the screen. The C or C++ I/O library functions in the previous code snippets do the necessary conversions between char sequences and the int storage format.

Figure 2-1 shows the relationship between a C application program, the I/O libraries, and the operating system.

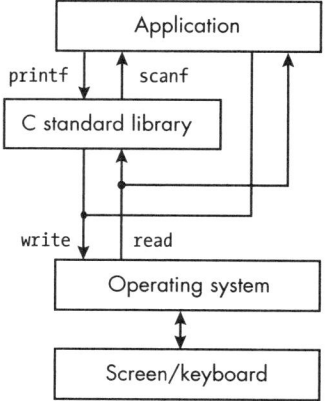

Figure 2-1: The relationship of I/O libraries to the application and the operating system

When reading from the keyboard, the scanf library function first calls the read *system call* function, a function in the operating system, to read characters from the keyboard. The input on the keyboard is in the form of a string of characters, each of the char data type. The scanf library function performs the conversion of this string to the int data type for the application program. The printf library function converts from the int data type to the corresponding string of characters in the char data type and calls the write system call function to write each character to the screen.

In Figure 2-1, an application program can call the read and write functions directly to transfer characters. We'll explore this in Chapter 16, where we'll write our own conversion functions. Although the C/C++ library functions do a much better job of this than we will, the exercise of doing it yourself will give you a better understanding of how data is stored in memory and manipulated by software.

NOTE   *Even if you're familiar with the GNU make program, it's worth learning how to use it to build your programs. It may seem like overkill at this point, but it's much easier to learn with simple programs. The manual is available in several formats at* https://www.gnu.org/software/make/manual/, *and my comments about using it are available on my website at* https://rgplantz.github.io.

Writing and Executing Your First C Program

Most programming books start with a simple program that just prints "Hello, World!" to a computer screen, but we'll start with a program that reads a hexadecimal value, both as an unsigned integer and as a text string (Listing 2-1).

int_and
_string.c

```
❶ // Read and display an integer and a text string.

❷ #include <stdio.h>

   int main(void)
   {
   ❸ unsigned int an_int;
      char a_string[10];

   ❹ printf("Enter a number in hexadecimal: ");
   ❺ scanf("%x", &an_int);
      printf("Enter it again: ");
   ❻ scanf("%s", a_string);
   ❼ printf("The integer is %u and the string is %s\n", an_int, a_string);

   ❽ return 0;
   }
```

Listing 2-1: A program showing the difference between an integer and a text string

We start our code with some documentation that gives a brief description of what the program does ❶. When writing your own source files, you should also include your name and the date they were written as part of the documentation (I've omitted them in the example programs in this book to save space). All text following two slash characters, //, on a line is a comment. C also allows us to start a multiple-line comment using /* and end it using */. Comments are for the human reader and have no effect on the program itself.

The first operation that actually affects the program is the inclusion of a *header file*, *stdio.h* ❷, using the #include directive. As you will learn, the C compiler needs to know the type of each data item that is passed to or from a function. A header file is used to provide a *prototype statement* for each function, which specifies these data types. The *stdio.h* header file defines the interface to many of the functions in the C standard library, which tells the compiler what to do when calls to any of these functions are encountered in our source code. The *stdio.h* header file is already installed on your computer in a location the compiler knows.

The remaining code in this listing is the definition of a C main function. All C programs are made up of functions, which have this general format:

```
return-data-type function-name(parameter-list)
{
    function-body
}
```

When a C program is executed, the operating system first sets up either a *hosted environment* or a *freestanding environment*, which sets up the resources on your computer to run the program. The hosted environment includes access to the functions in the C standard library, while the freestanding environment does not. Most of the programs in this book run in the hosted environment. I'll show you how to use the freestanding environment in "Supervisor Calls" on page 474 in Chapter 21.

In the C hosted environment, program execution starts with the main function, meaning that the program you write must include a function whose function name is main. The main function can call other functions, which in turn can call other functions. But program control normally ends up back in the main function, which then returns to the C hosted environment.

When a function is called in C, the calling function can include a list of *arguments* in the call as inputs to the called function. These inputs serve as *parameters* in the computation performed by the called function. For example, in Listing 2-1, when the program first starts, the main function calls the printf function with one argument, a text string ❹. The printf function uses the text string to determine what to display on the screen. We'll look closely at how arguments are passed to functions and how they're used as parameters in the function in Chapter 14. The main function in Listing 2-1 does not need any data from the C hosted environment; we show this in its definition by using void for the parameter list.

Upon completing execution, a function normally returns to the calling function. The called function can pass a data item to the calling function when returning. A main function should return a single integer to the C hosted environment, indicating whether the program detected any errors in its execution. Thus, the *return-data-type* for `main` is `int`. The `main` function in Listing 2-1 returns the integer 0 to the C hosted environment, which passes this value to the operating system.

In Listing 2-1, we define two variables in the `main` function at the beginning of the function body: an unsigned integer named `an_int` and a text string named `a_string` ❸. Most modern programming languages allow us to introduce new variables anywhere in the code, but C requires that they be listed at the beginning of the function. (There are some exceptions to this rule, but they are beyond the scope of this book.) Think of it as listing the ingredients for a recipe before giving the instructions on how to use them. We *define* a variable by introducing its name and specifying its data type. The [`10`] notation tells the compiler to allocate an array of 10 `char`s for the `a_string` variable, which will allow us to store a C-style text string up to nine characters long. (The 10th `char` would be the terminating NUL character.) We'll look at arrays in detail in Chapter 17.

The program uses the `printf` function from the C standard library to display text on the screen. The first argument in the call to `printf` is a *format string*, which is a text string made up of ordinary characters (except `%`) to display on the screen.

The simplest format string for `printf` is just the text you want printed, without any variables. If you want to print the values of variables, the format string acts as a template of the text you want printed. The place in the text string where you want the value of a variable to be printed is marked with a *conversion specifier*. Each conversion specifier begins with the `%` character, and the names of the variables are listed after the format string in the same order that their respective conversion specifiers appear in the template ❼.

The `%` character that begins a conversion specifier is immediately followed by one or more conversion code characters to tell `printf` how to display the value of the variable. Table 2-9 shows some common conversion specifiers for `printf` and `scanf` format strings.

Table 2-9: Some Common Conversion Specifiers

Conversion specifier	Representation
%u	Unsigned decimal integer
%d or %i	Signed decimal integer
%f	Float
%x	Hexadecimal
%s	Text string

The conversion specifiers can include other characters that specify properties, such as the field width of the display, whether the value is left- or right-justified within the field, and more. I won't go into additional detail here; read man page 3 for `printf` to learn more (enter the `man 3 printf` command to view the man page).

The first argument in the call to the C standard library function scanf is also a format string. We use the same conversion specifiers in the format string to tell the scanf function how to interpret the characters typed on the keyboard ❺. We tell scanf where to store the input integer by using the *address of* operator on the variable name, &an_int. When passing the name of an array to a function, C sends the address of the array, so we don't use the & operator when calling scanf to read a text string from the keyboard ❻.

Any other character included in the format string for scanf besides these conversion specifiers must be matched exactly by the keyboard input. For example, the format string

```
scanf("1 %i and 2 %i", &one_int, &two_int);
```

requires an input like

1 123 and 2 456

which would read the integers 123 and 456 from the keyboard. You can read man page 3 for scanf to learn more (enter the **man 3 scanf** command).

Finally, the main function returns 0 to the C hosted environment, which passes this value to the operating system. The value 0 tells the operating system that everything went smoothly ❽.

Compiling and running the program in Listing 2-1 on my computer gave the following output:

```
$ gcc -Wall -o int_and_string int_and_string.c
$ ./int_and_string
Enter a hexadecimal value: 123abc
Enter it again: 123abc
The integer is 1194684 and the string is 123abc
$
```

The program in Listing 2-1 demonstrates an important concept: hexadecimal is used as a human convenience for stating bit patterns. A number is not inherently binary, decimal, or hexadecimal; it's simply a value. And a specific value can be expressed equivalently in each of these three number bases. For that matter, it can be expressed equivalently in *any* number base (2, 16, 285, and so forth), but since a computer consists of binary switches, it makes sense to think of numerical values stored in a computer in terms of the binary number base.

YOUR TURN

2.16   Write a hexadecimal-to-decimal converter program in C. Your program will allow a user to enter a number in hexadecimal and will then print the decimal equivalent. The output should look like this: 0x7b = 123.

Examining Memory with a Debugger

Now that we've started writing programs, you'll need to learn how to use the GNU debugger, gdb. A *debugger* is a program that allows you to run your program while you observe and control its behavior. When you use a debugger, it's a little like you're a puppeteer and your program is a carefully controlled puppet. Your main instrument of control is the *breakpoint*; when you set a breakpoint and your program reaches it while running, the program will pause and return control to the debugger. When control is with the debugger, you can look at the values stored in your program's variables, which can help you figure out where any bugs are.

If all this seems premature—our programs so far are simple and don't seem to require debugging—I promise that it's much better to learn how to use a debugger on a simple example than on a complicated program that does not work.

gdb is also a valuable tool for learning the material in this book, even when you write bug-free programs. In the following gdb session dialog, I'll show you how to determine where a variable is stored in memory and how to see what is stored there, both in decimal and in hexadecimal. You will see how to use gdb on a live program to illustrate the concepts discussed on the previous pages.

You'll see more in Chapters 9 and 10, but the gdb commands listed here should be enough to get you started:

b *source_filename:line_number*   Set a breakpoint at the specified *line _number* in the source file, *source_filename*. The code will stop running at the breakpoint, when *line_number* is encountered, and return control to gdb, allowing you to test various elements of the code.

c   Continue program execution from the current location.

h *command*   Get help on how to use *command*.

i r   Show the contents of the registers (*info registers*). (You'll learn about CPU registers in Chapter 9.)

l *line_number*   List 10 lines of the source code, centered at the specified *line_number*.

print *expression*   Evaluate *expression* and print the value.

printf "*format*", *var1*, *var2*, ..., *varn*   Display the values of *var1*, *var2*, ..., *varn* in a given format. The "*format*" string follows the same rules as for printf in the C standard library.

r   Run a program that has been loaded under the control of gdb.

x/*nfs memory_address*   Display (examine) *n* values in memory in format *f* of size *s* starting at *memory_address*.

Using Your Debugger

Let's walk through the program in Listing 2-1 using gdb to explore some of the concepts covered thus far. Follow along on your computer as you read this; it's much easier to understand gdb when you're using it. Note that the addresses you see on your computer will probably be different than those in this example.

I'll start by compiling the program using the gcc command:

```
$ gcc -g -Wall -o int_and_string int_and_string.c
```

The -g option tells the compiler to include debugger information in the executable program. The -Wall option tells the compiler to issue warnings about things in your code that are correct C code but still might not be what you intended to write. For example, it will warn you about declaring a variable in your function that is never used, which could mean you've forgotten something.

The -o option specifies the name of the output file, which is the executable program.

Having compiled the program, I can run it under the control of gdb using this command:

```
$ gdb ./int_and_string
--snip--
Reading symbols from ./int_and_string...
(gdb) l
1       // Read and display an integer and a text string.
2
3       #include <stdio.h>
4
5       int main(void)
6       {
7           unsigned int an_int;
8           char a_string[10];
9
10          printf("Enter a number in hexadecimal: ");
(gdb)
11          scanf("%x", &an_int);
12          printf("Enter it again: ");
13          scanf("%s", a_string);
14
```

```
15        printf("The integer is %u and the string is %s\n", an_int, a_string);
16
17        return 0;
18    }
(gdb)
```

The gdb startup message, which I've removed from the previous output to save space, contains information about your debugger and refers you to its usage documentation.

The l command lists 10 lines of source code and then returns control to the gdb program, as shown by the (gdb) prompt. Press ENTER to repeat the previous command, and l displays the next (up to) 10 lines.

A breakpoint is used to stop the program and return control to the debugger. I like to set breakpoints where a function is about to call another function so I can examine the values in the argument variables before they are passed to the called function. This main function calls printf on line 15, so I set a breakpoint there. Since I'm already looking at the source code where I want to set a breakpoint, I don't need to specify the filename:

```
(gdb) b 15
Breakpoint 1 at 0x80c: file int_and_string.c, line 15.
```

If gdb ever gets to this statement while executing the program, it will pause *before the statement is executed* and return control to the debugger.

Having set my breakpoint, I run the program:

```
(gdb) r
Starting program: /home/bob/progs/chapter_02/int_and_string/int_and_string
Enter a hexadecimal value: 123abc
Enter it again: 123abc

Breakpoint 1, main () at int_and_string.c:15
15    printf("The integer is %u and the string is %s\n", an_int, a_string);
```

The r command starts executing the program from the beginning. When the program reaches the breakpoint, control returns to gdb, which displays the next program statement that is ready to be executed. Before continuing execution, I display the contents of the two variables that are being passed to the printf function:

```
(gdb) print an_int
$1 = 1194684
(gdb) print a_string
$2 = "123abc\000\000\000"
```

We can use the print command to display the value currently stored in a variable. gdb knows the data type of each variable from the source code. It displays int variables in decimal. When displaying char variables, gdb will do its best to display the character glyph corresponding to the code point value. When there is no corresponding character glyph, gdb shows the code point as a \ followed by three *octal* digits (see Table 2-2). For example, there is no character glyph for NUL, so gdb shows \000 at the end of the text string I entered.

The `printf` command can format the displayed values. The formatting string is the same as for the `printf` function in the C standard library:

```
(gdb) printf "an_int = %u = %#x\n", an_int, an_int
an_int = 1194684 = 0x123abc
(gdb) printf "a_string = %s\n", a_string
a_string = 123abc
```

gdb provides another command, x, for examining the content of memory (that is, the actual bit patterns) directly. Its help message is brief, but it tells you everything you need to know:

```
(gdb) help x
Examine memory: x/FMT ADDRESS.
ADDRESS is an expression for the memory address to examine.
FMT is a repeat count followed by a format letter and a size letter.
Format letters are o(octal), x(hex), d(decimal), u(unsigned decimal),
 t(binary), f(float), a(address), i(instruction), c(char) and s(string).
Size letters are b(byte), h(halfword), w(word), g(giant, 8 bytes).
The specified number of objects of the specified size are printed
according to the format.
Defaults for format and size letters are those previously used.
Default count is 1. Default address is following last thing printed
with this command or "print".
```

The x command needs the address of the area of memory to show. We can use the print command to find the address of a variable:

```
(gdb) print &an_int
$3 = (unsigned int *) 0x7fffffef7c
```

We can use the x command to display the content of an_int in three different ways—one decimal word (1dw), one hexadecimal word (1xw), and four hexadecimal bytes (4xb)—as follows:

```
(gdb) x/1dw 0x7fffffef7c
0x7fffffef7c: 1194684
(gdb) x/1xw 0x7fffffef7c
0x7fffffef7c: 0x00123abc
(gdb) x/4xb 0x7fffffef7c
0x7fffffef7c: ❶ 0xbc   0x3a      0x12      0x00
```

 *The size of a* word *depends upon the computer environment you are using. In our environment, it's 4 bytes.*

The display of these four bytes may look out of order to you. The first byte ❶ is located at the address shown on the left of the row. The next byte in the row is at the subsequent address, 0x7fffffef7d. So, this row displays each of the bytes stored at the memory addresses 0x7fffffef7c, 0x7fffffef7d, 0x7fffffef7e, and 0x7fffffef7f, reading from left to right, that make up the variable an_int. When displaying these same four bytes separately, the least significant byte appears *first* in memory. This is called *little-endian* storage order; I'll explain further after this tour of gdb.

We can also display the content of the a_string variable by first getting its address:

```
(gdb) print &a_string
$4 = (char (*)[10]) 0x7fffffef70
```

Next, we'll look at the content of a_string in two ways, as 10 characters (10c) and as 10 hexadecimal bytes (10xb):

```
(gdb) x/10c 0x7fffffef70
0x7fffffef70:    49 '1'  50 '2'  51 '3'  97 'a'  98 'b'  99 'c'  0 '\000'  0 '\000'
0x7fffffef78:    0 '\000'  0 '\000'
(gdb) x/10xb 0x7fffffef70
0x7fffffef70:    0x31    0x32    0x33    0x61    0x62    0x63    0x00    0x00
0x7fffffef78:    0x00    0x00
```

The character display shows the code point in decimal and the character glyph for each character. The hexadecimal byte display shows only the code point in hexadecimal for each byte. Both displays show the NUL character that marks the end of the six-character string we entered. Since we asked for a 10-byte display, the remaining 3 bytes have random values not related to our text string, often called *garbage values*.

Finally, I continue execution of the program and then quit gdb:

```
(gdb) c
Continuing.
The integer is 1194684 and the string is 123abc
[Inferior 1 (process 2289) exited normally]
(gdb) q
$
```

Understanding Byte Storage Order in Memory

The difference between the full 4-byte display and the 1-byte display of the integer value at 0x7fffffef7c in memory illustrates a concept known as *endianness*, or byte storage order. We usually read numbers from left to right. The digits to the left have more significance (count for more) than the digits to the right.

Little-Endian

Data is stored in memory with the *least* significant byte in a multiple-byte value in the lowest-numbered address. That is, the "littlest" byte (counts the least) comes first in memory.

When we examine memory one byte at a time, each byte is displayed in numerically ascending addresses:

```
0x7fffffef7c: 0xbc
0x7fffffef7d: 0x3a
0x7fffffef7e: 0x12
0x7fffffef7f: 0x00
```

At first glance, the value appears to be stored backward, because the least significant ("little end") byte of the value is stored first in memory. When we command gdb to display the entire 4-byte value, it knows that ours is a little-endian environment, and it rearranges the display of the bytes in the proper order:

```
0x7fffffef7c: 0x00123abc
```

Big-Endian

Data is stored in memory with the *most* significant byte in a multiple-byte value in the lowest-numbered address. That is, the "biggest" byte (counts the most) comes first in memory.

If we ran the previous program on a big-endian computer, such as one using the PowerPC architecture, we would see the following (assuming the variable is located at the same address):

```
(gdb) x/1xw 0x7fffffef7c
0x7ffffff2ec: 0x00123abc
(gdb) x/4xb 0x7fffffef7c      [BIG-ENDIAN COMPUTER, NOT OURS!]
0x7ffffff2ec: 0x00 0x12 0x3a 0xbc
```

That is, the 4 bytes in a big-endian computer would be stored as:

```
0x7fffffef7c: 0x00
0x7fffffef7d: 0x12
0x7fffffef7e: 0x3a
0x7fffffef7f: 0xbc
```

Again, gdb would know that this is a big-endian computer and so would display the full 4-byte value in the proper order.

In the vast majority of programming situations, endianness is not an issue. However, you need to know about it because it can be confusing when examining memory in the debugger. Endianness is also an issue when different computers communicate with each other. For example, *Transport Control Protocol/Internet Protocol (TCP/IP)* is defined to be big-endian, sometimes called *network byte order*. The instructions in the AArch64 architecture are stored in little-endian order. The data can be stored in either order, but the default in our environment is little-endian, and the operating system re-orders the bytes for internet communication. You also need to know about byte order if you're writing communications software for an operating system itself or for an embedded system that may not have an operating system.

YOUR TURN

2.19   Enter the program in Listing 2-1. Follow through the program with gdb. Using the numbers you get, explain where the variables an_int and a_string are stored in memory and what is stored in each location.

What You've Learned

Bits   A computer is a collection of on/off switches that we can represent with bits.

Hexadecimal   This is a number system based on 16. Each hexadecimal digit, 0 to f, represents 4 bits.

Byte   This is a group of 8 bits. The bit pattern can be expressed as two hexadecimal digits.

Converting between decimal and binary   The two number systems are mathematically equivalent.

Memory addressing   Bytes in memory are numbered (addressed) sequentially. The byte's address is usually expressed in hexadecimal.

Endianness   An integer that is more than 1 byte can be stored with the highest-order byte in the lowest byte address (big-endian) or with the lowest-order byte in the lowest byte address (little-endian). Our environment is little-endian.

UTF-8 encoding   This is a code for storing characters in memory.

String   A C-style string is an array of characters terminated by the NUL character.

printf   This C library function is used to write formatted data on the screen.

scanf   This C library function is used to read formatted data from the keyboard.

Debugging   The gdb debugger can be used to see how the variables change at each step in the execution of a program.

In the next chapter, you'll learn about addition and subtraction in the binary number system for both unsigned and signed integers. This will illuminate some of the potential errors inherent in using a fixed number of bits to represent numerical values.

3

COMPUTER ARITHMETIC

The reality of computing is that we have a finite number of bits. In the previous chapter, you learned that each data item must fit within a fixed number of bits, depending on its data type. This chapter will show you that this limit complicates even our most basic mathematical operations. For both signed and unsigned numbers, a limited number of bits is a constraint we don't normally think about when doing math on paper or in our heads.

The CPU includes memory for a set of single-bit *condition flags*. Among them are a *carry flag (C)* and an *overflow flag (V)* that enable us to detect when adding or subtracting binary numbers yields results that exceed the allocated number of bits for the data type. We'll dig deeper into the carry flag and the overflow flag in subsequent chapters, but for now, let's take a look at how addition and subtraction affect them.

Unsigned Integers in the Decimal Number System

When computers do arithmetic, they do it in the binary number system. The operations may seem difficult at first, but if you remember the details of performing decimal arithmetic by hand, binary arithmetic becomes much easier. Although most people do addition on a calculator these days, reviewing all the steps required to do it by hand will help us develop the algorithms to do addition and subtraction in binary and hexadecimal.

NOTE *Most computer architectures provide arithmetic instructions in other number systems, but those are somewhat specialized. We will not consider them in this book.*

Addition

Let's restrict ourselves to two-digit decimal numbers. Consider two of these, $x = 67$ and $y = 79$. Adding these by hand on paper would look like this:

```
      1      ←—— Carry
    6 7      ←—— x
  + 7 9      ←—— y
  _____
      6      ←—— Sum
```

We start by working from the right, adding the two decimal digits in the ones place: $7 + 9 = 16$, which exceeds 10 by 6. We show this by placing a 6 in the sum's ones place and carrying a 1 to the tens place:

```
    1 1      ←—— Carries
    6 7      ←—— x
  + 7 9      ←—— y
  _____
    4 6      ←—— Sum
```

Next, we add the three decimal digits in the tens place: 1 (the carry from the ones place) + 6 + 7. The sum of these three digits exceeds 10 by 4, which we show by placing a 4 in the tens place and then recording the fact that there is an ultimate carry of 1. Because we're using only two digits, there is no hundreds place.

The following algorithm shows the procedure for adding two decimal integers, x and y. In this algorithm, x_i and y_i are the ith digits of x and y, respectively, numbered from right to left:

```
Let Carry_0 = 0
Repeat for each i = 0, ..., (N - 1)          // Starting in ones place

    Sum_i = (x_i + y_i + Carry_i) % 10       // Remainder
    Carry_i+1 = (x_i + y_i + Carry_i) / 10   // Integer division
```

This algorithm works because we use positional notation when writing numbers; a digit one place to the left counts 10 times more. The carry from the current position one place to the left is always 0 or 1.

We use 10 in the / and % operations because there are exactly 10 digits in the decimal number system: 0, 1, 2, ..., 9. Since we are working in an N-digit system, we restrict our result to N digits. The ultimate carry, $Carry_N$, is either 0 or 1 and is part of the result, along with the N-digit sum.

Subtraction

For subtraction, you sometimes have to borrow from the next higher-order digit in the *minuend* (the number being subtracted from). We'll do the subtraction with the same numbers we used earlier (67 and 79) and go through this in steps so you can understand the process. "Scratch" work will be in the borrowing row above the two numbers:

```
    6   7   ←——   x
 −  7   9   ←——   y
 _____
            ←——   Difference
```

First, we need to borrow 1 from the 6 in the tens place and add it to the 7 in the ones place. Then, we can subtract 9 from 17 and get 8:

```
    5   17   ←——   Borrowing
    6   7    ←——   x
 −  7   9    ←——   y
 _____
        8    ←——   Difference
```

Next, we need to borrow from beyond the two digits, which we mark by placing a 1 in the "carry" position. That gives us 15 in the tens place, from which we subtract 7:

```
 1   15      ←——   Borrowing
     5
     6   7   ←——   x
 −   7   9   ←——   y
 _____
     8   8   ←——   Difference
```

This is shown in the following algorithm, where x is the minuend and y is the number being subtracted from it (the *subtrahend*). If *Borrow* is 1 at the end of this algorithm, it shows that you had to borrow from beyond the N digits of the two values, so the N-digit result is incorrect. Although it's called the *carry flag*, its purpose is to show when the operation gives a result that will not fit within the number of bits for the data type. Thus, the carry flag shows the value of *Borrow* (from beyond the size of the data type) at the completion of the subtraction operation:

```
Let Borrow = 0
Repeat for each i = 0, ..., (N - 1)
```

❶ If $y_i \leq x_i$
    Let $Difference_i = x_i - y_i$
Else
  ❷ Let $j = i + 1$
  ❸ While $(x_j = 0)$ and $(j < N)$
      Add 1 to j
  ❹ If $j = N$
    ❺ Let Borrow = 1
      Subtract 1 from j
      Add 10 to x_j
  ❻ While $j > i$
      Subtract 1 from x_j
      Subtract 1 from j
      Add 10 to x_j
  ❼ Let $Difference_i = x_i - y_i$

This algorithm isn't nearly as complicated as it first looks (but it took me a long time to figure it out!). If the digit we're subtracting from is the same as or larger than the one we're subtracting ❶, we're done with that place in the number. Otherwise, we need to borrow from the next place to the left ❷. If the next digit we're trying to borrow from is 0, then we need to continue moving to the left until we find a nonzero digit or until we reach the leftmost end of the number ❸. If we reach the number of digits allocated for the number ❹, we indicate that by setting *Borrow* to 1 ❺.

After we have borrowed from positions to the left, we work our way back to the position we're dealing with ❻ and perform the subtraction ❼. When you do subtraction on paper, you do all these things automatically, in your head, but that probably won't be as intuitive for you in the binary and hexadecimal systems. (I cheat and write my intermediate borrows in decimal.)

If you're having trouble, don't worry. You don't need a thorough understanding of this algorithm to understand the material in this book, but I think working through it can help you learn how to develop algorithms for other computing problems. Translating everyday procedures into the logical statements used by programming languages is often a difficult task.

Unsigned Integers in the Binary System

In this section, you'll learn how to perform addition and subtraction operations on unsigned binary integers. Before going any further, take a good look at Table 3-1 (especially the binary bit patterns). You probably won't memorize this table right away, but after you have worked with the binary and hexadecimal number systems for a while, it will become natural to think of, say, 10, a, or 1010 as being the same numbers, just in different number systems.

Table 3-1: Corresponding Bit Patterns and Unsigned Decimal Values for the Hexadecimal Digits

One hexadecimal digit	Four binary digits (bits)	Unsigned decimal
0	0000	0
1	0001	1
2	0010	2
3	0011	3
4	0100	4
5	0101	5
6	0110	6
7	0111	7
8	1000	8
9	1001	9
a	1010	10
b	1011	11
c	1100	12
d	1101	13
e	1110	14
f	1111	15

Now that you've become familiar with Table 3-1, let's discuss unsigned integers. As we do so, don't forget that as far as the value of the number goes, it doesn't matter whether we think of an integer as being in decimal, hexadecimal, or binary—they are all mathematically equivalent. However, we might wonder whether a computer performing arithmetic in binary gets the same results we do when doing the same calculation using decimal arithmetic. Let's take a closer look at some specific operations.

Addition

In the following examples, we use 4-bit values. First, consider adding the two unsigned integers 2 and 4:

$$
\begin{array}{rcccc}
0 \quad 000 & \longleftarrow & \text{Carries} & & \\
0010_2 & = & 2_{16} & = & 2_{10} \\
+ \quad 0100_2 & = & 4_{16} & = & 4_{10} \\
\hline
0110_2 & = & 6_{16} & = & 6_{10}
\end{array}
$$

The decimal value 2 is represented in binary as 0010, and decimal 4 is represented by 0100. The carry flag, or C, is equal to 0, because the result of the addition operation is also 4 bits long. We add the digits (shown in both binary and hex here, though the carries are shown only in binary) in the same relative positions as we do in decimal.

Next, consider two larger integers. Keeping our 4-bit storage space, we'll add the two unsigned integers 4 and 14:

$$
\begin{array}{rllllll}
1 & 100 & \longleftarrow & \text{Carries} & & & \\
& 0100_2 & = & 4_{16} & = & 4_{10} \\
+ & 1110_2 & = & e_{16} & = & 14_{10} \\
\hline
& 0010_2 & = & 2_{16} & \neq & 18_{10}
\end{array}
$$

In this case, the carry flag equals 1, because the result of the operation exceeded the 4 bits that we allocated for storing the integers. Thus, our result is incorrect. If we included the carry flag in the result, we would get a 5-bit value and the result would be $10010_2 = 18_{10}$, which is correct. In this case, we'd have to account for the carry flag in software.

Subtraction

Let's subtract 14 from 4, or 1110 from 0100:

$$
\begin{array}{rlllll}
1 & 110 & \longleftarrow & \text{Borrowing} & & \\
& 0100_2 & = & 4_{10} \\
- & 1110_2 & = & 14_{10} \\
\hline
& 0110_2 & = & 6_{10} & \neq & -10_{10}
\end{array}
$$

The CPU can indicate that we had to borrow from beyond the 4 bits by setting the carry flag to 1, which means the 4-bit result in this subtraction is incorrect.

These 4-bit arithmetic examples generalize to any size arithmetic performed by the computer. The AArch64 architecture has an addition instruction that sets the carry flag to 0 if there is no ultimate (or final) carry and sets it to 1 if there is an ultimate carry as a result of the addition. Similarly, there is a subtraction instruction that sets the carry flag to 0 if no borrow from the "outside" is required or to 1 if a borrow is required as a result of the subtraction.

NOTE *Our C compiler does not use these addition and subtraction instructions. There is no indication of carry or borrow when performing an addition or subtraction operation. We'll look at this more closely in Chapter 15, when we discuss embedding assembly language in C code.*

YOUR TURN

3.1   How many bits are required to store a single decimal digit? Invent a code for storing eight decimal digits in 32 bits. Using this code, does binary addition produce the correct results? You saw such a code in Chapter 2, with some reasons for its usefulness.

Adding and Subtracting Signed Integers

When representing nonzero signed decimal integers, there are two possibilities: they can be positive or negative. With only two options, we need to use only 1 bit for the sign. We could use a *sign-magnitude code* by simply using the highest-order bit for signed numbers—say, where 0 means + and 1 means −. But if we do this, we'll run into some problems. As an example, consider adding +2 and −2:

$$
\begin{array}{rcr}
0010_2 & = & +2_{10} \\
-\quad 1010_2 & = & -2_{10} \\
\hline
1100_2 & \neq & 0_{10}
\end{array}
$$

The result, 1100_2, is equal to -4_{10} in our code, which is arithmetically incorrect. The simple addition we used for unsigned numbers will not work correctly for signed numbers when using a sign-magnitude code.

Some computer architectures do use 1 bit for the sign when using signed decimal integers. They have a special *signed add* instruction that handles cases like this. (A fun aside: such computers have both a +0 and a −0!) But most computers employ a different encoding to represent signed numbers that allows the use of a simple add instruction for signed addition. Let's look at this now.

Understanding Two's Complement

In mathematics, the *complement* of a quantity is the amount that must be added to make it "whole." When applying this concept to numbers, the definition of *whole* depends on the radix (or base) you're working in and the number of digits you allow to represent the numbers. If x is an n-digit number in radix r, its *radix complement*, $\neg x$, is defined such that $x + (\neg x) = radix^n$, where $radix^n$ is 1 followed by n 0s. For example, if we're working with two-digit decimal numbers, then the radix complement of 37 is 63, because $37 + 63 = 10^2 = 100$. Another way of saying this is that adding a number to its radix complement results in 0, with a carry beyond the n digits.

Another useful concept is the *diminished radix complement*, which is defined such that $x + diminished\_radix\_complement = radix^n - 1$. For example, the diminished radix complement of 37 is 62, because $37 + 62 = 10^2 - 1 = 99$. If you add a number to its diminished radix complement, the result is n of the largest digits in the radix: two 9s in this example of two digits in radix 10.

To see how the radix complement can be used to represent negative numbers, consider an audiotape cassette player, which plays a cassette tape containing magnetic tape wound back and forth between two spools.

The audio recording on the tape is an analog signal that does not include information about the position along the tape. Many audiotape cassette players have a four-digit counter that represents the tape position. You can insert a tape cassette and push a reset button to set the counter to 0000. As you move the tape forward and backward, the counter registers the movement. These counters provide a "coded" representation of the relative tape position in arbitrary units. Now, assume we can insert a cassette, somehow move it to its center, and push the reset button. Moving the tape forward—in the positive direction—will cause the counter to increment. Moving the tape backward—in the negative direction—will cause the counter to decrement. In particular, if we start at 0000 and move to +1, the "code" on the tape counter will show 0001. On the other hand, if we start at 0000 and move to −1, the "code" on the tape counter will show 9999.

We can use our tape system to perform the arithmetic in the previous example, (+2) + (−2):

1. Move the tape forward to (+2); the counter shows 0002.
2. Add (−2) by moving the tape backward two steps on the counter; the counter now shows 0000, which is 0 according to our code.

Next, we'll perform the same arithmetic starting with (−2) and then adding (+2):

1. Move the tape backward to (−2); the counter shows 9998.
2. Add (+2) by moving the tape forward two steps on the counter; the counter now shows 0000, but there is a carry (9998 + 2 = 0000 with carry = 1).

If we ignore the carry, the answer is correct: 9998 is the 10's complement (the radix is 10) of 0002. When adding two signed integers using radix complement notation, the carry is irrelevant. Adding two signed numbers can give a result that will not fit within the number of bits allocated for storing the result, just as with unsigned numbers. But our tape example just illustrated that the carry flag will probably not show us that the result will not fit. We will discuss this issue in the next section.

Computers work in the binary number system, where the radix is 2. Let's look at the *two's complement* notation for representing signed integers. It uses the same general pattern as the tape counter for representing signed decimal integers in bit patterns.

Table 3-2 shows the correspondence between hexadecimal, binary, and signed decimal (in two's complement notation) for 4-bit values. In binary, moving the "tape" one place back (negative) from 0 would go from 0000 to 1111. In hexadecimal, it would go from 0 to f.

Table 3-2: Four-Bit Two's Complement Notation

One hexadecimal digit	Four binary digits (bits)	Signed decimal
8	1000	−8
9	1001	−7
a	1010	−6
b	1011	−5
c	1100	−4
d	1101	−3
e	1110	−2
f	1111	−1
0	0000	0
1	0001	+1
2	0010	+2
3	0011	+3
4	0100	+4
5	0101	+5
6	0110	+6
7	0111	+7

Here are some important observations about this table:

- The high-order bit of each positive number is 0, and the high-order bit of each negative number is 1.

- Although changing the sign of (*negating*) a number is more complicated than simply changing the high-order bit, it is common to call the high-order bit the *sign bit*.

- The notation allows for one more negative number than positive numbers.

- The range of integers, x, that can be represented in this notation (with 4 bits) is

$$-8_{10} \le x \le +7_{10}$$

or:

$$-2^{(4-1)} \le x \le +(2^{(4-1)} - 1)$$

The last observation can be generalized for n bits to the following:

$$-2^{(n-1)} \le x \le +(2^{(n-1)} - 1)$$

When using two's complement notation, the negative of any n-bit integer x is defined as:

$$x + (-x) = 2^n$$

Notice that 2^n written in binary is 1 followed by n 0s. In other words, in the n-bit two's complement notation, adding a number to its negative produces n 0s and a carry of 1.

Computing Two's Complement

We'll derive a way to compute the negative of a number by using two's complement notation. Solving the defining equation for $-x$, we get:

$$-x = 2^n - x$$

This may look odd to a mathematician, but keep in mind that x in this equation is restricted to n bits, while 2^n has $n + 1$ bits (1 followed by n 0s).

For example, if we want to compute -123 in binary (using two's complement notation) in 8 bits, we perform the arithmetic:

$$-123_{10} = 100000000_2 - 01111011_2$$
$$= 10000101_2$$

This subtraction operation is error-prone, so let's do a bit of algebra on our equation for computing $-x$. We'll subtract 1 from both sides and rearrange a little:

$$-x - 1 = 2^n - x - 1$$
$$= (2^n - 1) - x$$

This gives us:

$$-x = ((2^n - 1) - x) + 1$$

If this looks more complicated than our first equation, don't worry. Let's consider the quantity $(2^n - 1)$. Since 2^n is written in binary as 1 followed by n 0s, $(2^n - 1)$ is written as n 1s. For example, for $n = 8$:

$$2^8 - 1 = 11111111_2$$

Thus, we can say

$$(2^n - 1) - x = 11 \ldots 1_2 - x$$

where $11 \ldots 1_2$ designates n 1s.

Although it may not be immediately obvious, you'll see how easy this subtraction is when you consider the previous example of computing -123 in 8-bit binary. Let $x = 123$, giving:

$$
\begin{array}{rl}
11111111 & \longleftarrow \quad (2^n - 1) \\
-\quad 01111011 & \longleftarrow \quad x \\
\hline
=\quad 10000100 & \longleftarrow \quad \text{One's complement}
\end{array}
$$

Or, in hexadecimal, giving:

$$
\begin{array}{rl}
ff & \longleftarrow \quad (2^n - 1) \\
-\quad 7b & \longleftarrow \quad x \\
\hline
=\quad 84 & \longleftarrow \quad \text{One's complement}
\end{array}
$$

Since all the quantities here have n bits, this computation is easy—simply flip all the bits, giving the diminished radix complement, also called the *one's complement* in the binary number system. A 1 becomes a 0 and a 0 becomes a 1.

All that remains to compute the negative is to add 1 to the result. Finally, we have the following:

$$-123_{10} = 84_{16} + 1_{16}$$
$$= 85_{16}$$
$$= 10000101_2$$

HINT   *To double-check your arithmetic, pay attention to whether the value you are converting is even or odd. It will be the same in all number bases.*

YOUR TURN

3.6   Develop an algorithm to convert signed decimal integers to two's complement binary.

3.7   Develop an algorithm to convert integers in two's complement binary notation to signed decimal.

3.8   The following 16-bit hexadecimal values are stored in two's complement notation. What are the equivalent signed decimal numbers?

    (a)   1234
    (b)   ffff
    (c)   8000
    (d)   7fff

3.9   Show how each of the following signed decimal integers would be stored in 16-bit two's complement notation. Give your answers in hexadecimal:

    (a)   +1,024
    (b)   −1,024
    (c)   −256
    (d)   −32,767

Adding and Subtracting Signed Integers in Binary

The number of bits used to represent a value is determined at the time a program is written by the computer architecture and programming language used. This is why you can't just add more digits (bits) if the result is too large, as you would on paper. For unsigned integers, the solution to this problem is the carry flag, which indicates when the sum of two unsigned integers exceeds the number of bits allocated for it. In this section, you'll learn that adding two signed numbers can also produce a result that exceeds the allocated number of bits, but in this case, the carry flag alone does not indicate the error.

The CPU can indicate when the sum of signed numbers has gotten too big for its bits by using the *overflow flag*, V. The value of the overflow flag is given by an operation that may not seem intuitive at first: the *exclusive or (XOR)* of the penultimate and ultimate carries. As an example, let's say we're adding the two 8-bit numbers 15_{16} and $6f_{16}$:

$$
\begin{array}{rclcl}
\text{Ultimate carry} \quad \rightarrow \quad 0 & 1 & \leftarrow & \text{Penultimate carry} \\
0001 & 0101 & \leftarrow & x \\
+ \quad \underline{0110} & \underline{1111} & \leftarrow & y \\
1000 & 0100 & \leftarrow & \text{Sum}
\end{array}
$$

In this example, the carry is 0 and the penultimate carry is 1. The V flag is equal to the XOR of the ultimate carry and penultimate carry, $V = C \veebar (penultimate\_carry)$, where $\veebar$ is the XOR operator. In this case, $V = 0 \veebar 1 = 1$.

Case by case, we'll see why the V flag indicates the validity of adding two signed integers in the two's complement representation. In the next three sections, we'll discuss the three possible cases: the two numbers can have opposite signs, both be positive, or both be negative.

Two Numbers of the Opposite Sign

Let x be the negative number and y the positive number. We can express x and y in binary as follows:

$$x = 1\ldots, y = 0\ldots$$

That is, the high-order (sign) bit of one number is 1 and the high-order (sign) bit of the other is 0, regardless of what the other bits are.

The result of $x + y$ always remains within the range of the two's complement representation:

$$-2^{(n-1)} \leq x < 0$$
$$0 \leq y \leq +(2^{(n-1)} - 1)$$
$$-2^{(n-1)} \leq x + y \leq +(2^{(n-1)} - 1)$$

If we add x and y, there are two possible carry results:

- If the penultimate carry is 0:

$$
\begin{array}{rclcl}
\text{Carry} \quad \rightarrow \quad 0 & 0 & \leftarrow & \text{Penultimate carry} \\
1\ldots & & \leftarrow & x \\
+ \quad \underline{0\ldots} & & \leftarrow & y \\
1\ldots & & \leftarrow & \text{Sum}
\end{array}
$$

This addition produces $V = 0 \veebar 0 = 0$.

- If the penultimate carry is 1:

$$
\begin{array}{rcll}
\text{Carry} \rightarrow & 1 \quad 1 & \leftarrow & \text{Penultimate carry} \\
& 1\ldots & \leftarrow & x \\
+ & \underline{0\ldots} & \leftarrow & y \\
& 0\ldots & \leftarrow & \text{Sum}
\end{array}
$$

This addition produces $V = 1 \veebar 1 = 0$.

Adding two integers of opposite signs always yields 0 for the overflow flag, so the sum is always within the allocated range.

Two Positive Numbers

If both x and y are positive, we can express them in binary as follows:

$$x = 0\ldots, y = 0\ldots$$

Here, the high-order (sign) bit of both numbers is 0, regardless of what the other bits are.

Again, if we add x and y, there are two possible carry results:

- If the penultimate carry is 0:

$$
\begin{array}{rcll}
\text{Carry} \rightarrow & 0 \quad 0 & \leftarrow & \text{Penultimate carry} \\
& 0\ldots & \leftarrow & x \\
+ & \underline{0\ldots} & \leftarrow & y \\
& 0\ldots & \leftarrow & \text{Sum}
\end{array}
$$

This addition produces $V = 0 \veebar 0 = 0$. The high-order bit of the sum is 0, so it's a positive number, and the sum is in range.

- If the penultimate carry is 1:

$$
\begin{array}{rcll}
\text{Carry} \rightarrow & 0 \quad 1 & \leftarrow & \text{Penultimate carry} \\
& 0\ldots & \leftarrow & x \\
+ & \underline{0\ldots} & \leftarrow & y \\
& 1\ldots & \leftarrow & \text{Sum}
\end{array}
$$

This addition produces $V = 0 \veebar 1 = 1$. The high-order bit of the sum is 1, so it's a negative number. Adding two positive numbers cannot give a negative sum, so the sum must have exceeded the allocated range.

Two Negative Numbers

If both x and y are negative, we can express them in binary as follows:

$$x = 1\ldots, y = 1\ldots$$

In this case, the high-order (sign) bit of both numbers is 1, regardless of what the other bits are.

If we add x and y, there are two possible carry results:

- If the penultimate carry is 0:

$$
\begin{array}{rll}
\text{Carry} \rightarrow \quad 1 \quad 0 & \leftarrow & \text{Penultimate carry} \\
1\ldots & \leftarrow & x \\
+ \quad 1\ldots & \leftarrow & y \\
\hline
0\ldots & \leftarrow & \text{Sum}
\end{array}
$$

This gives $V = 1 \veebar 0 = 1$. The high-order bit of the sum is 0, so it's a positive number. But adding two negative numbers cannot give a positive sum, so the sum has exceeded the allocated range.

- If the penultimate carry is 1:

$$
\begin{array}{rll}
\text{Carry} \rightarrow \quad 1 \quad 1 & \leftarrow & \text{Penultimate carry} \\
1\ldots & \leftarrow & x \\
+ \quad 1\ldots & \leftarrow & y \\
\hline
1\ldots & \leftarrow & \text{Sum}
\end{array}
$$

This gives $V = 1 \veebar 1 = 0$. The high-order bit of the sum is 1, so it's a negative number and the sum is within range.

We won't go into subtraction here. The same rules apply there, and I invite you to explore them on your own.

We can state the following rules for adding or subtracting two n-bit numbers, based on what you just learned and what we did in "Unsigned Integers in the Binary System" on page 40:

- When the program treats the result as unsigned, the carry flag, C, is 0 if and only if the result is within the n-bit range; V is irrelevant.
- When the program treats the result as signed, the overflow flag, V, is 0 if and only if the result is within the n-bit range; C is irrelevant.

NOTE *Using two's complement notation means the CPU does not need additional instructions for signed addition and subtraction, thus simplifying the hardware. The CPU just sees bit patterns. The AArch64 architecture includes add and subtract instructions that set C and V according to the rules of the respective binary arithmetic operation, regardless of how the program treats the numbers. The distinction between signed and unsigned is completely determined by the program. After each addition or subtraction operation, the program should check the state of C for unsigned integers or V for signed integers and at least indicate when the sum is in error. Many high-level languages do not perform this check, which can lead to some obscure program bugs.*

The Circular Nature of Integer Codes

The notations used for both unsigned integers and signed integers are circular in nature—for a given number of bits, each code "wraps around." Figure 3-1 shows this using the "decoder ring" for 3-bit numbers.

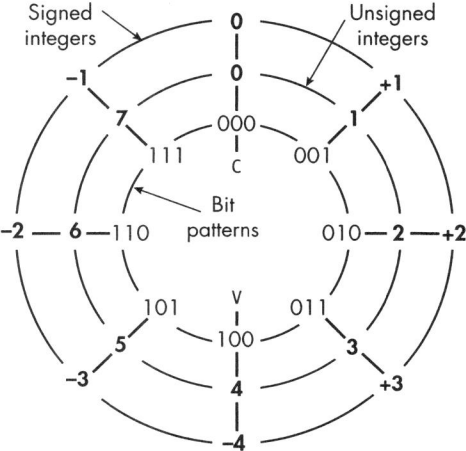

Figure 3-1: A "decoder ring" for 3-bit signed and unsigned integers

To use this decoder ring to add or subtract two integers, follow these steps:

1. Pick the ring corresponding to the type of integer you're using (signed or unsigned).

2. Move to the location on that ring corresponding to the first integer.

3. Move along that ring the number of "spokes" equal to the second integer. Move clockwise to add and counterclockwise to subtract.

The result is correct if you do not cross the top for unsigned integers or cross the bottom for signed integers.

YOUR TURN

3.10   Use the decoder ring in Figure 3-1 to perform the following arithmetic. Indicate whether the result is "right" or "wrong":

    (a)   Unsigned integers: 1 + 3
    (b)   Unsigned integers: 3 + 4
    (c)   Unsigned integers: 5 + 6
    (d)   Signed integers: (+1) + (+3)
    (e)   Signed integers: (−3) − (+3)
    (f)   Signed integers: (+3) + (−4)

(continued)

3.11 Add the following pairs of 8-bit numbers (shown in hexadecimal) and indicate whether your result is "right" or "wrong." First treat them as unsigned values and then as signed values (stored in two's complement):

(a) 55 + aa
(b) 55 + f0
(c) 80 + 7b
(d) 63 + 7b
(e) 0f + ff
(f) 80 + 80

3.12 Add the following pairs of 16-bit numbers (shown in hexadecimal) and indicate whether your result is "right" or "wrong." First treat them as unsigned values and then as signed values (stored in two's complement):

(a) 1234 + edcc
(b) 1234 + fedc
(c) 8000 + 8000
(d) 0400 + ffff
(e) 07d0 + 782f
(f) 8000 + ffff

What You've Learned

Binary arithmetic   Computers perform addition and subtraction in the binary number system. Addition of two numbers may yield a result that is 1 bit wider than each of the two numbers. Subtraction of one number from another may require borrowing from 1 bit beyond the width of the two numbers.

Representing signed/unsigned   Bit patterns can be treated as representing either signed or unsigned integers. Two's complement notation is commonly used to represent signed integers.

Carry flag   The CPU includes a 1-bit carry flag, C, that can show whether the result of addition or subtraction exceeds the number of bits allowed for an unsigned integer.

Overflow flag   The CPU includes a 1-bit overflow flag, V, that can show whether the result of addition or subtraction exceeds the number of bits allowed for a signed integer using two's complement notation.

In the next chapter, you'll learn how to perform Boolean algebra. Although it may seem a bit strange at first, once we get going, you'll see that it's actually easier than elementary algebra. For one thing, everything evaluates to either 0 or 1!

4

BOOLEAN ALGEBRA

Boolean algebra was developed in the 19th century by an English mathematician, George Boole, who was working on ways to use mathematical rigor to solve logic problems. He formalized a mathematical system for manipulating logical values in which the only possible values for the variables are *true* and *false*, usually designated 1 and 0, respectively.

The basic operations in Boolean algebra are *conjunction* (AND), *disjunction* (OR), and *negation* (NOT). This distinguishes it from elementary algebra, which includes the infinite set of real numbers and uses the arithmetic operations addition, subtraction, multiplication, and division. (Exponentiation is a simplified notation for repeated multiplication.)

While mathematicians and logicians were expanding the field of Boolean algebra in increasingly complex and abstract ways, engineers were learning to harness electrical flows using switches in circuits to perform logic operations. The two fields developed in parallel until the mid-1930s, when a graduate student named Claude Shannon proved that electrical switches could be used to implement the full range of Boolean algebraic expressions. (When used to describe switching circuits, Boolean algebra is sometimes called *switching algebra*.) With Shannon's discovery, a world of possibilities was opened and Boolean algebra became the mathematical foundation of the computer.

In this chapter, I'll start with descriptions of the basic Boolean operators. Then, you'll learn about their logical rules, which form the basis of Boolean algebra. Next, I'll explain ways to combine Boolean variables and operators into algebraic expressions to form Boolean logic functions. Finally, I'll discuss techniques for simplifying Boolean functions. In subsequent chapters, you'll learn how electronic on/off switches can be used to implement logic functions that can be connected together in logic circuits to perform the primary functions of a computer: arithmetic, logic operations, and memory storage.

Basic Boolean Operators

A Boolean operator acts on a value or pair of values called the *operand(s)*. There are several symbols used to denote each Boolean operator, which I'll include in the description of each of the operators. In this book, I'll present the symbols used by logicians.

I'll use truth tables to show the results of each operation. A *truth table* shows the results for all possible combinations of the operands. For example, consider the addition of two bits, x and y. There are four possible combinations of the values, one of which is addition, which will give a sum and a possible carry. Table 4-1 shows how to express this in a truth table.

Table 4-1: A Truth Table for Addition of Two Bits

x	y	Carry	Sum
0	0	0	0
0	1	0	1
1	0	0	1
1	1	1	0

I'll also provide the electronic circuit representations for *gates*, which are the electronic devices that implement the Boolean operators. You'll learn more about these devices in Chapters 5 through 8, where you'll also see that the real-world behavior of the physical devices varies slightly from the ideal mathematical behavior shown in the truth tables.

As with elementary algebra, you can combine these basic operators to define secondary operators. You'll see an example of this when I define the XOR operator near the end of this chapter. For now, let's take a look at the basic operators:

AND

AND is a *binary operator*, meaning it acts on two operands. The result of AND is 1 if and only if *both* operands are 1; otherwise, the result is 0. In logic, this operation is known as *conjunction*. I'll use $\land$ to designate the AND operation. It's also common to use the · symbol or simply AND.

Figure 4-1 shows the circuit symbol for an AND gate and a truth table defining the output, with operands x and y.

x	y	x ∧ y
0	0	0
0	1	0
1	0	0
1	1	1

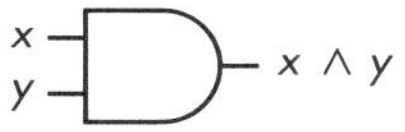

Figure 4-1: An AND gate acting on two variables, x and y

As you can see in the truth table, the AND operator has properties similar to multiplication in elementary algebra, which is why some use the · symbol to represent it.

OR

OR is also a binary operator. The result of OR is 1 if at least one of the operands is 1; otherwise, the result is 0. In logic, this operation is known as *disjunction*. I'll use ∨ to designate the OR operation. It's also common to use the + symbol or simply OR. Figure 4-2 shows the circuit symbol for an OR gate and a truth table defining the output, with operands x and y.

x	y	x ∨ y
0	0	0
0	1	1
1	0	1
1	1	1

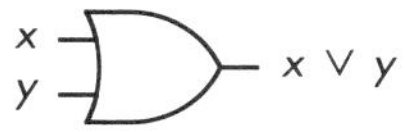

Figure 4-2: An OR gate acting on two variables, x and y

The truth table shows that the OR operator follows rules somewhat similar to addition in elementary algebra, which is why some use the + symbol to represent it.

NOT

NOT is a *unary operator*, which acts on only one operand. The result of NOT is 1 if the operand is 0 and 0 if the operand is 1. Other names for the NOT operation are *complement* and *invert*. I'll use ¬ to designate the NOT operation. It's also common to use the ' symbol, an overscore above the variable, or simply NOT. Figure 4-3 shows the circuit symbol for a NOT gate and a truth table defining the output, with the operand x.

x	¬x
0	1
1	0

Figure 4-3: A NOT gate acting on one variable, x

As you'll see, NOT has some properties of the arithmetic negation used in elementary algebra, but there are some significant differences.

It's no accident that AND is multiplicative and OR is additive. George Boole developed his algebra to apply mathematical rigor to logic and use addition and multiplication to manipulate logical statements. He developed the rules based on using AND for multiplication and OR for addition. In the next section, you'll learn how to use these operators, together with NOT, to represent logical statements.

Boolean Expressions

Just as you can use elementary algebra operators to combine variables into expressions such as $(x + y)$, you can use Boolean operators to combine variables into expressions.

There is a significant difference, though. A Boolean expression is created from values (0 and 1) and literals. In Boolean algebra, a *literal* is a single instance of a variable or its complement that's being used in an expression. In the expression

$$x \wedge y \vee \neg x \wedge z \vee \neg x \wedge \neg y \wedge \neg z$$

there are three variables (x, y, and z) and seven literals. In a Boolean expression, you have a variable in both its complemented form and its uncomplemented form, because each form is a separate literal.

We can combine literals using either the $\wedge$ or the $\vee$ operator. Like in elementary algebra, Boolean algebra expressions are made up of *terms*—groups of literals that are acted upon by operators, such as $(x \vee y)$ or $(a \wedge b)$—and *operation precedence* (or *order of operations*) specifies how these operators are applied when evaluating an expression. Table 4-2 lists the precedence rules for the Boolean operators. As with elementary algebra, expressions in parentheses are evaluated first.

Table 4-2: Precedence Rules for Boolean Algebra Operators

Operation	Notation	Precedence
NOT	$\neg x$	Highest
AND	$x \wedge y$	Middle
OR	$x \vee y$	Lowest

Now that you know how the three fundamental Boolean operators work, we'll look at some of the rules they obey when used in algebraic expressions. As you'll see later in the chapter, we can use the rules to simplify Boolean expressions, which will allow us to simplify the way we implement those expressions in the hardware.

Knowing how to simplify Boolean expressions is an important tool for both those making hardware and those writing software. A computer is just a physical manifestation of Boolean logic. Even if your only interest is in programming, every programming statement you write is ultimately carried out by hardware that is completely described by the system of Boolean algebra. Our programming languages tend to hide much of this through abstraction, but they still use Boolean expressions to implement programming logic.

Boolean Algebra Rules

When comparing AND and OR in Boolean algebra to multiplication and addition in elementary algebra, you'll find that some of the rules of Boolean algebra are familiar but others are significantly different.

Rules That Are the Same as Elementary Algebra

Let's start with the rules that are the same; in the next section, we'll look at the ones that differ. These rules are as follows:

AND and OR are associative

We say that an operator is *associative* if we can change the order of applying two or more occurrences of the operator in an expression without changing the value of the expression. Mathematically:

$$x \land (y \land z) = (x \land y) \land z$$
$$x \lor (y \lor z) = (x \lor y) \lor z$$

To prove the associative rule for AND and OR, let's use exhaustive truth tables, as shown in Tables 4-3 and 4-4. Table 4-3 lists all possible values of the variables x, y, and z, as well as the intermediate computations of the terms $(y \land z)$ and $(x \land y)$. In the last two columns, I compute the values of each expression on both sides of the previous equations, which shows that the two equalities hold.

Table 4-3: The Associativity of the AND Operation

x	y	z	$(y \land z)$	$(x \land y)$	$x \land (y \land z)$	$(x \land y) \land z$
0	0	0	0	0	0	0
0	0	1	0	0	0	0
0	1	0	0	0	0	0
0	1	1	1	0	0	0
1	0	0	0	0	0	0
1	0	1	0	0	0	0
1	1	0	0	1	0	0
1	1	1	1	1	1	1

Table 4-4 lists all possible values of the variables x, y, and z, as well as the intermediate computations of the terms $(y \lor z)$ and $(x \lor y)$. In the last two columns, I compute the values of each expression on both sides of the previous equations, which again shows that the two equalities hold.

Table 4-4: The Associativity of the OR Operation

x	y	z	$(y \lor z)$	$(x \lor y)$	$x \lor (y \lor z)$	$(x \lor y) \lor z$
0	0	0	0	0	0	0
0	0	1	1	0	1	1
0	1	0	1	1	1	1
0	1	1	1	1	1	1
1	0	0	0	1	1	1
1	0	1	1	1	1	1
1	1	0	1	1	1	1
1	1	1	1	1	1	1

This strategy works for each of the rules shown in this section, but I'll only go through the truth table for the associative rule here. You'll get to do this for the other rules in "Your Turn" exercise 4.1 on page 61.

AND and OR have identity values

An *identity value* is a value specific to an operation, such that using that operation on a quantity with the identity value yields the value of the original quantity. For AND and OR, the identity values are 1 and 0, respectively:

$$x \land 1 = x$$
$$x \lor 0 = x$$

AND and OR are commutative

We can say that an operator is *commutative* if we can reverse the order of its operands without changing the result of the operation:

$$x \land y = y \land x$$
$$x \lor y = y \lor x$$

AND is distributive over OR

The AND operator applied to quantities OR-ed together can be *distributed* to apply to each of the OR-ed quantities:

$$x \land (y \lor z) = (x \land y) \lor (x \land z)$$

Unlike in elementary algebra, the additive OR *is* distributive over the multiplicative AND. You'll see this in the next section.

AND has an annulment (also called annihilation) value

An *annulment value* is a value such that operating on a quantity with the annulment value yields the annulment value. The annulment value for AND is 0:

$$x \land 0 = 0$$

We're used to 0 being the annulment value for multiplication in elementary algebra, but addition has no concept of annulment. You'll learn about the annulment value for OR in the next section.

NOT shows involution

An operator shows *involution* if applying it to a quantity twice yields the original quantity:

$$\neg(\neg x) = x$$

Involution is simply the application of a double complement: NOT(NOT true) = true. This is similar to double negation in elementary algebra.

Rules That Differ from Elementary Algebra

Although AND is multiplicative and OR is additive, there are significant differences between these logical operations and the arithmetic ones. The differences stem from the fact that Boolean algebra deals with logic expressions that evaluate to either true or false, while elementary algebra deals with the infinite set of real numbers. In this section, you'll see expressions that might remind you of elementary algebra, but the Boolean algebra rules are different. Those rules are:

OR is distributive over AND

The OR operator applied to quantities AND-ed together can be distributed to apply to each of the AND-ed quantities:

$$x \vee (y \wedge z) = (x \vee y) \wedge (x \vee z)$$

Because addition is not distributive over multiplication in elementary algebra, you might overlook this way of manipulating Boolean expressions.

First, let's look at elementary algebra. Using addition for OR and multiplication for AND in the previous equation, we have:

$$x + (y \cdot z) \neq (x + y) \cdot (x + z)$$

When we plug in the numbers $x = 1$, $y = 2$, and $z = 3$, the left-hand side gives

$$1 + (2 \cdot 3) = 7$$

and the right-hand side gives:

$$(1 + 2) \cdot (1 + 3) = 12$$

Thus, addition is *not* distributive over multiplication in elementary algebra.

The best way to show that OR is distributive over AND in Boolean algebra is to use a truth table, as shown in Table 4-5.

Table 4-5: OR Distributes over AND

x	y	z	$x \vee (y \wedge z)$	$(x \vee y) \wedge (x \vee z)$
0	0	0	0	0
0	0	1	0	0
0	1	0	0	0
0	1	1	1	1
1	0	0	1	1
1	0	1	1	1
1	1	0	1	1
1	1	1	1	1

Comparing the two right-hand columns, you can tell that OR-ing the variable, x, with each of the two AND-ed variables, y and z, gives the same result as OR-ing it with each of the variables and AND-ing the two OR-ed terms. Thus, the distributive property holds.

OR has an annulment (also called annihilation) value

There is no annulment value for addition in elementary algebra, but in Boolean algebra, the annulment value for OR is 1:

$$x \vee 1 = 1$$

AND and OR both have a complement value

The *complement value* is the diminished radix complement of the variable. You learned in Chapter 3 that the sum of a quantity and that quantity's diminished radix complement is equal to (*radix* − 1). Since the radix in Boolean algebra is 2, the complement of 0 is 1 and the complement of 1 is 0. So, the complement of a Boolean quantity is simply the NOT of that quantity, which gives:

$$x \wedge \neg x = 0$$
$$x \vee \neg x = 1$$

The complement value illustrates one of the differences between the AND and OR logical operations and the multiplication and addition arithmetic operations. In elementary algebra:

$$x \cdot (-x) = -x^2$$
$$x + (-x) = 0$$

Even if we restrict x to be 0 or 1, in elementary algebra $1 \cdot (-1) = -1$ and $1 + (-1) = 0$.

AND and OR are idempotent

If an operator is *idempotent*, applying it to two of the same operands results in that operand. In other words:

$$x \wedge x = x$$
$$x \vee x = x$$

This looks different than in elementary algebra, where repeatedly multiplying a number by itself is exponentiation and repeatedly adding a number to itself is equivalent to multiplication.

De Morgan's law applies

In Boolean algebra, the special relationship between the AND and OR operations is captured by *De Morgan's law*, which states:

$$\neg(x \wedge y) = \neg x \vee \neg y$$
$$\neg(x \vee y) = \neg x \wedge \neg y$$

The first equation states that the NOT of the AND of two Boolean quantities is equal to the OR of the NOT of the two quantities. The second equation states that the NOT of the OR of two Boolean quantities is equal to the AND of the NOT of the two quantities.

This relationship is an example of the *principle of duality*, which in Boolean algebra states that if you replace every 0 with a 1, every 1 with a 0, every AND with an OR, and every OR with an AND, the equation is still true. Look back over the rules just given and you'll see that all of them except involution have dual operations. De Morgan's law is one of the best examples of duality; you'll see this principle in play when you complete "Your Turn" exercise 4.2.

YOUR TURN

4.1   Use truth tables to prove the Boolean algebra rules given in this section.

4.2   Prove De Morgan's law.

Boolean Functions

The functionality of a computer is based on Boolean logic, which means the various operations of a computer are specified by Boolean functions. A Boolean function looks somewhat like a function in elementary algebra, but the variables can appear in either uncomplemented or complemented form. The variables and constants are connected by Boolean operators. A Boolean function evaluates to either 1 or 0 (true or false).

When we discussed addition in the binary number system on page 41 in Chapter 3, you saw that when adding two bits, x and y, we have to include a possible carry into their bit position in the computation. The conditions that cause the carry out from the bit position to be 1 are:

there's no carry into the current bit position, $x = 1$, and $y = 1$, or

there's a carry into the current bit position, $x = 0$, and $y = 1$, or

there's a carry into the current bit position, $x = 1$, and $y = 0$, or

there's a carry into the current bit position, $x = 1$, and $y = 1$.

We can express this more concisely with the Boolean function

$$C_{out}(c_{in}, x, y) = (\neg c_{in} \wedge x \wedge y) \vee (c_{in} \wedge \neg x \wedge y) \vee (c_{in} \wedge x \wedge \neg y) \vee (c_{in} \wedge x \wedge y)$$

where x is one bit, y is the other bit, c_{in} is the carry in from the next lower-order bit position, and $C_{out}(c_{in}, x, y)$ is the carry resulting from the addition in the current bit position. We'll use this equation throughout this section, but first, let's think a bit about the differences between Boolean and elementary functions.

Like an elementary algebra function, a Boolean algebra function can be manipulated mathematically, but the mathematical operations are different. Operations in elementary algebra are performed on the infinite set of real numbers, but Boolean functions work on only two possible values, 0 or 1. Elementary algebra functions can evaluate to any real number, but Boolean functions can evaluate only to 0 or 1.

This difference means we have to think differently about Boolean functions. For example, look at this elementary algebra function:

$$F(x, y) = x \cdot (-y)$$

You probably read it as "if I multiply the value of x by the negative of the value of y, I'll get the value of $F(x, y)$." However, with the Boolean function

$$F(x, y) = x \wedge (\neg y)$$

there are only four possibilities. If $x = 1$ and $y = 0$, then $F(x, y) = 1$; for the other three possibilities, $F(x, y) = 0$. Whereas you can plug any numbers into an elementary algebra function, a Boolean algebra function shows you what the values of the variables are that cause the function to evaluate to 1. I think of elementary algebra functions as *asking* me to plug in values for the variables for evaluation, while Boolean algebra functions *tell* me what values of the variables cause the function to evaluate to 1.

There are simpler ways to express the conditions for carry, and those simplifications lead to being able to implement a Boolean function for carry with fewer logic gates, thus lowering the cost and power usage. In this and the following sections, you'll learn how the mathematical nature of Boolean algebra makes function simplification easier and more concise.

Canonical Sum or Sum of Minterms

A *canonical form* of a Boolean function explicitly shows whether each variable in the problem is complemented or not in each term that defines the function, just as we did with our plain-language statement of the conditions that produce a carry of 1 earlier. This ensures that you have taken all possible combinations into account in the function definition.

We'll use the equation for carry on page 62 to illustrate these concepts. Although the parentheses in the equation are not required, I've added them to help you see the form of the equation. The parentheses show four *product terms*, which are terms where all the literals are operated on only by AND. The four product terms are then OR-ed together. Since the OR operation is like addition, the right-hand side is called a *sum of products*. It's also said to be in *disjunctive normal form*.

Let's look more closely at the product terms. Each of them includes all the variables in this equation in the form of a literal (uncomplemented or complemented). An equation that has n variables has 2^n permutations of the values for the variables; a *minterm* is a product term that specifies exactly one of the permutations. Since there are four combinations of values for c_{in}, x, and y that produce a carry of 1, the previous equation has four of the possible eight minterms. A Boolean function that is defined by summing (OR-ing) all the minterms that evaluate to 1 is said to be a *canonical sum*, a *sum of minterms*, or in *full disjunctive normal form*. A function defined by a sum of minterms evaluates to 1 when at least one of the minterms evaluates to 1.

For every minterm, exactly one set of values for the variables makes the minterm evaluate to 1. For example, the minterm $(c_{in} \land x \land \neg y)$ in the previous equation evaluates to 1 only when $c_{in} = 1$, $x = 1$, $y = 0$. A product term that does not contain all the variables in the problem, in either uncomplemented or complemented form, will always evaluate to 1 for more sets of values for the variables than a minterm. For example, $(c_{in} \land x)$ evaluates to 1 for $c_{in} = 1$, $x = 1$, $y = 0$ and for $c_{in} = 1$, $x = 1$, $y = 1$. (We call them *minterms* because they minimize the number of cases that evaluate to 1.)

Rather than write out all the literals in a function, logic designers commonly use the notation m_i to specify the ith minterm, where i is the integer represented by the values of the literals in the problem if the values are placed in order and treated as binary numbers. For example, $c_{in} = 1$, $x = 1$, $y = 0$ gives 110, which is the (base 10) number 6; thus, that minterm is m_6.

Table 4-6 shows all eight possible minterms for the three-variable function that specifies carry.

Table 4-6: The Conditions That Cause Carry to Be 1

c_{in}	x	y	Minterm		$C_{out}(c_{in}, x, y)$
0	0	0	m_0	$(\neg c_{in} \land \neg x \land \neg y)$	0
0	0	1	m_1	$(\neg c_{in} \land \neg x \land y)$	0
0	1	0	m_2	$(\neg c_{in} \land x \land \neg y)$	0
0	1	1	m_3	$(\neg c_{in} \land x \land y)$	1
1	0	0	m_4	$(c_{in} \land \neg x \land \neg y)$	0
1	0	1	m_5	$(c_{in} \land \neg x \land y)$	1
1	1	0	m_6	$(c_{in} \land x \land \neg y)$	1
1	1	1	m_7	$(c_{in} \land x \land y)$	1

The $C_{out}(c_{in}, x, y)$ column shows which minterms in our equation cause it to evaluate to 1.

Using this notation to write a Boolean equation as a canonical sum and using the $\sum$ symbol to denote summation, we can restate the function for carry as:

$$C_{out}(c_{in}, x, y) = (\neg c_{in} \wedge x \wedge y) \vee (c_{in} \wedge \neg x \wedge y) \vee (c_{in} \wedge x \wedge \neg y) \vee (c_{in} \wedge x \wedge y)$$
$$= m_3 \vee m_5 \vee m_6 \vee m_7$$
$$= \sum(3, 5, 6, 7)$$

We are looking at a simple example here. For more complicated functions, writing out all the minterms is error-prone. The simplified notation is easier to work with and helps avoid making errors.

Canonical Product or Product of Maxterms

Depending on factors like available components and personal choice, a designer may prefer to work with the cases where a function evaluates to 0 instead of 1. In our example, that means a design that specifies when the complement of carry is 0. To see how this works, let's take the complement of both sides of the equation for specifying carry, using De Morgan's law:

$$\neg C_{out}(c_{in}, x, y) = (c_{in} \vee \neg x \vee \neg y) \wedge (\neg c_{in} \vee x \vee \neg y) \wedge (\neg c_{in} \vee \neg x \vee y) \wedge (\neg c_{in} \vee \neg x \vee \neg y)$$

Because we complemented both sides of the equation, we now have the Boolean equation for $\neg C_{out}$, the complement of carry. Thus, we are looking for conditions that cause $\neg C_{out}$ to evaluate to 0, not 1. In this equation, the parentheses are required due to the precedence rules of Boolean operators. The parentheses show four *sum terms*, which are terms where all the literals are operated on only by OR. The four sum terms are then AND-ed together. Since the AND operation is like multiplication, the right-hand side is called a *product of sums*. It's also said to be in *conjunctive normal form*.

Each of the sum terms includes all the variables in this equation in the form of literals (uncomplemented or complemented). Whereas a minterm was a *product* term that specified a single permutation of the 2^n permutations of possible values for the variables, a *maxterm* is a *sum* term specifying exactly one of those permutations. A Boolean function that is defined by multiplying (AND-ing) all the maxterms that evaluate to 0 is said to be a *canonical product*, a *product of maxterms*, or in *full conjunctive normal form*.

Each maxterm identifies exactly one set of values for the variables in a function that cause the term to evaluate to 0 when OR-ed together. For example, the maxterm $(\neg c_{in} \vee \neg x \vee y)$ in the previous equation evaluates to 0 only when $c_{in} = 1$, $x = 1$, $y = 0$. But a sum term that does not contain all the variables in the problem, in either uncomplemented or complemented form, will always evaluate to 0 for more than one set of values. For example, the sum term $(\neg c_{in} \vee \neg x)$ evaluates to 0 for two sets of values for the three variables in this example, $c_{in} = 1$, $x = 1$, $y = 0$ and $c_{in} = 1$, $x = 1$, and $y = 1$. (We call them *max*terms because they minimize the number of cases that evaluate to 0 and thus *maximize* the number of cases that evaluate to 1.)

Rather than write out all the literals in a function, logic designers commonly use the notation M_i to specify the ith maxterm, where i is the integer value of the base 2 number created by concatenating the values of the literals in the problem. For example, stringing together $c_{in} = 1$, $x = 1$, $y = 0$ gives 110, which is the maxterm M_6. The truth table in Table 4-7 shows the maxterms that cause the carry to be 0. Notice that maxterm $M_6 = (\neg c_{in} \vee \neg x \vee y)$ evaluates to 0 when $c_{in} = 1$, $x = 1$, and $y = 0$.

Table 4-7 shows all eight possible maxterms for the three-variable function that specifies the complement of carry.

Table 4-7: The Conditions That Cause the Complement of Carry to Be 0

c_{in}	x	y	Maxterm		$\neg C_{out}(c_{in}, x, y)$
0	0	0	M_0	$(c_{in} \vee x \vee y)$	1
0	0	1	M_1	$(c_{in} \vee x \vee \neg y)$	1
0	1	0	M_2	$(c_{in} \vee \neg x \vee y)$	1
0	1	1	M_3	$(c_{in} \vee \neg x \vee \neg y)$	0
1	0	0	M_4	$(\neg c_{in} \vee x \vee y)$	1
1	0	1	M_5	$(\neg c_{in} \vee x \vee \neg y)$	0
1	1	0	M_6	$(\neg c_{in} \vee \neg x \vee y)$	0
1	1	1	M_7	$(\neg c_{in} \vee \neg x \vee \neg y)$	0

The $\neg C_{out}(c_{in}, x, y)$ column shows which maxterms in our equation cause it to evaluate to 0.

Using this notation to write a Boolean equation as a canonical product and using the $\prod$ symbol to denote multiplication, we can restate the function for the complement of carry as:

$$\neg C_{out}(c_{in}, x, y) = (c_{in} \vee \neg x \vee \neg y) \wedge (\neg c_{in} \vee x \vee \neg y) \wedge (\neg c_{in} \vee \neg x \vee y) \wedge (\neg c_{in} \vee \neg x \vee \neg y)$$
$$= M_3 \wedge M_5 \wedge M_6 \wedge M_7$$
$$= \prod(3, 5, 6, 7)$$

In Table 4-7, you'll see that these are the conditions that cause the complement of carry to be 0 and hence the carry to be 1. This shows that using either minterms or maxterms is equivalent.

Comparison of Canonical Boolean Forms

Table 4-8 shows all the minterms and maxterms for a three-variable problem. Comparing the corresponding minterms and maxterms reveals the duality of minterms and maxterms: one can be formed from the other using De Morgan's law by complementing each variable and interchanging OR and AND.

Table 4-8: The Canonical Terms for a Three-Variable Problem

Minterm = 1		x	y	z	Maxterm = 0	
m_0	$\neg x \wedge \neg y \wedge \neg z$	0	0	0	M_0	$x \vee y \vee z$
m_1	$\neg x \wedge \neg y \wedge z$	0	0	1	M_1	$x \vee y \vee \neg z$
m_2	$\neg x \wedge y \wedge \neg z$	0	1	0	M_2	$x \vee \neg y \vee z$
m_3	$\neg x \wedge y \wedge z$	0	1	1	M_3	$x \vee \neg y \vee \neg z$
m_4	$x \wedge \neg y \wedge \neg z$	1	0	0	M_4	$\neg x \vee y \vee z$
m_5	$x \wedge \neg y \wedge z$	1	0	1	M_5	$\neg x \vee y \vee \neg z$
m_6	$x \wedge y \wedge \neg z$	1	1	0	M_6	$\neg x \vee \neg y \vee z$
m_7	$x \wedge y \wedge z$	1	1	1	M_7	$\neg x \vee \neg y \vee \neg z$

The Venn diagrams in Figure 4-4 provide a pictorial view of the reason we use the terms minterm and maxterm.

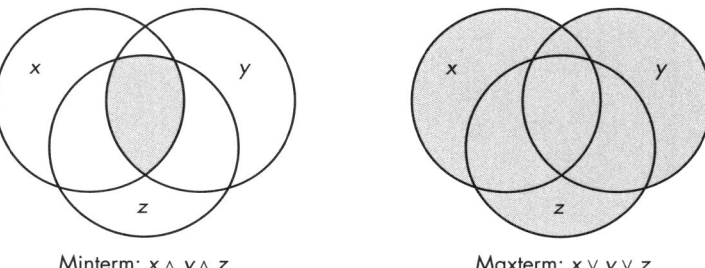

Minterm: $x \wedge y \wedge z$ Maxterm: $x \vee y \vee z$

Figure 4-4: The relationships between three variables for a minterm and a maxterm

The canonical forms give us a complete and unique statement of the function because they take all possible combinations of the variables' values into account. However, there often are simpler solutions to the problem. The remainder of this chapter will be devoted to methods of simplifying Boolean functions.

Boolean Expression Minimization

When implementing a Boolean function in hardware, each $\wedge$ operator specifies an AND gate, each $\vee$ operator specifies an OR gate, and each $\neg$ operator specifies a NOT gate. In general, the complexity of the hardware is related to the number of AND and OR gates used (NOT gates are simple and tend not to contribute significantly to the complexity). Simpler hardware uses fewer components, thus saving cost and space, and uses less power. These savings are especially important with handheld and wearable devices. In this section, you'll learn how you can manipulate Boolean expressions to reduce the number of AND and OR gates, thus simplifying their hardware implementation.

Minimal Expressions

When simplifying a function, start with one of the canonical forms to ensure you have taken all possible cases into account. To translate a problem into a canonical form, create a truth table that lists all possible combinations of the variables in the problem. From the truth table, it will be easy to list the minterms or maxterms that define the function.

Armed with a canonical statement, the next step is to look for a functionally equivalent *minimal expression*, which is an expression that does the same thing as the canonical one using a minimum number of literals and Boolean operators. To minimize an expression, we apply the rules of Boolean algebra to reduce the number of terms and the number of literals in each term, without changing the logical meaning of the expression.

There are two types of minimal expressions, depending on whether you use minterms or maxterms:

Minimal sum of products

When starting with a minterms description of the problem, the minimal expression, known as a *minimal sum of products*, is a sum of products expression where all other mathematically equivalent sum of products expressions have at least as many product terms and those with the same number of product terms have at least as many literals. As an example of a minimal sum of products, consider these equations:

$$S(x, y, z) = (\neg x \wedge \neg y \wedge \neg z) \vee (x \wedge \neg y \wedge \neg z) \vee (x \wedge \neg y \wedge z)$$
$$S1(x, y, z) = (\neg x \wedge \neg y \wedge \neg z) \vee (x \wedge \neg y)$$
$$S2(x, y, z) = (x \wedge \neg y \wedge z) \vee (\neg y \wedge \neg z)$$
$$S3(x, y, z) = (x \wedge \neg y) \vee (\neg y \wedge \neg z)$$

S is in canonical form as each of the product terms explicitly shows the contribution of all three variables. The other three functions are simplifications of S. Although all three have the same number of product terms, $S3$ is a minimal sum of products for S because it has fewer literals in its product terms than $S1$ and $S2$.

Minimal product of sums

When starting with a maxterms description of the problem, the minimal expression, known as a *minimal product of sums*, is a product of sums expression where all other mathematically equivalent product of sums expressions have at least as many sum terms and those with the same number of sum terms have at least as many literals. For an example of a minimal product of sums, consider these equations:

$$P(x, y, z) = (\neg x \vee \neg y \vee z) \wedge (\neg x \vee y \vee z) \wedge (x \vee \neg y \vee z)$$
$$P1(x, y, z) = (x \vee \neg y \vee z) \wedge (\neg x \vee z)$$
$$P2(x, y, z) = (\neg x \vee y \vee z) \wedge (\neg y \vee z)$$
$$P3(x, y, z) = (\neg x \vee z) \wedge (\neg y \vee z)$$

P is in canonical form, and the other three functions are simplifications of *P*. Although all three have the same number of sum terms as *P*, *P3* is a minimal product of sums for *P* because it has fewer literals in its product terms than *P1* and *P2*.

A problem may have more than one minimal solution. Good hardware design typically involves finding several minimal solutions and assessing each one within the context of the available hardware. This means more than using fewer gates; for example, as you'll learn when we discuss hardware implementation, adding judiciously placed NOT gates can reduce hardware complexity.

In the following two sections, you'll learn two ways to find minimal expressions.

Minimization Using Algebraic Manipulations

To illustrate the importance of reducing the complexity of a Boolean function, let's return to the function for carry:

$$C_{out}(c_{in}, x, y) = (\neg c_{in} \wedge x \wedge y) \vee (c_{in} \wedge \neg x \wedge y) \vee (c_{in} \wedge x \wedge \neg y) \vee (c_{in} \wedge x \wedge y)$$

The expression on the right-hand side of the equation is a sum of minterms. Figure 4-5 shows the circuit to implement this function. It requires four AND gates and one OR gate. The small circles at the inputs to the AND gates indicate a NOT gate at that input.

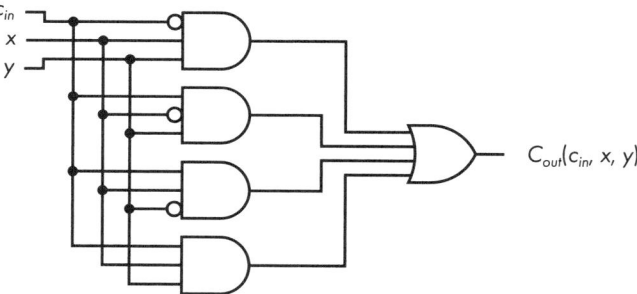

Figure 4-5: A hardware implementation of a function to generate the value of carry when adding two numbers

Let's try to simplify the Boolean expression implemented in Figure 4-5 to see whether we can reduce the hardware requirements. Note that there may not be a single path to a solution, and there may be more than one correct solution. I will present only one way here.

First, we'll do something that might look strange. We'll use the idempotency rule to duplicate the fourth term twice:

$$C_{out}(c_{in}, x, y) = (\neg c_{in} \wedge x \wedge y) \vee (c_{in} \wedge \neg x \wedge y) \vee (c_{in} \wedge x \wedge \neg y)$$
$$\vee (c_{in} \wedge x \wedge y) \vee (c_{in} \wedge x \wedge y) \vee (c_{in} \wedge x \wedge y)$$

Next, we'll rearrange the product terms a bit to OR each of the three original terms with $(c_{in} \wedge x \wedge y)$:

$$C_{out}(c_{in}, x, y) = ((\neg c_{in} \wedge x \wedge y) \vee (c_{in} \wedge x \wedge y)) \vee ((c_{in} \wedge x \wedge \neg y) \vee (c_{in} \wedge x \wedge y))$$
$$\vee ((c_{in} \wedge \neg x \wedge y) \vee (c_{in} \wedge x \wedge y))$$

Now, we can use the rule for distribution of AND over OR to factor out terms that OR to 1:

$$C_{out}(c_{in}, x, y) = (x \wedge y \wedge (\neg c_{in} \vee c_{in})) \vee (c_{in} \wedge x \wedge (\neg y \vee y)) \vee (c_{in} \wedge y \wedge (\neg x \vee x))$$
$$= (x \wedge y \wedge 1) \vee (c_{in} \wedge x \wedge 1) \vee (c_{in} \wedge y \wedge 1)$$
$$= (x \wedge y) \vee (c_{in} \wedge x) \vee (c_{in} \wedge y)$$

Figure 4-6 shows the circuit for this function. Not only have we eliminated an AND gate, but each of the AND gates and the OR gate has one fewer input.

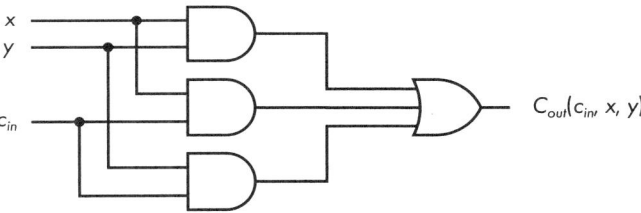

Figure 4-6: A simplified hardware implementation to generate the value of carry when adding two numbers

Comparing the circuits in Figures 4-5 and 4-6, we can see that Boolean algebra has helped us simplify the hardware implementation. This simplification results from stating the conditions that result in a carry of 1 in plain language. The original, canonical form of the equation stated that a carry, $C_{out}(c_{in}, x, y)$, will be 1 in any of these four cases:

If $c_{in} = 0$, $x = 1$, and $y = 1$

If $c_{in} = 1$, $x = 0$, and $y = 1$

If $c_{in} = 1$, $x = 1$, and $y = 0$

If $c_{in} = 1$, $x = 1$, and $y = 1$

The minimization can be stated much more simply: carry is 1 if at least two of c_{in}, x, and y are 1.

NOTE *These examples of specifying a logic circuit for carry from addition, and the algorithm for subtraction in Chapter 3, illustrate one of the more common sources of programming errors. Specifying an activity that seems very simple to us humans in simple logical steps that a computer can execute can be a very tedious, error-prone process.*

We arrived at the solution in Figure 4-6 by starting with the sum of minterms; in other words, we were working with the values of c_{in}, x, and y that generate a 1 for carry. As you saw in the section "Canonical Product or Product of Maxterms" on page 64, since carry must be either 1 or 0, it's equally as valid to start with the values of c_{in}, x, and y that generate a 0 for the complement of carry and to write the equation as a product of maxterms:

$$\neg C_{out}(c_{in}, x, y) = (c_{in} \vee \neg x \vee \neg y) \wedge (\neg c_{in} \vee x \vee \neg y) \wedge (\neg c_{in} \vee \neg x \vee y) \wedge (\neg c_{in} \vee \neg x \vee \neg y)$$

To simplify this equation, we'll take the same approach we took with the sum of minterms and start by duplicating the last term twice to give:

$$\neg C_{out}(c_{in}, x, y) = (c_{in} \vee \neg x \vee \neg y) \wedge (\neg c_{in} \vee x \vee \neg y) \wedge (\neg c_{in} \vee \neg x \vee y)$$
$$\wedge (\neg c_{in} \vee \neg x \vee \neg y) \wedge (\neg c_{in} \vee \neg x \vee \neg y) \wedge (\neg c_{in} \vee \neg x \vee \neg y)$$

Adding some parentheses helps to clarify the simplification process:

$$\neg C_{out}(c_{in}, x, y) = ((c_{in} \vee \neg x \vee \neg y) \wedge (\neg c_{in} \vee \neg x \vee \neg y)) \wedge ((\neg c_{in} \vee x \vee \neg y)$$
$$\wedge (\neg c_{in} \vee \neg x \vee \neg y)) \wedge ((\neg c_{in} \vee \neg x \vee y) \wedge (\neg c_{in} \vee \neg x \vee \neg y))$$

Next, we'll use the distribution of OR over AND. Because this is tricky, I'll go over the steps to simplify the first grouping of product terms in this equation; the steps for the other two groupings are similar to this one. Distribution of OR over AND has this generic form:

$$(X \vee Y) \wedge (X \vee Z) = X \vee (Y \wedge Z)$$

The sum terms in our first grouping share a $(\neg x \vee \neg y)$, so we'll make the following substitutions into the generic form:

$$X = (\neg x \vee \neg y)$$
$$Y = c_{in}$$
$$Z = \neg c_{in}$$

Making the substitutions and using the complement rule for AND, we get:

$$(c_{in} \vee \neg x \vee \neg y) \wedge (\neg c_{in} \vee \neg x \vee \neg y) = (\neg x \vee \neg y) \vee (c_{in} \wedge \neg c_{in})$$
$$= (\neg x \vee \neg y)$$

And applying these same manipulations to the other two groupings, we get:

$$\neg C_{out}(c_{in}, x, y) = (\neg x \vee \neg y) \wedge (\neg c_{in} \vee \neg x) \wedge (\neg c_{in} \vee \neg y)$$

Figure 4-7 shows the circuit implementation of this function. This circuit produces the complement of carry. We would need to complement the output, $\neg C_{out}(c_{in}, x, y)$, to get the value of carry.

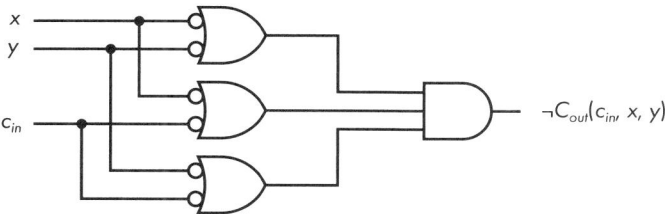

Figure 4-7: A simplified hardware implementation to generate the complement of carry when adding two numbers

If you compare Figures 4-7 and 4-6, you can graphically see De Morgan's law, where the ORs have become ANDs with complemented values as inputs. The circuit in Figure 4-6 might look simpler to you because the circuit in Figure 4-7 requires NOT gates at the six inputs to the OR gates. But as you will learn in the next chapter, this may not be the case because of the inherent electronic properties of the devices used to construct logic gates.

The important point to understand here is that there is more than one way to solve the problem. One of the jobs of the hardware engineer is to decide which solution is best, based on elements such as cost, component availability, and so on.

Minimization Using Karnaugh Maps

The algebraic manipulations used to minimize Boolean functions may not always be obvious. You may find it easier to work with a graphic representation of the logical statements.

A commonly used graphic tool for working with Boolean functions is the *Karnaugh map*, also called a *K-map*. The Karnaugh map, invented in 1953 by Maurice Karnaugh, a telecommunications engineer at Bell Labs, gives a way to visually find the same simplifications you can find algebraically. It can be used either with a sum of products, using minterms, or with a product of sums, using maxterms. Here, I illustrate how they work, starting with minterms.

Simplifying Sums of Products Using Karnaugh Maps

The Karnaugh map is a rectangular grid with a cell for each minterm. There are 2^n cells for n variables. Figure 4-8 is a Karnaugh map showing all four possible minterms for two variables, x and y. The vertical axis is used to plot x and the horizontal axis is used for y. The value of x for each row is shown by the number (0 or 1) immediately to the left of the row, and the value of y for each column appears at the top of the column.

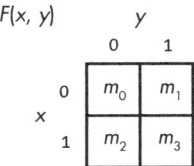

Figure 4-8: The mapping
of two-variable minterms
on a Karnaugh map

To illustrate how to use a Karnaugh map, let's look at an arbitrary function of two variables:

$$F(x, y) = (x \wedge \neg y) \vee (\neg x \wedge y) \vee (x \wedge y)$$

Start by placing a 1 in each cell corresponding to a minterm that appears in the equation, as shown in Figure 4-9.

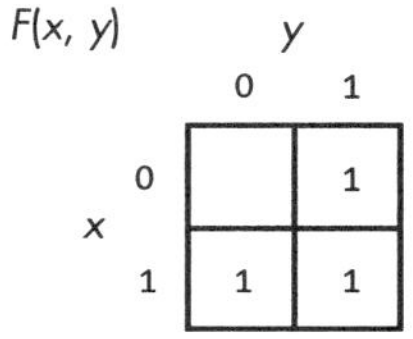

Figure 4-9: A Karnaugh
map of the arbitrary
function F(x, y)

Placing a 1 in the cell corresponding to each minterm that evaluates to 1 shows graphically when the equation evaluates to 1. The two cells on the right-hand side correspond to the minterms m_1 and m_3, $(\neg x \wedge y)$ and $(x \wedge y)$. Since these terms are OR-ed together, $F(x, y)$ evaluates to 1 if either of these minterms evaluates to 1. Using the distributive and complement rules, we get the result:

$$(\neg x \wedge y) \vee (x \wedge y) = (\neg x \vee x) \wedge y$$
$$= y$$

This shows algebraically that $F(x, y)$ evaluates to 1 whenever y is 1, which you'll see next by simplifying this Karnaugh map.

The only difference between the two minterms, $(\neg x \wedge y)$ and $(x \wedge y)$, is the change from x to $\neg x$. Karnaugh maps are arranged such that only one variable changes between two cells that share an edge, a requirement called the *adjacency rule*.

To use a Karnaugh map to perform simplification, you group two adjacent cells in a sum of products Karnaugh map that have 1s in them. Then you eliminate the variable that differs between them and coalesce the two product terms. Repeating this process allows you to simplify the equation. Each grouping eliminates a product term in the final sum of products. This can be extended to equations with more than two variables, but the number of cells that are grouped together must be a multiple of 2, and you can group only adjacent cells. The adjacency wraps around from side to side and from top to bottom. You'll see an example in Figure 4-18 on page 79.

To see how all this works, consider the grouping in the Karnaugh map in Figure 4-10.

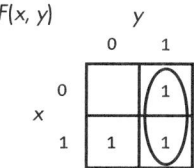

Figure 4-10: Two of the minterms in F(x, y) grouped

This grouping is a graphical representation of the algebraic manipulation we did earlier, where $F(x, y)$ evaluates to 1 whenever $y = 1$, regardless of the value of x. Thus, the grouping coalesces two minterms into one product term by eliminating x.

From the last grouping, we know our final simplified function will have a y term. Let's do another grouping to find the next term. First, we'll simplify the equation algebraically. Returning to the original equation for $F(x, y)$, we can use idempotency to duplicate one of the minterms:

$$F(x, y) = (x \wedge \neg y) \vee (\neg x \wedge y) \vee (x \wedge y) \vee (x \wedge y)$$

Now, we'll do some algebraic manipulation on the first product term and the one we just added:

$$(x \wedge \neg y) \vee (x \wedge y) = (\neg y \vee y) \wedge x$$
$$= x$$

Instead of using algebraic manipulations, we can do this directly on our Karnaugh map, as shown in Figure 4-11. This map shows that separate groups can include the same cell (minterm).

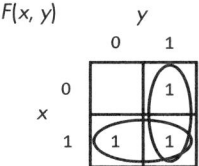

Figure 4-11: A Karnaugh map grouping showing that (x ∧ ¬y) ∨ (¬x ∧ y) ∨ (x ∧ y) = x ∨ y

The group in the bottom row represents the product term x and the one in the right-hand column represents y, giving us the following minimization:

$$F(x, y) = x \vee y$$

Note that the cell that is included in both groupings, $(x \wedge y)$, is the term that we duplicated using the idempotent rule in our algebraic solution previously. You can think of including a cell in more than one group as adding a duplicate copy of the cell, as we did in our algebraic manipulation earlier, and then coalescing it with the other cell(s) in the group, thus removing it.

The adjacency rule is automatically satisfied when there are only two variables in the function. When we add another variable, we need to think about how to order the cells of a Karnaugh map such that we can use the adjacency rule to simplify Boolean expressions.

Ordering Cells in a Karnaugh Map

One of the problems with both the binary and binary coded decimal (BCD) codes is that the difference between two adjacent values often involves more than one bit being changed. In 1943, Frank Gray introduced a code, the *Gray code*, in which adjacent values differ by only one bit. Although encoding values in the Gray code complicates arithmetic operations on the values, it simplifies showing when the values are adjacent to one another, which shows us how to order the cells in a Karnaugh map.

Constructing the Gray code is quite easy. Start with one bit:

Decimal	Gray code
0	0
1	1

To add a bit, first write the mirror image of the existing pattern:

Gray code
0
1
1
0

Then, add a 0 to the beginning of each of the original bit patterns and add a 1 to the beginning of each of the mirror-image set to give the Gray code for two bits, as shown in Table 4-9.

Table 4-9: The Gray Code for Two Bits

Decimal	Gray code
0	00
1	01
2	11
3	10

This is the reason the Gray code is sometimes called *reflected binary code (RBC)*. Table 4-10 shows the Gray code for four bits.

Table 4-10: The Gray Code for Four Bits

Decimal	Gray code	Binary
0	0000	0000
1	0001	0001
2	0011	0010
3	0010	0011
4	0110	0100
5	0111	0101
6	0101	0110
7	0100	0111
8	1100	1000
9	1101	1001
10	1111	1010
11	1110	1011
12	1010	1100
13	1011	1101
14	1001	1110
15	1000	1111

Let's compare the binary codes with the Gray codes for the decimal values 7 and 8 in Table 4-10. The binary codes for 7 and 8 are 0111 and 1000, respectively; all four bits change when stepping only 1 in decimal value. But the Gray codes for 7 and 8 are 0100 and 1100, respectively; only one bit changes, thus satisfying the adjacency rule for a Karnaugh map.

Notice that the pattern of changing only one bit between adjacent values also holds when the bit pattern wraps around. That is, when going from the highest value (15 for four bits) to the lowest (0), only one bit is changed.

Using a Karnaugh Map for Three Variables

To see how the adjacency property is important, let's consider a more complicated function. We'll use a Karnaugh map to simplify our function for carry, which has three variables. Adding another variable means we need to double the number of cells to hold the minterms. To keep the map two-dimensional, we add the new variable to an existing variable on one side of the map. We need a total of eight cells (2^3), so we'll draw it four cells wide and two cells high. We'll add z to the y-axis and draw our Karnaugh map with y and z on the horizontal axis and x on the vertical axis, as shown in Figure 4-12.

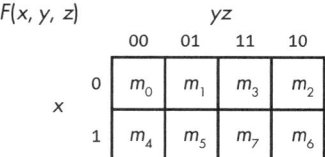

Figure 4-12: The mapping of three-variable minterms on a Karnaugh map

The order of the bit patterns along the top of the three-variable Karnaugh map is 00, 01, 11, 10, as opposed to 00, 01, 10, 11, which is the Gray code order in Table 4-9. The adjacency rule also holds when wrapping around the edges of the Karnaugh map—that is, going from m_2 to m_0 or from m_6 to m_4—which means that groups can wrap around the edges of the map. (Other axis labeling schemes will also work, as you'll see at the end of this section.)

You saw earlier in this chapter that carry can be expressed as the sum of four minterms:

$$C_{out}(c_{in}, x, y) = (\neg c_{in} \wedge x \wedge y) \vee (c_{in} \wedge \neg x \wedge y) \vee (c_{in} \wedge x \wedge \neg y) \vee (c_{in} \wedge x \wedge y)$$
$$= m_3 \vee m_5 \vee m_6 \vee m_7$$
$$= \sum(3, 5, 6, 7)$$

Figure 4-13 shows these four minterms on a Karnaugh map.

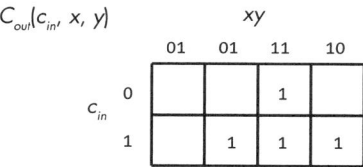

Figure 4-13: A Karnaugh map of the function for carry

We look for adjacent cells that can be grouped together to eliminate one variable from the product term. As noted, the groups can overlap, giving the three groups shown in Figure 4-14.

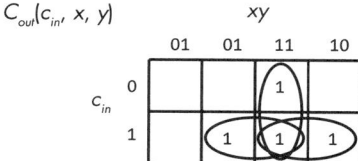

Figure 4-14: A minimum sum of products of the function for carry = 1

Using the three groups in the Karnaugh map in Figure 4-14, we end up with the same equation we got through algebraic manipulations:

$$C_{out}(c_{in}, x, y) = (x \wedge y) \vee (c_{in} \wedge x) \vee (c_{in} \wedge y)$$

Simplifying Products of Sums Using Karnaugh Maps

It's equally valid to work with a function that shows when the complement of carry is 0. We did that using maxterms:

$$\neg C_{max}(c_{in}, x, y) = (c_{in} \vee \neg x \vee \neg y) \wedge (\neg c_{in} \vee x \vee \neg y) \wedge (\neg c_{in} \vee \neg x \vee y) \wedge (\neg c_{in} \vee \neg x \vee \neg y)$$

$$= M_3 \wedge M_5 \wedge M_6 \wedge M_7$$

$$= \prod(3, 5, 6, 7)$$

Figure 4-15 shows the arrangement of maxterms on a three-variable Karnaugh map.

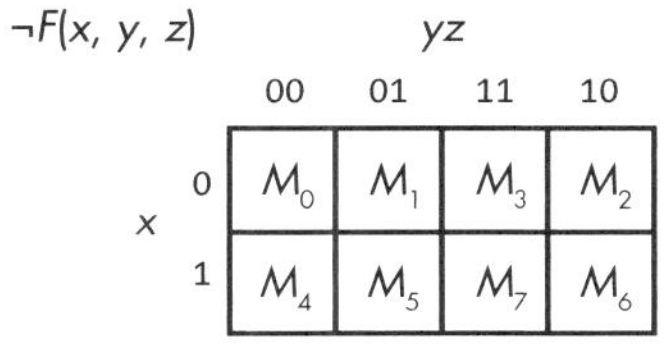

$\neg F(x, y, z)$

	yz			
	00	01	11	10
x 0	M_0	M_1	M_3	M_2
1	M_4	M_5	M_7	M_6

Figure 4-15: The mapping of three-variable maxterms on a Karnaugh map

When working with a maxterm statement of the solution, you mark the cells that evaluate to 0. The minimization process is the same as when working with minterms, except that you group the cells with 0s in them.

Figure 4-16 shows a minimization of $\neg C_{out}(c_{in}, x, y)$, the complement of carry.

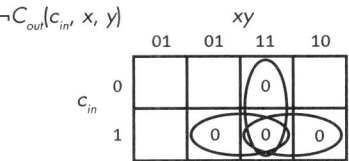

$\neg C_{out}(c_{in}, x, y)$

Figure 4-16: A minimum product of sums of the function for NOT carry = 0

The Karnaugh map in Figure 4-16 leads to the same product of sums we got algebraically for the complement of carry = 0:

$$\neg C_{out}(c_{in}, x, y) = (\neg x \vee \neg y) \wedge (\neg c_{in} \vee \neg x) \wedge (\neg c_{in} \vee \neg y)$$

Comparing Figures 4-14 and 4-16 gives a graphic view of De Morgan's law. When making this comparison, keep in mind that Figure 4-14 shows the product terms that get added and Figure 4-16 shows the sum terms that get multiplied, and the result is complemented. Thus, we exchange 0 and 1 and exchange AND and OR to go from one Karnaugh map to the other.

To further emphasize the duality of minterms and maxterms, compare Figures 4-17(a) and (b).

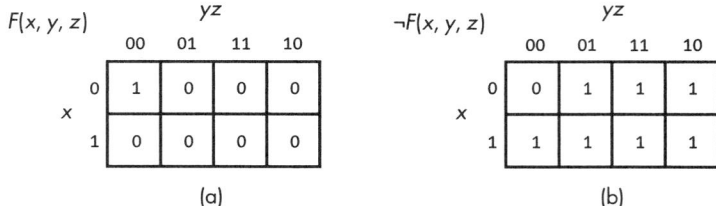

Figure 4-17: A comparison of (a) one minterm and (b) one maxterm

Figure 4-17(a) shows the function:

$$F(x, y, z) = \neg x \wedge \neg y \wedge \neg z$$

Although it's not necessary and usually not done, we have placed a 0 in each of the cells representing minterms not included in this function.

Similarly, in Figure 4-17(b), we have placed a 1 in each of the cells representing the maxterms that are not included in the function:

$$\neg F(x, y, z) = x \vee y \vee z$$

This comparison shows graphically how a minterm specifies the minimum number of 1s in a Karnaugh map and a maxterm specifies the maximum number of 1s.

Exploring Larger Groupings on a Karnaugh Map

Thus far, we have grouped only two cells together on our Karnaugh maps. Here, I'll show you an example of larger groups. Consider a function that outputs 1 when a 3-bit number is even. Table 4-11 shows the truth table. It uses 1 to indicate that the number is even and uses 0 to indicate odd.

Table 4-11: The Even Values of a 3-Bit Number

Minterm	x	y	z	Number	Even(x, y, z)
m_0	0	0	0	0	1
m_1	0	0	1	1	0
m_2	0	1	0	2	1
m_3	0	1	1	3	0
m_4	1	0	0	4	1
m_5	1	0	1	5	0
m_6	1	1	0	6	1
m_7	1	1	1	7	0

The canonical sum of products for this function is:

$$Even(x, y, z) = \sum(0, 2, 4, 6)$$

Figure 4-18 shows these minterms on a Karnaugh map with the four terms grouped together. We can group all four together because they all have adjacent edges.

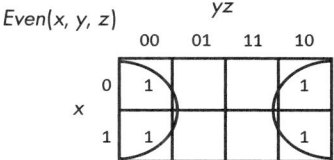

Figure 4-18: A Karnaugh map showing even values of a 3-bit number

From the Karnaugh map in Figure 4-18, we can write the equation for when a 3-bit number is even:

$$Even(x, y, z) = \neg z$$

The Karnaugh map shows that it does not matter what the values of x and y are, only that $z = 0$.

Adding More Variables to a Karnaugh Map

Each time you add another variable to a Karnaugh map, you will need to double the number of cells. The only requirement for the Karnaugh map to work is that you arrange the minterms (or maxterms) according to the adjacency rule. Figure 4-19 shows a four-variable Karnaugh map for minterms. The y and z variables are on the horizontal axis, and w and x are on the vertical axis.

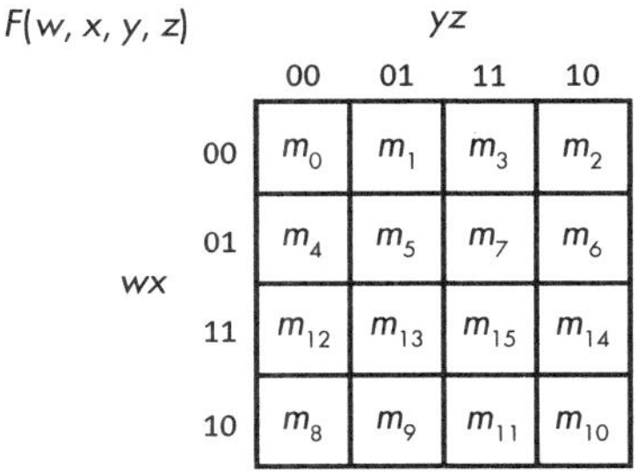

$F(w, x, y, z)$

		yz			
		00	01	11	10
	00	m_0	m_1	m_3	m_2
	01	m_4	m_5	m_7	m_6
wx	11	m_{12}	m_{13}	m_{15}	m_{14}
	10	m_8	m_9	m_{11}	m_{10}

Figure 4-19: The mapping of four-variable minterms on a Karnaugh map

So far we have assumed that every minterm (or maxterm) is accounted for in our functions. But design does not take place in a vacuum. We might have knowledge about other components of the overall design telling us that some combinations of variable values can never occur. Next, I'll show you how to take this knowledge into account in your function simplification process. The Karnaugh map provides an especially clear way to visualize the situation.

Using "Don't Care" Cells

Sometimes, you have information about the values that the variables can have. If you know which combinations of values will never occur, then the minterms (or maxterms) that represent those combinations are irrelevant.

For example, you may want a function that indicates whether one of two possible events has occurred or not, but you know that the two events cannot occur simultaneously. Let's name the events x and y and let 0 indicate that the event has not occurred and 1 indicate that it has. Table 4-12 shows the truth table for our function, $F(x, y)$.

Table 4-12: A Truth Table for x or y Occurring, but Not Both

x	y	$F(x, y)$
0	0	0
0	1	1
1	0	1
1	1	×

We can show that both events cannot occur simultaneously by placing an × in that row. We can draw a Karnaugh map with an × for the minterm that can't exist in the system, as shown in Figure 4-20. The × represents a *don't care* cell; grouping this cell with other cells doesn't affect the evaluation of the function.

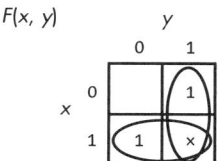

Figure 4-20: A Karnaugh map for F(x, y), showing a "don't care" cell

Since the cell that represents the minterm $(x \wedge y)$ is a "don't care" cell, we can include it, or not, in our minimization groupings, leading to the two groupings shown. The Karnaugh map in Figure 4-20 leads us to the solution

$$F(x, y) = x \vee y$$

which is a simple OR gate. You probably guessed this solution without having to use a Karnaugh map. You'll see a more interesting use of "don't care" cells when you learn about the design of two digital logic circuits at the end of Chapter 7.

Karnaugh maps can be used to minimize only two levels of logic: groups of AND gates feeding an OR gate, or groups of OR gates feeding an AND gate. As you'll see in the next several chapters, most logic designs involve more than two levels. Karnaugh maps can provide some useful guidelines, but you need to think carefully about the overall design. You will see an example of using Karnaugh maps to design an adder circuit with three levels of logic in Chapter 6.

Combining Basic Boolean Operators

As mentioned earlier in this chapter, we can combine basic Boolean operators to implement more complex Boolean operators. Now that you know how to work with Boolean functions, we'll design one of the more common operators, the *exclusive or*, often called *XOR*, using the three basic operators, AND, OR, and NOT. It's so commonly used that it has its own circuit symbol. Let's take a look:

XOR

XOR is a binary operator. The result is 1 if one, and only one, of the two operands is 1; otherwise, the result is 0. I'll use $\veebar$ to designate the XOR operation. It's also common to use the $\oplus$ symbol. Figure 4-21 shows XOR gate operation with inputs x and y.

x	y	$x \veebar y$
0	0	0
0	1	1
1	0	1
1	1	0

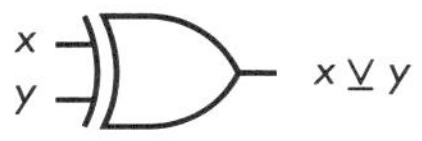

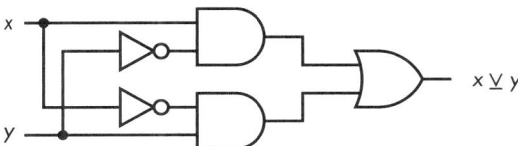

Figure 4-21: An XOR gate acting on two variables, x and y

The minterm implementation of this operation is:

$$x \veebar y = (x \wedge \neg y) \vee (\neg x \wedge y)$$

The XOR operator can be implemented with two AND gates, two NOT gates, and one OR gate, as shown in Figure 4-22.

Figure 4-22: An XOR gate made from AND, OR, and NOT gates

We can, of course, design many more Boolean operators, but we'll move on in the next few chapters to learn how these operators can be implemented in hardware using simple on/off switches. As you'll discover, the idealized minimal solutions you've learned about in this chapter may not always be the best solutions, due to factors such as the inherent electrical characteristics of the switches, multiple levels of logic, availability of hardware components, and so forth.

4.3 Design a function that will detect all the 4-bit integers that are even.

4.4 Find a minimal sum of products expression for this function:

$$F(x, y, z) = (\neg x \land \neg y \land \neg z) \lor (\neg x \land \neg y \land z) \lor (\neg x \land y \land \neg z)$$
$$\lor (x \land \neg y \land \neg z) \lor (x \land y \land \neg z) \lor (x \land y \land z)$$

4.5 Find a minimal product of sums expression for this function:

$$\neg F(x, y, z) = (x \lor y \lor z) \land (x \lor y \lor \neg z) \land (x \lor \neg y \lor \neg z)$$
$$\land (\neg x \lor y \lor z) \land (\neg x \lor \neg y \lor \neg z)$$

4.6 The arrangement of the variables for a Karnaugh map is arbitrary, but the minterms (or maxterms) need to be consistent with the labeling. Show where each minterm is located with this Karnaugh map axis labeling using the notation of Figure 4-12:

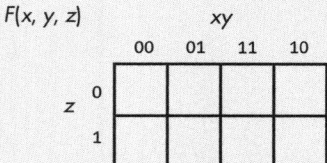

4.7 The arrangement of the variables for a Karnaugh map is arbitrary, but the minterms (or maxterms) need to be consistent with the labeling. Show where each minterm is located with this Karnaugh map axis labeling using the notation of Figure 4-12:

$F(x, y, z)$ xz

	00	01	11	10
y 0				
1				

4.8 Create a Karnaugh map for five variables. You'll probably need to review the Gray code in Table 4-10 and increase it to five bits.

4.9 Design a logic function that detects the single-digit prime numbers. Assume that the numbers are coded in 4-bit BCD (see Table 2-7). The function is 1 for each prime number.

What You've Learned

Boolean operators The three basic Boolean operators are AND, OR, and NOT.

Rules of Boolean algebra Boolean algebra provides a mathematical way to work with the rules of logic. AND works like multiplication, and OR is similar to addition in elementary algebra.

Simplifying Boolean algebra expressions Boolean functions specify the functionality of a computer. Simplifying these functions leads to a simpler hardware implementation.

Karnaugh maps These provide a graphical way to simplify Boolean expressions.

Gray code This shows how to order the cells in a Karnaugh map.

Combining basic Boolean operators XOR can be created from AND, OR, and NOT operators.

The next chapter starts with an introduction to basic electronics that will provide a basis for understanding how transistors can be used to implement switches. From there, we'll look at how transistor switches are used to implement logic gates.

5

LOGIC GATES

In the previous chapter, you learned about Boolean algebra expressions and how to implement them using logic gates. In this chapter, you'll learn how to implement logic gates in hardware using *transistors*, the solid-state electronic devices used to implement the on/off switches we've been discussing so far in this book.

To help you to understand how transistors operate, we'll start with a simple introduction to electronics. From there, you'll learn how transistors can be connected in pairs to switch faster and use less electrical power. We'll end the chapter with some practical considerations regarding the use of transistors to construct logic gates.

Crash Course in Electronics

You don't need to be an electrical engineer to understand how logic gates work, but some understanding of the basic concepts can be helpful. In this section, I provide a brief overview of the fundamental concepts of electronic circuits. We'll begin with two definitions:

Current   Refers to the movement of electrical charge. Electrical charge is measured in *coulombs (C)*. A flow of 1 C per second (1 C/s) is defined as 1 *ampere (A)*, often abbreviated as *amp*. Current flows through an electrical circuit only if there is a completely connected path from one side of the power source to the other.

Voltage   Also called *potential difference*, refers to the difference in electrical energy per unit charge between two points in an electrical circuit. One *volt (V)* is defined as the electrical difference between two points on a *conductor* (the medium the current flows through) when 1 A of current flowing through the conductor dissipates 1 watt (W) of power.

A computer is constructed from the following electronic components:

- Power sources that provide the electrical power
- Passive components that affect current flow and voltage levels but whose characteristics cannot be altered by another electronic component
- Active components that switch between various combinations of the power source, passive components, and other active components under the control of one or more other electronic components
- Conductors that connect the other components

Let's look at how each of these electronic components works.

Power Supplies and Batteries

In almost all countries, electrical power comes in the form of *alternating current (AC)*. For AC, a plot of the magnitude of the voltage versus time shows a sinusoidal wave shape. Computer circuits use *direct current (DC)* power, which, unlike AC, does not vary over time. A power supply is used to convert AC to DC, as shown in Figure 5-1.

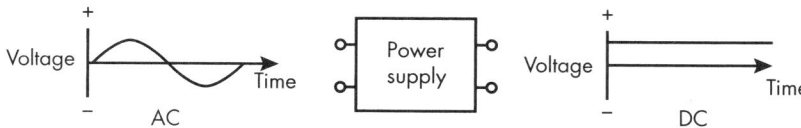

Figure 5-1: An AC/DC power supply

Batteries also provide DC electrical power. When drawing circuits, we'll use the symbol for a battery (Figure 5-2) to designate a DC power supply. The power supply in Figure 5-2 provides 5 V DC.

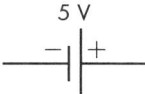

Figure 5-2: The circuit
symbol for a 5 V DC
power source

In the previous chapters, you've seen that everything that happens in a computer is based on a system of 1s and 0s. But how are these 1s and 0s physically represented? Computer circuits distinguish between two different voltage levels to provide logical 0s and 1s. For example, logical 0 may be represented by 0 V DC and logical 1 by 5 V DC. The reverse could also be implemented: 5 V as logical 0 and 0 V as logical 1. The only requirement is that the hardware design be consistent. Luckily, programmers don't need to worry about the actual voltages used; that's best left to the computer hardware engineers.

NOTE   *Electronic devices are designed to operate reliably within a range of voltages. For example, a device designed to operate at a nominal 5 V typically has a tolerance of ±5%, or 4.75 to 5.25 V.*

The components in a computer circuit constantly switch between the two voltage levels. Each voltage switch takes time, which limits how fast a given circuit can complete an operation. As you'll see in the "Transistors" section on page 96, speeding up the switching times uses more power, which creates heat. Excessive heat can damage the components, which limits the speed of calculations. The time-dependent characteristics of the circuit components are an important design consideration for computer hardware engineers. We'll look at these characteristics in the next section.

Passive Components

All electrical circuits have the following electromagnetic properties, which are distributed throughout the circuit:

Resistance   Impedes current flow, thus dissipating energy. The electrical energy is transformed into heat.

Capacitance   Stores energy in an electric field. Voltage across a capacitance cannot change instantaneously.

Inductance   Stores energy in a magnetic field. Current through an inductance cannot change instantaneously.

It takes time for energy to be stored as an electric field, so *capacitance impedes time changes in voltage*. And it takes time for energy to be stored as a magnetic field, so *inductance impedes time changes in current*. These two properties are lumped together with resistance and called *impedance*. The impedance to changes slows down the switching that takes place in a computer, and the resistance consumes electrical power. We'll be looking at the general timing characteristics of these properties in the remainder of this section, but will leave a discussion of power consumption to more advanced books on the topic.

To get a feel for the effects of each of these properties, we'll consider the discrete electronic devices that are used to place these properties in a specific location in a circuit: resistors, capacitors, and inductors. These are part of a broader class of electronic components called *passive components*, which cannot be controlled electronically; they simply consume or store energy. Figure 5-3 shows the circuit symbols for the passive electronic devices we'll be discussing here.

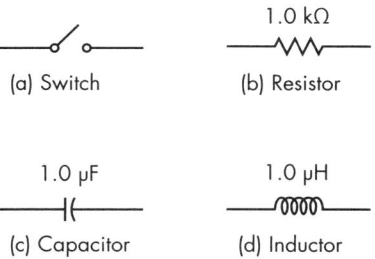

(a) Switch

(b) Resistor

(c) Capacitor

(d) Inductor

Figure 5-3: Circuit symbols for passive devices

Switches

A *switch* can be in one of two positions: open or closed. In the open position, there is no connection between the two ends, and no conduction occurs. When a switch is closed, the connection between the two ends is complete, thus conducting electricity. The symbol in Figure 5-3(a) typically indicates a switch that is activated manually. In the section "Transistors" on page 96, you'll learn that a computer uses transistors for open/closed switches, which are controlled electronically, thus implementing the on/off logic that forms the basis of a computer.

Resistors

A *resistor* is used to limit the amount of current in a specific location in a circuit. By limiting the current flow into a capacitor or inductor, a resistor affects the time it takes for these other devices (discussed in "Capacitors" on page 90 and "Inductors" on page 93) to build up their energy storage. The amount of resistance is usually chosen in conjunction with the amount of capacitance or inductance to provide specific timing characteristics. Resistors are also used to limit current flowing through a device to nondestructive levels.

As it limits current flow, a resistor irreversibly transforms the electrical energy into heat. A resistor doesn't store energy, unlike a capacitor or inductor, which can return the stored energy to the circuit at a later time.

The relationship between voltage and current for a single resistor is given by *Ohm's law*,

$$V(t) = I(t) \times R$$

where $V(t)$ is the voltage difference across the resistor at time t, $I(t)$ is the current flowing through it at time t, and R is the value of the resistor. Resistor values are specified in *ohms*.

The circuit shown in Figure 5-4 shows two resistors connected through a switch to a power supply, which supplies 5 V. The Greek letter Ω is used to indicate ohms, and kΩ indicates 10^3 Ω. Since current can flow only in a closed path, no current flows until the switch is closed.

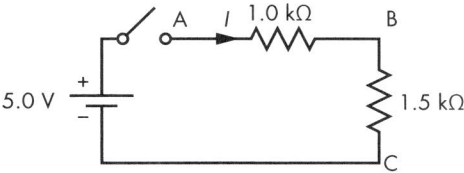

Figure 5-4: Two resistors in series with a power supply and switch

In Figure 5-4, both resistors are in the same path, so when the switch is closed, the same current, I, flows through each of them. Resistors that are in the same current flow path are said to be *connected in series*. To determine the amount of current flowing from the power supply, we need to compute the total resistance in the path of the current. In this example, this is the sum of the two resistors:

$$R = 1.0 \text{ k}\Omega + 1.5 \text{ k}\Omega$$
$$= 2.5 \text{ k}\Omega$$

Thus, the 5 V is applied across a total of 2.5 kΩ. Solving for I, and leaving out t because the power supply voltage doesn't vary with time, we get

$$I = \frac{V}{R}$$
$$= \frac{5.0 \text{ V}}{2.5 \times 10^3 \text{ } \Omega}$$
$$= 2.5 \times 10^{-3} \text{ A}$$
$$= 2.0 \text{ mA}$$

where mA is milliamps.

We can now determine the voltage difference between points A and B in the circuit in Figure 5-4 by multiplying the resistor value and current:

$$V_{AB} = 1.0 \text{ k}\Omega \times 2.0 \text{ mA}$$
$$= 2.0 \text{ V}$$

Similarly, the voltage difference between points B and C is:

$$V_{BC} = 1.5 \text{ k}\Omega \times 2.0 \text{ mA}$$
$$= 3.0 \text{ V}$$

Thus, connecting the resistors in series serves as a *voltage divider*, dividing the 5 V between the two resistors: 2.0 V across the 1.0 kΩ resistor and 3.0 V across the 1.5 kΩ resistor.

Figure 5-5 shows the same two resistors *connected in parallel*.

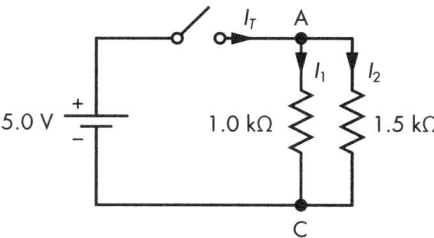

Figure 5-5: Two resistors in parallel

In Figure 5-5, the full voltage of the power supply, 5 V, is applied across points A and C when the switch is closed. Thus, each resistor has 5 V applied across it, and we can use Ohm's law to compute the current through each one:

$$I_1 = \frac{V}{R_1}$$
$$= \frac{5.0 \text{ V}}{1.0 \text{ k}\Omega}$$
$$= 5.0 \times 10^{-3} \text{ A}$$
$$= 5.0 \text{ mA}$$

$$I_2 = \frac{V}{R_2}$$
$$= \frac{5.0 \text{ V}}{1.5 \text{ k}\Omega}$$
$$= 3.3 \text{ mA}$$

The total current from the power supply when the switch is closed, $I_T = I_1 + I_2$, is divided at point A to supply both resistors. It must equal the sum of the two currents through the resistors:

$$I_T = I_1 + I_2$$
$$= 5.0 \text{ mA} + 3.3 \text{ mA}$$
$$= 8.3 \text{ mA}$$

Capacitors

A *capacitor* stores energy in the form of an *electric field*, which is essentially the electric charge at rest. A capacitor initially allows current to flow into it. But instead of providing a continuous path for the current flow, it stores the electric charge, creating an electric field and causing the current flow to decrease over time.

Since it takes time for the electric field to build up, capacitors are often used to smooth out rapid changes in voltage. When there is a sudden increase in current flow into a capacitor, the capacitor tends to absorb the electric charge. Then, when the current flow suddenly decreases, the stored electric charge is released from the capacitor.

The voltage across a capacitor changes with time according to

$$V(t) = \frac{1}{C} \int_0^t I(t)dt$$

where $V(t)$ is the voltage difference across the capacitor at time t, $I(t)$ is the current flowing through it at time t, and C is the value of the capacitor in *farads* (F).

NOTE   *In case you haven't studied calculus, the $\int$ symbol represents integration, which can be thought of as "infinitesimal summation." This equation says that the voltage sums up as time increases from 0 to the current time, t. You'll see a graphic view of this in Figure 5-7.*

Figure 5-6 shows a 1.0 microfarad (µF) capacitor being charged through a 1.0 kΩ resistor.

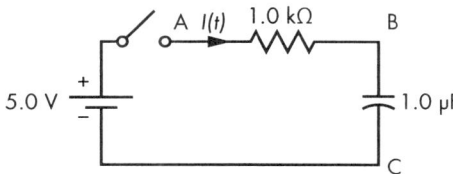

Figure 5-6: A capacitor in series with a resistor

As you will see later in this chapter, this circuit is a rough simulation of the output of one transistor connected to the input of another. The output of the first transistor (which acts like the power supply plus resistor in Figure 5-6) has resistance, and the input to the second transistor has capacitance. The switching behavior of the second transistor depends upon the voltage across the (equivalent) capacitor, $V_{BC}(t)$, reaching a threshold value.

Let's look at the time it takes for the voltage across the capacitor to reach a threshold value. Assuming the voltage across the capacitor, V_{BC}, is 0 V when the switch is first closed, current flows through the resistor and into the capacitor. The voltage across the resistor plus the voltage across the capacitor must be equal to the voltage that is available from the power supply. That is:

$$5.0 = I(t)R + V_{BC}(t)$$

Starting with the voltage across the capacitor, V_{BC}, at 0 V, when the switch is first closed, the full 5.0 V of the power supply will appear across the resistor. Thus, the initial current flow in the circuit will be:

$$I_{initial} = \frac{5.0 \text{ V}}{1.0 \text{ k}\Omega}$$
$$= 5.0 \text{ mA}$$

This initial surge of current into the capacitor causes the voltage across the capacitor to build up toward the power supply voltage. The previous integral equation shows that this buildup decreases exponentially as the voltage across the capacitor approaches its final value.

As the voltage across the capacitor, $V_{BC}(t)$, increases, the voltage across the resistor, $V_{AB}(t)$, must decrease. When the voltage across the capacitor finally equals the voltage of the power supply, the voltage across the resistor is 0 V and the current flow in the circuit is zero. The rate of the exponential decrease in current flow is given by the product of the resistor value and the capacitor value, RC, called the *time constant*. For the values of R and C in this example, we get

$$RC = 1.0 \times 10^3 \ \Omega \times 1.0 \times 10^{-6} \ \text{F}$$
$$= 1.0 \times 10^{-3} \ \text{s}$$
$$= 1.0 \ \text{ms}$$

where s is seconds and ms is milliseconds.

Assuming the capacitor in Figure 5-6 has 0 V across it when the switch is closed, the voltage that develops across the capacitor over time is given by:

$$V_{BC}(t) \quad = 5.0 \times \left(1 - e^{\frac{-t}{RC}}\right)$$
$$= 5.0 \times \left(1 - e^{\frac{-t}{10^{-3}}}\right)$$

Figure 5-7 shows this graphically for the circuit in Figure 5-6. The left y-axis shows voltage across the capacitor, while the right y-axis voltage is across the resistor. Note that the scales go in opposite directions.

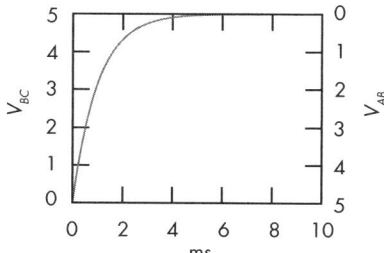

Figure 5-7: A capacitor charging over time

At time t = 1.0 ms (one time constant), the voltage across the capacitor is

$$V_{BC} \quad = 5.0 \left(1 - e^{\frac{-10^{-3}}{10^{-3}}}\right)$$
$$= 5.0 \left(1 - e^{-1}\right)$$
$$= 5.0 \times 0.63$$
$$= 3.15 \ \text{V}$$

which is more than the threshold voltage of the typical transistors used in a computer. You'll learn more about this later in the chapter.

After six time constants have passed, the voltage across the capacitor is:

$$V_{BC} = 5.0 \left(1 - e^{\frac{-6 \times 10^{-3}}{10^{-3}}}\right)$$
$$= 5.0 \left(1 - e^{-6}\right)$$
$$= 5.0 \times 0.9975$$
$$= 4.9875 \text{ V}$$

At this time, the voltage across the resistor is essentially 0 V and current flow is very low.

Inductors

An *inductor* stores energy in the form of a *magnetic field*, which is created by electric charge in motion. An inductor initially prevents the flow of electrical charge, requiring time for the magnetic field to build. By providing a continuous path for the flow of electrical charge (current), an inductor creates the magnetic field.

In a computer, inductors are mainly used in the power supply and the circuitry that connects the power supply to the CPU. If you have access to the inside of a computer, you can likely see a small (about 1 cm diameter) donut-shaped device with wire wrapped around it on the motherboard near the CPU. This is an inductor used to smooth the power supplied to the CPU.

Although either an inductor or a capacitor can be used to smooth the power, the inductor does it by resisting current changes and the capacitor does it by resisting voltage changes. A discussion of which one, or both, to use for smoothing is beyond the scope of this book.

The relationship between voltage $V(t)$ at time t across an inductor and current flow through it, $I(t)$, is given by

$$V(t) = L\frac{dI(t)}{dt}$$

where L is the value of the inductor in *henrys (H)*.

NOTE *Again, we're using some calculus here. The $dI(t)/dt$ notation represents differentiation, which is the rate of change of $I(t)$ with respect to time, t. This equation says that the voltage at time t is proportional to the rate of change of $I(t)$ at that time. (You'll see a graphic view of this shortly, in Figure 5-9.)*

Figure 5-8 shows a 1.0 μH inductor connected in series with a 1.0 kΩ resistor.

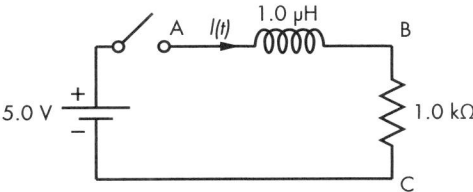

Figure 5-8: An inductor in series with a resistor

When the switch is open, no current flows through this circuit. When it closes, the inductor initially impedes the flow of current, and it takes time for a magnetic field to be built up in the inductor. Before the switch is closed, no current is flowing through the resistor, so the voltage across it, V_{BC}, is 0 V. The voltage across the inductor, V_{AB}, is the full 5 V of the power supply. As current begins to flow through the inductor, the voltage across the resistor, $V_{BC}(t)$, grows. This results in an exponentially decreasing voltage across the inductor. When the voltage across the inductor finally reaches 0 V, the voltage across the resistor is 5 V and current flow in the circuit is 5.0 mA.

The rate of the exponential voltage decrease is given by the time constant L/R. Using the values of R and L in Figure 5-8, we get

$$
\begin{aligned}
\frac{L}{R} &= \frac{1.0 \times 10^{-6} \text{ H}}{1.0 \times 10^{3} \text{ }\Omega} \\
&= 1.0 \times 10^{-9} \text{ s} \\
&= 1.0 \text{ ns}
\end{aligned}
$$

where ns is nanoseconds.

When the switch is closed, the voltage that develops across the inductor over time is given by

$$
\begin{aligned}
V_{AB}(t) &= 5.0 \times \left(1 - e^{-t\frac{R}{L}} \right) \\
&= 5.0 \times \left(1 - e^{\frac{-t}{10^{-9}}} \right)
\end{aligned}
$$

as shown in Figure 5-9. The left y-axis shows voltage across the resistor for the circuit in Figure 5-8, with the right y-axis voltage being across the inductor. Note that the scales go in opposite directions.

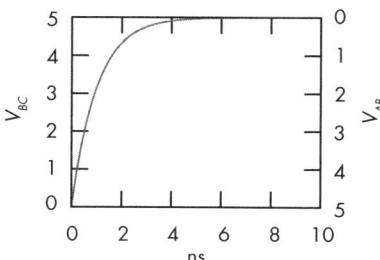

Figure 5-9: An inductor charging over time

At time t = 1.0 ns (one time constant), the voltage across the inductor is:

$$
\begin{aligned}
V_{AB} &= 5.0 \left(1 - e^{\frac{-10^{-9}}{10^{-9}}} \right) \\
&= 5.0 \left(1 - e^{-1} \right) \\
&= 5.0 \times 0.63 \\
&= 3.15 \text{ V}
\end{aligned}
$$

After about 6 ns (six time constants), the voltage across the inductor is essentially equal to 0 V. At this time, the full voltage of the power supply is across the resistor and a steady current of 5.0 mA flows.

The circuit in Figure 5-8 shows how inductors can be used with a CPU power supply. The power supply in this circuit simulates the computer power supply, and the resistor simulates the CPU, which consumes the electrical energy from the power supply. The voltage produced by a power supply includes *noise*, which consists of small, high-frequency fluctuations added to the DC level. As shown in Figure 5-9, the voltage supplied to the CPU, $V_{BC}(t)$, changes little over short periods of time. The inductor connected in series between the power supply and the CPU acts to smooth out the voltage that powers the CPU.

Power Consumption

An important part of hardware design is power consumption, especially in battery-powered devices. Of the three electromagnetic properties we've discussed here, resistance is the primary consumer of power.

Energy is the ability to cause change, and *power* is a measure of how fast energy can be used to make that change. The basic unit of energy is the *joule (J)*. The basic unit of power is the *watt (W)*, which is defined as expending 1 joule per second (J/s). For example, I have a backup battery that can store 240 watt-hours (Wh). That means it can store enough energy to provide 240 watts for 1 hour, or 240 Wh × 3,600 s/h = 864,000 J. The units for volt and ampere are defined such that 1 W = 1 V × 1 A. This gives rise to the formula for power,

$$P = V \times I$$

where P is the power used, V is the voltage across the component, and I is the current flowing through it.

After a brief charging time, a capacitor prevents current flow. This equation shows that the power consumption of a capacitor then goes to zero. The energy used to charge the capacitor is stored in the form of an electrical field. Similarly, the voltage across an inductor goes to zero after a brief charging time, resulting in the amount of power consumed by the inductor going to zero. An inductor stores the charging energy in the form of a magnetic field.

However, a resistor doesn't store energy. As long as there is a voltage difference across a resistor, current flows through it.

The power used by a resistor, R, is given by:

$$P = V \times I$$
$$= I \times R \times I$$
$$= I^2 \times R$$

This power is converted to heat in the resistor. Since power consumption increases by the square of the current, a common hardware design goal is to reduce the amount of current flow.

This section has been an idealized discussion of the passive components that computer engineers include in their designs. In the real world, each component includes elements of all three characteristics—resistance, capacitance, and inductance—that the hardware design engineer needs to take into account. These secondary effects are subtle and often troublesome in the design.

The rest of this chapter is devoted to discussing the *active components*, which are controlled electronically and used to implement the switches that are the basis for a computer. As you will see, the active components include resistance and capacitance, which affect the design of the circuits they're used in.

Transistors

In previous chapters, I described a computer as a collection of two-state switches and discussed how data can be represented by the settings, 0 or 1, of these switches. Then we moved on to look at how 0s and 1s can be combined using logic gates to implement logical functions. In this section, you'll learn how transistors can be used to implement the two-state switches that make up a computer.

A *transistor* is a device whose resistance can be controlled electronically, thus making it an active component. The ability to be controlled electronically is what distinguishes the switches made from transistors from the simple on/off switches you saw earlier in the chapter, which could be controlled mechanically. Before examining how a transistor can be used as a switch, let's look at how we would implement a logic gate using mechanical on/off switches. We'll use the NOT gate for this example.

Figure 5-10 shows two push-button switches connected in series between 5 V and 0 V.

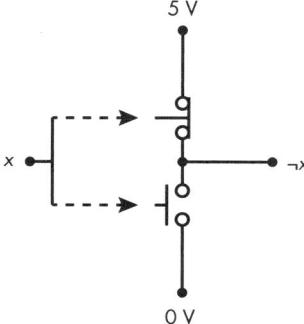

Figure 5-10: A NOT gate made
from two push-button switches

The top switch is normally closed. When its button is pushed (from the left side), the connection between the two small circles is broken, thus opening the circuit at this point. The bottom switch is normally open. When its button is pushed, a connection is made between the two small circles, thus completing the circuit at this point.

We'll let 5 V represent a 1 and 0 V a 0. The input to this NOT gate, x, pushes the two buttons simultaneously. We will control x in the following way: when $x = 1$, we'll push the two buttons, and when $x = 0$, we will not push the buttons. When the buttons are not pushed ($x = 0$), the 5 V are connected to the output, $\neg x$, which represents 1. When the buttons are pushed ($x = 1$), the 5 V are disconnected and the 0 V, which represents 0, are connected to the output. Thus, an input of 1 gets an output of 0 and an input of 0 gets an output of 1.

Early computing devices used mechanical switches to implement their logic, but the results were very slow by today's standards. Modern computers use transistors, which are electronic devices made from semiconductor materials that can be switched quickly between their conducting and non-conducting states under electronic control.

Just as with the mechanically controlled push-button example, we use two different voltages to represent 1 and 0. For example, we might use a high voltage, say +5 V, to represent 1 and a low voltage, say 0 V, to represent 0. But transistors can be switched on or off electronically, which makes them much faster than the mechanical switches used in the original computers. Transistors also take up much less space and consume much less electrical power.

In the following sections, we'll look at two transistors commonly used in modern computers: the MOSFET switch and the CMOS switch.

MOSFET Switch

The most commonly used switching transistor in today's computer logic circuits is the *metal-oxide-semiconductor field-effect transistor (MOSFET)*. There are several types of MOSFET, which use different voltage levels and polarities. I'll describe the behavior of the most common type, the *enhancement-mode MOSFET*, and leave the details of the other variations to more advanced books on the topic. The brief discussion here will help you understand the basics of how they work.

The basic material in a MOSFET is typically silicon, which is a *semiconductor*, meaning it conducts electricity, but not very well. Its conductivity is improved by adding an impurity, a process called *doping*. Depending on the type of impurity, the electrical conductivity can be either the flow of electrons or the flow of lack of electrons (called *holes*). Since electrons have a negative electrical charge, the type that conducts electrons is called *N-type* and the type that conducts holes is called *P-type*. The main conduction path through a MOSFET is the *channel*, which is connected between the *source* and the *drain* terminals on the MOSFET. The *gate* is made from the opposite type of semiconductor and controls the conductivity through the channel.

Figure 5-11 shows the two basic types of MOSFET: N-channel and P-channel. Here, I've shown each MOSFET connected to a 5 V power source through a resistor.

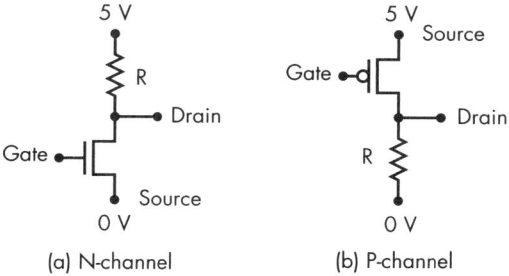

(a) N-channel   (b) P-channel

Figure 5-11: The two basic types of MOSFETs

These are simplified circuits, as the intention is just to provide context for discussing how MOSFETs work. Each MOSFET has three connection points, or *terminals*. The gate is used as the input terminal. Voltage applied to the gate, relative to the voltage applied to the source, controls current flow through the MOSFET. The drain is used as the output. The source of an N-channel MOSFET is connected to the lower voltage of the power supply, while the source of a P-channel is connected to the higher voltage.

After learning about complements in Boolean algebra, it probably does not surprise you that the two types of MOSFETs have complementary behavior. You'll see in the following sections how we can connect them in complementary pairs that make for faster, more efficient switches than using only one type.

First, we'll look at how each works as a single switching device, starting with the N-channel MOSFET.

N-Channel MOSFET

In Figure 5-11(a), the drain of the N-channel MOSFET is connected to the 5 V side of the power supply through the resistor, R, and the source is connected to the 0 V side.

When the voltage applied to the gate is positive with respect to the source, the resistance between the drain and the source of the N-channel MOSFET decreases. When this voltage reaches a threshold value, typically in the range of 1 V, the resistance becomes very low, thus providing a good conduction path for current between the drain and the source. The resulting circuit is equivalent to Figure 5-12(a).

In Figure 5-12(a), current flows from the 5 V connection of the power supply to the 0 V connection through the resistor, R. The voltage at the drain will be 0 V. A problem with this current flow is that the resistor consumes power, simply converting it to heat. In a moment, you'll see the reason we don't want to increase the amount of resistance to limit the current flow to reduce power consumption.

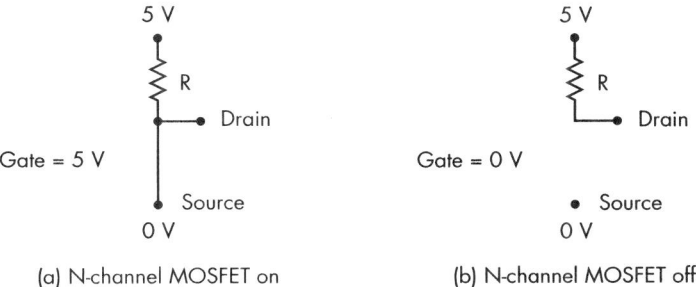

(a) N-channel MOSFET on   (b) N-channel MOSFET off

Figure 5-12: An N-channel MOSFET switch equivalent circuit: (a) switch closed, (b) switch open

If the voltage applied to the gate is switched to be nearly the same as the voltage applied to the source—0 V in this example—the MOSFET turns off, resulting in the equivalent circuit shown in Figure 5-12(b). The drain is typically connected to another MOSFET's gate, which draws current only briefly as it switches from one state to the other. After this brief switching of state, the connection of the drain to another MOSFET's gate does not draw current. Since no current flows through the resistor, there is no voltage difference across it. Thus, the voltage at the drain will be 5 V.

The resistor is said to be acting as the *pull-up device*, because when the MOSFET is turned off, the circuit is completed through the resistor, which acts to pull the voltage on the drain up to the higher voltage of the power supply.

P-Channel MOSFET

Now, let's look at the P-channel MOSFET, shown in Figure 5-11(b). The drain is connected to the lower voltage (0 V) through a resistor, R, and the source is connected to the higher-voltage power supply (5 V). When the voltage applied to the gate is switched to be nearly the same as the voltage applied to the source, the MOSFET turns off. In this case, the resistor acts as a *pull-down device* to pull the voltage on the drain down to 0 V. Figure 5-13(a) shows the equivalent circuit.

When the voltage applied to the gate is negative with respect to the source, the resistance between the drain and the source of the P-channel MOSFET decreases. When this voltage reaches a threshold value, typically in the range of −1 V, the resistance becomes very low, providing a good conduction path for current between the drain and the source. Figure 5-13(b) shows the resulting equivalent circuit when the gate is −5 V with respect to the source.

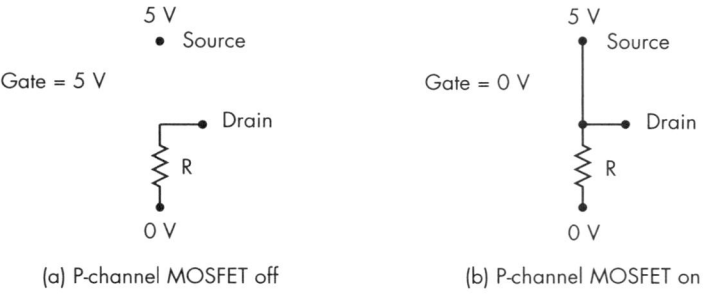

Figure 5-13: A P-channel MOSFET switch equivalent circuit: (a) switch open,
(b) switch closed

The resistors in the MOSFET circuits in Figures 5-11 present a couple of problems with both MOSFET types. We'll look at those next.

Resistors in MOSFET Circuits

The equivalent circuits in Figures 5-12(a) and 5-13(b) show that the respective MOSFET in its on state acts like a closed switch, thus causing current to flow through the pull-up or pull-down resistor. The current flow through the resistor when the MOSFET is in its on state consumes power that is simply converted to heat.

In addition to the pull-up and pull-down resistors using power when a MOSFET is in its on state, there's another problem with this hardware design. Although the gate of a MOSFET draws essentially no current to remain in either an on or an off state, a brief burst of current into the gate is required to change its state. That current is supplied by the device connected to the gate, probably from the drain of another MOSFET. I won't go into details in this book, but the amount of current that can be supplied at the drain from this other MOSFET is largely limited by its pull-up or pull-down resistor. The situation is essentially the same as that in Figures 5-6 and 5-7, where you saw that the time it takes to charge a capacitor is longer for higher resistance values.

So, there's a trade-off here: the larger the resistors, the lower the current flow, which reduces power consumption when the MOSFET is in the on state. But a larger resistor also reduces the amount of current available at the drain, thus increasing the amount of time it takes to switch a MOSFET connected to the drain. We're left with a dilemma: small pull-up and pull-down resistors increase power consumption, but large resistors slow down the computer.

CMOS Switch

We can solve this dilemma with *complementary metal-oxide semiconductor (CMOS)* technology. To see how this works, let's eliminate the pull-up and pull-down resistors and connect the drains of a P-channel and an N-channel. The P-channel will replace the pull-up resistor in the N-channel circuit, and the N-channel will replace the pull-down resistor in the P-channel circuit. We'll also connect the two gates, giving the circuit shown in Figure 5-14.

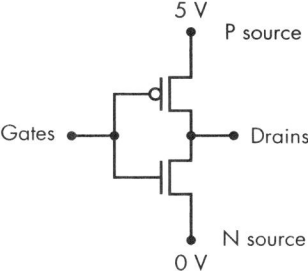

Figure 5-14: A CMOS inverter (NOT) circuit

Figure 5-15(a) shows the equivalent circuit with the gates at the higher power supply voltage of 5 V. The pull-up MOSFET (a P-channel) is off and the pull-down MOSFET (an N-channel) is on, so the drains are pulled down to the lower power supply voltage of 0 V. In Figure 5-15(b), the gates are at the lower power supply voltage of 0 V, which turns the P-channel MOSFET on and the N-channel MOSFET off. The P-channel MOSFET pulls the drains up to the higher power supply voltage of 5 V.

Figure 5-15: A CMOS inverter equivalent circuit: (a) pull-up open and pull-down closed, (b) pull-up closed and pull-down open

I summarize this behavior in Table 5-1.

Table 5-1: The Truth Table for a Single CMOS

Gates	Drains
0 V	5 V
5 V	0 V

If we use the gates connection as the input, use the drains connection as the output, and let 5 V be logical 1 and 0 V be logical 0, then the CMOS implements a NOT gate.

The two main advantages of using CMOS circuits are:

- They consume very little power. Because of the switching speed difference between N-channel and P-channel MOSFETs, only a small amount of current flows during the switching period. Less current means less heat, which is often the limiting factor in chip design.

- The circuit responds much faster. A MOSFET can supply the current at its output faster than a resistor can, charging the gate of the following MOSFET. This allows us to build faster computers.

Figure 5-16 shows an AND gate implemented with three CMOSs.

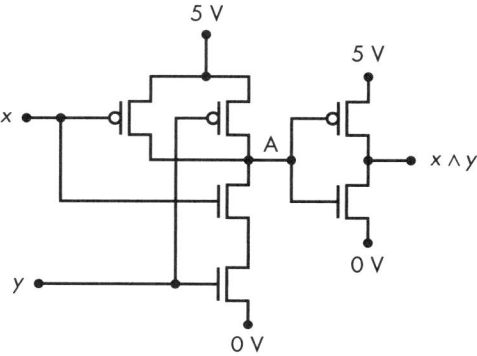

Figure 5-16: An AND gate using three CMOS transistors

The truth table in Table 5-2 shows the intermediate output from the first two CMOSs (point A in Figure 5-16).

Table 5-2: The Truth Table for the AND Gate of Figure 5-16

x	y	A	x ∧ y
0	0	1	0
0	1	1	0
1	0	1	0
1	1	0	1

From the truth table, we see that the signal at point A is $\neg(x \wedge y)$. The circuit from point A to the output is a NOT gate. The result at point A is called the *NAND* operation. It requires two fewer transistors than the AND operation. We'll look at the implications of this in the next section.

NAND and NOR Gates

As you learned in the previous section, the inherent design of transistors means that most circuits invert the signal. That is, for most circuits, a high voltage at the input produces a low voltage at the output, and vice versa.

As a result, an AND gate will typically require a NOT gate at the output to achieve a true AND operation.

You also learned that it takes fewer transistors to produce NOT(AND) than a regular AND. This combination is so common that it has been given a name: the *NAND gate*. And, of course, we have an equivalent with the OR gate, called the *NOR gate*:

NAND   A binary operator that gives a result of 0 if and only if *both* operands are 1 and gives 1 otherwise. We'll use $\neg(x \wedge y)$ to designate the NAND operation. Figure 5-17 shows the hardware symbol for the NAND gate along with a truth table showing its operation on inputs x and y.

x	y	$\neg(x \wedge y)$
0	0	1
0	1	1
1	0	1
1	1	0

Figure 5-17: The NAND gate acting on two variables, x and y

NOR   A binary operator that gives a result of 0 if at least one of the two operands is 1 and gives 1 otherwise. We'll use $\neg(x \vee y)$ to designate the NOR operation. Figure 5-18 shows the hardware symbol for the NOR gate along with a truth table showing its operation on inputs x and y.

x	y	$\neg(x \vee y)$
0	0	1
0	1	0
1	0	0
1	1	0

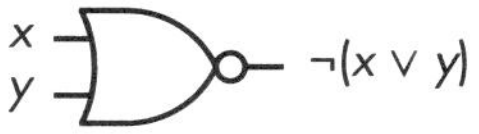

Figure 5-18: The NOR gate acting on two variables, x and y

Notice the small circle at the output of the NAND and NOR gates in Figures 5-17 and 5-18. This signifies *NOT*, just as with the NOT gate you saw in Figure 4-3.

Although in the previous chapter we explicitly showed NOT gates when inputs to gates are complemented, it's common to simply use these small circles at the input to signify the complement. For example, Figure 5-19 shows an OR gate with both inputs complemented.

x	y	$(\neg x \vee \neg y)$	$\neg(x \wedge y)$
0	0	1	1
0	1	1	1
1	0	1	1
1	1	0	0

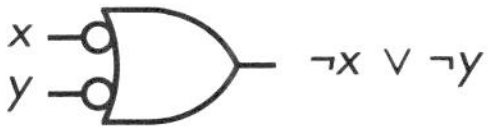

Figure 5-19: An alternative way to draw a NAND gate

As the truth table shows, this is another way to implement a NAND gate. As you learned in Chapter 4, De Morgan's law confirms this:

$$\neg(x \land y) = \neg x \lor \neg y$$

NAND as a Universal Gate

One of the interesting properties about NAND gates is that they can be used to build AND, OR, and NOT gates. This means the NAND gate can be used to implement any Boolean function. In this sense, you can think of the NAND gate as a *universal gate*. Recalling De Morgan's law, it probably won't surprise you that a NOR gate can also be used as a universal gate. But the physics of CMOS transistors is such that NAND gates are faster and take up less space, so they are almost always the preferred solution.

Let's go through how to use a NAND gate to build an AND, OR, or NOT gate. To build a NOT gate using a NAND gate, simply connect the signal to both inputs of the NAND gate, as shown in Figure 5-20.

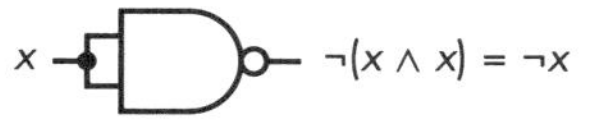

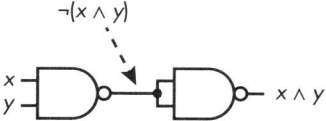

Figure 5-20: A NOT gate built from a NAND gate

To make an AND gate, we can observe that the first NAND gate in Figure 5-21 produces $\neg(x \land y)$ and connect it to a NOT gate like the one in Figure 5-20 to produce $(x \land y)$.

$\neg(x \land y)$

$x \land y$

Figure 5-21: An AND gate built from two NAND gates

We can use De Morgan's law to derive an OR gate. Consider the following:

$$\neg(\neg x \land \neg y) = \neg(\neg x) \lor \neg(\neg y)$$
$$= x \lor y$$

So, to implement OR, we need three NAND gates, as in Figure 5-22. The two NAND gates at the x and y inputs are connected as NOT gates to produce $\neg x$ and $\neg y$, which gives $\neg(\neg x \land \neg y)$ at the output of the third NAND gate.

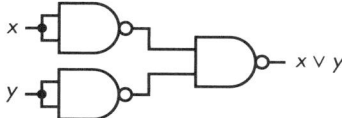

Figure 5-22: An OR gate built from three NAND gates

It looks like we are creating more complexity to build circuits from NAND gates, but consider this function:

$$F(w, x, y, z) = (w \wedge x) \vee (y \wedge z)$$

Without knowing how logic gates are constructed, it would be reasonable to implement this function with the circuit shown in Figure 5-23.

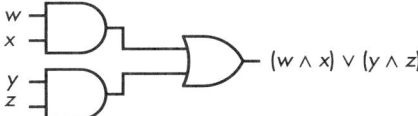

Figure 5-23: F(w, x, y, z) using two AND gates and one OR gate

Although it might seem like we're going in the wrong direction, let's add some hardware to this circuit. The involution property states that $\neg(\neg x) = x$, so we can add two NOT gates to each path, as shown in Figure 5-24.

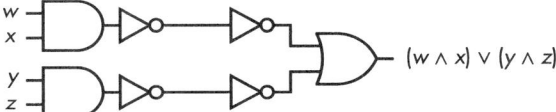

Figure 5-24: F(w, x, y, z) using two AND gates, one OR gate, and four NOT gates

Comparing the two AND gate/NOT gate combinations that operate on the w, x, y, and z inputs with Figure 5-17, we see that each is simply a NAND gate. They will produce $\neg(w \wedge x)$ and $\neg(y \wedge z)$ at the outputs of the two left-most NOT gates.

You saw from the application of De Morgan's law in Figure 5-19 that $(\neg a) \vee (\neg b) = \neg(a \wedge b)$. In other words, we can replace the combination of the two rightmost NOT gates and the OR gate with a single NAND gate:

$$\neg(\neg(w \wedge x) \wedge \neg(y \wedge z)) = (w \wedge x) \vee (y \wedge z)$$

The resulting circuit, shown in Figure 5-25, uses three NAND gates.

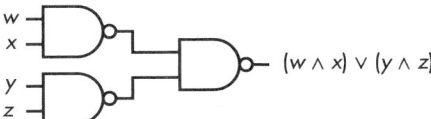

Figure 5-25: F(w, x, y, z) using three NAND gates

From simply viewing the logic circuit diagrams in Figures 5-23 and 5-25, it may seem that we haven't gained anything in this circuit transformation. But we saw in the previous section that a NAND gate (point A in Figure 5-16) requires two fewer transistors than an AND gate. Thus, the NAND gate implementation is less power-intensive and faster. The same is true of an OR gate.

The conversion from an AND/OR/NOT gate design to one that uses only NAND gates is straightforward:

1. Express the function as a minimal sum of products.
2. Convert the products (AND terms) and the final sum (OR) to NANDs.
3. Add a NAND gate for any product with only a single literal.

Everything I've said about NAND gates here applies to NOR gates. You simply apply De Morgan's law to find the complement of everything. But as mentioned previously, NAND gates are typically faster and take up less space than NOR gates, so they are almost always the preferred solution.

As with software, hardware design is an iterative process. Most problems do not have a unique solution, and you often need to develop several designs and analyze each one within the context of the available hardware. As the previous example shows, two solutions that look the same on paper may be very different at the hardware level.

YOUR TURN

5.1   Design a NOT gate, an AND gate, and an OR gate using NOR gates.

5.2   Design a circuit using NAND gates that detects the "below" condition for two 2-bit integers, x and y, $F(x, y) = 1$. It's common to use below/above for unsigned integer comparisons and less than/greater than for signed integer comparisons.

What You've Learned

Basic electronics concepts   Resistance, capacitance, and inductance affect the voltages and current flow in an electronic circuit.

Transistors   Semiconductor devices that can be used as electronically controlled switches.

MOSFET   The most commonly used switching device for implementing logic gates in computers. Metal-oxide-semiconductor field-effect transistors come in N-channel and P-channel types.

CMOS   N-channel and P-channel MOSFETs are paired in a complementary configuration to increase switching speed and reduce power consumption.

NAND and NOR gates   These require fewer transistors than AND and OR gates because of the inherent electronic characteristics of transistors.

In the next chapter, you'll learn how simple logic gates are connected in circuits to implement the complex operations needed to build a computer.

6

COMBINATIONAL LOGIC CIRCUITS

In the previous chapter, you learned about a computer's basic component, the logic gate. Computers are constructed from assemblages of logic gates, called *logic circuits*, that process digital information.

In this and the following two chapters, we'll look at how to build some of the logic circuits that make up CPUs, memory, and other devices. I won't describe any of these units in their entirety; instead, we'll look at a few small parts and discuss the concepts behind them. The goal is to provide an introductory overview of the ideas that underlie these logic circuits.

The Two Types of Logic Circuits

There are two types of logic circuits. A *combinational logic circuit* has output that depends only on the inputs given at any specific time and not on any previous inputs. A *sequential logic circuit* has output that depends on both previous and current inputs.

To elucidate these two types, let's consider a TV remote. You can select a specific channel by entering a number on the remote. The channel selection depends only on the number you entered and ignores the channels you were viewing before. Thus, the relationship between the input and the output is combinational.

The remote control also has an input for going up or down one channel. This input depends on the previously selected channel and the previous sequence of up/down button pushes. The channel up/down buttons illustrate a sequential input/output relationship.

We'll explore sequential logic circuits in the next chapter. In this chapter, we'll go through several examples of combinational logic circuits to see how they function.

SIGNAL VOLTAGE LEVELS

Electronic logic circuits represent 1s and 0s with either a high voltage or a low voltage. We call the voltage that represents 1 the *active voltage*. If we use a higher voltage to represent 1, then the signal is called *active high*. If we use a lower voltage to represent 1, then the signal is called *active low*.

An active-high signal can be connected to an active-low input, but the hardware designer must take the difference into account. For example, if the required logical input to an active-low input is 1, the required voltage is the lower of the two voltages; if the signal to be connected to this input is active high, then a logical 1 is the higher of the two voltages, and the signal must first be complemented to be interpreted as a 1 at the active-low input.

I will use only logic levels—0 and 1—in the discussions of logic circuits in this book and avoid the actual voltage levels being used in the hardware, but you should know the terminology because it can come up when talking to others or reading component specification sheets.

Adders

We'll start with one of the most fundamental operations performed in the CPU: adding two bits. Our eventual goal is to add two *n*-bit numbers.

Recall from Chapter 2 that the bits in a binary number are numbered from right (the least significant bit) to left (the most significant bit), starting with 0. I'll start by showing you how to add two bits in the ith bit position and complete the discussion by showing you how to add two 4-bit numbers, taking into account the carry from each bit position.

Half Adder

Addition can be done with several kinds of circuits. We'll start with the *half adder*, which simply adds the two bits in the current bit position of a number (expressed in binary). This is shown by the truth table in Table 6-1, where x_i is the ith bit of the number x and the values in the y_i column represent the ith bit of the number y. Sum_i is the ith bit of the number Sum, and $Carry_{i+1}$ is the carry from adding bits x_i and y_i.

Table 6-1: A Truth Table for Adding Two Bits Using a Half Adder

x_i	y_i	$Carry_{i+1}$	Sum_i
0	0	0	0
0	1	0	1
1	0	0	1
1	1	1	0

The sum is the XOR of the two inputs, and the carry is the AND of the two inputs. Figure 6-1 shows the logic circuit for a half adder.

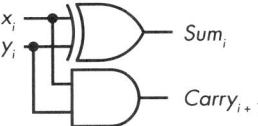

Figure 6-1: A half adder logic circuit

But there's a flaw here: the half adder works with only two input bits. It can be used to add the two bits from the same bit position of two numbers, but it doesn't take into account a possible carry from the next lower-order bit position. Including this carry as a third input will give us a full adder.

Full Adder

Unlike the half adder, a *full adder* circuit has three 1-bit inputs: $Carry_i$, x_i, and y_i. $Carry_i$ is the carry that resulted when you added the two bits in the previous bit position (the bit to the right). For example, if we're adding the two bits in bit position 5, the inputs to the full adder are the two bits in position 5 plus the carry from adding the bits in position 4. Table 6-2 shows the results.

Table 6-2: A Truth Table for Adding Two Bits Using a Full Adder

$Carry_i$	x_i	y_i	$Carry_{i+1}$	Sum_i
0	0	0	0	0
0	0	1	0	1
0	1	0	0	1
0	1	1	1	0
1	0	0	0	1
1	0	1	1	0
1	1	0	1	0
1	1	1	1	1

To design a full adder circuit, we start with the function that specifies when Sum_i is 1 as a sum of product terms from Table 6-2:

$$Sum_i(Carry_i, x_i, y_i) = (\neg Carry_i \wedge \neg x_i \wedge y_i) \vee (\neg Carry_i \wedge x_i \wedge \neg y_i)$$
$$\vee (Carry_i \wedge \neg x_i \wedge \neg y_i) \vee (Carry_i \wedge x_i \wedge y_i)$$

There are no obvious simplifications in this equation, so let's look at the Karnaugh map for Sum_i, shown in Figure 6-2.

$Sum_i(Carry_i, x_i, y_i)$

	00	01	11	10
0		1		1
1	1		1	

Figure 6-2: A Karnaugh map for the sum of three bits, $Carry_i$, x_i, and y_i

There are no obvious groupings in Figure 6-2, so we are left with the four product terms to compute Sum_i in the previous equation.

You learned in Chapter 4 that $Carry_{i+1}(Carry_i, x_i, y_i)$ can be expressed by the equation:

$$Carry_{i+1}(Carry_i, x_i, y_i) = (x_i \wedge y_i) \vee (Carry_i \wedge x_i) \vee (Carry_i \wedge y_i)$$

Together, these two functions give the circuit for a full adder, as shown in Figure 6-3.

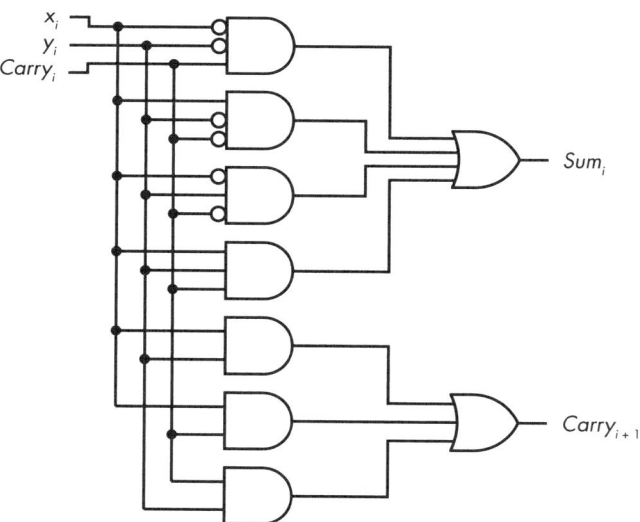

Figure 6-3: A full adder circuit

The full adder uses nine logic gates. In the next section, we'll see if we can find a simpler circuit.

Full Adder from Two Half Adders

To see if we can find a simpler solution for adding two bits and the carry from the next lower-order bit position, let's go back to the equation for Sum_i. Using the distribution rule, we can rearrange it as follows:

$$Sum_i(Carry_i, x_i, y_i) = \neg Carry_i \wedge ((\neg x_i \wedge y_i) \vee (x_i \wedge \neg y_i))$$
$$\vee \, Carry_i \wedge ((\neg x_i \wedge \neg y_i) \vee (x_i \wedge y_i))$$

In Chapter 4, you learned that the quantity in the parentheses in the first product term is the XOR of x_i and y_i:

$$(\neg x_i \wedge y_i) \vee (x_i \wedge \neg y_i) = x_i \veebar y_i$$

Thus, we have:

$$Sum_i(Carry_i, x_i, y_i) = \neg Carry_i \wedge (x_i \veebar y_i) \vee Carry_i \wedge ((\neg x_i \wedge \neg y_i) \vee (x_i \wedge y_i))$$

Let's manipulate the quantity in the parentheses in the second product term. Recall that in Boolean algebra $x \wedge \neg x = 0$, so we can write the following:

$$(\neg x_i \wedge \neg y_i) \vee (x_i \wedge y_i) = (x_i \wedge \neg x_i) \vee (\neg x_i \wedge \neg y_i) \vee (x_i \wedge y_i) \vee (y_i \wedge \neg y_i)$$
$$= x_i \wedge (\neg x_i \vee y_i) \vee \neg y_i \wedge (\neg x_i \vee y_i)$$
$$= (x_i \vee \neg y_i) \wedge (\neg x_i \vee y_i)$$
$$= \neg(x_i \veebar y_i)$$

Thus:

$$Sum_i(Carry_i, x_i, y_i) = \neg Carry_i \wedge (x_i \veebar y_i) \vee Carry_i \wedge \neg(x_i \veebar y_i)$$
$$= Carry_i \veebar (x_i \veebar y_i)$$

We'll do something to develop a Boolean function for $Carry_{i+1}$ that will probably seem counterintuitive. Let's start with the Karnaugh map for carry when adding three bits (see Figure 4-14), but remove two of the groupings, as shown by the dotted lines in Figure 6-4.

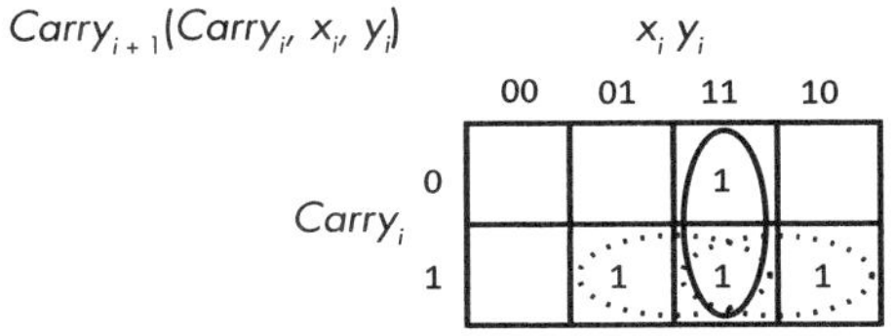

$Carry_{i+1}(Carry_i, x_i, y_i)$

Figure 6-4: The Karnaugh map for carry from Figure 4-14, redrawn without two overlapping groupings (dotted lines)

This will give us the following equation:

$$Carry_{i+1}(Carry_i, x_i, y_i) = (x_i \wedge y_i) \vee (Carry_i \wedge \neg x_i \wedge y_i) \vee (Carry_i \wedge x_i \wedge \neg y_i)$$
$$= (x_i \wedge y_i) \vee Carry_i \wedge ((\neg x_i \wedge y_i) \vee (x_i \wedge \neg y_i))$$
$$= (x_i \wedge y_i) \vee (Carry_i \wedge (x_i \veebar y_i))$$

Notice that two of the terms in this equation, $(x_i \wedge y_i)$ and $(x_i \veebar y_i)$, are already generated by a half adder (see Figure 6-1). With a second half adder and an OR gate, we can implement a full adder, as shown in Figure 6-5.

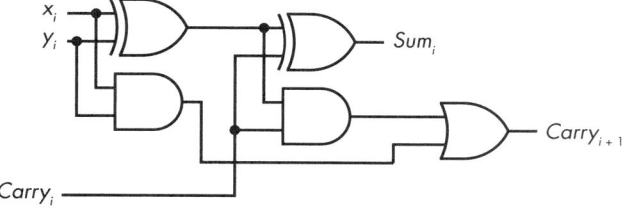

Figure 6-5: A full adder using two half adders

Now you should understand where the terms *half adder* and *full adder* come from.

A simpler circuit is not always better. In truth, we cannot say which of the two full adder circuits in Figures 6-3 and 6-5 is better just by looking at the logic circuits. Good engineering design depends on many factors, such as how each logic gate is implemented, the cost of the logic gates and their availability, and so forth. I've presented two alternatives here to show that different approaches can lead to different, but functionally equivalent, designs.

Ripple-Carry Addition and Subtraction Circuits

Now you know how to add the two bits in a given bit position, plus a carry from the next lower-order bit position. But most values that a program works with have many bits, so we need a way to add the corresponding bits in each bit position of two n-bit numbers. This can be done with an *n-bit adder*, which can be implemented with n full adders. Figure 6-6 shows a 4-bit adder.

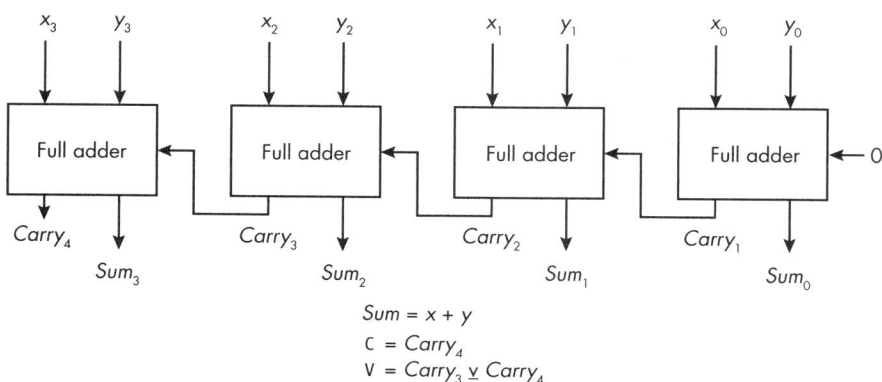

Figure 6-6: A 4-bit adder

Addition begins with the full adder on the right receiving the two lowest-order bits, x_0 and y_0. Since this is the lowest-order bit, there is no carry, and $c_0 = 0$. The bit sum is s_0, and the carry from this addition, c_1, is connected to the carry input of the next full adder to the left, where it is added to x_1 and y_1. Thus, the ith full adder adds the two ith bits of the operands, plus the carry (which is either 0 or 1) from the $(i - 1)$th full adder.

Each full adder handles one bit (often referred to as a *slice*) of the total width of the values being added. The carry from each bit position is added to the bits in the next higher-order bit position. The addition process flows from the lowest-order bit to the highest-order in a sort of rippling effect, which gives this method of adding the name *ripple-carry addition*.

Notice that in Figure 6-6, we have C and V, the *carry flag* and *overflow flag*. You learned about carry and overflow in Chapter 3. The AArch64 architecture includes addition and subtraction instructions that record whether carry and overflow occurred in the CPU. You'll learn more about this in Chapter 9.

Let's see how we can use a similar idea to implement subtraction. Recall that in two's complement, a number is negated by taking its two's complement, flipping all the bits, and adding 1. Thus, we can subtract y from x by doing this:

$$x - y = x + (\textit{two's complement of } y)$$
$$= x + ((\textit{y's bits flipped}) + 1)$$

We can perform subtraction with our adder in Figure 6-5 if we complement each y_i and set the initial carry in to 1 instead of 0. Each y_i can be complemented by XOR-ing it with 1. This leads to the 4-bit circuit in Figure 6-7, which will add two 4-bit numbers when *func* = 0 and subtract them when *func* = 1.

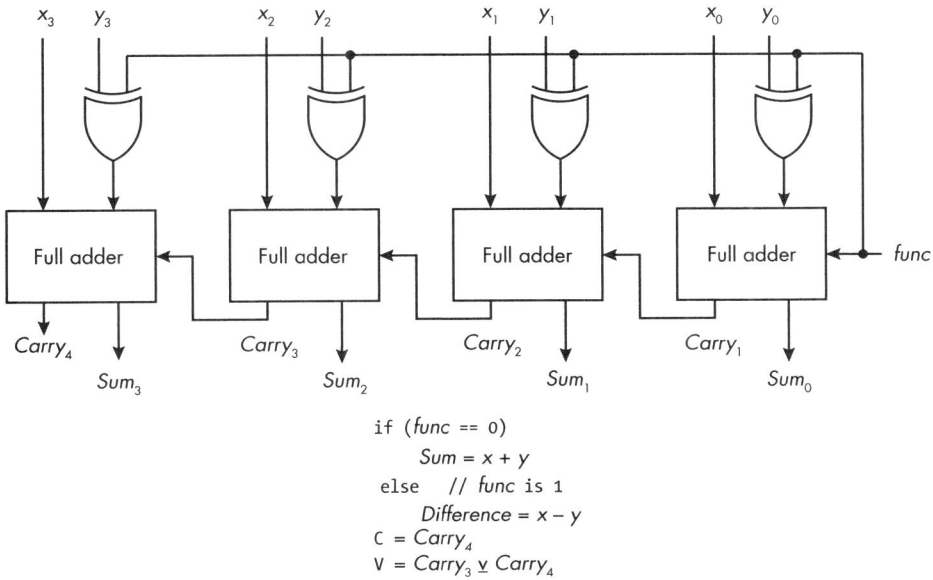

```
if (func == 0)
    Sum = x + y
else    // func is 1
    Difference = x – y
C = Carry₄
V = Carry₃ ⊻ Carry₄
```

Figure 6-7: A 4-bit adder/subtractor

There is, of course, a time delay as the sum is computed from right to left. The computation time can be significantly reduced through circuit designs that make use of what can be known about the values of the intermediate carries, c_i, but I won't go into such details in this book. Let's turn to our next type of circuit.

Decoders

Many places in a computer require selecting one of several connections based on a number. For example, as you will see in Chapter 8, the CPU has a small amount of memory organized in *registers*, which are used for computations. The AArch64 architecture provides 31 general-purpose 64-bit registers. If an instruction uses one of the registers, 5 bits in the instruction must be used to select which of the 31 registers should be used.

This selection can be done with a *decoder*. The input to the decoder is the 4-bit number of the register, and the output is one of 16 possible connections to the specified register.

A decoder has n binary inputs that can produce up to 2^n binary outputs. The most common type of decoder, sometimes called a *line decoder*, selects only one of the output lines to set to 1 for each input bit pattern. It's also common for a decoder to include an *Enable* input. Table 6-3 is a truth table for a 3×8 (three inputs, eight outputs) decoder with an *Enable* input that shows how this works.

Table 6-3: A Truth Table for a 3×8 Decoder with *Enable*

Enable	Input			Output							
	x_2	x_1	x_0	y_7	y_6	y_5	y_4	y_3	y_2	y_1	y_0
0	0	0	0	0	0	0	0	0	0	0	0
0	0	0	1	0	0	0	0	0	0	0	0
0	0	1	0	0	0	0	0	0	0	0	0
0	0	1	1	0	0	0	0	0	0	0	0
0	1	0	0	0	0	0	0	0	0	0	0
0	1	0	1	0	0	0	0	0	0	0	0
0	1	1	0	0	0	0	0	0	0	0	0
0	1	1	1	0	0	0	0	0	0	0	0

1	0	0	0	0	0	0	0	0	0	0	1
1	0	0	1	0	0	0	0	0	0	1	0
1	0	1	0	0	0	0	0	0	1	0	0
1	0	1	1	0	0	0	0	1	0	0	0
1	1	0	0	0	0	0	1	0	0	0	0
1	1	0	1	0	0	1	0	0	0	0	0
1	1	1	0	0	1	0	0	0	0	0	0
1	1	1	1	1	0	0	0	0	0	0	0

When *Enable* = 0, all the output lines are 0. When *Enable* = 1, the 3-bit number at the input, $x = x_2x_1x_0$, selects which output line is set to 1. So, this decoder could be used to select one of eight registers with a 3-bit number. (I'm not using all of the 31 registers in the AArch64 architecture to keep the table a reasonable size here.)

The 3×8 line decoder specified in Table 6-3 can be implemented with four-input AND gates, as shown in Figure 6-8.

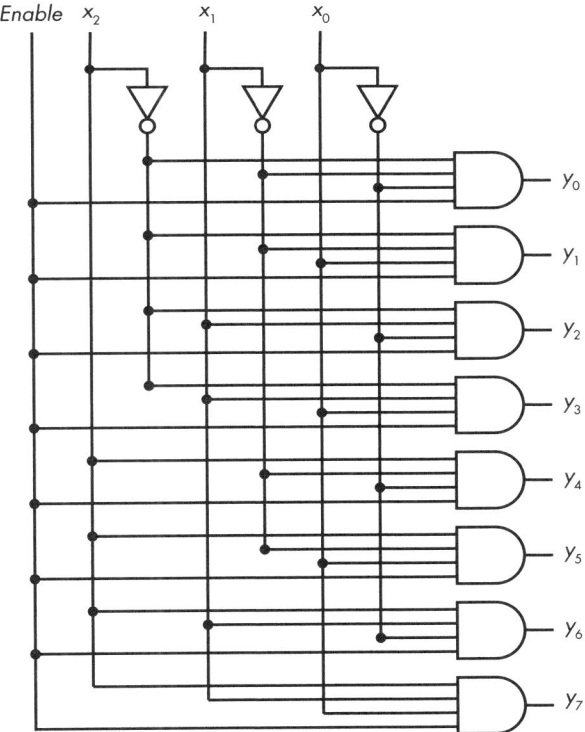

Figure 6-8: The circuit for a 3×8 decoder with Enable

Decoders are more versatile than they might seem at first glance. Each possible input can be seen as a minterm (for a refresher on minterms, see "Canonical Sum or Sum of Minterms" on page 62 in Chapter 4). The line decoder in Table 6-3 shows that only a single output is 1 when a minterm evaluates to 1 and *Enable* is 1. Thus, a decoder can be viewed as a "minterm generator."

We know from Chapter 4 that any logical expression can be represented as the OR of minterms, so it follows that we can implement any logical expression by OR-ing the output(s) of a decoder. For example, if you look back at the Karnaugh maps for the full adder (Figures 6-2 and 6-4), you might see that $Sum_i(Carry_i, x_i, y_i)$ and $Carry_{i+1}(Carry_i, x_i, y_i)$ can be expressed as the OR of minterms,

$$Sum_i(Carry_i, x_i, y_i) = m_1 \lor m_2 \lor m_4 \lor m_7$$

$$Carry_{i+1}(Carry_i, x_i, y_i) = m_3 \lor m_5 \lor m_6 \lor m_7$$

where the subscript i on x, y, and *Carry* refers to the bit slice and the subscripts on m are part of the minterm notation.

We can implement each bit slice of a full adder with a 3×8 decoder and two four-input OR gates, as shown in Figure 6-9. An n-bit adder would require n of these circuits.

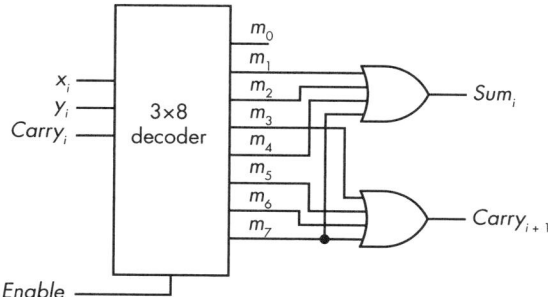

Figure 6-9: A 1-bit slice of a full adder implemented with a 3×8 decoder

The decoder circuit in Figure 6-8 requires eight AND gates and three NOT gates. The full adder in Figure 6-9 adds two OR gates, for a total of 13 logic gates. Comparing this with the full adder design in Figure 6-5, which requires only five logic gates (two XOR, two AND, and one OR), it would seem that using a decoder to construct a full adder increases the complexity of the circuit. Keep in mind, however, that designs must take into account other factors, such as availability of components, cost of components, and so forth.

6.2 You have probably seen seven-segment displays, which are used to display numerals. Each segment in a seven-segment display is lit by applying a 1 to the input pin connected to that segment. Suppose you have a seven-segment display with an 8-bit input that lights the segments and the decimal point, as shown in the following figure:

Bit	Segment
0	a
1	b
2	c
3	d
4	e
5	f
6	g
7	dp

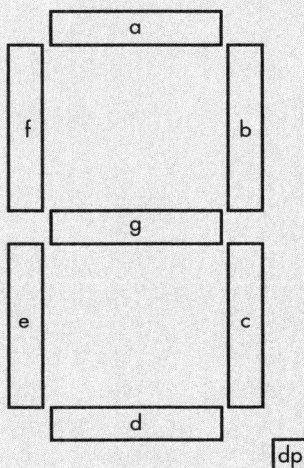

For example, you could display a 5 with the bit pattern 0110 1101. However, it would be more convenient to write a program to use BCD for individual numerals. Design a decoder that transforms numerals in BCD to segment patterns on the seven-segment display.

Multiplexers

In the previous section, you learned how an n-bit number can be used to select which one of 2^n output lines should be set to 1. The opposite situation also occurs, where we need to select which of several inputs should be passed on. For example, when performing arithmetic operations, such as addition, the numbers can come from different locations within the CPU. (You will learn more about this in the next few chapters.) The operation itself will be performed by one arithmetic unit, and the CPU needs to select the inputs to the operation from all the possible locations.

A device that can make this selection is called a *multiplexer (MUX)*. It can switch between 2^n input lines by using n selection lines. Figure 6-10 shows a circuit for a four-way multiplexer.

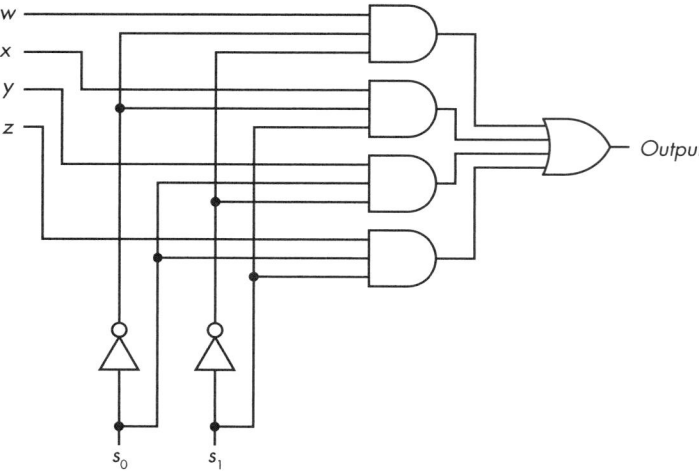

Figure 6-10: A four-way multiplexer circuit

The output is given by:

$$Output = (\neg s_0 \wedge \neg s_1 \wedge w) \vee (\neg s_0 \wedge s_1 \wedge x) \vee (s_0 \wedge \neg s_1 \wedge y) \vee (s_0 \wedge s_1 \wedge z)$$

When using AND and OR gates, the number of transistors required to implement a multiplexer gets large as the number of inputs grows. A three-input AND gate is required for each input to the multiplexer, with the output of each AND gate connected to one of the inputs to the OR gate. So, the number of inputs to the OR gate equals the number of multiplexer inputs.

This four-way multiplexer requires a four-input OR gate. If we try to scale this up, the n-input OR gate will present some technical electronic problems for a large n. The use of an n-input OR gate can be avoided by using a type of gate that can disconnect its output signal from its input, which we'll look at next.

Tristate Buffer

The logic gate called a *tristate buffer* has three possible outputs: 0, 1, and "no connection." The "no connection" output is actually a high-impedance connection, also called *high Z* or *open*. A tristate buffer has both a data input and an *Enable* input, which behaves as shown in Figure 6-11.

Enable	In	Out
0	0	High Z
0	1	High Z
1	0	0
1	1	1

Enable

In ▷ Out

Figure 6-11: A tristate buffer

When *Enable* = 1, the output, which is equal to the input, is connected to whatever circuit element follows the tristate buffer. But when *Enable* = 0, the output is essentially disconnected. This is different from 0; being disconnected means it has no effect on the circuit element to which it is connected.

The "no connection" output lets us physically connect the outputs of many tristate buffers but select only one to pass its input to the common output line. The four-way multiplexer in Figure 6-12 shows how we avoid using an n-input OR gate by using n tristate buffers.

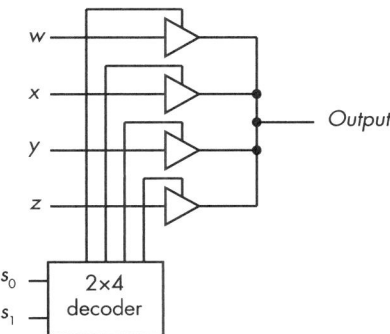

Figure 6-12: A four-way multiplexer built from a decoder and tristate buffers

The $2{\times}4$ decoder in Figure 6-12 selects which of the tristate buffers connects one of the inputs, w, x, y, or z, to the output to create a four-way multiplexer. Figure 6-13 shows the circuit symbol used for a multiplexer, along with the truth table that shows its behavior.

s_1	s_0	**Output**
0	0	w
0	1	x
1	0	y
1	1	z

Figure 6-13: A four-way multiplexer

As an example of where we might use a four-way multiplexer like this one, consider a computer with four registers and one adder. Let's name the registers w, x, y, and z. If we connect the bits in the corresponding bit position from each register to a multiplexer, then we can use the 2-bit selector $s_1 s_0$ to choose which register will provide the input to the adder. For example, each bit in position 5, w_5, x_5, y_5, and z_5, would be connected to one of the inputs in multiplexer 5. If $s_1 s_0 = 10$, the input to the adder would be y_5.

Programmable Logic Devices

So far, we've been discussing hardware designs that use individual logic gates. If the design changes, the logic gate configuration changes. This almost always means that the circuit board that holds the logic gates and connects them will need to be redesigned. A change also often means ordering a different kind of logic gate, which can be expensive and take time. These problems can be reduced by using *programmable logic devices (PLDs)* to implement the required logic function.

PLDs contain many AND gates and OR gates, which can be programmed to implement Boolean functions. The inputs, and their complemented value, are connected to the AND gates. The AND gates, taken together, are referred to as the *AND plane* or *AND array*. The outputs from the AND gates are connected to OR gates, which taken together are referred to as the *OR plane* or *OR array*. Depending on the type, one or both planes can be programmed to implement combinational logic. When using a PLD, a design change requires changing only how the device is programmed, not buying different devices, meaning the circuit board does not need to be redesigned.

PLDs come in several types. Most can be programmed by a user. Some are preprogrammed at the time of manufacture, and some can even be erased and reprogrammed by the user. Programming technologies range from specifying the manufacturing mask (for the preprogrammed devices) to inexpensive electronic programming systems. We'll look at the three main categories of PLDs in this section.

Programmable Logic Array

In a *programmable logic array (PLA)*, both the AND and OR planes are programmable. PLAs are used to implement logic functions. Figure 6-14 gives the general idea for a PLA that has two input variables and two possible output functions of these variables.

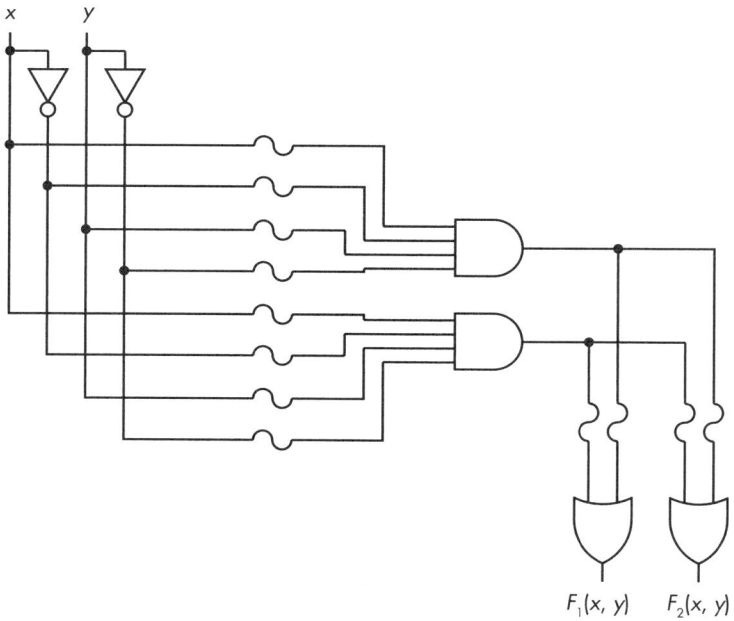

Figure 6-14: A simplified circuit for a programmable logic array

Each input variable, in both its uncomplemented and complemented form, is an input to the AND gates through fuses. A *fuse* is a thin piece of conductor used to protect an electrical circuit. If the current flowing through it is high enough, the conductor melts, opening the circuit and stopping current flow. PLDs can be programmed by breaking (or *blowing*) the appropriate fuses, removing the input to the logic gate. Some devices use *antifuses* instead of fuses; these are normally open, and programming them consists of completing the connection instead of removing it. Devices that can be reprogrammed have fuses that can be broken and then remade.

In Figure 6-14, the S-shaped lines in the circuit diagram represent the fuses. The fuses can be blown or left in place so as to program each AND gate to output a product of the inputs, x, $\neg x$, y, and $\neg y$. Since every input, plus its complement, is input to each AND gate, any of the AND gates can be programmed to output a minterm.

The products produced by the AND gate plane are all connected to the inputs of the OR gates, also through fuses. Thus, depending on which OR gate fuses are left in place, the output of each OR gate is a sum of products. There may be additional logic circuitry to select between the different outputs. You have already seen that any Boolean function can be expressed as a sum of products, so this logic device can be programmed to implement any Boolean function by blowing the fuses.

A PLA is typically larger than the one shown in Figure 6-14, which is already complicated to draw. To simplify the drawing, it is typical to use a diagram similar to Figure 6-15 to specify the design.

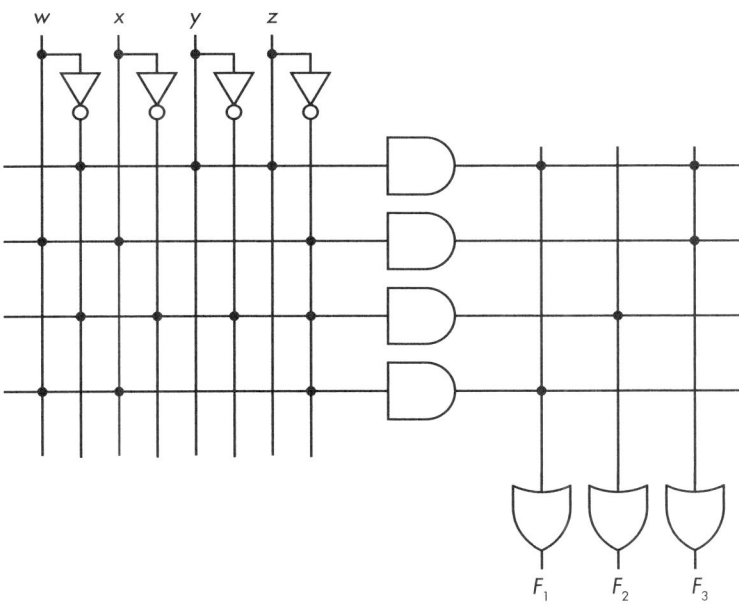

Figure 6-15: A diagram for a programmable logic array where the dots represent connections

This diagram can be a little tricky to understand. In Figure 6-14, each AND gate has multiple inputs: one for each variable and one for its complement. In Figure 6-15, we use a single horizontal line leading to the input of each AND gate to represent multiple wires (variable and complement), so each AND gate in Figure 6-15 has eight inputs, even though we draw only one line.

The dots at the intersections of the vertical and horizontal lines represent places where the fuses have been left intact, thus creating a connection. For example, the three dots on the topmost horizontal line indicate that there are three inputs left connected to that AND gate. The output of the topmost AND gate is:

$$\neg w \wedge y \wedge z$$

Referring again to Figure 6-14, you can see that the output from each AND gate is connected to each of the OR gates (through fuses). Therefore, the OR gates also have multiple inputs—one for each AND gate—and the vertical lines leading to the OR gate inputs represent multiple wires. The PLA in Figure 6-15 has been programmed to provide these three functions:

$$F_1(w, x, y, z) = (\neg w \wedge y \wedge z) \vee (w \wedge x \wedge \neg z)$$
$$F_2(w, x, y, z) = \neg w \wedge \neg x \wedge \neg y \wedge \neg z$$
$$F_3(w, x, y, z) = (\neg w \wedge y \wedge z) \vee (w \wedge x \wedge \neg z)$$

Since the AND plane can produce all possible minterms and the OR plane can provide any sum of the minterms, a PLA can be used to implement any possible logical function. If we want to change the function, it's a simple matter of programming another PLA and replacing the old one.

Read-Only Memory

Although PLDs have no memory (meaning the current state isn't affected by previous states of the inputs), they can be used to make *nonvolatile* memory— memory whose contents remain intact when the power is turned off. *Read-only memory (ROM)* is used to store bit patterns that can represent data or program instructions. A program can only read the data or program stored in ROM; the contents of the ROM cannot be changed by writing new data or program instructions to it. ROM is commonly used in devices that have a fixed set of functionalities, such as watches, automobile engine control units, and appliances. In fact, our lives are surrounded by devices that are controlled by programs stored in ROM.

ROM can be implemented as a PLD where only the OR gate plane can be programmed. The AND gate plane remains wired to provide all the minterms. We can think of the inputs to the ROM as addresses; then, the OR gate plane is programmed to provide the bit pattern at each address. For example, the ROM diagrammed in Figure 6-16 has two inputs, a_1 and a_0, which provide a 2-bit address.

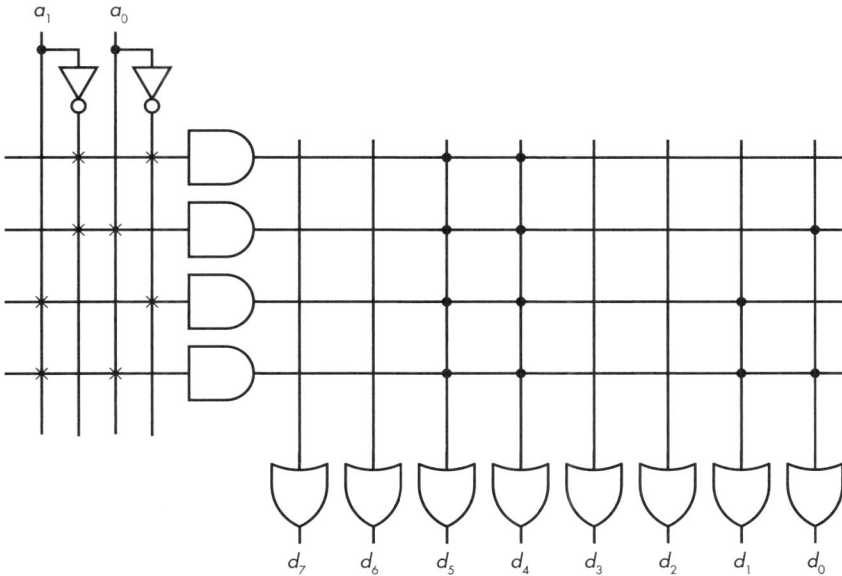

Figure 6-16: A 4-byte ROM device

The × connections in Figure 6-16 represent permanent connections, showing that the AND gate plane is fixed. Each AND gate produces a minterm at each address in this ROM device. The OR gate plane produces up to 2^n 8-bit bytes, where n is the width, in number of bits, of the address input to the AND gate plane. The connections (dots) to the OR gates represent the bit pattern stored at the corresponding address. Table 6-4 shows a ROM device in which the OR gate plane has been programmed to store the four characters 0, 1, 2, and 3 (in ASCII code).

Table 6-4: A ROM Device Holding Four ASCII Characters

Minterm	Address	Contents	ASCII character
$\neg a_1 \neg a_0$	00	00110000	0
$\neg a_1 a_0$	01	00110001	1
$a_1 \neg a_0$	10	00110010	2
$a_1 a_0$	11	00110011	3

Although we have stored only data in this example, computer instructions are bit patterns, so we could just as easily store an entire program in a ROM device. As with a PLA, if you need to change the program, you can just program another ROM device and replace the old one.

There are several types of ROM devices. While the bit pattern is set in a ROM device during manufacturing, a *programmable read-only memory (PROM)* device is programmed by the person who uses it. There are also *erasable programmable read-only memory (EPROM)* devices that can be erased with an ultraviolet light and then reprogrammed.

Programmable Array Logic

In a *programmable array logic (PAL)* device, each OR gate is permanently wired to a group of AND gates. Only the AND gate plane is programmable. The PAL device diagrammed in Figure 6-17 has four inputs and two outputs, each of which can be the sum of up to four products.

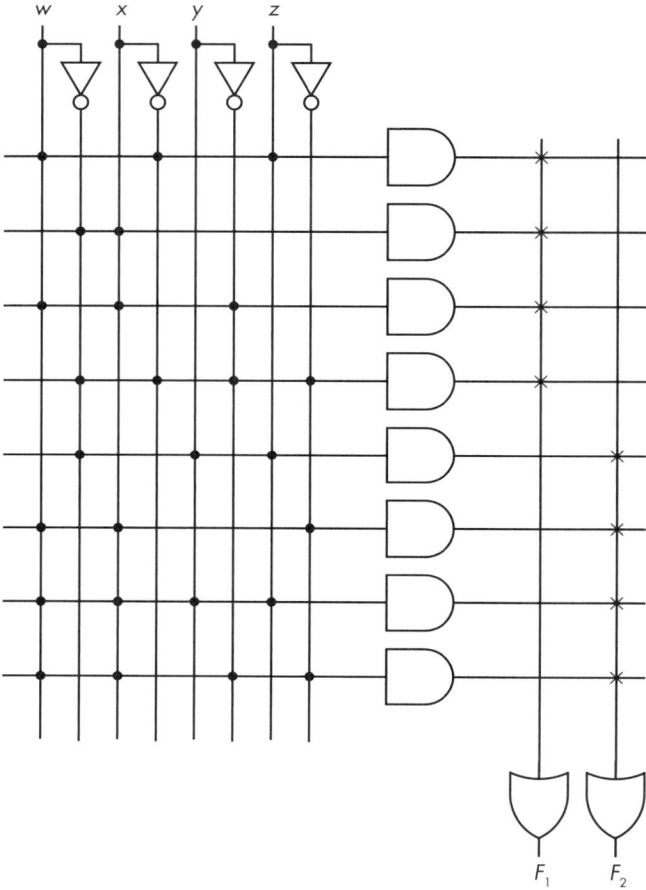

Figure 6-17: A two-function programmable array logic device

The "×" connections in the OR gate plane show that the top four AND gates are OR-ed to produce $F_1(w, x, y, z)$ and the lower four are OR-ed to produce $F_2(w, x, y, z)$. The AND gate plane in this figure has been programmed to produce these two functions:

$$F_1(w, x, y, z) = (w \wedge \neg x \wedge z) \vee (\neg w \wedge x) \vee (w \wedge x \wedge \neg y) \vee (\neg w \wedge \neg x \wedge \neg y \wedge \neg z)$$
$$F_2(w, x, y, z) = (\neg w \wedge y \wedge z) \vee (x \wedge y \wedge \neg z) \vee (w \wedge x \wedge y \wedge z) \vee (w \wedge x \wedge \neg y \wedge \neg z)$$

Of the three types of programmable logic devices presented here, the PLA device is the most flexible, as we can program both the OR and the

AND plane, but it is also the most expensive. The ROM device is less flexible: it can be programmed to produce any combination of minterms, which are then OR-ed together. We know that any function can be implemented as the OR of minterms, so we can produce any function with a ROM device, but a ROM device doesn't allow us to minimize the function since all the product terms must be minterms.

The PAL device is the least flexible, because all the product terms programmed in the AND plane will be OR-ed together. So, we cannot select which minterms are in the function by programming the OR plane. However, PAL devices allow us to do some Boolean function minimization. If the required function can be implemented in a PAL device, this will be less expensive than using a ROM or PLA device.

YOUR TURN

6.3 Design a ROM device that holds the four characters a, b, c, and d.

6.4 Design a ROM device that holds the four characters A, B, C, and D.

6.5 Comparing two values to determine which is larger, or whether they are the same, is a common operation in computing. The hardware device used to perform such a comparison is called a *comparator*. Use a programmable logic device to design a comparator that compares two 2-bit values. Your comparator will have three outputs: equal, greater than, and less than.

What You've Learned

Combinational logic circuits   These depend only on their input at any point in time. They have no memory of previous effects of the inputs. Examples include adders, decoders, multiplexers, and programmable logic devices.

Half adder   This circuit has two 1-bit inputs and produces two 1-bit outputs: the sum of the inputs and the carry from that sum.

Full adder   This circuit has three 1-bit inputs and produces two 1-bit outputs: the sum of the inputs and the carry from that sum.

Ripple-carry adder   This circuit uses n full adders to add n-bit numbers. The carry output from each full adder is one of the three inputs to the full adders in the next higher-order bit position.

Decoder   A device used to select one of n outputs based on 2^n inputs.

Multiplexer (MUX)   A device used to select one of 2^n inputs based on an n-bit selector signal.

Programmable logic array (PLA)   A device used to generate an OR-ed combination of minterms to implement Boolean functions in hardware.

Read-only memory (ROM)   Nonvolatile memory, with the input being the address of the data or instruction.

Programmable array logic (PAL)   A device used to implement Boolean functions in hardware. It's less flexible than a PLA or ROM device, but also less expensive.

In the next chapter, you will learn about sequential logic circuits, which use feedback to maintain a memory of their activity.

7

SEQUENTIAL LOGIC CIRCUITS

In the previous chapter, you learned about combinational logic circuits, which are circuits that depend only on their current input. Another way of thinking about this is that combinational logic circuits are instantaneous (except for the time required for the electronics to settle): their output depends only on the input at the time the output is observed. *Sequential logic circuits*, on the other hand, depend on both the current and past inputs. They have a time history, which can be summarized by the current state of the circuit.

Formally, the *system state* is a description of the system such that the state at time t_0 and the inputs from time t_0 through time t_1 uniquely determines the state at time t_1 and the outputs from time t_0 through time t_1. In other words, the system state provides a summary of everything that has affected the system. Knowing the state of a system at any given time t tells you everything you need to know to specify the system's behavior from that time on. How it got into that state is irrelevant.

The concept of system state is captured in a *finite state machine*, a mathematical model of computation that exists in any one of a finite number of states. External inputs to a finite state machine cause it to transition from one state to another or to the same state, while possibly producing an output. Sequential logic circuits are used to implement finite state machines. If a sequential logic circuit is designed such that its output depends only on the state it's in, it's called a *Moore state machine*. If the output also depends on the input causing a transition to a state, it's called a *Mealy state machine*.

In this chapter, you'll learn how *feedback* is used in a logic circuit to keep the gates in a particular state over time, thus implementing memory. We'll use *state diagrams* to show how inputs cause a sequential logic circuit to transition between states and what the corresponding outputs are. You'll also learn how sequential logic circuits can be synchronized with a clock to provide reliable results.

Latches

The first sequential logic circuit we'll look at is a *latch*, a 1-bit storage device that can be in one of two states, depending on its input. A latch can be constructed by connecting two or more logic gates such that the output from one gate feeds into the input of another gate; this keeps the output of both gates in the same state as long as power is applied. The state of a latch does not depend on time. (The term *latch* is also used for a multiple-bit storage device that behaves like the 1-bit device described here.)

SR Latch Using NOR Gates

The most basic latch is the *Set–Reset (SR)* latch. It has two inputs, S and R, and two states, *set* and *reset*. The state is used as the primary output, Q. It's common to also provide the complemented output, $\neg Q$. The SR latch is said to be in the set state when the outputs are $Q = 1$ and $\neg Q = 0$. It's in the reset state when $Q = 0$ and $\neg Q = 1$. Figure 7-1 shows a simple implementation of an SR latch using NOR gates.

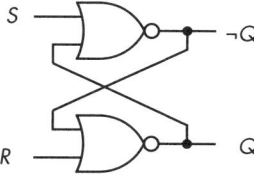

Figure 7-1: A NOR gate implementation of an SR latch

The output of each NOR gate is fed into the input of the other. As I describe the behavior of the circuit in this chapter, you'll see that this feedback is what keeps the latch in one state.

There are four possible input combinations for an SR latch, as detailed in the following list:

$S = 0, R = 0$: **Keep current state**

If the latch is in the set state ($Q = 1$ and $\neg Q = 0$), an input of $S = 0$ and $R = 0$ will cause $\neg Q$, the output of the upper NOR gate, to yield $\neg(0 \lor 1)$ = 0 and Q, the output of the lower NOR gate, to yield $\neg(0 \lor 0)$ = 1. Conversely, if the latch is in the reset state ($Q = 0$ and $\neg Q = 1$), then the output of the upper NOR gate yields $\neg(0 \lor 0)$ = 1, and the lower NOR gate yields $\neg(1 \lor 0)$ = 0. Thus, the cross-feedback between the two NOR gates maintains the current state of the latch.

$S = 1, R = 0$: **Set ($Q = 1$)**

If the latch is in the reset state, these inputs cause the output of the upper NOR gate to be $\neg(1 \lor 0)$ = 0, thus changing $\neg Q$ to 0. This is fed back to the input of the lower NOR gate to yield $\neg(0 \lor 0)$ = 1. The feedback from the output of the lower NOR gate to the input of the upper NOR gate keeps the output of the upper gate at $\neg(1 \lor 1)$ = 0. The latch has then moved into the set state ($Q = 1$ and $\neg Q = 0$).

If the latch is in the set state, the upper NOR gate yields $\neg(1 \lor 1)$ = 0 and the output of the lower NOR gate is $\neg(0 \lor 0)$ = 1. The latch thus remains in the set state.

$S = 0, R = 1$: **Reset ($Q = 0$)**

If the latch is in the set state, the lower NOR gate yields $\neg(0 \lor 1)$ = 0, thus changing Q to be 0. This is fed back to the input of the upper NOR gate to yield $\neg(0 \lor 0)$ = 1. The feedback from the output of the upper NOR gate to the input of the lower NOR gate keeps the output of the lower gate at $\neg(1 \lor 1)$ = 0. The latch has then moved into the reset state ($Q = 0$ and $\neg Q = 1$).

If the latch is already in the reset state, the lower NOR gate yields $\neg(1 \lor 1)$ = 0 and the output of the upper NOR gate is $\neg(0 \lor 0)$ = 1, so the latch remains in the reset state.

$S = 1, R = 1$: **Not allowed**

If $Q = 0$ and $\neg Q = 1$, the upper NOR gate yields $\neg(1 \lor 0)$ = 0. This is fed back to the input of the lower NOR gate to yield $\neg(0 \lor 1)$ = 0. This would give $Q = \neg Q$, which is inconsistent with the laws of Boolean algebra.

If $Q = 1$ and $\neg Q = 0$, the lower NOR gate yields $\neg(0 \lor 1)$ = 0. This is fed back to the input of the upper NOR gate to yield $\neg(1 \lor 0)$ = 0. This would also give $Q = \neg Q$, which is inconsistent. Circuits must be designed to prevent this input combination.

To simplify things, we can represent this logic visually. Figure 7-2 introduces a graphic way to show the behavior of a NOR gate SR latch: the state diagram. In this figure, the current state is shown in the bubbles and the corresponding primary output is below the state. The lines with arrows show the possible transitions between the states and are labeled with the inputs that cause the transition to the next state.

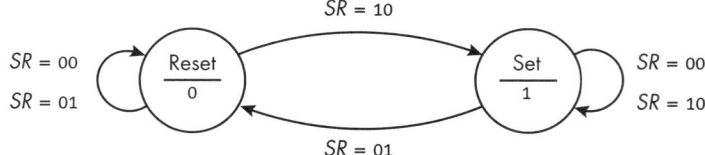

Figure 7-2: A state diagram for a NOR gate SR latch

The two circles in Figure 7-2 show the two possible states of the SR latch: set or reset. The labels on the lines show the combination of inputs, *SR*, that causes each state transition. For example, when the latch is in the reset state, there are two possible inputs, *SR* = 00 and *SR* = 01, that cause it to remain in that state. The input *SR* = 10 causes it to transition to the set state. Since the output is dependent only on the state—and not on the input—a latch is a Moore state machine.

Those familiar with graph theory will recognize that a state diagram is a directed graph: the states are the vertices and the inputs that cause transitions are the edges. Although they are beyond the scope of this book, tools from graph theory can be useful in the design process.

As in graph theory, we can also show the same behavior in a tabular form using a *state transition table*, as shown in Table 7-1.

Table 7-1: A NOR Gate SR Latch State Transition Table

S	R	Q	Q_{next}
0	0	0	0
0	0	1	1
0	1	0	0
0	1	1	0
1	0	0	1
1	0	1	1
1	1	0	x
1	1	1	x

In Table 7-1, *S* and *R* are the inputs, *Q* is the output in the current state, and Q_{next} shows the output in the state that results from the corresponding input. The x in the bottom two rows indicates an impossible condition.

Both inputs to a NOR gate SR latch are normally held at 0, which maintains the current state, giving the output *Q*. Momentarily changing only *R* to 1 causes the state to go to reset, which changes the output to *Q* = 0, as shown in the Q_{next} column of the state transition table. Momentarily changing only *S* to 1 causes the state to go to set, giving the output *Q* = 1.

As described earlier, the input combination *S* = *R* = 1 is not allowed because that would cause an inconsistent state for the SR latch, as indicated in the prohibited rows of the state transition table by an x in the Q_{next} column.

SR Latch Using NAND Gates

The physics of their construction tends to make NAND gates faster than NOR gates. Let's start with the equation for the output of a NOR gate:

$$F(x, y) = \neg(x \lor y)$$

From De Morgan's law, we get the following:

$$\neg F(x, y) = \neg(\neg x \land \neg y)$$

This shows that a NAND gate is functionally equivalent to a NOR gate if we complement the two inputs, except that the output is complemented.

This leads to the circuit shown in Figure 7-3, with $\neg S$ and $\neg R$ as the inputs. To emphasize the logical duality of the two designs, NAND and NOR, I have drawn the circuit with the output Q at the top and $\neg Q$ on the bottom.

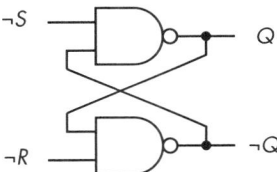

Figure 7-3: A NAND gate implementation of an SR latch

Like the NOR gate SR latch, the NAND gate SR latch is said to be in the set state when the outputs are $Q = 1$ and $\neg Q = 0$; it's in the reset state when $Q = 0$ and $\neg Q = 1$. There are four possible input combinations:

$\neg S = 1$, $\neg R = 1$: **Keep current state**
If the latch is in the set state ($Q = 1$ and $\neg Q = 0$), the upper NAND gate yields $\neg(1 \land 0) = 1$, and the lower NAND gate yields $\neg(1 \land 1) = 0$. If $Q = 0$ and $\neg Q = 1$, the latch is in the reset state; the upper NAND gate yields $\neg(1 \land 1) = 0$, and the lower NAND gate yields $\neg(0 \land 1) = 1$. The cross feedback between the two NAND gates maintains the state of the latch.

$\neg S = 0$, $\neg R = 1$: **Set ($Q = 1$)**
If the latch is in the reset state, the upper NAND gate yields $\neg(0 \land 1) = 1$, thus changing Q to be 1. This is fed back to the input of the lower NAND gate to yield $\neg(1 \land 1) = 0$. The feedback from the output of the lower NAND gate to the input of the upper NAND gate keeps the output of the upper gate at $\neg(0 \land 0) = 1$. The latch has moved into the set state ($Q = 1$ and $\neg Q = 0$).

If the latch is already in the set state, then the upper NAND gate yields $\neg(0 \land \mathtt{0}) = 1$, and the output of the lower NAND gate is $\neg(1 \land 1) = 0$. The latch thus remains in the set state.

$\neg S = 1$, $\neg R = 0$: **Reset ($Q = 0$)**
If the latch is in the set state, the lower NAND gate yields $\neg(1 \land 0) = 1$. This is fed back to the input of the upper NAND gate, thereby making

$Q = \neg(1 \wedge 1) = 0$. The feedback from the output of the upper NAND gate to the input of the lower NAND gate keeps the output of the lower gate at $\neg(0 \wedge 0) = 1$, so the latch moves into the reset state ($Q = 0$ and $\neg Q = 1$).

If the latch is already in the reset state, the lower NAND gate yields $\neg(0 \wedge 0) = 1$, and the output of the upper NAND gate is $\neg(1 \wedge 1) = 0$. The latch remains in the reset state.

$\neg S = 0$, $\neg R = 0$: Not allowed

If the latch is in the reset state, the upper NAND gate yields $\neg(0 \wedge 1) = 1$. This is fed back to the input of the lower NAND gate to yield $\neg(1 \wedge 0) = 1$. This would give $Q = \neg Q$, which is inconsistent.

If the latch is in the set state, the lower NAND gate yields $\neg(1 \wedge 0) = 1$. This is fed back to the input of the upper NAND gate to yield $\neg(0 \wedge 1) = 1$. This would also give $Q = \neg Q$, which is inconsistent. Circuits must be designed to prevent this input combination.

Figure 7-4 shows the behavior of a NAND gate SR latch using a state diagram.

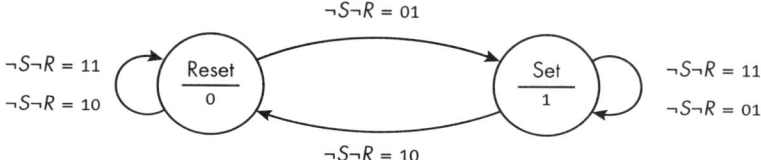

Figure 7-4: A NAND gate SR latch

Comparing this with the NOR gate SR latch in Figure 7-2, you can see that they both describe the same behavior. For example, an input of $SR = 10$ to the NOR gate SR latch will place it in the set state, while an input of $\neg S \neg R = 01$ to the NAND gate SR latch will place it in the set state. I find that I have to think carefully about this when analyzing circuits. An off-by-one error when there are only two choices can cause behavior opposite to what I want.

Table 7-2 is a state transition table for a NAND gate SR latch.

Table 7-2: A NAND Gate SR Latch State Transition Table

$\neg S$	$\neg R$	Q	Q_{next}
1	1	0	0
1	1	1	1
1	0	0	0
1	0	1	0
0	1	0	1
0	1	1	1
0	0	0	x
0	0	1	x

Placing 0 on both inputs at the same time causes a problem—namely, that the outputs of both NAND gates would become 1. In other words, $Q = \neg Q = 1$, which is logically impossible. The circuit design must prevent this input combination. The x in the bottom two rows indicates an impossible condition.

The SR latch implemented with two NAND gates can be thought of as the complement of the NOR gate SR latch. The state is maintained by holding both $\neg S$ and $\neg R$ at 1. Momentarily changing $\neg S$ to 0 causes the state to be set with the output $Q = 1$, and setting $\neg R = 0$ causes it to be reset with the output $Q = 0$.

Thus far, we have been looking at a single latch. The problem here is that the state of the latch, and its output, will change whenever the input changes. In a computer, it would be interconnected with many other devices, each changing state with new inputs. It takes time for each device to change state and for its output(s) to propagate to the next device(s). The precise timing depends on slight manufacturing differences in the devices, so the results can be unreliable. We need a means for synchronizing the activity to bring some order to the operations. We'll start by adding an *Enable* input to the SR latch, which will allow us to control more precisely when the inputs will be allowed to affect the state.

SR Latch with Enable

We can get better control over the SR latch by adding two NAND gates to provide an *Enable* input. Connecting the outputs of these two NAND gates to the inputs of a $\neg S \neg R$ latch gives us a *gated SR latch*, as depicted in Figure 7-5.

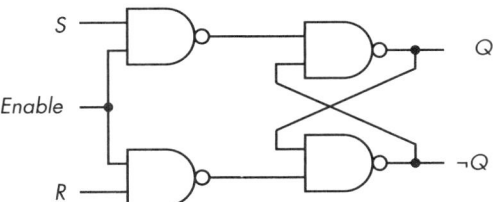

Figure 7-5: A gated SR latch

In this circuit, the outputs of both the control NAND gates remain at 1 as long as *Enable* = 0. This sends $\neg S = 1$ and $\neg R = 1$ to the inputs of the $\neg S \neg R$ latch portion of this circuit, which causes the state to remain the same. By AND-ing the additional *Enable* input with the S and R input lines, we can control the time when the state should be changed to the next value.

Table 7-3 shows the state behavior of the SR latch with the *Enable* control.

Table 7-3: A Gated SR Latch
State Transition Table

Enable	S	R	Q	Q_{next}
0	—	—	0	0
0	—	—	1	1
1	0	0	0	0
1	0	0	1	1
1	0	1	0	0
1	0	1	1	0
1	1	0	0	1
1	1	0	1	1
1	1	1	0	x
1	1	1	1	x

In Table 7-3, a — indicates that an input does not matter and an x indicates a prohibited result. As explained earlier, the design must prevent input combinations that would produce prohibited results. The state of the latch can follow the S and R inputs only when *Enable* = 1. Such a device is said to be *level-triggered*.

In the next section, I'll simplify the gated SR latch and create a latch that takes a single data input, D, with control over when this input will affect the state of the latch.

The D Latch

A *D latch* allows us to store the value of 1 bit. We start with the truth table in Table 7-4, which includes the rows from Table 7-3 where *Enable* = 1 and $R = \neg S$.

Table 7-4: A Truth Table for a D Latch
with *Enable*

Enable	S	R	D	Q	Q_{next}
0	—	—	—	0	0
0	—	—	—	1	1
1	0	1	0	0	0
1	0	1	0	1	0
1	1	0	1	0	1
1	1	0	1	1	1

We're looking for a design that will have two inputs: one for *Enable* and the other for D (short for data). We want D = 1 to set the state, giving the output Q = 1, and D = 0 to reset it, giving the output Q = 0, when the *Enable* line becomes 1. The value of D should have no effect on the state when *Enable* = 0.

We can construct a gated D latch from a gated SR latch by adding a NOT gate, as shown in Figure 7-6.

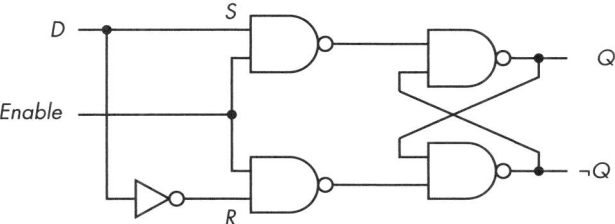

Figure 7-6: A gated D latch constructed from an SR latch

The one data input, *D*, is fed to the *S* side of the SR latch; the complement of the data value is fed to the *R* side.

Now, we have a circuit that can store 1 bit of data using the *D* input and can be synchronized with other operations using the *Enable* input. However, there are some problems with the D latch. The state of a D latch can be affected by the input while the D latch is enabled. Thus, its output can change while the latch is enabled, making it difficult to synchronize reliably with other devices.

This scheme does work well when the latch should remain in one state for an extended period. In general, latches work for operations where we want to select a state and leave it for a period of time that is not synchronized with other operations in the computer. An example is an I/O port, where the timing is dependent on the behavior of the device connected to the port. For instance, a running program cannot know when the user will press a key on the keyboard. When a key is pressed, the program may not be ready for the character, so the binary code for the character should be latched at the input port. Once the character code is stored at the input port, the latch will be disabled until the program reads the character code from the latch.

Most of the computing operations within the CPU and main memory must be coordinated in time. Connecting many circuits to the same clock signal allows us to synchronize their operations. Let's consider how we might synchronize a D latch connected in a circuit. We could feed an input to this D latch and enable the latch with a clock signal, but its output can change if the input changes, making its output unreliable during the time it's enabled. If the output from our D latch is connected to the input of another device, the input to this second device is thus unreliable while our D latch is enabled. To avoid this problem and provide a reliable input, we should disable our D latch once it has settled.

It also takes some time, called *propagation delay*, for the output of our D latch to reach the input of the second device, due to the physics of the connections. So, this second device should be disabled until the input to our D latch is reliable and we have allowed for the propagation delay.

While the second device is disabled and waiting for a reliable input from our D latch, its output (from the previous clock cycle) is reliable. So, if it's connected to the input of yet another device, this third device can be enabled. This leads to a scheme where every other device is enabled, while the alternate devices are disabled. After waiting for a period equal to the sum of the longest settling time and propagation delay time of all the devices connected together, the disabled devices are enabled and the enabled devices are disabled. The digital 1s and 0s are propagated through this circuit of devices by means of this alternating enable/disable cycle.

As you can probably imagine, coordinating this flipping back and forth between enabled and disabled can be difficult. I'll give you a solution to this problem in the next section.

Flip-Flops

While a latch could be controlled by the levels of a clock signal, its output would be affected by any changes in its input during the portion of time when the clock signal enables the latch. A *flip-flop* provides an output at a specific time in the clock cycle, such as when the clock signal transitions from 0 to 1. Because the output becomes available at a clock signal transition point, it is said to be *edge triggered*. After the trigger event, the output of a flip-flop remains throughout the duration of the clock cycle. This provides the reliability needed to connect many flip-flops in a circuit and synchronize their operations with one clock. I'll start this section with a discussion of clocks, and then we'll look at a few examples of flip-flops.

NOTE *The terminology varies. Some people also call latches* flip-flops. *I will use the term* latch *to mean a level-triggered device, with no timing considerations, and* flip-flop *to mean an edge-triggered device controlled by a clock signal.*

Clocks

Sequential logic circuits have a time history, summarized in their state. We keep track of time with a *clock*, a device that provides an electronic *clock signal*. This is typically a square wave that alternates between the 0 and 1 levels, as shown in Figure 7-7. This signal is used as the enabling/disabling input to devices that need to be synchronized.

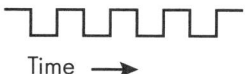

Time →

Figure 7-7: A typical clock signal used to synchronize sequential logic circuits

In order to achieve reliable behavior, most synchronous circuits use edge-triggered devices. The amount of time spent at each level is usually the same, and either the positive-going (0 to 1) or negative-going (1 to 0) edge of a clock signal may be used.

The clock frequency must be slow enough that the circuit elements have time to complete their operations before the next clock transition occurs. For example, reliable operation of a latch or flip-flop requires that the input signal be stable for a period of time, called the *setup time*, before the device is enabled. The input signal must remain stable for another period of time, the *hold time*, after the start of the enabling signal. In practice, these times can vary with temperature, manufacturing variations, and so forth. Hardware designers need to consult manufacturers' specifications for the limits of these time values.

Let's look at a few examples of flip-flop circuits that can be controlled by a clock.

D Flip-Flop

We'll begin by connecting a clock signal to the *Enable* input of the gated D latch in Figure 7-6. Here, the input affects the output as long as *Enable* = 1. The problem is that if the input changes while *Enable* = 1, the output will also change, leading to an unreliable design.

One way to isolate the output from input changes is to connect the outputs of our D latch to the inputs of an SR latch in a primary/secondary configuration, as shown in Figure 7-8.

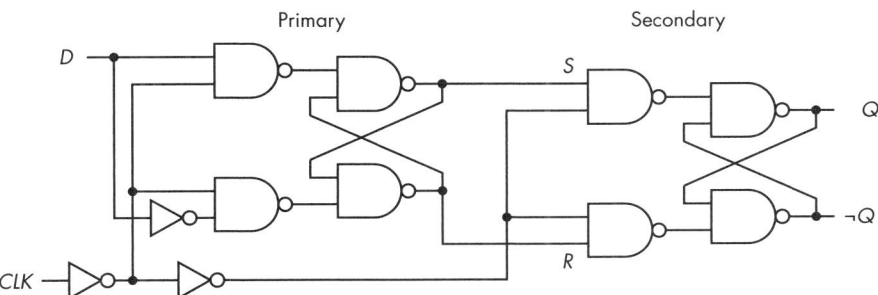

Figure 7-8: A D flip-flop, positive-edge triggering

The primary portion of the D flip-flop processes the input and provides a reliable input to the secondary portion for final output. The bit we want to store, 0 or 1, is fed to the *D* input of the D latch, and the clock signal is fed to the *CLK* input. The uncomplemented output of the D latch is fed to the *S* input, and its complemented output is fed to the *R* input of the SR latch. The final output of the D flip-flop is the output from the SR latch.

I'll walk you through how this circuit works. The behavior of the primary portion is shown in the truth table for a D latch in Table 7-4. The behavior of the secondary portion is shown in the truth table for an SR latch in Table 7-3. Figure 7-9 shows the timing of the key points in our D flip-flop.

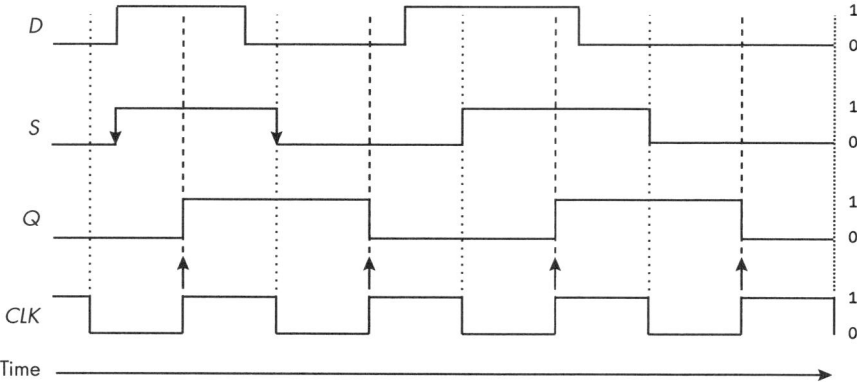

Figure 7-9: The timing of a D flip-flop

The data input, *D*, in Figure 7-9 is not in complete synchrony with the clock signal, and its timing is somewhat irregular. This can occur due to propagation delays, interference from other components, temperature gradients in the circuits, and other factors.

We'll start at the point where CLK first goes to 0. This signal is inverted, which enables the D latch. The output of the D latch, *S*, follows the *D* input, going from 0 to 1. The second inverter in the CLK path to the SR latch disables it, latching the flip-flop output, *Q*, at the 0 level.

When the CLK signal goes to 1, the D latch is disabled, which latches its outputs, *S* and *R*, at 1 and 0. This presents stable inputs to the SR latch during this clock half-cycle. The twice-inverted CLK signal enables the SR latch, which causes the output of the flip-flop, *Q*, to go to 1.

The CLK signal then goes to 0, disabling the SR latch in the secondary portion, which remains latched at the 1 level for this clock half-cycle.

Thus, the flip-flop introduces a time delay of one-half clock cycle between accepting an input and providing an output, but the output is stable for an entire clock period. The output is available at a precise point in time, the 0 to 1 transition. This is called *positive-edge triggering*. If the first NOT gate connected to the CLK signal in Figure 7-8 were removed, we would have a D flip-flop with *negative-edge triggering*.

Sometimes a flip-flop must be set to a known value before the clocking begins—for example, when a computer is first starting up. These known values are input independently of the clock process; hence, they are *asynchronous inputs*.

Figure 7-10 shows a D flip-flop with an *asynchronous preset* (*PR*) input added to it.

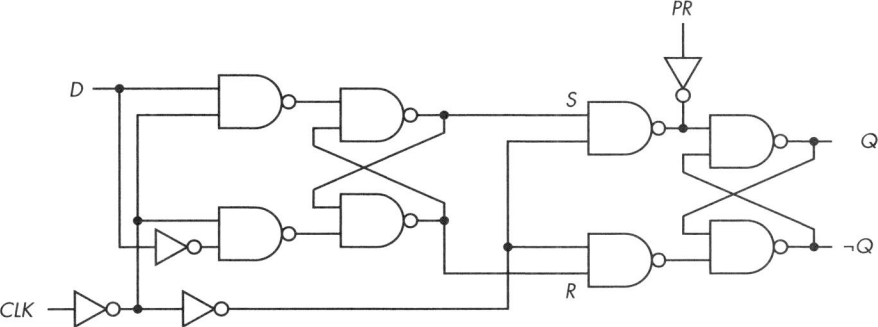

Figure 7-10: A positive-edge triggering D flip-flop with an asynchronous preset

When a 1 is applied to the *PR* input, Q becomes 1 and $\neg Q$ becomes 0, regardless of what the other inputs are—even CLK. It is also common to have an asynchronous clear input (*CLR*) that sets the state (and output) to 0.

There are more efficient circuits for implementing edge-triggered D flip-flops, but this discussion shows that they can be constructed from ordinary logic gates. They are economical and efficient, so they are widely used in *very large scale integration (VLSI)* circuits, which are circuits that include billions of transistor gates on a single semiconductor microchip.

Rather than draw the implementation details for each D flip-flop, circuit designers use the symbols shown in Figure 7-11.

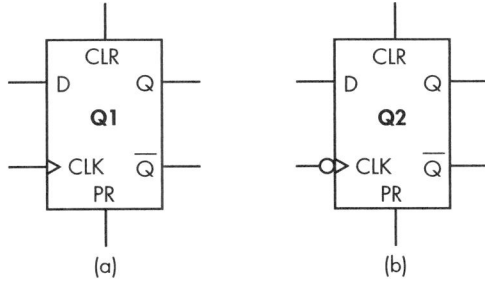

Figure 7-11: The symbols used for D flip-flops: (a) positive-edge triggering, (b) negative-edge triggering

The various inputs and outputs are labeled in Figure 7-11. Hardware designers typically use $\overline{Q}$ instead of $\neg Q$. It's common to label the flip-flop as Qn, where $n = 1, 2, \ldots$, which is used to identify the flip-flop within the overall circuit. The small circle at the clock input in Figure 7-11(b) means that this D flip-flop is triggered by a negative-going clock transition.

Now that you've seen some logic components that save state, let's look at the process of designing sequential logic circuits using these components.

Designing Sequential Logic Circuits

We'll consider a general set of steps for designing sequential logic circuits. Design in any field is usually iterative, as you have no doubt learned from your programming experience. You start with a design, analyze it, and then refine the design to make it faster, less expensive, and so on. After you've gained some experience, the design process usually requires fewer iterations.

The following steps are a good method for building a first working design:

1. From the plain-language description of the problem, create a state transition table and state diagram showing what the circuit must do. These form the basic technical specifications for the circuit you will be designing.

2. Choose a binary code for the states and create a binary-coded version of the state table and/or state diagram. For N states, the code will need $\log_2 N$ bits. Any code will work, but some codes may lead to simpler combinational logic in the circuit.

3. Choose a type of flip-flop. This choice is often dictated by the components you have on hand.

4. Determine the inputs required to each flip-flop to cause each of the required transitions.

5. Simplify the inputs to each flip-flop. Karnaugh maps or algebraic methods are good tools for the simplification process.

6. Draw the circuit.

Step 5 may cause you to rethink your choice of type of flip-flop. The three steps of flip-flop choice, determining inputs, and simplification may need to be repeated several times to reach a good design. The following two examples illustrate this process. You can think of these as guided "Your Turn" exercises; if you have access to a digital circuit simulator, or the required hardware, I suggest you use those resources to follow along.

A Counter

We want to design a counter that has an *Enable* input. When *Enable* = 1, it increments through the sequence 0, 1, 2, 3, 0, 1, . . . , incrementing with each clock tick. *Enable* = 0 causes the counter to remain in its current state. The output is the sequence number in 2-bit binary. Here are the steps:

Step 1: Create a state transition table and state diagram.
At each clock tick, the counter increments by 1 if *Enable* = 1. If *Enable* = 0, it remains in the current state. Figure 7-12 shows the four states—0, 1, 2, and 3—and the corresponding 2-bit output for each state.

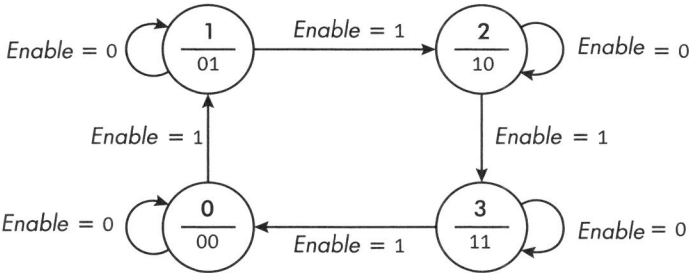

Figure 7-12: A state diagram for a counter that cycles through 0, 1, 2, 3, 0, 1, . . .

Table 7-5 shows the state transition table for this counter.

Table 7-5: A State Transition Table for the Counter

	Enable = 0	Enable = 1
Current *n*	Next *n*	Next *n*
0	0	1
1	1	2
2	2	3
3	3	0

When *Enable* = 0, the counter is essentially turned off; when *Enable* = 1, the counter automatically increments by 1, wrapping around to 0 after it reaches its limit of 3.

Step 2: Create a binary-coded version of the state table/state diagram.

With four states, we need 2 bits. We'll let n be the state, which we represent with the 2-bit binary number $n_1 n_0$. Table 7-6 shows the behavior.

Table 7-6: A State Transition Table for a 2-Bit Counter

	Current		Next	
Enable	n_1	n_0	n_1	n_0
0	0	0	0	0
0	0	1	0	1
0	1	0	1	0
0	1	1	1	1
1	0	0	0	1
1	0	1	1	0
1	1	0	1	1
1	1	1	0	0

Step 3: Select a flip-flop.

We'll use D flip-flops. After going through the design, we may decide that another flip-flop might work better. We could then come back to this step and go through the remaining steps again. An experienced designer may have some insight into the problem that would suggest starting with another type of flip-flop. Often, any potential savings in cost or power consumption do not justify changing to another type of flip-flop.

Step 4: Determine the inputs to the flip-flops.

We need two flip-flops, one for each bit. A D flip-flop simply stores the value of its input on the next clock cycle, so the inputs that cause each flip-flop to change to the next state are shown under the two "Next" columns in Table 7-6.

We can write the Boolean equations that show the logical combinations of the inputs, *Enable* and the current n_1 and n_0, that produce the required inputs. We'll use E for *Enable* and D_1 and D_0 for the inputs to the respective D flip-flops:

$$D_1(E, n_1, n_0) = (\neg E \wedge n_1 \wedge \neg n_0) \vee (\neg E \wedge n_1 \wedge n_0)$$
$$\vee (E \wedge \neg n_1 \wedge n_0) \vee (E \wedge n_1 \wedge \neg n_0)$$
$$D_0(E, n_1, n_0) = (\neg E \wedge \neg n_1 \wedge n_0) \vee (\neg E \wedge n_1 \wedge n_0)$$
$$\vee (E \wedge \neg n_1 \wedge \neg n_0) \vee (E \wedge n_1 \wedge \neg n_0)$$

Step 5: Simplify the required inputs.

We can use Karnaugh maps to find a simpler solution, as shown in Figure 7-13.

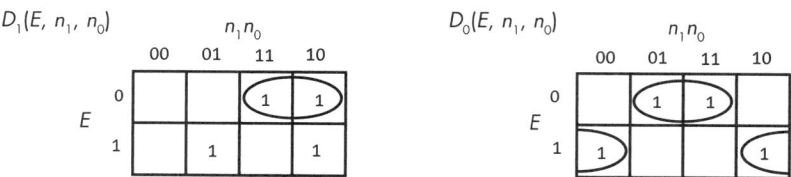

Figure 7-13: Karnaugh maps for a 2-bit counter implemented with D flip-flops

The Karnaugh maps allow us to simplify the Boolean equations for the input to each flip-flop:

$$D_1(E, n_1, n_0) = (\neg E \wedge n_1) \vee (E \wedge \neg n_1 \wedge n_0) \vee (E \wedge n_1 \wedge \neg n_0)$$
$$D_0(E, n_1, n_0) = (\neg E \wedge n_0) \vee (E \wedge \neg n_1)$$

Step 6: Draw the circuit.

We'll use a PLA (introduced in "Programmable Logic Array" on page 120 in Chapter 6) to generate the inputs to the two D flip-flops. Figure 7-14 shows our resulting circuit used to implement this counter.

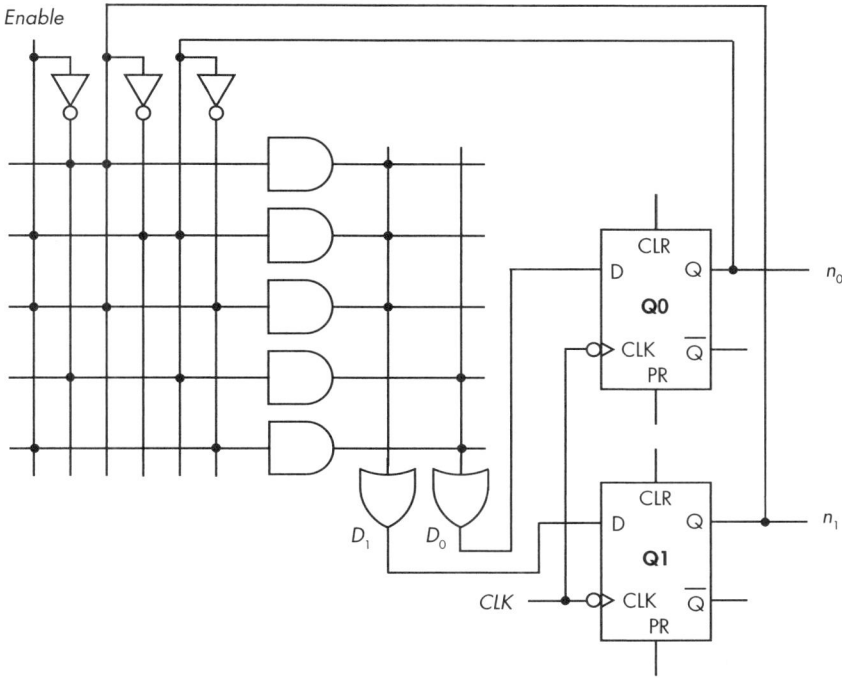

Figure 7-14: A 2-bit counter implemented with a PLA and two D flip-flops

Figure 7-15 shows the timing of the binary counter when progressing through the sequence 3, 0, 1, 2, 3 (11, 00, 01, 10, 11).

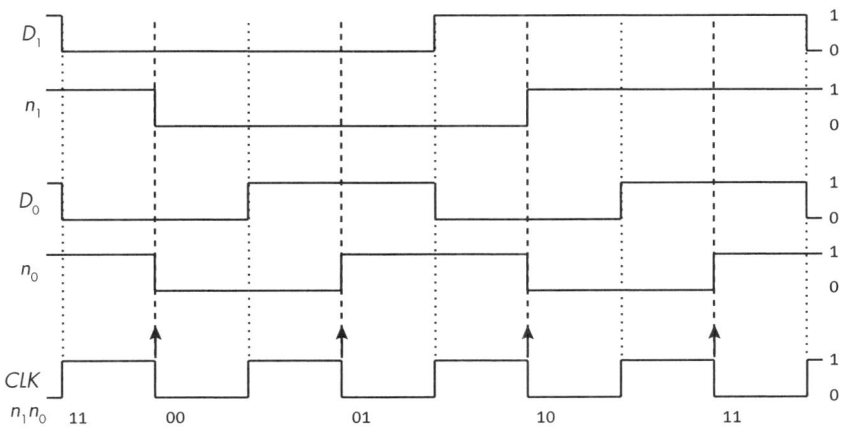

Figure 7-15: The timing of a 2-bit counter implemented with D flip-flops

D_i is the input to the ith D flip-flop, and n_i is its output. Remember that when the ith input, D_i, is applied to its D flip-flop, the output of the flip-flop does not change until the second half of the clock cycle. This can be seen when comparing the trace for the corresponding output, n_i, in the figure.

A Branch Predictor

For our second example, we'll design a branch predictor. This example is a bit more complicated than the previous one.

Except for very inexpensive microcontrollers, most modern CPUs execute instructions in stages. Each stage consists of hardware that is specialized to perform the operations in that stage. An instruction passes through each stage in an assembly-line fashion. For example, if you were to create an assembly line to manufacture wooden chairs, you could do it in three stages: saw the wood to make the parts for the chair, assemble the parts, and paint the chair. The hardware needed at each stage would be saw, hammer and screwdriver, and paintbrush.

The arrangement of specialized hardware in the CPU is called a *pipeline*. The hardware in the first stage is designed to fetch an instruction from memory, as you'll see in Chapter 9. After an instruction is fetched from memory, it passes on to the next stage of the pipeline, where it is decoded. Simultaneously, the first stage of the pipeline fetches the next instruction from memory. The result is that the CPU is working on several instructions at the same time. This provides some parallelism, thus improving execution speed.

Almost all programs contain *conditional branch points*—places where the next instruction to be fetched can be in one of two different memory locations. Unfortunately, there is no way to know which of the two instructions to fetch until the decision-making instruction has moved several stages into the pipeline.

To maintain execution speed, as soon as a conditional branch instruction has passed on from the fetch stage, it's helpful if the CPU can predict where to fetch the next instruction from. Then it can go ahead and do so. If the prediction was wrong, the CPU simply ignores the work it has done on the predicted instruction by flushing out the pipeline and fetching the other instruction, which enters the beginning of the pipeline.

In this section, we'll design a circuit that predicts whether a conditional branch will be taken. The predictor will continue to predict the same outcome, and the branch will be either taken or not taken, until it makes two mistakes in a row.

Here are the steps we will follow in designing our branch predictor circuit:

Step 1: Create a state table and state diagram.

We'll use Yes to indicate when the branch is taken and No to indicate when it isn't. The state diagram in Figure 7-16 shows the four possible states.

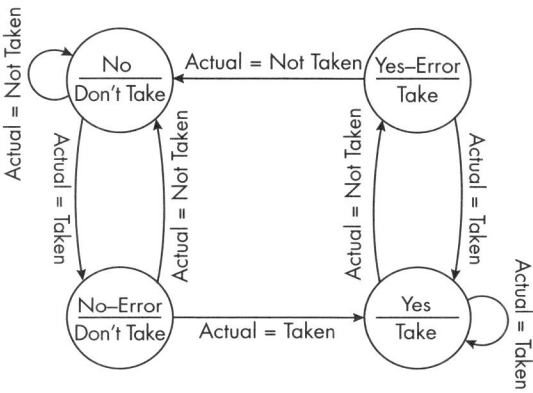

Figure 7-16: The four possible states for our branch predictor

Let's begin in the No state. Here, the branch was not taken at least the last two times this instruction was executed. The output is to predict that it will also not be taken this time. The input to the circuit is whether the branch has actually been taken when the instruction has completed execution.

The arc labeled Actual = Not Taken in Figure 7-16 loops back to the No state, with the prediction (the output) that the branch will not be taken the next time the instruction is executed. If the branch is taken, the Actual = Taken arc shows that the circuit moves into the No–Error state to indicate one error in the prediction. But because it must be wrong twice in a row to change our prediction, the circuit is still predicting Don't Take as the output.

From the No–Error state, if the branch is not taken (the prediction is correct), the circuit returns to the No state. However, if the branch is taken, the circuit predicted incorrectly twice in a row, so the circuit moves to the Yes state and the output is to predict Take.

I'll leave tracing through the remainder of this state diagram as an exercise for you. Once you're satisfied with how it works, take a look at Table 7-7, which provides the technical specifications for our circuit.

Table 7-7: The Branch Predictor State Table

Current state	Prediction	Actual = Not Taken Next state	Actual = Not Taken Prediction	Actual = Taken Next state	Actual = Taken Prediction
No	Don't Take	No	Don't Take	No–Error	Don't Take
No–Error	Don't Take	No	Don't Take	Yes	Take
Yes–Error	Take	No	Don't Take	Yes	Take
Yes	Take	Yes–Error	Take	Yes	Take

When the result of the conditional branch (taken or not taken) is determined in the pipeline, Table 7-7 shows the next state and the corresponding prediction. This prediction will be used to determine which of the two possible addresses—the address of the next instruction or the address of the branch target—to store for use the next time this instruction is encountered in the program.

Step 2: Represent the states.

For this problem, we'll choose a binary code for the state, $s_1 s_0$, as shown in Table 7-8.

Table 7-8: The States of the Branch Predictor

State	s_1	s_0	Prediction
No	0	0	Don't Take
No–Error	0	1	Don't Take
Yes–Error	1	0	Take
Yes	1	1	Take

The prediction is 1 bit, s_1, which is 0 if the prediction is Don't Take and 1 if the prediction is Take.

Letting the input, Actual, be 0 when the branch is not taken and 1 when it is taken and using the state notation of Table 7-8, we get the state transition table shown in Table 7-9.

Table 7-9: The State Transition Table for the Branch Predictor

	Current		Next	
Actual	s_1	s_0	s_1	s_0
0	0	0	0	0
0	0	1	0	0
0	1	0	0	0
0	1	1	1	0
1	0	0	0	1
1	0	1	1	1
1	1	0	1	1
1	1	1	1	1

When the conditional branch instruction reaches a point in the pipeline where it is determined whether the branch should be taken or not, this information is used as the input, Actual, to the predictor circuit, which transforms the state from Current to Next for the next time this instruction is encountered.

Step 3: Select a flip-flop.

We'll use D flip-flops again here, with the same caveats as in the previous example.

Step 4: Determine the inputs to the flip-flops.

We need two flip-flops, one for each bit. A D flip-flop simply stores the value of its input on the next clock cycle, so the inputs that cause each flip-flop to change to the next state are shown under the two "Next" columns in Table 7-9.

We can write the Boolean equations that show the logical combinations of the three signals, Actual and the Current s_1 and s_0 that produce the required input to each D flip-flop to cause it to go to the Next s_1 and s_0. We'll use A for Actual and D_1 and D_0 for the inputs to the respective D flip-flops:

$$D_1(A, s_1, s_0) = (\neg A \land s_1 \land s_0) \lor (A \land \neg s_1 \land s_0)$$
$$\lor (A \land s_1 \land \neg s_0) \lor (A \land s_1 \land s_0)$$
$$D_0(A, s_1, s_0) = (A \land \neg s_1 \land \neg s_0) \lor (A \land \neg s_1 \land s_0)$$
$$\lor (A \land s_1 \land \neg s_0) \lor (A \land s_1 \land s_0)$$

Step 5: Simplify the required inputs.

We'll start by using the following Boolean identities:

$$(\neg A \wedge s_1 \wedge s_0) \vee (A \wedge s_1 \wedge s_0) = (s_1 \wedge s_0)$$
$$(A \wedge \neg s_1 \wedge s_0) \vee (A\neg \wedge s_1 \wedge \neg s_0) = (A \wedge \neg s_1)$$
$$(A \wedge s_1 \wedge \neg s_0) \vee (A \wedge s_1 \wedge \neg s_0) = (A \wedge s_0)$$
$$(\neg s_1 \wedge \neg s_0) \vee (\neg s_1 \wedge s_0) \vee (s_1 \wedge \neg s_0) \vee (s_1 \wedge s_0) = 1$$

Our equations become:

$$D_1(A, s_1, s_0) = (s_1 \wedge s_0) \vee (A \wedge s_0) \vee (A \wedge s_1)$$
$$D_0(A, s_1, s_0) = A$$

Step 6: Draw the circuit.

In this circuit, the input is Actual = 0 if the branch was not taken the last time and Actual = 1 if it was taken. As with our counter, we'll use a PLA with our two D flip-flops, as shown in Figure 7-17.

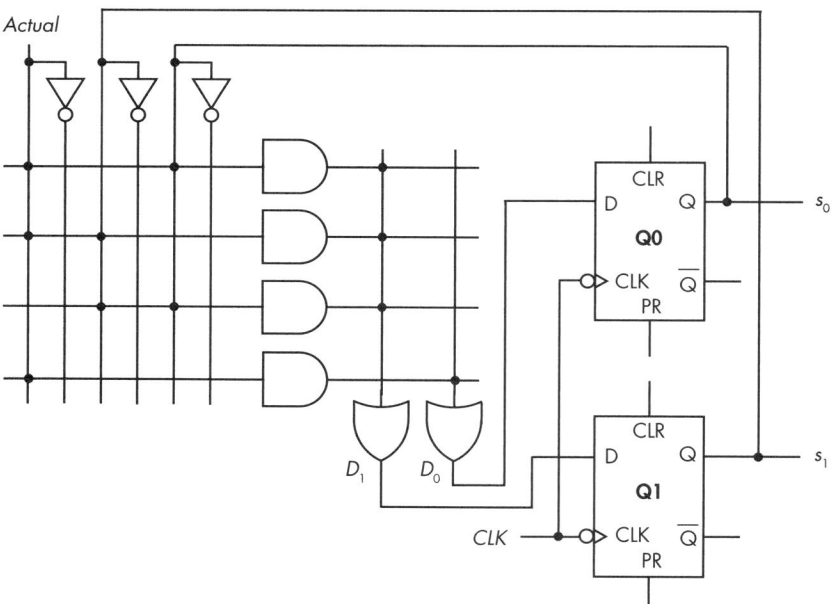

Figure 7-17: The branch predictor circuit using a PLA and two D flip-flops

This example shows the simplest method of branch prediction. More complex methods exist, and there is also ongoing research into branch prediction's effectiveness. Although it can speed up some algorithms, the additional hardware required for branch prediction consumes more electrical power, which is a concern in battery-powered devices.

We used D flip-flops and PLAs in both of these example designs, but as usual, the choice of components depends on multiple factors: cost, availability of components, design tools, design time, power usage, and so forth.

YOUR TURN

7.1   Redesign the 2-bit counter in Figure 7-14 to use individual gates instead of a PLA.

7.2   Redesign the branch predictor in Figure 7-17 to use individual gates instead of a PLA.

What You've Learned

Sequential logic circuits   These depend on both the current and past inputs. They have a time history, which can be summarized by the current state of the circuit.

Latch   A device that stores 1 bit of data. The ability to change the value of the bit is controlled by the level of an enabling signal; this is called level triggering.

Flip-flop   A device that stores 1 bit of data. The ability to change the value of the bit is controlled by the transition of a clock signal; this is called edge triggering.

SR latch   The state of an SR latch depends on its input and is either set or reset.

D flip-flop   A D flip-flop stores 1 bit of data. By connecting two latches in a primary–secondary configuration, the output is isolated from the input, allowing a flip-flop to be synchronized with a clock signal. The output of a D flip-flop can be changed only once per clock cycle.

You saw two examples of designing sequential logic circuits with D flip-flops and PLAs in this chapter. In the next chapter, you'll learn about some of the various memory structures used in a computer system.

8

MEMORY

In the previous three chapters, you learned about some of the hardware used to implement logical functions. Now, we'll look at how this functionality can be used to implement the subsystems that make up a computer, starting with memory.

Every computer user wants lots of memory and fast computing. However, faster memory costs more money, so there are some trade-offs. I'll begin this chapter with a discussion of how different types of memory are used to provide a reasonable compromise between speed and cost. Then, I'll describe a few different ways of implementing memory in hardware.

The Memory Hierarchy

In general, the closer memory is to the CPU, the faster and more expensive it is. The slowest memory is memory in the cloud. It's also the least expensive. My email account provides 15GB of storage in the cloud and doesn't cost me any money (if I ignore the "cost" of seeing a few advertisements), but its speed is limited by my internet connection. At the other extreme, the memory within the CPU runs at the same speed as the CPU but is relatively expensive. The Raspberry Pi has a little over 500 bytes of memory in the CPU available for us to use in our programs.

Figure 8-1 shows this general hierarchy. As we get closer to the CPU (at the top of the figure), memory is faster and costs more money, so there's less of it.

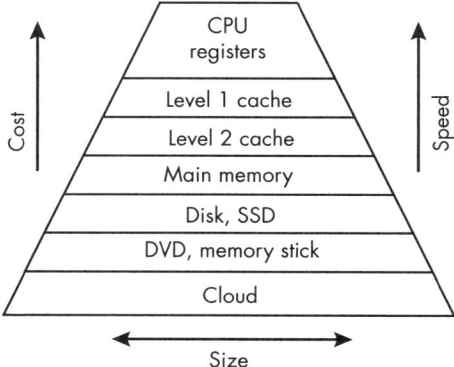

Figure 8-1: The computer memory hierarchy

The top three layers in Figure 8-1 are typically included in the CPU chip in modern computers. There may be one or two more levels of cache before getting to main memory. Main memory and a disk or solid-state drive (SSD), or both, are usually within the same enclosure as the CPU.

The next layer away from the CPU represents offline data storage devices, of which DVDs and memory sticks are only two examples. You may also have an external USB disk, a tape drive, and so forth. To make these devices available to the computer, you usually need to take some physical action, such as inserting a DVD in the drive or plugging a memory stick into a USB port.

The final layer in this hierarchy is storage in the cloud. Although most of us set up our computers to log on to the cloud automatically, it may not always be available.

In this chapter, I'll start with the two layers just above the cloud layer, offline storage and disk/SSD, and work toward the CPU registers. Then, I'll describe the hardware used to build registers and work back out toward main memory. We'll leave discussion of implementation of the three outermost layers to other books.

Mass Storage

Collectively, the two layers above the cloud layer in Figure 8-1 are known as *mass storage*. Mass storage devices store large amounts of data, and the data persists when the power to the device is turned off.

Let's take another look at the major subsystems of a computer, introduced in Chapter 1. As shown in Figure 8-2, the three subsystems communicate with one another via the data, control, and address buses. In addition, the input/output (I/O) block includes specialized circuitry that interfaces with mass storage devices.

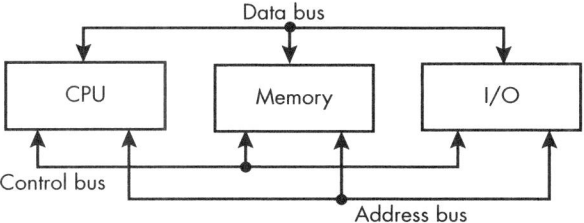

Figure 8-2: The subsystems of a computer

The Raspberry Pi, for example, has circuitry that implements the SD bus protocol and uses a micro SD card as its SSD. The operating system includes software (a *device driver*) that applications call to access the data and applications on the micro SD card through the SD port. I'll discuss I/O programming in Chapter 20, but the specifics of device drivers are beyond the scope of this book.

In the rest of this chapter, I'll cover *volatile memory*, which loses its contents when the power is turned off.

Main Memory

Main memory is the random-access memory (RAM) that you see in the specifications when you buy a computer. Main memory is synchronized in the hardware with the CPU via the bus interface, which I'll discuss in Chapters 9 and 20. Thus, a programmer can access items in memory by simply specifying the address and whether to load the item from memory or to store a new value there.

The amount of memory in your Raspberry Pi depends on the model. The Raspberry Pi 3 A+ has 512MB and the 3 B and 3 B+ each have 1GB. The Raspberry Pi 4 B can have 2, 4, or 8GB. The Raspberry Pi 5 can have 4 or 8GB. Other memory configurations may be available.

Usually, the entire program and dataset are not loaded into main memory. Instead, the operating system loads only the portion currently being worked on from mass storage into main memory. Most mass storage devices in modern computers can be accessed only in *blocks* of predetermined size. For example, the Raspberry Pi OS uses a disk block size of 4KB. When a needed instruction or data item is loaded into main memory, the computer loads the whole block of instructions or data that includes the needed item. The chances are good that the nearby parts of the program (instructions or data) will be needed soon. Since they're already in main memory, the operating system doesn't need to access the mass storage device again, thus speeding up program execution.

The most common organization of main memory is to store both the program instructions and data in main memory. This is referred to as the *von Neumann architecture* as it was initially described by John von Neumann

("First Draft of a Report on the EDVAC," Moore School of Electrical Engineering, University of Pennsylvania, 1945), although other computer science pioneers of the day were working on the same concepts.

One downside of the von Neumann architecture is that if an instruction calls for reading data from (or writing data to) memory, the next instruction in the program sequence cannot be read from (or written to) memory over the same bus until the current instruction has completed the data transfer. This is known as the *von Neumann bottleneck*. This conflict slows program execution, and it gave rise to another stored program architecture: the *Harvard architecture*, in which the program and data are stored in different memories, each with its own bus connected to the CPU. This makes it possible for the CPU to access program instructions and data simultaneously. This specialization reduces memory usage flexibility, which generally increases the total amount of memory needed. It also requires additional memory access hardware. The additional memory and access hardware increase the cost. It's common for the Level 1 cache to have a Harvard architecture, thus providing separate paths to the CPU for the instructions and the data.

Another downside of the von Neumann architecture is that a program can be written to view itself as data, thus enabling self-modification, which is generally a bad idea. Linux, like most modern, general-purpose operating systems, prohibits applications from modifying themselves.

Cache Memory

Most of the programs I use take up tens or hundreds of megabytes in main memory, but most of the execution time is taken up by loops, which execute the same few instructions repeatedly, access the same few variables, and occupy only tens or hundreds of bytes. Most modern computers include very fast *cache memory* between the main memory and the CPU, which provides a much faster location for the instructions and variables currently being processed by the program.

Cache memory is organized in levels, with Level 1 being the closest to the CPU and also the smallest. Cache sizes of the Raspberry Pi vary, as shown in Table 8-1.

Table 8-1: The Raspberry Pi's Cache Sizes

Model	Level 1		Level 2	Level 3
	Instruction	Data	Unified	Unified
3 A+, B, B+	4 × 32KB	4 × 32KB	512KB	n/a
4 B	4 × 48KB	4 × 32KB	1MB	n/a
5	4 × 64KB	4 × 64KB	4 × 512KB	2MB

NOTE *I have seen conflicting information about cache sizes on the various Raspberry Pi models, so I don't guarantee the accuracy of the sizes in Table 8-1, but they are close enough to illustrate how caches work.*

The portion of the CPU that performs the computations is called the *processor core*, or simply the *core*. The CPUs in all the Raspberry Pi models in Table 8-1 have four processor cores. The notation 4 × prefacing a memory size in this table means that each processor core has that amount of cache memory.

The Raspberry Pi 3 and 4 have two cache levels, and the Raspberry Pi 5 has three. Level 1 on all models uses a Harvard architecture. The Level 2 and 3 caches are all unified caches that hold both instructions and data. Cache memory in the Raspberry Pi is organized in 64-byte blocks called *lines*. Instructions and data are transferred to and from main memory one line at a time on a 64-byte address boundary.

When a program needs to access an instruction or data item, the hardware first checks to see if it's located in the Level 1 cache. If not, it checks the Level 2 cache. If it's in the Level 2 cache, the hardware copies the cache line that includes the needed instruction or data into the Level 1 cache and then into the CPU, where it stays until the program needs it again or the Level 1 cache needs to reuse that location for other instructions or data from the Level 2 cache. The hardware continues this process to subsequent cache levels until it either finds the needed item in a cache or reaches main memory.

When data is written to main memory, it's first written to the Level 1 cache, then the next cache levels. There are many schemes for using caches, which can become rather complex. I'll leave further discussion of caches for more advanced treatments, such as the Wikibooks article on microprocessor design and caches at *https://en.wikibooks.org/wiki/Microprocessor_Design/Cache*.

The time taken to access the Level 1 cache is close to the speed of the CPU. Level 2 is about 10 times slower, Level 3 about 100 times slower, and main memory about 1,000 times slower. These values are approximate and differ widely among implementations. Modern processors include cache memory in the same chip as the CPU, and some have more than three levels of cache.

Computer performance is usually limited by the time it takes for the CPU to read instructions and data into the CPU, not by the speed of the CPU itself. Having the instructions and data in the Level 1 cache reduces this time. Of course, if they are not in the Level 1 cache and the hardware needs to copy other instructions or data from Level 2 or Level 3, or from main memory into Level 3, then Level 2, and finally Level 1, access will take longer than simply getting the instructions or data directly from main memory. The effectiveness of caches depends on the *locality of reference*, which is the tendency of a program to reference nearby memory addresses in a short period of time. This is one of the reasons good programmers break a program, especially repetitive sections, into small units. A small program unit is more likely to fit within a few lines of a cache, where it will be available for successive repetitions.

Registers

The fastest memory is within the CPU itself: the *registers*. Registers typically provide a few hundred bytes of storage and are accessed at the same speed as the CPU. They're mainly used for numerical computations, logical operations, temporary data storage, holding addresses, and similar short-term operations—somewhat like how we use scratch paper when doing computations by hand.

Many registers are directly accessible by the programmer, while others are hidden. Some are used in the hardware that serves to interface between the CPU and I/O devices. The organization of registers in the CPU is specific to the particular CPU architecture, and it's one of the most important aspects of programming a computer at the assembly language level.

In the next chapter, you'll learn about the main registers in the ARM CPU that we'll be using for our programming in this book. But before we get to that, let's look at how memory can be implemented in hardware using the logic devices discussed in previous chapters.

Implementing Memory in Hardware

Starting at the top of the hierarchy shown in Figure 8-1, we'll first see how we can implement the memory in the CPU registers. We will then work our way back down from the CPU, and you'll see some of the limitations that arise when applying these designs to larger memory systems, such as cache and main memory. We'll explore designs for the memory in these larger systems, but I won't cover the implementation of mass storage systems in this book.

Four-Bit Registers

Let's begin with a design for a simple *4-bit register*, which might be found in inexpensive CPUs used in price-sensitive consumer products, such as coffee makers and remote controls. Figure 8-3 shows a design for implementing a 4-bit register using a D flip-flop for each bit. Each time the clock does a positive transition, the state (contents) of the register, $r = r_3 r_2 r_1 r_0$, is set to the input, $d = d_3 d_2 d_1 d_0$.

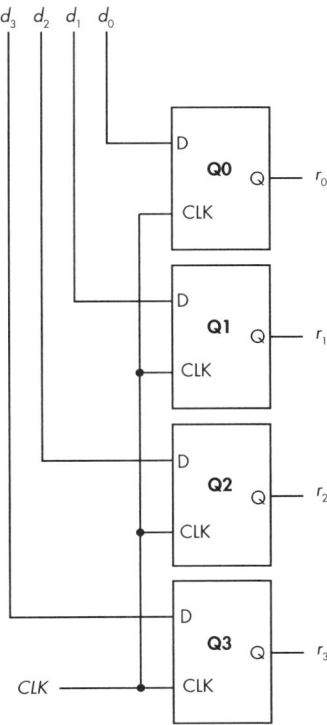

Figure 8-3: A 4-bit register using
a D flip-flop for each bit

   The problem with this circuit is that any changes in any d_i will change
the state of the corresponding stored bit, r_i, in the next clock cycle, so the
contents of the register are essentially valid for only one clock cycle. One-
cycle buffering of a bit pattern is fine for some applications, but we also
need registers that will store a value until it is explicitly changed, perhaps
billions of clock cycles later. Let's add a *Store* signal and feedback from the
output, r_i, of each bit. We want each r_i to remain unchanged when *Store* = 0
and to follow the input, d_i, when *Store* = 1, as shown in Table 8-2.

Table 8-2: Storing One
Bit in a D Flip-Flop

Store	d_i	r_i	Q
0	0	0	0
0	0	1	1
0	1	0	0
0	1	1	1
1	0	0	0
1	0	1	0
1	1	0	1
1	1	1	1

Table 8-2 leads to the Boolean equation for Q, the new output of each D flip-flop:

$$Q(Store, d_i, r_i) = \neg(\neg(\neg Store \wedge r_i) \wedge \neg(Store \wedge d_i))$$

This equation can be implemented with three NAND gates at the input of each D flip-flop, as shown in Figure 8-4.

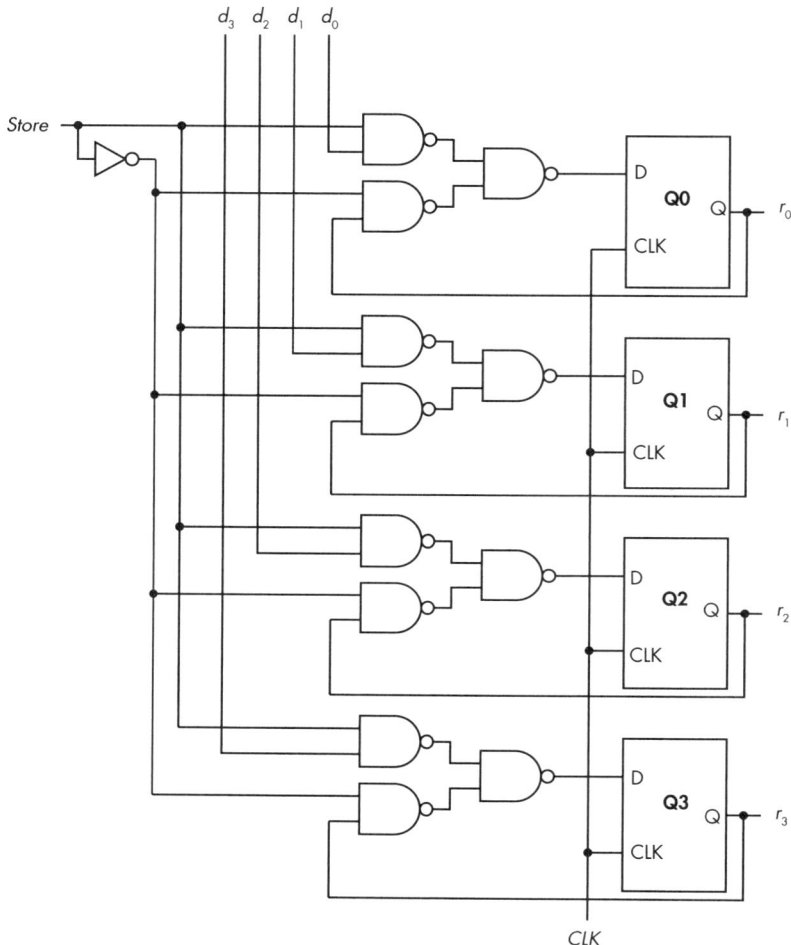

Figure 8-4: A 4-bit register with Store signal

There's another important feature of this design that follows from the primary/secondary property of the D flip-flops. The state of the secondary portion does not change until the second half of the clock cycle. So, the circuit connected to the output of this register can read the current state during the first half of the clock cycle, while the primary portion is preparing to possibly change the state to the new contents.

We now have a way to store, for example, the results from an adder circuit. The output from the register could be used as the input to another circuit that performs arithmetic or logical operations on the data.

Registers can also be designed to perform simple operations on the data stored in them. Next, we'll look at a register design that can convert serial data to a parallel format.

Shift Registers

A *shift register* uses a sequence of D flip-flops, like the simple storage register in Figure 8-4, but the output of each flip-flop is connected to the input of the next flip-flop in the sequence, as shown in Figure 8-5. We can use a shift register as a *serial-in parallel-out (SIPO)* device.

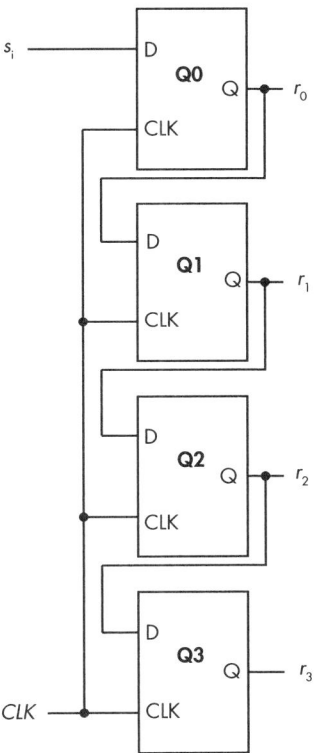

Figure 8-5: A 4-bit serial-to-parallel shift register

In the shift register in Figure 8-5, a serial stream of bits is input at s_i. At each clock tick, the output of Q0 is applied to the input of Q1, thus copying the previous value of r_0 to the new r_1. The state of Q0 changes to the value of the new s_i, thus copying this to be the new value of r_0. The serial stream of bits continues to ripple through the 4 bits of the shift register. At any time, the last 4 bits in the serial stream are available in parallel at the four outputs, r_3, r_2, r_1, r_0, with r_3 being the oldest in time.

The same circuit could be used to provide a time delay of four clock ticks in a serial bit stream; simply use r_3 as the serial output.

The Register File

The registers in the CPU that are used for similar operations are grouped together into a *register file*. For example, as you'll see in the next chapter, the CPU in the Raspberry Pi we'll be programming includes 31 64-bit general-purpose registers that are used for integer computations, temporary storage of addresses, and so forth. We need a mechanism for addressing each of the registers in the register file.

Consider a register file composed of eight of the 4-bit registers shown in Figure 8-4. We'll name the outputs from the eight registers $r0$ through $r7$. Thus, the ith bits from the eight registers are $r0_i$ through $r7_i$. To read the 4 bits of data in one of these eight registers (for example, $r5_3$, $r5_2$, $r5_1$, and $r5_0$ in register $r5$), we need to specify one of the eight registers using 3 bits. You learned in Chapter 6 that a multiplexer can select one of several inputs. We can connect an 8×1 multiplexer to each corresponding bit of the eight registers, as shown in Figure 8-6.

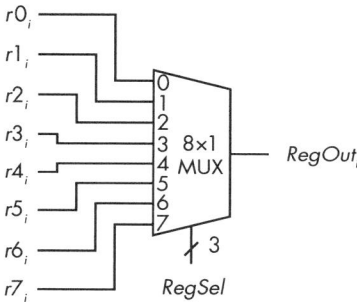

Figure 8-6: An eight-way multiplexer used to select the output of the register file

The inputs to the multiplexer, $r0_i$–$r7_i$, are the ith bits from each of eight registers, $r0$–$r7$. The slash through the *RegSel* line with a 3 next to it is the notation used to show there are three lines here.

Figure 8-6 shows only the output of the ith bit; n multiplexers are required for n-bit registers, so a 4-bit register would need four of these multiplexer output circuits. The same *RegSel* would be applied simultaneously to all four multiplexers to output all 4 bits of the same register. Larger registers would require correspondingly more multiplexers.

Read/Write Memory

You saw how to build a 4-bit register to store values from D flip-flops in Figure 8-3. We now need to be able to select when to read the value that's stored in the register and disconnect the output when we're not reading it. A tristate buffer (introduced in Chapter 6) allows us to do that, as shown in Figure 8-7. This circuit is for only one 4-bit register. We need one of these for each register in the computer. The $addr_j$ line comes from a decoder and selects one of the registers.

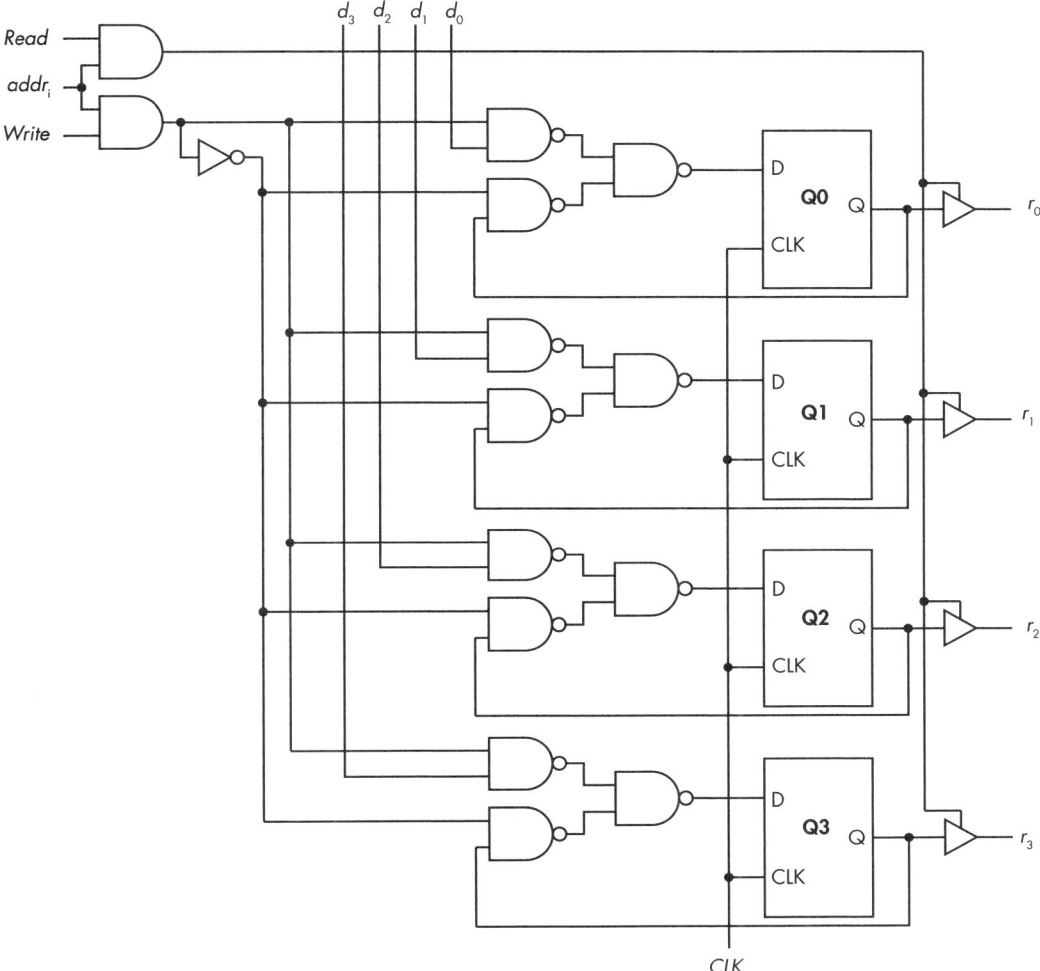

Figure 8-7: A 4-bit read/write register

Write = 1 causes the 4-bit data $d_3d_2d_1d_0$ to be stored in the D flip-flops Q3, Q2, Q1, and Q0. The 4-bit output, $r_3r_2r_1r_0$, remains disconnected from the D flip-flops when *Read* = 0. Setting *Read* = 1 connects the outputs.

Let's continue down the memory hierarchy in Figure 8-1 to cache memory, which is typically constructed from flip-flops, similar to a register file.

Static Random-Access Memory

The memory we have been discussing that uses flip-flops is called *static random-access memory (SRAM)*. It's called *static* because it maintains its values as long as power is maintained. As you learned in Chapter 2, it's called *random* because it takes the same amount of time to access any (random) byte in this memory.

SRAM is commonly used for cache memory. As shown in Table 8-1, the cache on a Raspberry Pi can range in size from 32KB to 2MB. Each bit in SRAM requires about six transistors to implement.

Continuing down the memory hierarchy, we get to main memory, the largest memory unit that is internal to the computer. The amount of main memory in a Raspberry Pi ranges from 1GB to 8GB, depending on the model, so using SRAM for main memory would be quite expensive. Next, we'll look at a less expensive type of memory that's suitable for large main memory systems.

Dynamic Random-Access Memory

Dynamic random-access memory (DRAM) is commonly implemented by charging a capacitor to one of two voltages for storing one bit. The circuit requires only one transistor to charge the capacitor, as shown in Figure 8-8. These circuits are arranged in a rectangular array.

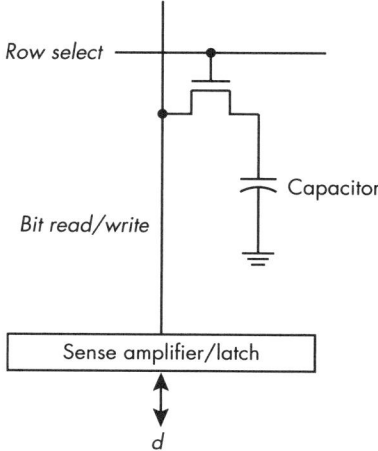

Figure 8-8: One DRAM bit

When the *row select* line is set to 1, all the transistors in that row are turned on, thus connecting the respective capacitor to the sense amplifier/latch. The value stored in the capacitor—high voltage or low voltage—is amplified and stored in the latch. There, it's available to be read. Since this action tends to discharge the capacitors, they must be refreshed from the values stored in the latch. Separate circuitry is provided to do the refresh.

When data is to be stored in DRAM, the new bit value, 0 or 1, is first stored in the latch. *Row select* is then set to 1, and the sense amplifier/latch circuitry applies the voltage corresponding to the logical 0 or 1 to the capacitor. The capacitor is either charged or discharged appropriately.

These operations take more time than simply switching flip-flops, so DRAM is appreciably slower than SRAM. In addition, each row of capacitors must be read and refreshed on the order of every 60 ms. This further slows memory access.

In addition to the memory itself, the amount of hardware required to address the individual bytes in a large memory system can be substantial. Let's look at a way to reduce the number of gates needed for addressing memory.

As an example, selecting 1 byte in 1MB of memory requires a 20-bit address. This in turn requires a 20×2^{20} address decoder, as shown in Figure 8-9.

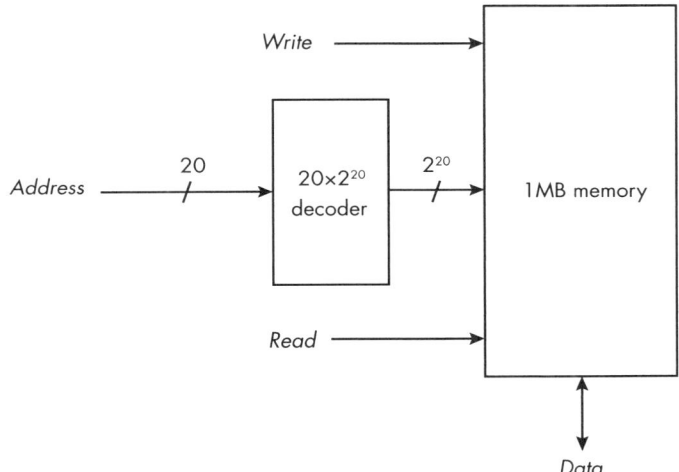

Figure 8-9: Addressing 1MB of memory with one 20×2^{20} address decoder

Recall that an $n \times 2^n$ decoder requires 2^n AND gates. So, a 20×2^{20} decoder requires 1,048,576 AND gates. We can simplify the circuitry by organizing memory into a grid of 1,024 rows and 1,024 columns, as shown in Figure 8-10. We can then select a byte by selecting a row and a column, each using a 10×2^{10} decoder.

Although two decoders are required, each requires only 2^{10} AND gates, for a total of $2 \times 2^{10} = 2,048$ AND gates for each of the two decoders. Of course, accessing individual bytes in memory is slightly more complex, and some complexity is added to split the 20-bit address into two 10-bit portions. Still, this example should give you an idea of how engineers can simplify designs.

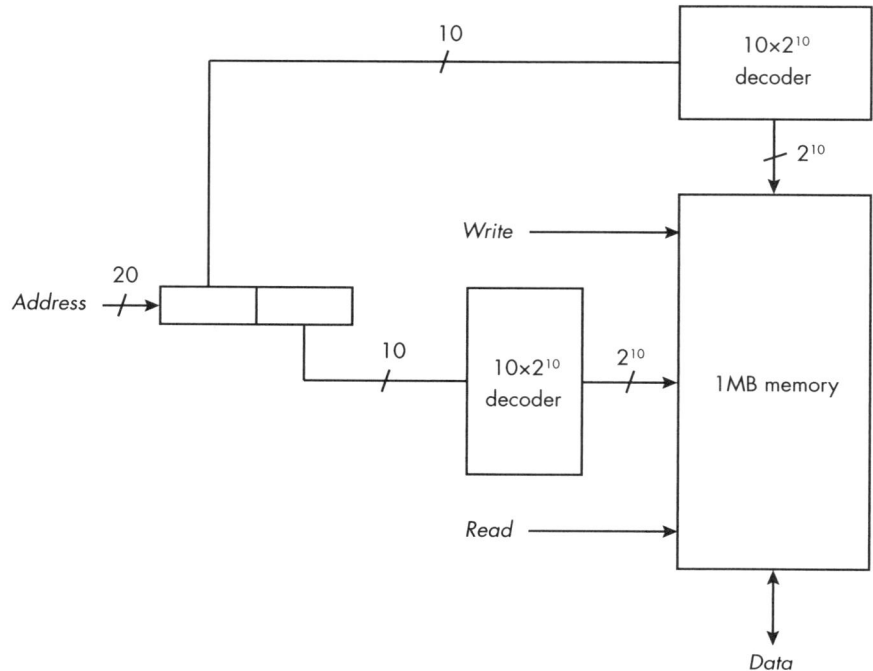

Figure 8-10: Addressing 1MB of memory with two 10×2^{10} address decoders

You now have a clear picture of how the hierarchical arrangement of memory in a modern computer allows fast program execution while keeping hardware costs at a reasonable level. Although DRAM is much slower than the CPU, its low cost per bit makes it a good choice for main memory. As we move closer to the CPU in the memory hierarchy, the much faster SRAM is used for the cache(s). Since cache memory is much smaller than main memory, the higher cost per bit of SRAM is tolerable here, and since the instructions and data needed by the program being executed by the CPU are often in the cache, we see the benefits of the higher speed of SRAM in program execution.

YOUR TURN

8.3   Derive the equation for $D(Store, d_i, r_i)$ from Table 8-2.

What You've Learned

Memory hierarchy   Computer storage is organized such that smaller amounts of faster, more costly memory are located closer to the CPU. Smaller amounts of program instructions and data are copied to the successively faster memory levels as a program executes. This works because there is a very high probability that the next memory location needed by a program will be at an address close to the current one.

Registers   A few thousand bytes of memory located in the CPU that are accessed at the same speed as the CPU. Implemented in flip-flops.

Cache   Thousands to millions of bytes of memory outside the CPU, but often on the same chip. Cache memory is slower than the CPU but is synchronized with it. It is often organized in levels, with faster, smaller amounts closer to the CPU. The cache is usually implemented using SRAM.

Main memory   Hundreds of millions to billions of bytes of memory separate from the CPU. Main memory is much slower than the CPU but is synchronized with it. It is usually implemented using DRAM.

Static random-access memory (SRAM)   Uses flip-flops to store bits. SRAM is fast but expensive.

Dynamic random-access memory (DRAM)   Uses capacitors to store bits. DRAM is slow but has a much lower cost than SRAM.

In the next chapter, you will learn how the CPU in the Raspberry Pi is organized from a programmer's point of view.

9

CENTRAL PROCESSING UNIT

Now that you've learned about the electronic components that are used to build a central processing unit (CPU), it's time for you to learn about some of the specifics of the ARM CPU.

Arm Ltd is a design company that licenses its designs as *intellectual property (IP)* to other companies. The Raspberry Pi uses a *System on a Chip (SoC)* made by Broadcom. An SoC is an assembly of IP blocks in a single integrated circuit that includes a CPU and many of the other components of a computer system. The SoC used on a Raspberry Pi includes an ARM CPU IP block and other device IP blocks to work with the CPU.

This book is based on the eighth version of the ARM CPU architecture, Armv8-A. This version is used in several Raspberry Pi models, including the Raspberry Pi 3 A+, B, and B+, the Raspberry Pi 4 B, and the Raspberry Pi 5.

An Armv8-A processor can be run in either the AArch64 or the AArch32 execution state. *AArch64* is a 64-bit execution state that supports 64-bit addresses and the *A64* instruction set. The A64 instructions can use 64-bit registers for processing. *AArch32* is a 32-bit execution state that supports 32-bit addresses and the *A32* and *T32* instruction sets. (In previous Arm documentation, A32 was called ARM and T32 was called Thumb.) The A32 and T32 instructions can use 32-bit registers for processing.

A64 and A32 instructions are all 32 bits long. T32 instructions are either 32 or 16 bits long. The T32 instruction set can be useful in implementations of the ARM architecture for small devices because it can reduce the amount of memory needed for a program. I use the A64 instruction set in the AArch64 execution state in this book.

We'll begin this chapter with an overview of a typical CPU, then look at the registers in the AArch64 execution state and how a programmer accesses them. I'll conclude the chapter with an example of using the gdb debugger to view the contents of the registers.

CPU Overview

As you probably already know, the CPU is the heart of the computer. It follows the execution path that you specify in your program and performs all the arithmetic and logic operations. It also fetches the instructions and data from memory as they are needed by your program.

Let's start with a look at the major subsystems of a typical CPU. I'll follow this with a description of how the CPU fetches instructions from memory as it executes a program.

CPU Subsystems

Figure 9-1 shows a block diagram of the major subsystems of a typical CPU. This is a highly simplified diagram that shows only one processing core; actual CPUs are much more complicated, but the general concepts discussed here apply to most of them.

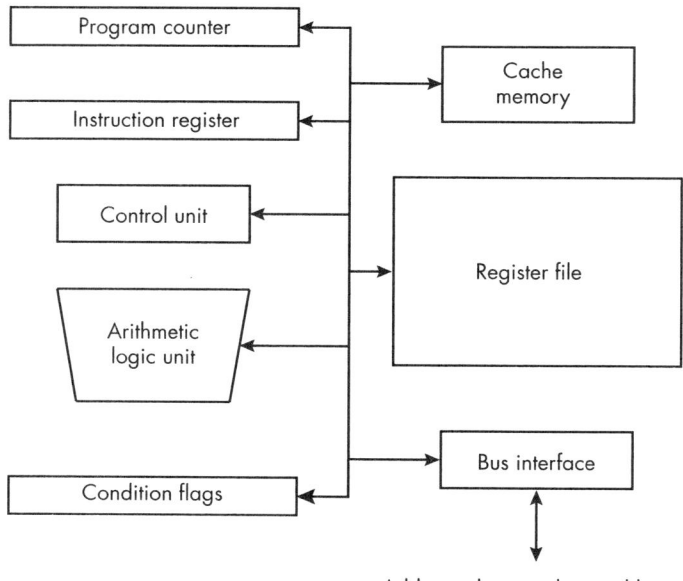

Figure 9-1: The major subsystems of a CPU

The subsystems are connected through internal buses, which are the hardware pathways and the protocols that control communications over these pathways. Let's briefly look at each of the subsystems in Figure 9-1. After this general introduction, we'll look at the subsystems a programmer will be most interested in and how they're used in the A64 architecture. The major CPU subsystems are:

Program counter   In the A64 architecture, the program counter register contains the memory address of the currently executing instruction. In many other architectures, it contains the address of the instruction immediately following the current one in memory. In the ARM A32 and T32 architectures, it contains the address of the instruction following the immediately following instruction. It's commonly called the *instruction pointer* in x86 architectures.

Cache memory   Although it could be argued that this is not part of the CPU, most modern CPUs include some cache memory on the CPU chip. The way the CPU uses cache memory was explained in Chapter 8.

Instruction register   When an instruction is fetched, it's loaded into the instruction register to be decoded and executed. The instruction register's bit pattern determines what the control unit causes the CPU to do. Once that action has been completed, the bit pattern in the instruction register will be changed to that of the next instruction in the program, and the CPU will perform the operation specified by this new bit pattern.

Register file   As you saw in Chapter 8, a register file is a group of registers used in similar ways. Most CPUs have several register files. For example, the A64 architecture includes a register file for integer operations and another register file for floating-point and vector operations. Compilers and assemblers have names for each register. All arithmetic and logic operations and data movement operations involve at least one register in a register file.

Control unit   The bits in the instruction register are decoded in the control unit. To carry out the action(s) specified by the instruction, the control unit generates the signals that control the other subsystems in the CPU. It's typically implemented as a finite state machine and contains decoders, multiplexers, and other logic components.

Arithmetic logic unit (ALU)   The ALU is used to perform the arithmetic and logic operations you specify in your program. It's also used by the CPU when it needs to do its own arithmetic (for example, to add two values to compute a memory address).

Condition flags   Each operation performed by the ALU results in various conditions that can be recorded for possible use by the program. For example, as discussed in Chapter 3, addition can produce a carry. The A64 instruction set includes add and subtract instructions that will set one of the condition flags to either 0 (no carry) or 1 (carry) after the ALU has completed the operation.

Bus interface   This is how the CPU communicates with the other computer subsystems—the memory and input/output (I/O) in Figure 1-1 (see Chapter 1). It contains the circuitry to place addresses on the address bus, to read and write data via the data bus, and to place control signals on the control bus. The bus interface on many CPUs interfaces with external bus control units that in turn interface with memory and with different types of I/O buses (for example, USB, SATA, or PCI-E).

Instruction Execution Cycle

Let's go into a bit more detail about how the CPU executes a program stored in main memory. It does this by fetching the instructions from main memory using the three buses that you learned about in Chapter 1—address, data, and control—through the bus interface.

In the A64 architecture, the address in the *program counter* register always points to (has the memory address of) the currently executing instruction in a program. After fetching the instruction at this address, the CPU decodes and executes it. The CPU then adds 4 (the number of bytes in an instruction) to the program counter, causing it to contain the address of the next instruction in the program. Thus, the program counter marks the current location in a program.

There are instructions that change the address in the program counter, thus causing a *branch* from one place in the program to another. In this case, the address in the program counter is not incremented after the instruction is executed.

When the CPU fetches an instruction from memory, it loads that instruction into the instruction register. The bit pattern in the instruction register causes the CPU to perform the operations specified in the instruction. Once that action has been completed, another instruction is automatically loaded into the instruction register, and the CPU will perform the operation specified by this next bit pattern.

Most modern CPUs use an *instruction queue*, where several instructions wait, ready to be executed. Separate electronic circuitry keeps the instruction queue full while the regular control unit is executing the instructions. This is an implementation detail that allows the control unit to run faster; the essence of how the control unit executes a program can be represented by the single instruction register model, which is what I'll describe here.

The steps to fetch each instruction from memory, and thus to execute a program, are as follows:

1. A sequence of instructions is stored in memory.

2. The memory address where the first instruction is located is copied to the program counter.

3. The CPU sends the address in the program counter to memory on the address bus.

4. The CPU sends a "read" signal on the control bus.

5. The memory responds by sending a copy of the state of the bits at that memory location on the data bus, which the CPU then copies into its instruction register.

6. The CPU executes the instruction in the instruction register.

7. If the instruction did not change the address in the program counter, the CPU automatically increments the program counter to contain the address of the next instruction in memory.

8. Go back to step 3.

Steps 3, 4, and 5 are called an *instruction fetch*. Notice that steps 3 through 8 constitute a cycle, known as the *instruction execution cycle*. Figure 9-2 shows this graphically for nonbranching A64 instructions.

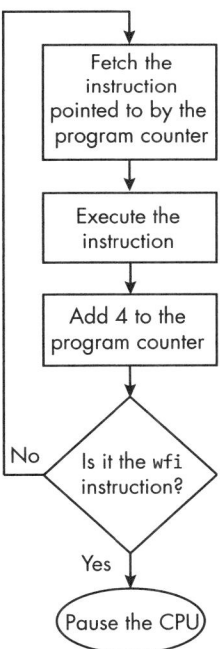

Figure 9-2: The instruction execution cycle for non-branching A64 instructions

The CPU adds 4 to the program counter because each A64 instruction is 32 bits long. Some computer architectures add the instruction length to the program counter before executing the instruction.

In the ARM A32 instruction set architecture, the CPU adds 8 (the length of two instructions) to the address of the currently executing instruction. You learned in Chapter 7 that instructions are fetched and executed in stages in a pipeline. In the older 32-bit ARM architecture, two more instructions have been fetched and are moving through the pipeline before the current instruction is executed. This difference was preserved in the A32 mode of the AArch64 architecture to give backward compatibility.

Most of the time, these differences will not matter to you, but as you will see when we discuss the coding of instructions in Chapter 12, knowing the details might help when debugging a program.

The wfi instruction in Figure 9-2 causes the CPU to stop executing instructions and wait for an interrupt. The A64 has another instruction, wfe, that also stops instruction execution and waits for an event. The differences between interrupts and events are beyond the scope of this book; the important point is that there are instructions to tell the CPU to stop executing instructions, thus pausing the instruction execution cycle. You'll learn more about interrupts in Chapter 21.

Most instructions in a program use at least one register in at least one of the register files. A program typically loads data from memory into a register, operates on the data, and stores the result in memory. Registers are also used to hold addresses of items that are stored in memory, thus serving as pointers to data or other addresses.

At this point in the book, I will focus mostly on the A64 instruction set architecture. I recommend you download *Learn the Architecture–Introducing the ARM Architecture* from *https://developer.arm.com/documentation/102404/ latest*. That document is more advanced than what I cover in this book, but one of my goals here is to help you learn how to read the more advanced presentations. Going back and forth between the two discussions will help you gain a better understanding of the material.

The remainder of this chapter is largely devoted to describing the general-purpose registers in the A64 architecture. You'll learn how to view their contents in the gdb debugger, and you'll learn how to start using them in assembly language in the next chapter.

A64 Registers

A portion of the memory in the CPU is organized into registers. Machine instructions access CPU registers by their addresses, just like they access main memory. Of course, the register addressing space is separate from the main memory addressing space; register addresses are placed on the internal CPU bus, not on the address portion of the bus interface, since the registers are in the CPU. The difference from a programmer's point of view is that the assembler has predefined names for the registers, whereas the programmer creates symbolic names for memory addresses.

Thus, in each program you write in assembly language, the following happens:

- CPU registers are accessed by using the names that are predefined in the assembler.
- Memory is accessed by the programmer providing a name for the memory location and using that name in the user program.

Table 9-1 lists the basic programming registers in the A64 architecture.

Table 9-1: The Basic A64 Registers

Number	Size	Name	Usage
31	64-bit	x0–x30 or w0–w30	General-purpose
1	64-bit	sp	Stack pointer
1	64-bit	xzr or wzr	Zero register
1	64-bit	pc	Program counter
1	64-bit	nzcv	Condition flags
32	128-bit	d0–x31, s0–s31, or h0–h31	Floating-point or vector
1	64-bit	fpcr	Floating-point control
1	64-bit	fpsr	Floating-point status

The names x0–x30 refer to the full 64 bits of the registers, and w0–w30 refer to the 32 low-order bits of the same registers. Similarly, xzr is a 64-bit 0 integer and wzr is a 32-bit 0 integer. For the floating-point registers, d0–d31 refer to the full 128 bits, s0–s31 to the low-order 64 bits, and h0–h31 to the low-order 32 bits of the registers.

Let's look at some of these registers in more detail. I'll start with the 31 general-purpose registers, then we'll look at several registers that have a special purpose. I'll cover the floating-point registers in Chapter 19.

General-Purpose Registers

The general-purpose registers are used for *integral data types*, such as int and char integer values (signed and unsigned), character representations, Boolean values, and memory addresses. Each bit in each register is numbered from right to left, beginning with 0. So, the rightmost bit is number 0, the next one to the left is 1, and so on. Since there are 64 bits in each general-purpose register, the leftmost bit is number 63.

Each instruction in a computer treats a group of bits as a single unit. In the early days, that unit was called a *word*. Each CPU architecture had a *word size*. In modern CPU architectures, different instructions operate on different numbers of bits, but the terminology has carried over from the original 32-bit ARM architecture to the current 64-bit architecture. Hence,

8 bits is called a *byte*, 16 bits a *halfword*, 32 bits a *word*, 64 bits a *doubleword*, and 128 bits a *quadword*.

Each of the general-purpose registers, r0–r30 in the A64 architecture, can be accessed as either a 32-bit word or a 64-bit doubleword. Our assembler uses w0–w30 for the word portion and x0–x30 for the doubleword, as shown in Figure 9-3.

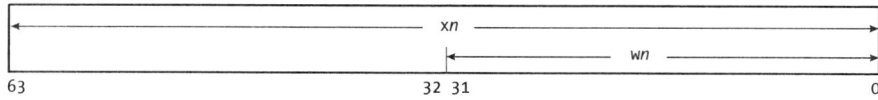

Figure 9-3: A64 general-purpose register names

When an instruction writes to the low-order 32 bits of a register, the high-order 32 bits are set to 0.

Special-Purpose Registers

As you just learned, the program counter register, named pc, contains the address of the current instruction. Software cannot write directly to pc; it can only be modified indirectly with a *branch* instruction.

Although it's considered a general-purpose register, *branch with link* instructions use the x30 register as a *link register*, named lr, to pass the return address when a function is called. I'll explain this in detail in Chapter 11, but for now keep in mind that you need to be careful how you use the x30 register when you write assembly language code.

You're probably used to most things in a computer occurring in multiples of 2, so you might be wondering why there are only 31 general-purpose registers. There is no register named w31 or x31. Instead, the A64 architecture treats the 32nd register as a *stack pointer*, named sp, or a *zero register*, named wzr or xzr.

The *stack* is a data structure located in memory, and the sp register contains its address. I'll cover all of this in detail in Chapter 11. The register name wsp refers to the low-order 32 bits of the stack pointer register. This would be used in specialized cases using 32-bit addressing that I won't cover in this book.

If your algorithm needs the value 0, many instructions allow you to use the wzr register for a 32-bit 0 or the xzr register for a 64-bit 0. If you use an instruction to store a value in the zero register, the value is simply discarded; however, this does actually have a use, as you'll see when we look at instructions that compare values in Chapter 13. The zero register does not need to be implemented as a physical register.

The condition flags, which you saw in Figure 9-1, are located in the nzcv register. Several arithmetic and logical operations affect the condition flags, which are in bits 31 to 28 of the nzcv register, as shown in Figure 9-4. The other 60 bits in this register are reserved for other uses.

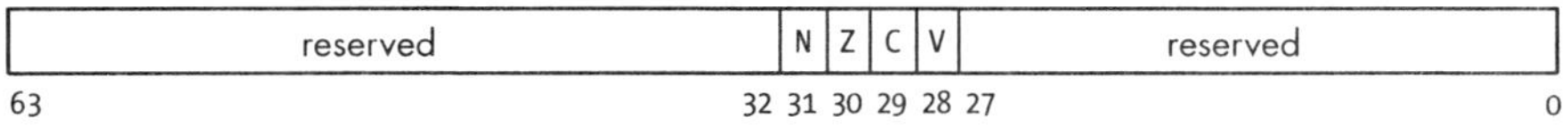

reserved	N	Z	C	V	reserved

63   32 31 30 29 28 27   0

Figure 9-4: The A64 nzcv register

The names of the flags and the conditions that cause them to be true (have a value of 1) are shown in Table 9-2.

Table 9-2: The Condition Flags

Name	Function	Condition that sets flag to 1
N	Negative flag	Highest-order bit of result is 1
Z	Zero flag	Result is 0
C	Carry flag	Shows carry or borrow
V	Overflow flag	Overflow of signed integer (two's complement) arithmetic

There are machine instructions for testing the state of the condition flags. For example, there's an instruction that will branch to another place in the program if the Z flag is 1.

Next, we'll look at some C/C++ data types as they relate to the sizes of the general-purpose registers.

C/C++ Integral Data Types and Register Sizes

Every piece of data in a computer program has a *data type*, which specifies the possible values for the data, the bit patterns used to represent those values, the operations that can be performed on the data, and the data's semantic usage in the program.

Some programming languages, including C, C++, and Java, require the programmer to explicitly state the data types of values used in the program. Other languages, such as Python, BASIC, and JavaScript, can determine a data type from the way the value is used.

Most programming languages specify the ranges for values that can be stored in a variable of each data type. For example, in C and C++, an int must be able to store a value in the range −32,768 to +32,767; thus, it must be at least 16 bits in size. An unsigned int must be able to store values in the range 0 to 65,535, so it also must be at least 16 bits. Programming environments can exceed the minimums given in the language specifications.

CPU manufacturers specify machine-level data types specific to the CPU architecture, often including specialized data types that are unique to the design. Table 9-3 gives A64 register sizes for C/C++ data types you can expect from our compilers, gcc and g++, but you should be careful not to count on these sizes to always be the same. The *<data type>* notation means a pointer to the memory address of the specified data type.

Table 9-3: The Sizes of Some C/C++ Data Types in the A64 Architecture

Data type	Size (bits)	Description
char	8	Byte
short	16	Integer
int	32	Integer
long	32	Integer
long long	64	Integer
float	32	Single-precision floating point
double	64	Double-precision floating point
*<data type>	64	Pointer

A value can usually be represented by more than one data type. For example, most people would think of 123 as representing the integer one hundred and twenty-three, but this value could be stored in a computer either as an int or as a char[] (a char array where each element of the array holds one code point for a character).

As Table 9-3 indicates, an int in our C/C++ environment is stored in a word, so 123 would be stored with the bit pattern 0x0000007b. As a C-style text string, we'd also need 4 bytes of memory, but the bit patterns would be 0x31, 0x32, 0x33, and 0x00—that is, the characters 1, 2, 3, and NUL. (Recall that a C-style string is terminated with a NUL character.)

If your solution to a problem depends on data sizes, C standard libraries often define specific sizes. For example, the GNU C libraries define int16_t to be a 16-bit signed integer and u_int16_t to be a 16-bit unsigned integer. In rare cases, you may want to use assembly language to ensure correctness.

You can learn a lot about how the CPU works by viewing what takes place in the registers. In the next section, you'll learn how to view the registers by using the gdb debugger.

Using gdb to View the CPU Registers

I'll use the program in Listing 9-1 to show you how to use gdb to view the contents of the CPU registers.

inches_to_feet.c
```
// Convert inches to feet and inches.

#include <stdio.h>
#define INCHES_PER_FOOT 12

int main(void)
{
❶ register int feet;
   register int inches;
❷ int total_inches;
   int *ptr;
```

```
    ptr = &total_inches;

    printf("Enter inches: ");
❸ scanf("%i", ptr);

    feet = total_inches / INCHES_PER_FOOT;
    inches = total_inches % INCHES_PER_FOOT;
    printf("%i\" = %i' %i\"\n", total_inches, feet, inches);

    return 0;
}
```

Listing 9-1: A simple program to illustrate the use of gdb to view CPU registers

I've used the register storage class modifier ❶ to request that the compiler use a CPU register for the feet and inches variables, instead of storing them in memory. The register modifier is advisory only; the C language standard doesn't require the compiler to honor the request. But notice that I didn't request that the compiler use a CPU register for the total_inches variable ❷. This variable must be placed in memory, as scanf needs a pointer to the location of total_inches ❸ to store the value read from the keyboard.

I introduced some gdb commands in Chapter 2. When you hit a breakpoint in a program that has been running, here are some additional commands that you may find useful for moving through the program under your control and viewing information about the program:

n (next)   Execute the current source code statement. If it's a call to a function, the entire function is executed.

s (step)   Execute the current source code statement. If it's a call to a function, step into the function, arriving at the first instruction of the called function.

si (step instruction)   Execute the current machine instruction. If it's a call to a function, step into the function.

sho arc (show architecture)   Display the architecture that gdb is currently using. You can use this command to make sure gdb is being used in the AArch64 mode.

Here's how I used gdb to control the execution of the program shown in Listing 9-1 and observe the register contents—note that you'll probably see different addresses if you replicate this example on your own:

```
❶ $ gcc -g -Wall -o inches_to_feet inches_to_feet.c
❷ $ gdb ./inches_to_feet
  GNU gdb (Debian 10.1-1.7) 10.1.90.20210103-git
  --snip--
  Reading symbols from ./inches_to_feet...
❸ (gdb) l
  1        // Convert inches to feet and inches.
  2
```

```
3        #include <stdio.h>
4        #define INCHES_PER_FOOT 12
5
6        int main(void)
7        {
8            register int feet;
9            register int inches;
10           int total_inches;
❹ (gdb)
11           int *ptr;
12
13           ptr = &total_inches;
14
15           printf("Enter inches: ");
16           scanf("%i", ptr);
17
18           feet = total_inches / INCHES_PER_FOOT;
19           inches = total_inches % INCHES_PER_FOOT;
20           printf("%i\" = %i' %i\"\n", total_inches, feet, inches);
(gdb)
21
22           return 0;
23       }
```

I first compile the program ❶ and then load it in gdb ❷. The debugger starts by printing information about itself, which I've removed here to save space. I then list the source code ❸ so I know where to set breakpoints. Using the ENTER key ❹ (RETURN on some keyboards) repeats the previous command (without showing it).

I want to follow along as the program processes the data, which I can do by setting breakpoints at strategic points in the program:

```
(gdb) b 15
Breakpoint 1 at 0x7d8: file inches_to_feet.c, line 15.
(gdb) b 18
Breakpoint 2 at 0x7f4: file inches_to_feet.c, line 18.
```

I set the first breakpoint where the program is about to prompt the user to enter the input data, at line 15, and a second at the statement where the program's computations begins, at line 18.

When I run the program, it breaks at the first breakpoint it encounters:

```
(gdb) r
Starting program: /home/progs/chapter_09/inches_to_feet/inches_to_feet

Breakpoint 1, main () at inches_to_feet.c:15
15           printf("Enter inches: ");
```

The program stops at line 15 of the source code, and control returns to gdb. The i r command shows the contents of the registers (be sure to type a space between i and r):

```
(gdb) i r
x0              0x7fffffef54            549755809620
x1              0x7ffffff0b8            549755809976
x2              0x7ffffff0c8            549755809992
x3              0x55555507c4            366503856068
x4              0x0                     0
x5              0xbc0984bf4dff9186      -4897237162606489210
x6              0x7ff7fb6c58            549621296216
x7              0x1000000040            68719476800
x8              0xffffffffffffffff      -1
x9              0xf                     15
x10             0x0                     0
x11             0x0                     0
x12             0x7ff7e48e48            549619797576
x13             0x0                     0
x14             0x0                     0
x15             0x6fffff4a              1879048010
x16             0x0                     0
x17             0x0                     0
x18             0x7fffffdb20            549755804448
x19             0x5555550880            366503856256
x20             0x0                     0
x21             0x55555506b0            366503855792
x22             0x0                     0
x23             0x0                     0
x24             0x0                     0
x25             0x0                     0
x26             0x0                     0
x27             0x0                     0
x28             0x0                     0
x29             0x7fffffef30            549755809584
x30             0x7ff7e65e18            549619916312
sp              0x7fffffef30            0x7fffffef30
pc              0x55555507d8            0x55555507d8 <main+20>
cpsr            0x60000000              [ EL=0 C Z ]
fpsr            0x0                     0
fpcr            0x0                     0
```

This display tells us the contents of the registers before the user enters data (you'll see different numbers). We might want to know if the compiler honored our request to use registers for the feet and inches variables, and if it did, which registers it used.

We'd like to know this information so we can look at the contents of the registers before and after they're used by the program to determine if the program is storing the correct values in them. We can answer this question by asking gdb to print the addresses of these two variables:

```
(gdb) print &feet
Address requested for identifier "feet" which is in register $x20
(gdb) print &inches
Address requested for identifier "inches" which is in register $x19
```

When we ask for the address of a variable, gdb will give the memory address associated with a programmer-supplied identifier. But in this program I asked the compiler to use registers, and gdb tells us which register the compiler chose for each variable.

I didn't ask the compiler to use registers for the total_inches and ptr variables, so gdb should tell us where they are located in memory:

```
(gdb) print &total_inches
$1 = (int *) 0x7fffffef54
(gdb) print &ptr
$2 = (int **) 0x7fffffef58
```

Now that we know x19 is being used for inches and x20 for feet, we can see what's currently stored in these two registers before using them for our computations:

```
❶ (gdb) i r x19 x20
x19            0x5555550880          366503856256
x20            0x0                   0
```

Rather than display all the registers, we can specify the two we want to look at ❶. We know from Table 9-3 that inches and feet are using only the w19 and w20 portions of the x19 and x20 registers, but gdb always shows us the entire 64 bits.

Continuing the program's execution, the program asks the user to enter the number of inches. Here, I respond with 123. It then breaks back into gdb at the next breakpoint it encounters:

```
(gdb) c
Continuing.
Enter inches: 123

Breakpoint 2, main () at inches_to_feet.c:18
18          feet = total_inches / INCHES_PER_FOOT;
```

The program is about to compute the number of feet, and then it will compute the remainder of inches. Before starting the computations, let's make sure the user's input is stored in the right place:

```
(gdb) print total_inches
$3 = 123
```

We'll now let the program do its computations:

```
(gdb) n
19          inches = total_inches % INCHES_PER_FOOT;
❶ (gdb)
20          printf("%i\" = %i' %i\"\n", total_inches, feet, inches);
```

Pressing the ENTER key repeats the n command ❶. The program is now ready to print out the results of the computations. Let's check to make sure all the computations were performed correctly and the results are stored in the right places:

```
(gdb) i r x19 x20
x19          0x3               3
x20          0xa               10
```

There are other ways to see what's stored in inches and feet:

```
(gdb) print $x19
$4 = 3
(gdb) print $x20
$5 = 10
(gdb) print inches
$6 = 3
(gdb) print feet
$7 = 10
```

When using gdb's print command, you can print only one variable at a time, even if a register is being used to store the variable. The $ prefix on the register name isn't required for the i r command, but it is for the print command.

Before completing execution of the program, let's take a final look at all the registers:

```
(gdb) i r
x0           0x78              120
x1           0x7b              123
x2           0xa               10
x3           0x0               0
x4           0x3               3
x5           0x7fffffe9f3      549755808243
x6           0x21a             538
x7           0x7b              123
x8           0x7ff7f5a338      549620917048
x9           0x5               5
x10          0xa               10
x11          0xffffffffffffffff -1
x12          0xffffffc8        4294967240
x13          0x7fffffeef0      549755809520
```

x14	0x2	2
x15	0x410	1040
x16	0x0	0
x17	0x0	0
x18	0x0	0
x19	0x3	3
x20	0xa	10
x21	0x55555506b0	366503855792
x22	0x0	0
x23	0x0	0
x24	0x0	0
x25	0x0	0
x26	0x0	0
x27	0x0	0
x28	0x0	0
x29	0x7fffffef30	549755809584
x30	0x55555507f4	366503856116
sp	0x7fffffef30	0x7fffffef30
pc	0x5555550848	0x5555550848 <main+132>
cpsr	0x60200000	[EL=0 SS C Z]
fpsr	0x0	0
fpcr	0x0	0

There's nothing remarkable in this display, but after you gain some experience looking at such displays, you'll learn to sometimes spot that something is not right. Now that I'm satisfied that the program performed all the computations correctly, I'll continue to the end of the program by using c and then exit:

```
(gdb) c
Continuing.
123" = 10' 3"
[Inferior 1 (process 2265) exited normally]
(gdb) q
$
```

The program continues to execute, printing the result and returning control to gdb. Of course, the last thing to do is to exit from gdb with q.

YOUR TURN

9.1   Modify the program in Listing 9-1 to request that registers be used for the variables total_inches and ptr. Did the compiler allow you to do that? If not, why?

9.2   Write a program in C that allows you to determine the endianness of your computer (described on page 33 in Chapter 2).

9.3 Modify the program from exercise 9.2 so you can demonstrate, using gdb, that endianness is a property of the CPU. That is, even though a 32-bit int is stored little-endian in memory, it will be read into a register in the "proper" order.

What You've Learned

General-purpose registers   The thirty-one 64-bit registers in the A64 architecture that provide a small amount of memory for computations in the CPU.

Condition flags   Bits that show whether some arithmetic or logic operations produce carry, overflow, or negative or zero values.

Program counter   A pointer that holds the address of the instruction currently being executed.

Instruction register   Holds the instruction currently being executed.

Arithmetic logic unit (ALU)   Performs the specified arithmetic and logic operations.

Control unit   Controls the activity in the CPU.

Bus interface   Responsible for interfacing the CPU with the main memory and I/O devices.

Cache memory   Holds portions of the program, both instructions and data, that are currently being worked on by the CPU. Cache memory is faster than main memory.

Instruction execution cycle   Details how the CPU works its way through a list of instructions.

C/C++ data type sizes   Data type sizes are closely related to register sizes.

In the next chapter, you'll start programming your Raspberry Pi in assembly language.

10

PROGRAMMING IN ASSEMBLY LANGUAGE

In previous chapters, you learned how computers can be programmed using 1s and 0s to represent operations and data. Those 1s and 0s are the *machine language*. Now, we'll move on to programming at the machine level. Instead of using machine language, we'll use *assembly language*, which uses a short mnemonic for each machine language instruction. We'll use an *assembler* program to translate the assembly language into the machine language instructions that control the computer.

Creating a program in assembly language is similar to creating one in a higher-level compiled language such as C, C++, Java, or FORTRAN. I'll use C as the programming model to explore the primary programming constructs and data structures that are common to essentially all higher-level programming languages. The compiler we're using, gcc, allows us to look at the assembly language it generates. From there, I'll show you how I would implement the programming constructs and data structures directly in assembly language.

We'll start by looking at the steps the compiler takes to create an executable program from C source code. Next, I'll discuss which of these steps apply to assembly language programming and walk you through creating a program directly in assembly language that will run in the C hosted environment. You'll also learn about a gdb mode that's useful for learning assembly language.

While reading this chapter, you should also consult the man pages and info documentation resources available in Raspberry Pi OS for the programs discussed here. You'll probably need to install some of them on your Raspberry Pi, as described in "The Programming Environment" on page 4.

I'll be using the GNU assembler program, as, quite a bit through the rest of the book. Some call this assembler gas, short for *GNU assembler*. I'll explain what you need to know about using the as program, but I recommend getting a copy of the *Using as* manual so you can learn the details as we go. It's available in the Software Development section at *https://www.gnu.org/manual/manual.html*, as part of the GNU Binutils collection.

Starting in C

The gcc compiler creates an executable program from one or more source files by performing several distinct steps. Each step results in an intermediate file that serves as the input to the next step. The description of each step here assumes a single C source file, *filename.c*:

Preprocessing
Preprocessing is the first step. This step resolves *preprocessor directives* such as #include (file inclusion), #define (macro definition), and #if (conditional compilation) by invoking the program cpp. Each preprocessor directive begins with the # character, which may be pronounced or not—for example, you may hear the #include directive referred to as *include, pound-include, hash-include,* or *hashtag-include*.

The compilation process can be stopped at the end of the preprocessing phase using the -E option, which writes the resulting C source code to *standard output*. Standard output is the plaintext output from a command line program in Linux. It is usually connected to the terminal window. You can redirect the output to a file with the > operator, like so:

```
$ gcc -Wall -O0 -E <filename.c> > <filename.i>
```

The *.i* file extension denotes a file that does not require preprocessing.

Compilation
Next, the compiler translates the source code that results from preprocessing into assembly language. The compilation process can be stopped at the end of the compilation phase with the -S option (an uppercase S), which writes the assembly language source code to *<filename>.s*.

Assembly

After the compiler generates the assembly language that implements the C source code, the assembler program, as, translates the assembly language into machine code (instructions and data). The process can be stopped at the end of the assembly phase using the -c option, which writes the machine code to an *object file* named *<filename>.o*. In addition to the machine code, the object file includes metadata about the code used by the linker to resolve cross-references between different modules, determine where to locate the different parts of the program, and so forth. It also includes metadata about the module, for use by the debugger.

Linking

The ld program determines where each function and data item will be located in memory when the program is executed. It replaces the programmer's labels, where each is referenced with the memory address of the label. If a called function is in an external library, this is noted where the function is called, and the address of the external library function is determined during program execution.

The compiler directs the ld program to add the computer code to the executable file that sets up the C hosted environment. This includes operations such as opening paths to standard output (the screen) and standard input (the keyboard) for use by the program.

The result of this linking is written to an executable file. The default name of the executable file is *a.out*, but you can specify another name with the -o option.

If you don't use any of the gcc options to stop the process at the end of one of these steps (-E, -S, -c), the compiler will perform all four steps and automatically delete the intermediate files, leaving only the executable program as the final result. You can direct gcc to keep all the intermediate files with the -save-temps option.

The complement of being able to stop gcc along the way is that we can supply files that have effectively gone through the earlier steps, and gcc will incorporate those files into the remaining steps. For example, if we write a file in assembly language (*.s*), gcc will skip the preprocessing and compilation steps and perform only the assembly and linking steps for that file. If we supply only object files (*.o*), gcc will go directly to the linking step. An implicit benefit of this is that we can write programs in assembly language that call functions in the C standard library (which are already in object file format), and gcc will automatically link our assembly language with those library functions.

Be sure to use the filename extensions specified in the GNU programming environment when naming a file. The default action of the compiler at each step depends upon the filename extension appropriate to that step. To see these naming conventions, enter **info gcc** into the command line, select

Invoking GCC, and then select **Overall Options**. If you don't use the specified filename extension, the compiler might not do what you want or might even overwrite a required file.

From C to Assembly Language

Programs written in C are organized into functions. Each function has a name that is unique within the program. After the C hosted environment is set up, the main function is called, so our programs will start with a main function.

Let's start by looking at the assembly language that gcc generates for the minimum C program in Listing 10-1.

do_nothing.c
```
// Minimum components of a C program

int main(void)
{
    return 0;
}
```

Listing 10-1: The minimum C program

This program does nothing except return 0 to the operating system. A program can return various numerical error codes; 0 indicates that the program did not detect any errors.

Even though this program accomplishes very little, some instructions need to be executed just to return 0. To see what takes place, we'll first translate this program from C to assembly language with the following Linux command:

```
$ gcc -Wall -O0 -S do_nothing.c
```

NOTE   *If you're not familiar with the GNU make program, it's worth learning how to use it to build your programs. It may seem like overkill at this point, but it's much easier to learn with simple programs. The manual is available in several formats at* https://www.gnu.org/software/make/manual/, *and I have some comments about using it on my website at* https://rgplantz.github.io.

Before showing the result of this command, I'll explain the options I've used. The -O0 (uppercase O and zero) option tells the compiler not to use any optimization. This is in keeping with the goal of this book, which is to show what's taking place at the machine level; asking the compiler to optimize the code may obscure some important details.

You've already learned that the -Wall option asks the compiler to warn you about questionable constructions in your code. That's not likely to be an issue in this simple program, but it's a good habit to get into.

The -S option directs the compiler to stop after the compilation phase and write the assembly language resulting from the compilation to a file with the same name as the C source code file, but with the *.s* extension instead of *.c*. The previous compiler command generates the assembly language shown in Listing 10-2, which is saved in the file *do_nothing.s*.

```
        .arch armv8-a
        .file   "do_nothing.c"
        .text
        .align  2
        .global main
        .type   main, %function
main:
.LFB0:
        .cfi_startproc
        mov     w0, 0
        ret
        .cfi_endproc
.LFE0:
        .size   main, .-main
        .ident  "GCC: (Debian 10.2.1-6) 10.2.1 20210110"
        .section .note.GNU-stack,"",@progbits
```

Listing 10-2: The minimum C program in assembly language generated by the compiler

The first thing to notice in Listing 10-2 is that assembly language is organized by lines. Only one assembly language statement is on each line, and none of the statements spans more than one line. This differs from the free-form nature of many high-level languages, where the line structure is irrelevant. In fact, good programmers use the ability to write program statements across multiple lines and indentation to emphasize the structure of their code. Good assembly language programmers use blank lines to help separate parts of an algorithm, and they comment almost every line.

The lines are organized roughly into columns. They probably do not make much sense to you at this point because they're written in assembly language, but if you look carefully, each of the lines is organized into four possible fields:

label: operation operand(s)   // comment

Not all the lines will have entries in all the fields. The assembler requires at least one space or tab character to separate the fields. When writing assembly language, your program will be much easier to read if you use the TAB key to move from one field to the next so the columns line up.

Let's look at each field in a bit more detail:

label   This field allows us to give a symbolic name to a memory address in the program. Other parts of the program can then refer to the memory address by name. A label consists of an identifier immediately followed by the : character. I'll cover the rules for creating an identifier soon. Only the lines that need to be referred to are labeled.

operation   This field contains either an *instruction operation code (opcode)* or an *assembler directive* (sometimes called a *pseudo-op*). The assembler translates an opcode and its operands into machine instructions, which are copied into memory when the program is to be executed. Assembler directives are instructions to the assembler program that guide the assembly process.

operand(s)   This field specifies the arguments to be used in the operation. The arguments can be explicit values, names of registers, or programmer-created names. There may be zero to several operands, depending on the operation.

comment   Everything on a line following two / characters (//) is ignored by the assembler, thus providing a way for the programmer to provide human-readable comments. Since assembly language is not as easy to read as higher-level languages, good programmers will place a comment on almost every line. Of course, the compiler has not commented the code in Listing 10-2 because it has no way of knowing the programmer's intent.

You probably noticed that most of the operators in Listing 10-2 begin with a . character. These are assembler directives. Each assembler directive begins with the . character, which may be pronounced or not—for example, you might hear .text referred to as *text* or *dot-text*. These are instructions to the assembler program itself, not computer instructions. The compiler generates some assembler directives that we won't need for the assembly language we write in this book; we'll take a quick look at those next, then look at the required directives.

Unused Assembler Directives

The assembler directives in Listing 10-2 that begin with .cfi tell the assembler to generate information that can be used for debugging and certain error situations. The labels beginning with .LF mark places in the code used to generate this information. A discussion of this is beyond the scope of this book, but their appearance in the listing can be confusing, so we'll tell the compiler not to include them in the assembly language file using the -fno-asynchronous-unwind-tables and -fno-unwind-tables options:

```
$ gcc -Wall -O0 -S -fno-asynchronous-unwind-tables -fno-unwind-tables do_nothing.c
```

This produces the file *do_nothing.s*, shown in Listing 10-3. I've used boldface to show the directives that we will use and left the ones we won't use unbolded. The compiler did not comment the assembly language code in this listing, but I've added my own comment using /// to help you see the relationship with the C source code. I'll add my own comments to many of the compiler-generated assembly language listings I show in this book.

```
          .arch armv8-a
          .file   "do_nothing.c"
          .text
          .align  2
          .global main
          .type   main, %function
main:
          mov     w0, 0           /// return 0;
          ret
          .size   main, .-main
          .ident  "GCC: (Debian 10.2.1-6) 10.2.1 20210110"
          .section        .note.GNU-stack,"",@progbits
```

Listing 10-3: The minimum C program in assembly language generated by the compiler, without .cfi directives

We've stripped away the .cfi directives, but we still have several assembler directives that we won't need when we write our own functions in assembly language. These include:

.file   This is used by gcc to specify the name of the C source file that this assembly language came from. This directive isn't used when writing directly in assembly language.

.size   This computes the size of the machine code, in bytes, that results from assembling this file. The . symbol refers to the current address in the code, so the arithmetic expression .-main subtracts the address of main from the current address. The .size directive associates this value with the main label as part of the metadata in the object file, thus giving the number of bytes in this function. This can be useful information in systems with limited memory, but it's of no concern in our programs.

.ident   This provides information in the object file about the compiler that was used. This might be useful in large projects that have evolved over several years, but we won't need it.

.section   This provides guidance to the linker about how the stack should be treated for this function. We won't include it and will just accept the default settings of the linker.

Next, we'll look at the directives that will be required when we write in assembly language.

Required Assembler Directives

The required assembler directives are shown in boldface in Listing 10-3.

There are several variations of the ARM instruction set architecture, and it continues to evolve. The .arch assembler directive tells the assembler which ARM architecture we're using. It causes the assembler to warn us if we use an instruction that is not available in our specific architecture. The .arch directive is arguably not required for the simple programs we're writing in this book, but we'll use it to be on the safe side.

The .text assembler directive tells the assembler to place whatever follows in the text section. What does *text section* mean? In Linux, the object files produced by the assembler are in the *Executable and Linkable Format (ELF)*. The ELF standard specifies many types of sections, each specifying the type of information stored in it. We use assembler directives to tell the assembler in which section to place the code. The text section is where the program's executable instructions go.

The Linux operating system also divides memory into *segments* for specific purposes when a program is loaded from the disk. The linker gathers together all the sections that belong in each segment and outputs an executable ELF file that's organized by segment to make it easier for the operating system to load the program into memory. The four general types of segments are as follows:

Text (also called code)   The *text segment* is where program instructions and constant data are stored. The operating system prevents a program from changing anything stored in the text segment, making it read-only.

Data   Global variables and static local variables are stored in the *data segment*. Global variables can be accessed by any of the functions in a program. A static local variable can be accessed only by the function it's defined in, but its value remains the same between calls to its function. Programs can both read from and write to variables in the data segment. These variables remain in place for the duration of the program.

Stack   Automatic local variables and the information that links functions are stored on the *call stack*. Automatic local variables are created when a function is called and deleted when the function returns to its calling function. A program can both read from and write to memory on the stack; it's allocated and deallocated dynamically as the program executes.

Heap   The *heap* is a pool of memory that's available for a program to use when running. A C program calls the malloc function (C++ programs call new) to get a chunk of memory from the heap. Programs can both read from and write to heap memory; it's used to store data and is explicitly deallocated by calling free (delete in C++) in the program.

NOTE   *This is a simplistic overview of ELF sections and segments. For more details, read the man page for ELF and sources such as "ELF-64 Object File Format," which you can download at* https://uclibc.org/docs/elf-64-gen.pdf, *and John R. Levine's* Linkers & Loaders *(Morgan Kaufmann, 1999). The readelf program is also useful for learning about ELF files.*

The .align directive is used to align the code following it on an address boundary. The argument used in Listing 10-3, 2, has different meanings depending on the platform you're using. On the ARM platform, it specifies the number of low-order bits that should be 0 in the program counter. If the bits are not 0, the assembler increments the address until they are. Thus, the code that follows this .align 2 directive will start at a full word address.

The .global directive has one argument, the identifier main. The .global directive makes the name globally known, so functions that are defined in other files can refer to this name. The code that sets up the C hosted environment was written to call the function named main, so the name must be global in scope. All C/C++ programs start with a main function. In this book, I'll also start the assembly language programs with a main function and execute them within the C hosted environment.

You can write stand-alone assembly language programs that don't depend on the C hosted environment, in which case you can create your own name for the first function in the program. You need to stop the compilation process at the end of the assembly step with the -c option. You then link the object (.o) files using the ld command by itself, not as part of gcc. I'll describe this in more detail in Chapter 21.

The .type directive has two arguments: main and @function. This causes the identifier main to be recorded in the object file as the name of a function.

These last three directives are not translated into actual machine instructions. Rather, they're used to describe the characteristics of the statements that follow. In the next chapter, we'll start seeing assembler directives that store constant data in memory for the program to use.

Now that you've seen how the compiler translates C code into assembly language, let's look at how to write a program directly in assembly language. In the Introduction, I said you should avoid writing programs in assembly language. But the goal of this book is to help you learn how computers work at the machine level. Writing programs directly in assembly language is a better learning technique than just reading what the compiler does.

Starting in Assembly Language

Listing 10-4 was written in assembly language by a programmer (me), rather than by a compiler. Naturally, I've added comments to explain what my code accomplishes.

do_nothing.s

```
// Minimum components of a C program, in assembly language

        .arch   armv8-a
        .text
        .align  2
        .global main
        .type   main, %function
❶ main:
        ❷ mov     w0, wzr  // return 0;
        ret
```

Listing 10-4: The minimum C-style program written in assembly language

The first line begins with two slashes, //. Everything after those two characters, up to the end of the line, is a comment and does not generate any action by the assembler. Comments can be started with two slashes at any place on a line. As in a high-level language, they are intended solely for human readers and have no effect on the program.

This comment line is followed by a blank line, also causing no action by the assembler, but very helpful for human readability.

A word about program comments here. Beginners often comment on what the programming statement does, not its purpose relative to solving the problem. Your comments should describe what *you* are doing, not what the computer is doing. For example, a comment like

```
counter = 1;  // Let counter = 1
```

in C is not very useful. But a comment like

```
counter = 1;  // Need to start at 1
```

could be very helpful.

After the five assembler directives that we're using in our assembly language programs (described in the previous section), we see the label main on the first memory address in this function ❶. It's common to place a label on its own line, in which case it applies to the address of the next assembly language statement that takes up memory ❷. This allows you to create longer, more meaningful labels while maintaining the column organization of your code, to improve readability.

Symbolic Names in Assembly Language

Since this is the top-level function in this program, the label main is required, but we'll soon be writing programs that require us to create our own names. The rules for creating a symbolic name are similar to those for C/C++. Each name starts with either a letter or the character . or _ followed by a string of letters, numerals, and/or $ and _ characters. The first character must not be a numeral, except for local labels, as described shortly. A name may be any length, and all characters are significant. Although the letter case of keywords (operators, register names, directives) is not significant, it is significant for labels. For example, my_label and My_label are different. Compiler-generated labels begin with the . character, and many system-related names begin with the _ character; it's a good idea to avoid beginning your own labels with these characters so you don't inadvertently create one that's already being used by the system.

Our assembler also allows us to use an unsigned integer, N, to create a *local label*. Your assembly language code can refer to these labels as Nb for the most recently used (N *backward*) and Nf for the next used (N *forward*). This means you can have more than one local label with the same number. While it might seem to simplify your code writing, using local labels is usually not a good programming technique because the names don't show the purpose of the labels.

Basic Format of Assembly Language Instructions

ARM instructions fall into three categories: load and store, data processing, and program flow control. We'll start by looking at the general format of the assembly language instruction. Rather than list all the A64 instructions, I will introduce a few at a time—the ones that will be needed to illustrate the programming concept at hand. I will also give only the commonly used variants of those instructions.

For a detailed description of the instructions and all their variants, download a copy of the *Arm Architecture Reference Manual for A-Profile Architecture* from *https://developer.arm.com/documentation/ddi0487/latest*. This manual can be a little difficult to read, but going back and forth between my descriptions of the instructions in this book and the descriptions in the manual should help you learn how to read the manual.

Assembly language provides a set of mnemonics that correspond directly to the machine language instructions. A *mnemonic* is a short, English-like group of characters that suggests the action of the instruction. Even if you've never seen assembly language before, the mov w0, wzr instruction in Listing 10-4 ❷ probably makes much more sense to you than the machine code it represents, 0x2a1f03e0. You can probably figure out that it moves the contents of the 32-bit zero register wzr to the w0 register. You'll see what that means in the next few paragraphs.

Strictly speaking, the mnemonics are completely arbitrary, as long as you have an assembler program that will translate them into the desired machine instructions. However, most assembler programs follow the mnemonics used in the manuals provided by CPU vendors.

ARM uses a *load and store architecture*, which means data items must be loaded into registers or be part of the instruction itself before they can be used in an arithmetic or logic operation.

The general format of a load or store instruction is:

```
operation register, memory_address
```

The memory_address is either a label on a memory address or the name of a register that contains the address. Load instructions copy the data item from the memory_address to the register. Store instructions copy the data item from the register to the memory_address. In most cases, you will be dealing with only one data item for each load or store instruction, but the A64 architecture includes load and store instructions that allow you to work with two data items in separate registers with one instruction. You'll see how this works in Chapter 11.

Data processing instructions—arithmetic and logic operations—have the general format:

```
operation register(s), source(s)
```

The first operand is where the result of the *operation* is placed. Some instructions use two registers for the results. There can be from one to three *source(s)*, which are registers or an *immediate value*. An immediate value is an explicit constant.

Instructions that control program flow have the general format

---
operation memory_address
---

or:

---
operation data, memory_address

The memory_address is either a label on a memory address or the name of a register that contains the address. The *data* must be in a register or an immediate value.

Symbols Used for Instruction Descriptions

Here is a list of symbols I'll use for describing instructions in this book, which are a little different from those used in the Arm manual:

wd A 32-bit destination register for the result of an operation.

xd A 64-bit destination register for the result of an operation.

ws, wn A 32-bit source register for an operation. If there's more than one source register, they are numbered.

xs, xn A 64-bit source register for an operation. If there's more than one source register, they are numbered.

xb, xn A 64-bit register that holds a base address.

offset A constant number that is added to a base address.

imm A constant number whose size depends on the instruction.

amnt The number of bits to shift a source operand.

addr An address, typically a label.

cond A logical combination of the bits in the nzcv register.

xtnd Specifies a wider version of an operand to use in an operation.

{} Indicates one or more operands that are optional.

| Indicates that either the operand on the left or the operand on the right can be used.

The registers can be any of the 31 general-purpose registers described in Chapter 9. Most instructions also allow us to use the wzr, xzr, wsp, and sp registers.

First Instructions

Again, I won't describe all the instructions, nor will I describe all the variants of the instructions that I do describe. My aim is to equip you with the information you need to understand the programming concepts I introduce in this book and to be comfortable using other sources as needed.

Let's start with the most commonly used assembly language instruction, mov. Some of the variations of this instruction follow; you can find more in the Arm manual:

mov—Move register

mov wd, ws|wzr copies the 32-bit value in ws or wzr to wd and zeros bits 63 to 32 of xd.

mov xd, xs|xzr copies the 64-bit value in xs or xzr to xd.

mov—Move to or from sp

mov xd|sp, xs|sp copies the 64-bit value in xs or sp to xd or sp.

mov—Move immediate

mov wd, imm copies the 16-bit value imm to the low-order part of wd and zeros bits 63 to 16 of xd.

mov xd, imm copies the 16-bit value imm to the low-order part of xd and zeros bits 63 to 16 of xd.

movz—Move immediate and zero

movz wd, imm{, lsl amnt} copies the 16-bit value imm to wd, optionally shifted amnt bits to the left. The other 48 bits of xd are set to 0. amnt can be 0 (the default) or 16.

movz xd, imm{, lsl amnt} copies the 16-bit value imm to xd, optionally shifted amnt bits to the left. The other 48 bits of xd are set to 0. amnt can be 0 (the default), 16, 32, or 48.

movk—Move immediate and keep

movk wd, imm{, lsl amnt} copies the 16-bit value imm to wd, optionally shifted amnt bits to the left. The other 48 bits of xd are not changed. amnt can be 0 (the default) or 16.

movk xd, imm{, lsl amnt} copies the 16-bit value imm to xd, optionally shifted amnt bits to the left. The other 48 bits of xd are not changed. amnt can be 0 (the default), 16, 32, or 48.

movn—Move immediate and NOT

movn wd, imm{, lsl amnt} copies the inverse of the 16-bit value imm to wd, optionally shifted amnt bits to the left. The other 48 bits of xd are set to 1. amnt can be 0 (the default) or 16.

movn xd, imm{, lsl amnt} copies the inverse of the 16-bit value in imm to xd, optionally shifted amnt bits to the left. The other 48 bits of xd are set to 1. amnt can be 0 (the default), 16, 32, or 48.

The only other instruction in Listing 10-4 is a ret, which causes a return to the calling function, assuming the return address is in x30:

ret—Return from a function

ret moves the address in x30 to the program counter, pc.

Now you see why I said in Chapter 9 that x30 is commonly used as the link register: when a function is called, the return address is placed in x30. We'll see how this works when we look at function calls in Chapter 11.

One of the most valuable uses of gdb is as a learning tool. It has a mode that is especially helpful in learning what each assembly language instruction does. I'll show you how to do this in the next section, using the program in Listing 10-4. This will also help you to become more familiar with using gdb, which is an important skill to have when debugging your programs.

Using gdb to Learn Assembly Language

This would be a good place for you to run the program in Listing 10-4 so you can follow along with the discussion. You can assemble, link, and execute it with the following commands:

```
$ as --gstabs -o do_nothing.o do_nothing.s
$ gcc -o do_nothing do_nothing.o
$ ./do_nothing
```

The --gstabs option (note the two dashes here) tells the assembler to include debugging information with the object file. The gcc program recognizes that the only input file is already an object file, so it goes directly to the linking stage. There is no need to tell gcc to include the debugging information, because the assembler already included it in the object file.

As you might guess from the name, you won't see anything on the screen when you run this program. We'll use gdb to walk through the execution of the program, which will allow us to see that this program actually does do something.

The gdb debugger has a mode that's useful for seeing the effects of each assembly language instruction as it's executed. The *text user interface (TUI)* mode splits the terminal window into a display pane at the top and the usual command pane at the bottom. The display pane can be further split into two display panes.

Each display pane can show either the source code (src), the registers (regs), or the disassembled machine code (asm). *Disassembly* is the process of translating the machine code (1s and 0s) into the corresponding assembly language. The disassembly process does not know the programmer-defined names, so you will see only the numerical values that were generated by the assembly and linking processes. The asm display will probably be more useful when we look at the details of instructions in Chapter 12.

The documentation for using the TUI mode is in info for gdb. I'll give a simple introduction to using the TUI mode here, using our assembly language version of do_nothing from Listing 10-4. I'll step through each of the instructions. You'll get a chance to single-step through each of them in "Your Turn" exercise 10.1 on page 205.

 *My example here shows gdb being run from the command line. I've been told that this doesn't work well if you try to run gdb within Emacs.*

As we did in Chapter 2, we'll run do_nothing under gdb, but this time we'll use the TUI mode:

```
$ gdb -tui ./do_nothing
```

This should bring up a screen like the one in Figure 10-1. Note that Figures 10-1 through 10-7 are zoomed in for readability; your screen view may look different, depending on your terminal window settings.

```
┌─do_nothing.s────────────────────────────────────────────────────────┐
│     1    // Minimum components of a C program, in assembly language  │
│     2                                                                │
│     3            .arch    armv8-a                                    │
│     4            .text                                               │
│     5            .align   2                                          │
│     6            .global  main                                       │
│     7            .type    main, %function                            │
│     8    main:                                                       │
│     9            mov      w0, wzr          // return 0;              │
│    10            ret                                                 │
│    11                                                                │
│    12                                                                │
│    13                                                                │
│    14                                                                │
│    15                                                                │
│    16                                                                │
│    17                                                                │
│    18                                                                │
│    19                                                                │
│    20                                                                │
│    21                                                                │
│exec No process In:                               L??    PC: ??      │
│This GDB was configured as "aarch64-linux-gnu".                      │
│Type "show configuration" for configuration details.                 │
│For bug reporting instructions, please see:                          │
│<https://www.gnu.org/software/gdb/bugs/>.                            │
│--Type <RET> for more, q to quit, c to continue without paging--cFind th│
│e GDB manual and other documentation resources online at:            │
│    <http://www.gnu.org/software/gdb/documentation/>.                │
│                                                                      │
│For help, type "help".                                               │
│Type "apropos word" to search for commands related to "word"...      │
│Reading symbols from ./do_nothing...                                 │
│(gdb) ▯                                                              │
```

Figure 10-1: Starting gdb in TUI mode gives the src display.

Enter c to continue through the preliminary message shown in this screenshot.

Next, set a breakpoint at the first instruction of the program and set a display layout. There are several display layouts available in TUI mode. We'll use the regs layout, shown in Figure 10-2.

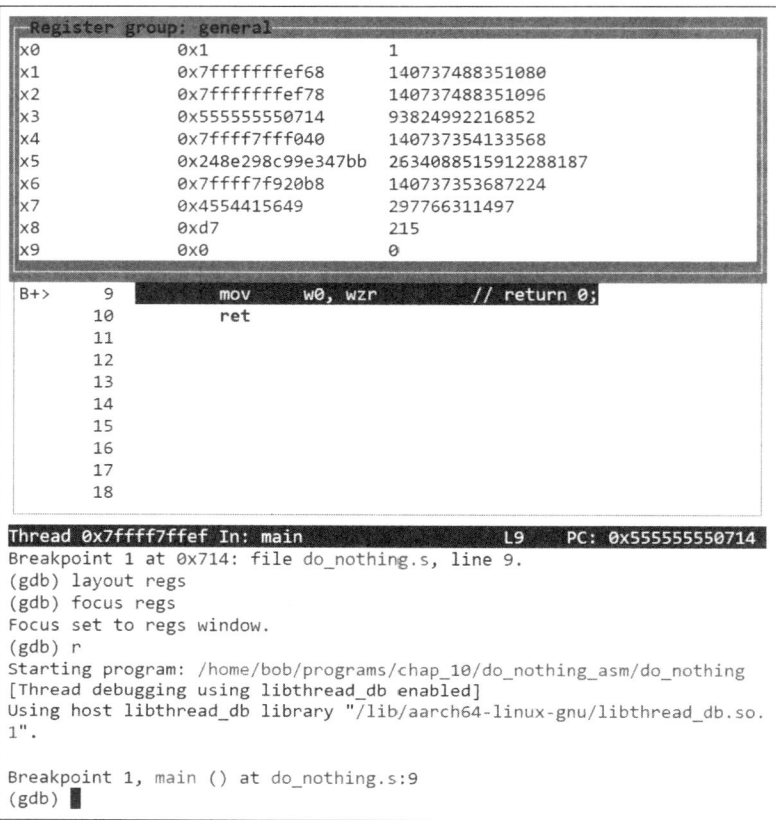

```
 Register group: general
x0              0x1                   1
x1              0x7fffffffef68        140737488351080
x2              0x7fffffffef78        140737488351096
x3              0x555555550714        93824992216852
x4              0x7ffff7fff040        140737354133568
x5              0x248e298c99e347bb    2634088515912288187
x6              0x7ffff7f920b8        140737353687224
x7              0x4554415649          297766311497
x8              0xd7                  215
x9              0x0                   0

B+>      9              mov     w0, wzr         // return 0;
        10              ret
        11
        12
        13
        14
        15
        16
        17
        18

Thread 0x7ffff7ffef In: main            L9    PC: 0x555555550714
Breakpoint 1 at 0x714: file do_nothing.s, line 9.
(gdb) layout regs
(gdb) focus regs
Focus set to regs window.
(gdb) r
Starting program: /home/bob/programs/chap_10/do_nothing_asm/do_nothing
[Thread debugging using libthread_db enabled]
Using host libthread_db library "/lib/aarch64-linux-gnu/libthread_db.so.
1".

Breakpoint 1, main () at do_nothing.s:9
(gdb)
```

Figure 10-2: Adding the regs *display pane to the TUI window*

The layout regs command divides the display pane into a regs pane and
an src pane. I've moved the focus to the regs pane before telling gdb to run
the program. The program starts with a 0x1 in the x0 register (your value
may differ). The instruction in the program that is about to be executed is
highlighted.

The display isn't large enough to show all the A64 registers. With the
focus on the regs pane, use the up and down arrow keys and the page up
and page down keys to scroll through the register display. I pressed the page
down key three times to get Figure 10-3.

```
Register group: general
x27              0x55555556fdd0      93824992345552
x28              0x0                 0
x29              0x7fffffffedf0      140737488350704
x30              0x7ffff7e17780      140737352136576
sp               0x7fffffffedf0      0x7fffffffedf0
pc               0x555555550714      0x555555550714 <main>
cpsr             0x80001000          [ EL=0 BTYPE=0 SSBS N ]
fpsr             0x0                 [ ]
fpcr             0x0                 [ Len=0 Stride=0 RMode=0 ]
tpidr            0x7ffff7fff640      0x7ffff7fff640

B+>      9              mov     w0, wzr         // return 0;
        10              ret
        11
        12
        13
        14
        15
        16
        17
        18

Thread 0x7ffff7ffef In: main              L9    PC: 0x555555550714
Breakpoint 1 at 0x714: file do_nothing.s, line 9.
(gdb) layout regs
(gdb) focus regs
Focus set to regs window.
(gdb) r
Starting program: /home/bob/programs/chap_10/do_nothing_asm/do_nothing
[Thread debugging using libthread_db enabled]
Using host libthread_db library "/lib/aarch64-linux-gnu/libthread_db.so.
1".

Breakpoint 1, main () at do_nothing.s:9
(gdb) █
```

Figure 10-3: Viewing other registers

The value in x30 shows the location the program will return to in the C hosted environment when it completes execution. You'll see how this works in Figure 10-6. The value in pc is the address of the first instruction in our main function.

Let's tell gdb to execute a single instruction, as shown in Figure 10-4.

Figure 10-4: Changes in the registers are highlighted.

In Figure 10-4, gdb highlights the next instruction to be executed as well as the registers that were changed. We knew pc would change, since we executed one instruction.

The instruction that was executed changed x0, but that doesn't show in our regs display pane in Figure 10-4. I used the page up key to give the view of x0 in Figure 10-5.

```
 Register group: general
x0              0x0                0
x1              0x7fffffffef68     140737488351080
x2              0x7fffffffef78     140737488351096
x3              0x555555550714     93824992216852
x4              0x7ffff7fff040     140737354133568
x5              0x248e298c99e347bb 2634088515912288187
x6              0x7ffff7f920b8     140737353687224
x7              0x4554415649       297766311497
x8              0xd7               215
x9              0x0                0

 B+     9          mov    w0, wzr           // return 0;
  >     10         ret
        11
        12
        13
        14
        15
        16
        17
        18

 Thread 0x7ffff7ffef In: main                L10    PC: 0x555555550718
(gdb) layout regs
(gdb) focus regs
Focus set to regs window.
(gdb) r
Starting program: /home/bob/programs/chap_10/do_nothing_asm/do_nothing
[Thread debugging using libthread_db enabled]
Using host libthread_db library "/lib/aarch64-linux-gnu/libthread_db.so.
1".

Breakpoint 1, main () at do_nothing.s:9
(gdb) si
(gdb)
```

Figure 10-5: Viewing the register changed by the instruction that was just executed

The x0 register is highlighted in Figure 10-5 to show that it changed.

Next, we'll tell gdb to execute the ret instruction, which should take us back to the C hosted environment, as shown in Figure 10-6.

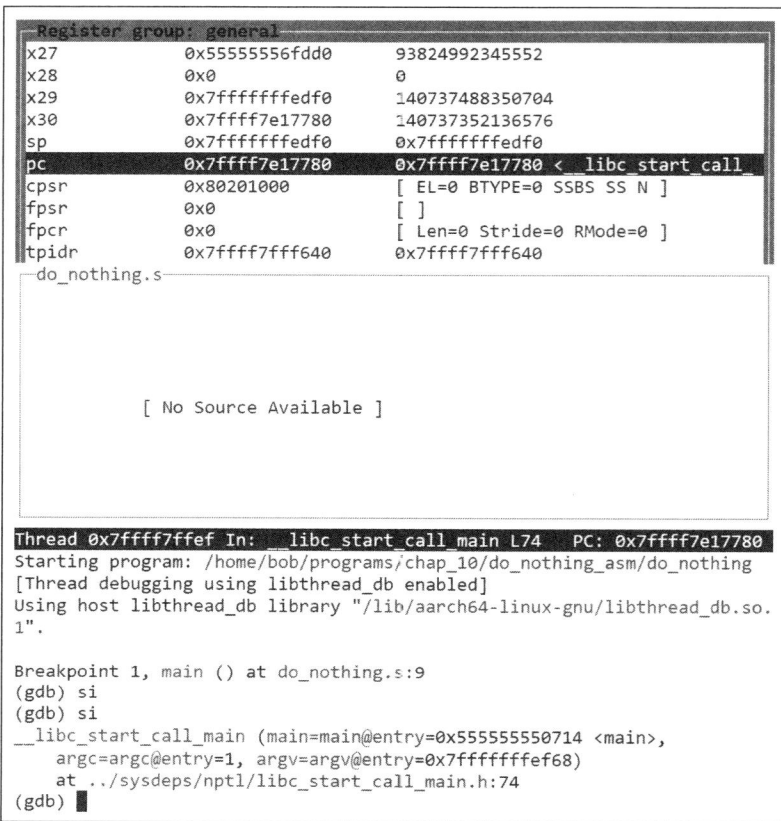

```
┌─Register group: general─────────────────────────────────────────
│x27          0x55555556fdd0        93824992345552
│x28          0x0                   0
│x29          0x7fffffffedf0        140737488350704
│x30          0x7ffff7e17780        140737352136576
│sp           0x7fffffffedf0        0x7fffffffedf0
│pc           0x7ffff7e17780        0x7ffff7e17780 <__libc_start_call_
│cpsr         0x80201000            [ EL=0 BTYPE=0 SSBS SS N ]
│fpsr         0x0                   [ ]
│fpcr         0x0                   [ Len=0 Stride=0 RMode=0 ]
│tpidr        0x7ffff7fff640        0x7ffff7fff640
┌─do_nothing.s─────────────────────────────────────────────────────



                    [ No Source Available ]




┌Thread 0x7ffff7ffef In: __libc_start_call_main L74   PC: 0x7ffff7e17780
Starting program: /home/bob/programs/chap_10/do_nothing_asm/do_nothing
[Thread debugging using libthread_db enabled]
Using host libthread_db library "/lib/aarch64-linux-gnu/libthread_db.so.
1".

Breakpoint 1, main () at do_nothing.s:9
(gdb) si
(gdb) si
__libc_start_call_main (main=main@entry=0x555555550714 <main>,
    argc=argc@entry=1, argv=argv@entry=0x7fffffffef68)
    at ../sysdeps/nptl/libc_start_call_main.h:74
(gdb) █
```

Figure 10-6: Back in the C hosted environment

The ret instruction has copied the address from the link register, x30, to pc, thus implementing the return from the main function.

Finally, we continue execution of the program in Figure 10-7.

```
Register group: general
x27              0x55555556fdd0        93824992345552
x28              0x0                   0
x29              0x7fffffffedf0        140737488350704
x30              0x7ffff7e17780        140737352136576
sp               0x7fffffffedf0        0x7fffffffedf0
pc               0x7ffff7e17780        0x7ffff7e17780 <__libc_start_call_
cpsr             0x80201000            [ EL=0 BTYPE=0 SSBS SS N ]
fpsr             0x0                   [ ]
fpcr             0x0                   [ Len=0 Stride=0 RMode=0 ]
tpidr            0x7ffff7fff640        0x7ffff7fff640
┌─do_nothing.s──────────────────────────────────────────────────────┐
│                                                                     │
│                                                                     │
│                                                                     │
│                                                                     │
│               [ No Source Available ]                               │
│                                                                     │
│                                                                     │
│                                                                     │
└─────────────────────────────────────────────────────────────────────┘
multi-thre No process In:                              L??    PC: ??
1".

Breakpoint 1, main () at do_nothing.s:9
(gdb) si
(gdb) si
__libc_start_call_main (main=main@entry=0x555555550714 <main>,
    argc=argc@entry=1, argv=argv@entry=0x7fffffffef68)
    at ../sysdeps/nptl/libc_start_call_main.h:74
(gdb) c
Continuing.
[Inferior 1 (process 4026) exited normally]
(gdb) █
```

Figure 10-7: The program has completed.

All that remains is to quit gdb.

YOUR TURN

10.1   Enter the program in Listing 10-4 and use gdb to single-step through
        the code.

10.2   Write the following C function in assembly language:

```
int f(void) {

    return 0;
}
```

(continued)

Make sure it assembles with no errors. Use the -S option to compile f.c and compare gcc's assembly language with yours. Write a main function in C that tests your assembly language function, f, and prints out the function's return value.

10.3   Write three assembly language functions that do nothing but return an integer. They should each return a different nonzero integer. Write a main function in C that tests your assembly language functions and prints out the functions' return values using printf.

10.4   Write three assembly language functions that do nothing but return a character. Each should return a different character. Write a main function in C that tests your assembly language functions and prints out the functions' return values using printf.

What You've Learned

Editor   A program used to write the source code for a program in the chosen programming language.

Preprocessing   The first stage of compilation. It brings other files into the source, interprets directives, and so forth, in preparation for actual compilation.

Compilation   Translates from the chosen programming language into assembly language.

Assembly   Translates assembly language into machine language.

Linking   Links separate object code modules and libraries together to produce the final executable program.

Assembler directives   Guide the assembler program during the assembly process.

mov instruction   Moves values within the CPU.

ret instruction   Returns program flow to the calling function.

gdb TUI mode   Displays changes in registers in real time as you step through a program. It's an excellent learning tool.

You might be wondering what happens to the return address in x30 if we call another function from main. To use x30 as the link register to call the other function, we need to save the return address somewhere while the other function is being executed. You'll learn how to do this in the next chapter, where we look at the details of how to pass arguments to functions, how to use the call stack, and how to create local variables in functions.

11

INSIDE THE MAIN FUNCTION

As you learned in Chapter 10, a C program begins by executing a function named main, which is called from a startup function in the C hosted environment. The main function will call other functions (*subfunctions*) to do most of the processing. Even a simple "Hello, World!" program needs to call another function to write the message on the screen.

In this chapter, we'll focus on the main function, but the concepts apply to all the functions we'll be writing. We'll begin with a detailed look at the call stack, which is used for saving values and for local variables. Then we'll look at how to process data in a function and how to pass arguments to other functions. I'll wrap up the chapter by showing you how to use this knowledge to write the main function in assembly language.

Using the Call Stack

The *call stack*, commonly referred to simply as the *stack*, is a very useful place for creating local variables and saving items within a function. Before we cover how to use the stack for these purposes, you need to understand what stacks are and how they work.

Stacks in General

A stack is a linear data structure created in memory to store data items. Insertion of a data item onto (or deletion from) a stack can be done at only one end, called the *top*. Programs keep track of the top of the stack with a *stack pointer*.

Informally, you can think of a stack as being organized like a stack of dinner plates on a shelf. You need to be able to access only the item at the top of the stack. (And, yes, if you pull out a plate from somewhere within the stack, you will probably break something.) There are two fundamental operations on a stack:

push *data_item*   Places the *data_item* at the top of the stack and moves the stack pointer to point to this latest item

pop *location*   Moves the data item at the top of the stack to *location* and moves the stack pointer to point to the item now at the top of the stack

The stack is a *last in, first out (LIFO)* data structure. The last thing to be pushed onto the stack is the first thing to be popped off.

To illustrate the stack concept, let's continue with the dinner plate example. Say we have three differently colored dinner plates: a red one on the dining table, a green one on the kitchen counter, and a blue one on the bedside table. We'll stack them on the shelf in the following way:

1.   Push red plate.

2.   Push green plate.

3.   Push blue plate.

At this point, our stack of plates looks like Figure 11-1.

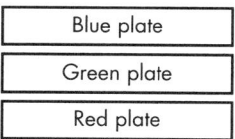

Figure 11-1: Three dinner plates in a stack

Now we perform the next operation:

4.   Pop kitchen counter.

This moves the blue plate to the kitchen counter (recall that the blue plate was previously on the bedside table) and leaves the stack of dinner plates as shown in Figure 11-2.

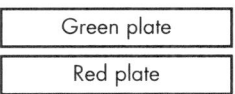

Figure 11-2: One dinner
plate has been popped
from the stack.

If you have guessed that it's easy to really mess up a stack, you're right. A stack must be used according to a strict discipline. Within any function:

- Always push an item onto the stack before popping anything off.

- Never pop more things off than you have pushed on.

- Always pop everything off the stack that you have pushed on.

If you have no use for the item(s) that you have pushed onto the stack, you may simply set the stack pointer to where it was when the function was first entered. This is equivalent to discarding the items that are popped off. (Our dinner plate analogy breaks down here.)

A good way to maintain this discipline is to think of the use of parentheses in an algebraic expression. A push is analogous to a left parenthesis and a pop to a right parenthesis. The pairs of parentheses can be nested, but they have to match. An attempt to push too many items onto a stack is called *stack overflow*. An attempt to pop items off the stack beyond the bottom is called *stack underflow*.

A stack is implemented by dedicating a contiguous area of main memory to it. Stacks can grow in either direction in memory, into higher addresses or lower. An *ascending stack* grows into higher addresses, and a *descending stack* grows into lower addresses. The stack pointer can point to the top item on the stack, a *full stack*, or to the memory location where the next item will be pushed onto the stack, an *empty stack*. These four possible stack implementations are shown in Figure 11-3, with the integers 1, 2, and 3 pushed onto the stack in that order. Notice that memory addresses are *increasing downward* in this figure, which is the way we usually view them in the gdb debugger.

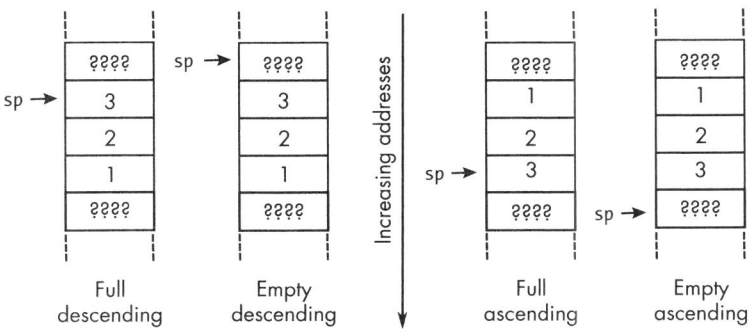

Figure 11-3: Four ways to implement a stack

The call stack in our environment is a *full descending stack*. To understand this choice, think about how you might organize things in memory. Recall that the control unit automatically increments the program counter as your program is executed. Programs come in vastly different sizes, so storing the program instructions at low memory addresses allows maximum flexibility with respect to program size.

The stack is a dynamic structure. You don't know how much stack space will be required by any given program as it executes, so it's impossible to know how much space to allocate. To allocate as much space as possible, while preventing it from colliding with program instructions, start the stack at the highest memory address and have it grow toward lower addresses.

This is a highly simplified rationalization for implementing stacks that grow "downward" in memory. The organization of various program elements in memory is much more complex than the description given here, but this may help you understand that there are some good reasons for what may seem to be a rather odd implementation.

The A64 architecture does not have push and pop instructions. It has instructions that allow you to effectively push items onto or pop items off of the stack, but most of the operations on the stack are done by allocating memory on the call stack and then directly storing items into or loading items from this allocated memory. Next, we'll look at how functions use the call stack.

The Stack Frame

Each function that calls another function needs to allocate memory on the stack for that function to use to save items and store local variables. This allocated memory is called a *stack frame* or *activation record*. To see how this works, we'll start with a program that has one local variable and calls two functions in the C standard library: printf and scanf. The program is shown in Listing 11-1.

inc_int.c
```
// Increment an integer.

#include <stdio.h>

int main(void)
{
    int x;

    printf("Enter an integer: ");
    scanf("%i", &x);
    x++;
    printf("Result: %i\n", x);
```

```
        return 0;
}
```

Listing 11-1: A program to increment an integer

You can see how a stack frame is created by looking at the assembly language generated by the compiler, shown in Listing 11-2. I'll be referring to the numbered lines in this listing in the next several sections of this chapter, through page 222.

inc_int.s
```
            .arch armv8-a
            .file   "inc_int.c"
            .text
❶ .section         .rodata
            .align  3
.LC0:
            .string "Enter an integer: "
            .align  3
.LC1:
❷ .string "%i"
            .align  3
.LC2:
            .string "Result: %i\n"
            .text
            .align  2
            .global main
            .type   main, %function
main:
❸ stp    x29, x30, [sp, -32]!  /// Create stack frame
    mov    x29, sp               /// Set our frame pointer
    adrp   x0, .LC0              /// Page address
    add    x0, x0, :lo12:.LC0    /// Offset in page
    bl     printf
❹ add    x0, sp, 28            /// Address of x
    mov    x1, x0
❺ adrp   x0, .LC1
    add    x0, x0, :lo12:.LC1
    bl     __isoc99_scanf
❻ ldr    w0, [sp, 28]          /// Load int
    add    w0, w0, 1
❼ str    w0, [sp, 28]          /// x++;
    ldr    w0, [sp, 28]
    mov    w1, w0
    adrp   x0, .LC2
    add    x0, x0, :lo12:.LC2
```

```
        bl      printf
        mov     w0, 0
❸ ldp      x29, x30, [sp], 32
        ret
        .size   main, .-main
        .ident  "GCC: (Debian 10.2.1-6) 10.2.1 20210110"
        .section        .note.GNU-stack,"",@progbits
```

Listing 11-2: The compiler-generated assembly language for the program in Listing 11-1

The instructions used to create the stack frame form the *function prologue*. The first instruction in a function prologue is usually an stp instruction:

stp—Store register pair

stp ws1, ws2, [xb{, offset}] stores the value in ws1 at the address in xb and the value in ws2 at xb + 4. If offset exists, it must be a multiple of 4 and is added to the address before storing the register values; xb is not changed.

stp xs1, xs2, [xb{, offset}] stores the value in xs1 at the address in xb and the value in xs2 at xb + 8. If offset exists, it must be a multiple of 8 and is added to the address before storing the register values; xb is not changed.

stp—Store register pair, pre-index

stp ws1, ws2, [xb, offset]! adds offset, which must be a multiple of 4, to xb. It then stores the value in ws1 at the new address in xb and the value in ws2 at xb + 4.

stp xs1, xs2, [xb, offset]! adds offset, which must be a multiple of 8, to xb. It then stores the value in xs1 at the new address in xb and the value in xs2 at xb + 8.

stp—Store register pair, post-index

stp ws1, ws2, [xb], offset stores the value in ws1 at the address in xb and the value in ws2 at xb + 4. It then adds offset, which must be a multiple of 4, to xb.

stp xs1, xs2, [xb], offset stores the value in xs1 at the address in xb and the value in xs2 at xb + 8. It then adds offset, which must be a multiple of 8, to xb.

NOTE *The operand order for almost all other A64 instructions is* destination(s), source(s), *but for the store instructions, it's the opposite.*

Almost all the functions we'll write will begin with an stp instruction that looks like this:

```
stp     x29, x30, [sp, -32]!
```

The compiler did this at the beginning of the function in Listing 11-2, creating the stack frame ❸.

The *Procedure Call Standard for the Arm 64-Bit Architecture (AArch64)* documentation (available in PDF and HTML formats at *https://github.com/ARM-software/abi-aa/releases*) specifies that the *frame pointer* (stored in register x29, also named fp) should point to the top of the stack frame, which is where the calling function's frame pointer is stored. The instruction mov x29, sp will set the called function's frame pointer, as shown in Listing 11-2.

The way the stp instruction has specified the stack memory address here, [sp, -32]!, probably doesn't make a lot of sense to you. Let's look at how instructions access memory in the A64 architecture.

A64 Memory Addressing

There are two ways that an instruction might refer to a memory address: the address could be encoded as part of the instruction, usually called an *absolute address*, or it could use *relative addressing*, where the instruction specifies an *offset* from a *base address*. In the latter case, the size of the offset and the location of the base address are encoded in the instruction.

All instructions in the A64 architecture are 32 bits long, but addresses are 64 bits long. We'll look at the details of the machine code in Chapter 12, but it's clear that a 64-bit address will not fit within a 32-bit instruction. To refer to a 64-bit address, instructions use one of the relative addressing modes listed in Table 11-1 to compute the address when they are executed.

Table 11-1: A64 Addressing Modes

Mode	Syntax	Note
Literal	*label*	pc-relative
Base register	[*base*]	Register only
Base plus offset	[*base, offset*]	Register-relative
Pre-indexed	[*base, offset*]!	Add offset to register before
Post-indexed	[*base*], *offset*	Add offset to register after

Each of the addressing modes in Table 11-1 starts with a 64-bit address in a *base register*. The literal mode uses *pc-relative addressing*, where the program counter serves as the base register. If *label* is in the same section as the instruction that references it, the assembler computes the address offset from the referencing instruction to the labeled instruction and fills in this offset as part of the referencing instruction. If the label is in another section, the linker will compute the offset and fill that in where the label is referenced. The number of bits allowed in the instruction limits the size of the address offset.

One of the advantages of pc-relative addressing is that it gives us *position-independent code (PIC)*, which means the function will execute correctly no matter where it is loaded into memory. The default for the gcc compiler in our environment is to produce PIC, with the linking phase producing a *position-independent executable (PIE)*. This means the linker doesn't specify a load address for the program, so the operating system can load the program wherever it chooses. Not including the load address with the executable file improves security.

In the other four modes, the base register is a general-purpose register, x0–x30, or sp. For the base-plus-offset mode, the offset can be an immediate value or in a register. The offset is sign-extended to 64 bits and added to the value in the base register to compute the address. If the offset is in a register, it can be scaled so that it is a multiple of the number of bytes being loaded or stored. You'll see how this works when you learn to process integer arrays in Chapter 17.

In the pre-indexed mode, the computed address is stored in the base register *before* loading or storing the value. In the post-indexed mode, the computed address is stored in the base register *after* loading or storing the value.

For the pre-indexed mode, the offset can only be an immediate value. The post-indexed mode allows an immediate value for the offset or, for some advanced programming techniques, an offset value in a register.

The call stack in our environment is full-descending (see Figure 11-3), so the stp instruction uses the pre-indexed addressing mode. In the function in Listing 11-2, the address is specified as [sp, -32]! ❸. This subtracts 32 from the stack pointer *before* storing the caller's frame pointer and return address on the stack. This effectively allocates 16 bytes on the stack for this function's use, then pushes the return address and the caller's frame pointer onto the call stack. The number of bytes allocated for the stack frame must always be a multiple of 16 because the stack pointer, sp, must always be aligned on a 16-byte address boundary.

After the function has completed its processing, we need a *function epilogue* to restore the caller's frame pointer and link register and to delete the stack frame. In the function in Listing 11-2, this is done with the following instruction:

```
ldp    x29, x30, [sp], 32
```

This instruction loads the two values at the top of the stack into the frame pointer and link register, then adds 32 to the stack pointer ❸. This effectively pops the two values off the top of the stack into the x29 and x30 registers and then deletes this function's stack frame. Let's look at some variants of the ldp instruction, which allows us to load two values at a time from memory:

ldp—Load register pair

ldp wd1, wd2, [xb{, offset}] loads the value at the address in xb into wd1 and the value at xb + 4 into wd2. If offset exists, it must be a multiple of 4 and is added to the address before loading the values; xb is not changed.

ldp xd1, xd2, [xb{, offset}] loads the value at the address in xb into xd1 and the value at xb + 8 into xd2. If offset exists, it must be a multiple of 8 and is added to the address before loading the values; xb is not changed.

ldp—Load register pair, pre-index

ldp wd1, wd2, [xb, offset]! adds offset, which must be a multiple of 4, to xb. It then loads the value at the new address in xb into wd1 and the value at xb + 4 into wd2.

ldp xd1, xd2, [xb, offset]! adds offset, which must be a multiple of 8, to xb. It then loads the value at the new address in xb into xd1 and the value at xb + 8 into xd2.

ldp—Load register pair, post-index

ldp wd1, wd2, [xb], offset loads the value at the address in xb into wd1 and the value at xb + 4 into wd2. It then adds offset, which must be a multiple of 4, to xb.

ldp xd1, xd2, [xb], offset loads the value at the address in xb into xd1 and the value at xb + 8 into xd2. It then adds offset, which must be a multiple of 8, to xb.

Next, we'll see how this function uses the other 16 bytes of stack memory.

Local Variables on the Call Stack

Local variables in C can be directly accessed by their names only in the function where they're defined. We can allow another function to access a local variable in our function, including changing its value, by passing the address of that variable to the other function. This is what enables scanf to store a value for x, as you'll see on page 221.

You learned in Chapter 9 that CPU registers can be used as variables. But if we were to use CPU registers to hold all of our variables, we'd soon run out of registers, even in a small program. So, we need to allocate space in memory for variables.

As we'll see later in this chapter, a function needs to preserve the contents of some registers for the calling function. If we want to use such a register in our function, a local variable would be a good place to store a copy of its content so we can restore it before returning to the calling function.

The stack frame meets the requirements of local variables. It's created when the function first starts, and it's deleted once the function completes. The memory in a stack frame is easily accessed using the base-plus-offset addressing mode (see Table 11-1), with sp as the base addressing register. An example in Listing 11-2 is where we load the integer:

```
ldr     w0, [sp, 28]
```

This instruction loads the 32-bit word located 28 bytes from the address in sp into w0 ❻. The function treats its stack frame as a record rather than a stack with this code. You'll learn about records in Chapter 17.

Figure 11-4 gives a pictorial view of the completed stack frame for the main function in Listings 11-1 and 11-2.

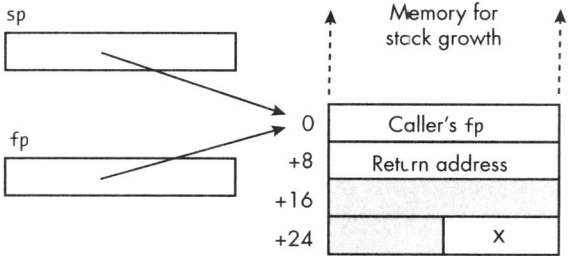

Figure 11-4: The stack frame for the function in Listings 11-1 and 11-2

The two addresses on the stack each take 8 bytes, and the int variable, x, takes 4 bytes. The memory in the gray area is unused but necessary for keeping the stack pointer, sp, aligned on a 16-byte address boundary.

Now that you know how to use a stack frame, let's look at how this function processes data.

Processing Data in a Function

A64 is a *load–store architecture*, which means the instructions that operate on data cannot access memory. There is a separate group of instructions for moving data to and from memory.

This is in contrast to a *register–memory architecture*, which includes instructions that can operate on data in memory. The data operations are still performed by the arithmetic/logic unit in the CPU (see Figure 9-1), but they use registers that are hidden from the programmer. The Intel x86 is an example of a register–memory architecture.

The processing in the main function in Listing 11-2 is very simple: the program adds 1 to an integer. But before it can perform this operation, it needs to load the value into a register using the ldr instruction ❻. Since this program changes the value in the variable, the new value must be stored back into memory with the str instruction ❼.

Let's look at some common instructions used for loading values from memory:

ldr—Load register, pc-relative

ldr *wd, addr* loads *wd* with the 32-bit value at memory location *addr*, which must be ±1MB from this instruction. Bits 63 to 32 of *xd* are set to 0.

ldr *xd, addr* loads *xd* with the 64-bit value at memory location *addr*, which must be ±1MB from this instruction.

ldr—Load register, base register–relative

ldr *wd,* [*xb*{, *offset*}] loads *wd* with the 32-bit value at the memory location obtained by adding the address in *xb* and the optional *offset*, which is a multiple of 4 in the range 0 to 16,380. Bits 63 to 32 of xd are set to 0.

ldr xd, [xb{, *offset*}] loads xd with the 64-bit value at the memory location obtained by adding the address in xb and the optional *offset*, which is a multiple of 8 in the range 0 to 32,760.

ldrsw—Load register, signed word, base register–relative
ldrsw wd, [xb{, *offset*}] loads wd with the 32-bit value at the memory location obtained by adding the address in xb and the optional *offset*, which is a multiple of 4 in the range 0 to 16,380. Bits 63 to 32 of xd are set to a copy of bit 31 of the loaded word.

ldrb—Load register, unsigned byte, base register–relative
ldrb wd, [xb{, *offset*}] loads the low-order byte of wd with the 8-bit value at the memory location obtained by adding the address in xb and the optional *offset*, which is in the range 0 to 4,095. Bits 31 to 8 of xd are set to 0; bits 63 to 32 are unchanged.

ldrsb—Load register, signed byte, base register–relative
ldrsb wd, [xb{, *offset*}] loads the low-order byte of wd with the 8-bit value at the memory location obtained by adding the address in xb and the optional *offset*, which is in the range 0 to 4,095. Bits 31 to 8 of xd are set to a copy of bit 7 of the loaded byte; bits 63 to 32 are unchanged.

Here are some similar instructions for storing values in memory:

str—Store register, pc-relative
str ws, *addr* stores the 32-bit value in ws at memory location *addr*, which must be ±1MB from this instruction.

str xs, *addr* stores the 64-bit value in xs at memory location *addr*, which must be ±1MB from this instruction.

str—Store register, base register–relative
str ws, [xb{, *offset*}] stores the 32-bit value in ws at the memory location obtained by adding the address in xb and the optional *offset*, which is a multiple of 4 in the range 0 to 16,380.

str xs, [xb{, *offset*}] stores the 64-bit value in xs at the memory location obtained by adding the address in xb and the optional *offset*, which is a multiple of 8 in the range 0 to 32,670.

strb—Store register, byte, base register–relative
strb ws, [xb{, *offset*}] stores the low-order 8 bits in ws at the memory location obtained by adding the address in xb and the optional *offset*, which is in the range 0 to 4,095.

The program simply adds 1 to the variable, which can be done with the add instruction. I'll include the sub instruction here because it's very similar, but I'll give only some basic syntax (both instructions have several options, which are described in the manuals):

add—Add extended register

add wd, ws1, ws2{, *xtnd amnt*} adds the values in ws1 and ws2 and stores the result in wd. The value added from ws2 can be a byte, halfword, word, or doubleword. It can be sign- or zero-extended and then left-shifted 0 to 4 bits before the addition, using the *xtnd amnt* option.

add xd, xs1, xs2{, *xtnd amnt*} adds the values in xs1 and xs2 and stores the result in xd. The value added from xs2 can be a byte, halfword, word, or doubleword. It can be sign- or zero-extended and then left-shifted 0 to 4 bits before the addition, using the *xtnd amnt* option.

add—Add immediate

add wd, ws, *imm*{, *shft*} adds *imm* to the value in ws and stores the result in wd. The *imm* operand is an unsigned integer in the range 0 to 4,095, which can be left-shifted 0 or 12 bits before the addition, using the *shft* option.

add xd, xs, *imm*{, *shft*} adds *imm* to the value in xs and stores the result in xd. The *imm* operand is an unsigned integer in the range 0 to 4,095, which can be left-shifted 0 or 12 bits before the addition, using the *shft* option.

sub—Subtract extended register

sub wd, ws1, ws2{, *xtnd amnt*} subtracts the value in ws2 from ws1 and stores the result in wd. The value subtracted from ws2 can be a byte, halfword, word, or doubleword. It can be sign- or zero-extended and then left-shifted 0 to 4 bits before the subtraction, using the *xtnd amnt* option.

sub xd, xs1, xs2{, *xtnd amnt*} subtracts the value in xs2 from xs1 and stores the result in xd. The value subtracted from xs2 can be a byte, halfword, word, or doubleword. It can be sign- or zero-extended and then left-shifted 0 to 4 bits before the subtraction, using the *xtnd amnt* option.

sub—Subtract immediate

sub wd, ws, *imm*{, *shft*} subtracts *imm* from the value in ws and stores the result in wd. The *imm* operand is an unsigned integer in the range 0 to 4,095, which can be left-shifted 0 or 12 bits before the subtraction, using the *shft* option.

sub xd, xs, *imm*{, *shft*} subtracts *imm* from the value in xs and stores the result in xd. The *imm* operand is an unsigned integer in the range 0 to 4,095, which can be left-shifted 0 or 12 bits before the subtraction, using the *shft* option.

Table 11-2 lists the allowable values for the *xtnd* option in the add and sub instructions.

Table 11-2: Allowable Values for *xtnd* in add and sub Instructions

xtnd	Effect
uxtb	Unsigned extension of byte
uxth	Unsigned extension of halfword
uxtw	Unsigned extension of word
uxtx	Unsigned extension of doubleword
sxtb	Signed extension of byte
sxth	Signed extension of halfword
sxtw	Signed extension of word
sxtx	Signed extension of doubleword

The extension begins with the indicated low-order portion of the source register and adds bits to the left to match the width of the other registers in the instruction. For unsigned extension, the added bits are all 0. For signed extension, the added bits are copies of the highest-order bit of the starting value. When using w registers, uxtw can be replaced with lsl; with x registers, uxtx can be replaced with lsl.

It might seem meaningless to extend a doubleword, which is already 64 bits wide, to match the size of an x register, but the instruction syntax requires that we use the entire *xtnd amnt* option if we wish to shift the value.

As an example of how these size extensions work, let's start with the following values in x2 and x3:

```
x2: 0xaaaaaaaaaaaaaaaa
x3: 0x89abba89fedccdef
```

The instruction sequence

```
add     w0, w3, w2, uxtb
add     w1, w3, w2, sxtb
```

gives:

```
x0: 0xfedcce99
x3: 0xfedccd99
```

We'll see other instructions that use these width extensions as we continue through the book.

Now that you know how to do the arithmetic, let's look at how to call the other functions.

Passing Arguments in Registers

There are several ways for a function to pass arguments to another function. I'll start by describing how to use registers for passing arguments. I'll discuss other ways when I cover subfunctions in more detail in Chapter 14.

Recall from Chapter 2 that when a function calls another function, it can pass arguments that the called function can use as parameters. In principle, the C compiler—or you, when you're writing in assembly language—could use any of the 31 general-purpose registers, except the link register, x30, to pass arguments from one function to another. Just store the arguments in the registers and call the desired function. Of course, the calling and called functions need to agree on exactly which register each argument is in.

The best way to avoid making mistakes is to follow a standard set of rules. This is especially important if more than one person is writing code for a program. Other people have realized the importance of having such standards and have developed an *application binary interface (ABI)* that includes a set of standards for passing arguments in the A64 architecture. The compiler we're using, gcc, follows the rules in the *Procedure Call Standard for the Arm 64-Bit Architecture* (referenced on page 213), and we'll do the same for the assembly language we write.

Table 11-3 summarizes the standards for how the called function uses the registers.

Table 11-3: General-Purpose Register Usage

Register	Usage	Save?
x0–x7	Parameter; result	No
x8	Address of result	No
x9–x18	Scratch	No
x19–x28	Variables	Yes
x29	Frame pointer	Yes
x30	Link register	Yes
sp	Stack pointer	Yes
xzr	Zero register	N/A

We would use *wn* instead of *xn* for 32-bit register names. We're using 64-bit addressing in this book. Because x29 and x30 will always contain addresses, we'll never use w29 or w30.

The "Save?" column shows whether a called function needs to preserve the value in that register for the calling function. If we need to use a register that must be preserved, we'll create a local variable in our stack frame for that purpose.

The calling function passes the arguments in the registers in the order in which they're listed, from left to right in a C function, starting with x0 (or w0 for a 32-bit value). This allows for the passing of up to eight arguments, x0–x7. You'll see how to use the call stack to pass more than eight arguments in Chapter 14.

For an example of how to pass arguments, let's look at the call to scanf in Listing 11-1:

```
scanf("%i", &x);
```

Let's start with the second argument, the address of x. In Figure 11-4, x is located at an offset of 28 bytes from the stack pointer, sp. Looking at the assembly language generated by the compiler in Listing 11-2, you can see that computing the address can be done by adding 28 to sp ❹. Since it's the second argument, it needs to be moved to x1.

The first argument—the text string "%i", which is created with a .string assembler directive ❷—is more complex. The general format for the .string directive is:

```
.string "text"
```

This creates a C-style text string as a char array with one byte for each character code point in *text*, plus one byte for the terminating NUL character.

The compiler places the three text strings in this program in the .rodata section ❶ of the object file. The loader/linker typically loads .rodata sections into the text segment following the executable code. Notice that each text string is aligned to an 8-byte (64 bits) address boundary with a .align 3 directive. This might make the code execute a little faster.

When you pass an array to a function in C, only the address of the first element in the array gets passed. So, the address of the first character of "%i" is passed to scanf. The A64 architecture provides two instructions for getting an address into a register:

adr—Address

adr *xd, addr* loads the memory address *addr* into *xd*; *addr* must be within ±1MB of this instruction.

adrp—Address page

adrp *xd, addr* loads the page address of *addr* into bits 63 to 12 of *xd*, with bits 11 to 0 set to 0. The page address is the next-lower 4KB address boundary of *addr*, and *addr* must be within ±4GB of this instruction.

Both instructions use the literal addressing mode (see Table 11-1) to refer to a memory address. They each allow a 21-bit offset value, hence the ±1MB range for adr. With 0s in the low-order 12 bits, the adrp instruction gives a 33-bit offset from the pc, for an addressing range of ±4GB from the pc, but with 4KB granularity.

The adrp instruction effectively treats memory as being divided into 4KB *pages*. (These pages are conceptually distinct from the memory pages that the operating system uses to manage main memory.) It loads the beginning address of a 4KB page, the *page address*, into the destination register. Compared to the adr instruction, this increases the range of addresses we can load into a register from $\pm$1MB to $\pm$4GB, but we still need to add the offset within the 4KB page to the page address in the register.

Thus, we can load a 64-bit address located within $\pm$4GB with a two-instruction sequence. The compiler did this in Listing 11-2 using the following code ❺:

```
adrp    x0, .LC1
add     x0, x0, :lo12:.LC1
```

Since the label `.LC1` is in the `.rodata` section, the linker computes the offset from the instruction to the label. The `adrp` instruction loads the page number of that offset into `x0`. The `:lo12:` modifier tells the assembler to use only the low-order 12 bits of the offset as the immediate value for the `add` instruction. This two-step process may seem a bit puzzling to you. It's due to the limited number of bits available for immediate values in an instruction; you'll see the details when we cover how instructions are coded in binary in Chapter 12.

After loading the arguments into registers, we transfer the program flow to the other function with a `bl` or a `blr` instruction:

bl—Branch and link

`bl` *addr* adds 4 to the address in the `pc` and loads the sum into `x30`. It then loads the memory address of *addr* into the `pc`, thus branching to *addr*, which must be within $\pm$128MB of this instruction.

blr—Branch and link, register

`blr` *xs* adds 4 to the address in the `pc` and loads the sum into `x30`. It then moves the 64-bit address in *xs* to the `pc`, thus branching to that address.

These instructions are used to call a function. Adding 4 to the address in the `pc` gives the address of the instruction immediately after the `bl` or `blr` in memory. We usually want the called function to return to this location. The `x30` register is used as a link register by these two branching instructions.

In the next section, we'll write the program in assembly language. It'll be very similar to what the compiler generated, but we'll use names that make it easier to read.

Writing main in Assembly Language

Listing 11-3 shows my assembly language version of the `inc_int` program. It closely follows the assembly language generated from the C version by the compiler in Listing 11-2, but I've added comments and used more meaningful labels for the string constants. This should make it a little easier to understand how the program uses the stack and passes arguments to other functions.

```
inc_int.s  // Increment an integer.
                   .arch armv8-a
           // Stack frame
             ❶ .equ   x, 28
```

```
      ❷ .equ    FRAME, 32
// Constant data
      ❸ .section  .rodata
prompt:
        .string "Enter an integer: "
input_format:
        .string "%i"
result:
        .string "Result: %i\n"
// Code
        .text
        .align  2
        .global main
        .type   main, %function
main:
      ❹ stp     fp, lr, [sp, FRAME]!  // Create stack frame
        mov     fp, sp               // Set our frame pointer

        adr     x0, prompt           // Prompt user
        bl      printf
        add     x1, sp, x            // Address for input
        adr     x0, input_format     // scanf format string
      ❺ bl      scanf

        ldr     w0, [sp, x]          // Get x
        add     w1, w0, 1            // Add 1
        str     w1, [sp, x]          // x++

        adr     x0, result           // printf format string
        bl      printf               // Result is in w1

        mov     w0, wzr
      ❻ ldp     fp, lr, [sp], FRAME  // Delete stack frame
        ret
```

Listing 11-3: A program to increment an integer, in assembly language

We see another assembler directive, .equ, in Listing 11-3. The format is:

```
.equ symbol, expression
```

The *expression* must evaluate to an integer, and the assembler sets *symbol* equal to that value. You can then use the symbol in your code, making it much easier to read, and the assembler will plug in the value of the expression. The expression is often just an integer. For example, I have equated the symbol FRAME to the integer 32 ❷. This allows us to write code that is self-documenting ❹. I've also used the assembler names, fp and lr, for the register names x29 and x30, respectively.

Note that we don't need to specify the .text segment for the .rodata section ❸. The assembler and linker produce a .rodata section, and it's up to the operating system to determine where to load it. I didn't align the text strings in the .rodata section either. Although alignment might make the code execute a little faster, it could waste a few bytes of memory. (Both factors are irrelevant for the programming we're doing in this book.) I've also used adr instead of adrp to load the addresses of the strings. The programs we'll be writing in this book are very simple, so I expect the strings in the .rodata section to be within ±1MB of the instructions that use them.

Finally, I've called scanf instead of __isoc99_scanf ❺. The __isoc99_ prefix disallows several nonstandard conversion specifiers; again, this is beyond the scope of this book.

Our variable, x, is in the stack frame ❶. The stack frame is created in the function prologue ❹ and deleted in the function epilogue ❻, making x an automatic local variable.

YOUR TURN

11.1   You can tell the gcc compiler to optimize the code it generates for speed with the -Ofast option or for size with the -Os option. Generate the assembly language for the program in Listing 11-1 for each option. What are the differences?

11.2   Modify the program in Listing 11-3 so that it inputs two integers and then displays the sum and difference of the two.

11.3   Enter the following C code in a file named *sum_diff.c*:

```
// Add and subtract two integers.

void sum_diff(int x, int y, int *sum, int *diff)
{
    *sum = x + y;
    *diff = x - y;
}
```

Modify the program in Listing 11-3 so that it inputs two integers, calls sum_diff to compute the sum and difference of the two integers, and then displays the two results.

What You've Learned

Call stack   An area of memory used for storing program data and addresses that grows and shrinks as needed.

Stack frame   Memory on the call stack used for saving the return address and caller's frame pointer, as well as for creating local variables.

Function prologue   The instructions that create a stack frame.

Function epilogue   The instructions that restore the caller's link register and frame pointer and delete the stack frame.

Automatic local variables   Variables created anew each time a function is called. They can easily be created on the call stack.

Passing arguments to a subfunction   Up to eight arguments are passed in the x0–x7 registers.

Calling a function   The branch and link instructions, `bl` and `blr`, transfer program flow to a function, storing the return address in `x30`.

A64 addressing   There are several modes for generating a 64-bit address with a 32-bit instruction.

Position-independent executable   The operating system can load the program anywhere in memory, and it will execute correctly.

Load–store architecture   Instructions can operate only on data that is in registers.

In the next chapter, we'll take a brief look at how instructions are coded in machine language. This will help you understand the reasons for some of the limitations of instructions, such as the size of offset when referring to a memory address.

12

INSTRUCTION DETAILS

In Chapters 2 and 3, you learned how bit patterns can be used to represent data. Then, in Chapters 4 to 8, you learned how bits can be implemented in hardware and used to perform computations. In this chapter, I'll explain some of the details of how instructions are encoded in bit patterns that specify the operations and the locations of the data they operate on.

The primary goal of this chapter is to give you an overall view of how computer instructions know where the data they operate on is located. The details of the machine code for each instruction are not the sort of thing that people memorize—you'll need to consult the manual for those—but being able to interpret them has helped me to better understand and debug many of my programs during my career.

The *Arm Architecture Reference Manual for A-Profile Architecture*, available at *https://developer.arm.com/documentation/ddi0487/latest*, gives an in-depth description of how each bit in a given instruction affects what the instruction does, which can be a little daunting to read. To help you learn how to read the details in the manual, I'll cover several instructions here, adding my own explanations to the manual's descriptions.

As mentioned in Chapter 10, A64 instructions fall into three general categories:

Load and store   These instructions are used to transfer data between memory and general-purpose registers.

Data processing   These instructions operate on data items in registers and constants that are encoded as part of the instruction.

Program flow control   These instructions are used to change the order of instruction execution from the order they are loaded into memory.

We'll look at a few examples of each type of instruction in this chapter.

Looking at Machine Code

An *assembly listing* is a specific type of file generated by the assembler from assembly language source code that shows the machine code corresponding to each assembly language instruction. I'll use the program in Listing 12-1 to show the machine language for several instructions.

```
add_consts.s // Add three constants to show some machine code.
            .arch armv8-a
// Stack frame
            .equ    z, 28
            .equ    FRAME, 32
// Constant data
            .section  .rodata
format:
            .string "%i + %i + 456 = %i\n"
// Code
            .text
            .align 2
            .global main
            .type main, %function
main:
            stp     fp, lr, [sp, FRAME]!  // Create stack frame
            mov     fp, sp

            mov     w19, 123             // 1st constant
            mov     w20, -123            // 2nd constant
            add     w21, w19, w20        // Add them
            add     w22, w21, 456        // Another constant
            str     w22, [sp, z]         // Store sum

            ldr     w3, [sp, z]          // Get sum
    ❶ mov     w2, w20              // Get 2nd constant
    ❷ orr     w2, wzr, w20         // Alias
            mov     w1, w19              // Get 1st constant
            adr     x0, format           // Assume on same page
```

```
        bl      printf

        mov     w0, wzr             // Return 0
        ldp     fp, lr, [sp], FRAME  // Delete stack frame
        ret
```

Listing 12-1: A program to add some constants

Of course, this is a silly program—all the data is constant—but it does allow me to illustrate a few points. For example, I've used two different instructions, mov ❶ and orr ❷, to copy the value in w20 into w2. This will allow us to compare the machine code for two ways of accomplishing the same effect.

We can produce an assembly listing by passing the -al option to the assembler. This causes the assembly listing to be written to standard output, which defaults to the screen. We can capture this with the redirection operator, >. For example, I used the command

```
$ as --gstabs -al -o add_consts.o add_consts.s > add_consts.lst
```

to produce the assembly listing file shown in Listing 12-2.

add_consts.lst AARCH64 GAS   add_consts.s   page 1

```
 1                  // Add three constants to show some machine code.
 2                          .arch armv8-a
 3                  // Stack frame
 4                          .equ    z, 28
 5                          .equ    FRAME, 32
 6                  // Constant data
 7                          .section  .rodata
 8              format:
 9 0000 2569202B          .string "%i + %i + 456 = %i\n"
 9      20256920
 9      2B203435
 9      36203D20
 9      25690A00
10              // Code
11                      .text
12                      .align 2
13                      .global main
14                      .type main, %function
15              main:
❶ 16 0000 FD7B82A9          stp     fp, lr, [sp, FRAME]!  // Create stack frame
17 0004 FD030091          mov     fp, sp
18
19 0008 730F8052          mov     w19, 123             // 1st constant
20 000c 540F8012          mov     w20, -123            // 2nd constant
21 0010 7502140B          add     w21, w19, w20        // Add them
```

```
22 0014 B6220711          add    w22, w21, 456          // Another constant
23 0018 F61F00B9          str    w22, [sp, z]           // Store sum
24
25 001c E31F40B9          ldr    w3, [sp, z]            // Get sum
❷ 26 0020 E203142A        mov    w2, w20                // Get 2nd constant
❸ 27 0024 E203142A        orr    w2, wzr, w20           // Alias instruction
28 0028 E103132A          mov    w1, w19                // Get 1st constant
29 002c 00000010          adr    x0, format             // Assume on same page
30 0030 00000094          bl     printf
31
32 0034 E0031F2A          mov    w0, wzr                // Return 0
33 0038 FD7BC2A8          ldp    fp, lr, [sp], FRAME    // Delete stack frame
34 003c C0035FD6          ret
```

Listing 12-2: The assembly listing file for the program in Listing 12-1

The first column in the assembly listing file shows the corresponding line number in the source file. The next column shows the 16-bit relative address from the beginning of each section, in hexadecimal.

The third column gives the machine code for the instruction or data, also in hexadecimal. All A64 instructions are 32 bits wide. The assembly listing shows the 4 bytes in each instruction in the order that they'll be stored in memory. Since ours is a little-endian environment, the 4 bytes appear backward in the assembly listing. For example, the first instruction in this program ❶ is the 32-bit word 0xa9827bfd. (We'll look at the other instructions that I've called out in this listing a bit later, in "Moving Data from Register to Register" on page 232.)

In some cases, the names for the bit fields in my descriptions are different from those in the manual. Note that some of the names I use might have a different meaning in other places in the manual. Here are the names I'm using:

sf   The size flag. The operands are 32-bit values when it's 0 or 64-bit when it's 1.

imm   A constant integer used by the instruction.

hw   The number of halfwords (16 bits) to shift a 16-bit imm value left before loading it into a register.

b_offset   The number of bytes from the current instruction to an address.

b_offset:hi   The high-order part of a b_offset.

b:lo   The low-order part of a b_offset.

w_offset   The number of 32-bit words from the current instruction to an address.

rb   The number of a register holding a 64-bit base address for this instruction.

rd The number of the destination register, which will hold the result of the instruction's operation. Where there are two destination registers, I use rd1 and rd2.

rs The number of a source register, which holds a value used in the instruction's operation. Where there are two source registers, I use rs1 and rs2.

pi Tells the instruction how to treat the base register: 01 for post-index, 11 for pre-index, or 10 for don't change.

sh Tells the instruction whether to shift an operand before using it in the operation: yes if it's 1, and no if it's 0. For a 2-bit sh field, 00 is lsl, 01 is lsr, 10 is asr, and 11 is ror.

shft_amnt The number of bits to shift an operand.

Bits 28 to 25 show which group the instruction is in: load and store (0x4, 0x6, 0xc, 0xe), data processing (0x5, 0x7, 0x8, 0x9, 0xd, 0xf), or program flow control (0xa, 0xb). Many instructions have variants. The assembler will pick the variant appropriate for the operands we use. I'll start by showing you the load and store instructions in Listing 12-1.

Encoding Load and Store Instructions

Figure 12-1 shows the basic load instruction.

31	30 29 28 27 26 25 24 23 22	21 20 19 18 17 16 15 14 13 12 11 10	9 8 7 6 5	4 3 2 1 0
1 sf	1 1 1 0 0 1 0 1	w_offset	rb	rd
0		0 0 0 0 0 0 0 0 0 1 1 1	1 1 1 1 1	0 0 0 1 1

Figure 12-1: A basic load instruction: ldr w3, [sp, z]

Figure 12-2 shows the basic store instruction.

31	30 29 28 27 26 25 24 23 22	21 20 19 18 17 16 15 14 13 12 11 10	9 8 7 6 5	4 3 2 1 0
1 sf	1 1 1 0 0 1 0 0	w_offset	rb	rs
0		0 0 0 0 0 0 0 0 0 1 1 1	1 1 1 1 1	1 0 1 1 0

Figure 12-2: A basic store instruction: str w22, [sp, z]

In both instructions, bit 24 is 1, which shows us that the assembler has used the immediate, unsigned offset variant. Other variants have 0 in bit 24. Both instructions use sp as the base address register, giving 11111 in the rb field, and in both instructions the offset from the base register is the number of 32-bit words. The offset in Listing 12-1 is z, which equates to 28. We use the number of bytes in assembly language, but the assembler divides this value by 4 to encode the number of words in the machine code for the instruction, giving 7 in the w_offset field.

In Figure 12-1, the 0 in the sf field together with 00011 in the rd field tells the CPU to use w3 for the destination register, and the 0 in the sf field together with 10110 in the rs field in Figure 12-2 tells the CPU to use w22 for the source register.

The stack frame is created with the stp instruction, shown in Figure 12-3.

31	30 29 28 27 26 25	24 23	22	21 20 19 18 17 16 15	14 13 12 11 10	9 8 7 6 5	4 3 2 1 0
sf	0 1 0 1 0 0	pi	0	w_offset	rs2	rb	rs1
1		1 1		0 0 0 0 1 0 0	1 1 1 1 0	1 1 1 1 1	1 1 1 0 1

Figure 12-3: The instruction to push fp and sp onto the stack: stp fp, lr, [sp, FRAME]!

It is deleted with the ldp instruction, shown in Figure 12-4.

31	30 29 28 27 26 25	24 23	22	21 20 19 18 17 16 15	14 13 12 11 10	9 8 7 6 5	4 3 2 1 0
sf	0 1 0 1 0 0	pi	0	w_offset	rd2	rb	rd1
1		0 1		0 0 0 0 1 0 0	1 1 1 1 0	1 1 1 1 1	1 1 1 0 1

Figure 12-4: The instruction to pop fp and sp from the stack: ldp fp, lr, [sp], FRAME

Both of these instructions use sp for their base register. In Figure 12-3, the 11 in the pi field tells the CPU to subtract the w_offset, 4 words (32 bytes), from sp before (pre-index) storing the contents of registers x29 and x30 at that address. The CPU stores the entire 64 bits of each register because sf is 1.

The pi field is 01 in Figure 12-4, so 32 is added to sp after (post-index) the two 64-bit values are loaded into registers x29 and x30. The CPU loads 64 bits from memory into each register because sf is 1. Next, I'll explain the data processing instructions in Listing 12-2.

Encoding Data Processing Instructions

Data processing instructions operate on values that are already in the CPU, either in registers or as part of the instruction itself. They are used to move data or perform arithmetic and logic operations on data. In some cases, these operations overlap.

Moving Data from Register to Register

We'll start by looking at the instruction that moves the value from the sp register to the fp register, shown in Figure 12-5.

31	30 29 28 27 26 25 24 23 22 21 20 19 18 17 16 15 14 13 12 11 10	9 8 7 6 5	4 3 2 1 0
sf	0 0 1 0 0 0 1 0 0 0 0 0 0 0 0 0 0 0 0 0 0	rs	rd
1		1 1 1 1 1	1 1 1 0 1

Figure 12-5: A basic register-to-register move instruction: mov fp, sp

Next, we'll look at an instruction that uses a logical operation to effectively move a value from one register to another, shown in Figure 12-6.

31 30 29 28 27 26 25 24 23	22 21	20	19 18 17 16	15 14 13 12 11 10	9 8 7 6 5	4 3 2 1 0
sf | 0 1 0 1 0 1 0	sh	0	rs2	shft_amnt	rs1	rd
0	0 0		1 0 1 0 0	0 0 0 0 0 0	1 1 1 1 1	0 0 0 1 0

Figure 12-6: A logical operation to move data: `orr w2, wzr, w20`

Notice that the rs field in Figure 12-5 is the same as the rs1 field in Figure 12-6, but in the first case it's the code for the stack pointer and in the second it's the zero register. This shows that the way register 31 is treated, as a stack pointer or zero register, depends on the instruction.

You're probably wondering why I'm showing an orr instruction instead of a mov instruction in Figure 12-6. As you might guess from the name, the orr instruction performs a bitwise OR operation between the values in the two source registers, rs1 and rs2, and stores the result in the destination register, rd. Since rs1 is the zero register in our instruction, this operation simply moves the value in rs2 to rd, which is equivalent to mov w2, w20 here. I'll describe the orr instruction in more detail when we look at logic operators in Chapter 16.

The mov w2, w20 ❷ and orr w2, wzr, w20 ❸ instructions in Listing 12-2 (on page 229) use exactly the same machine code. The two names for the same instruction are said to be *aliases*. For the instructions that have aliases, you should use the name that better expresses your intent in the algorithm. In our example program, mov w2, w20 is a better choice.

Moving a Constant to a Register

Figure 12-7 shows the instruction for moving a positive or unsigned constant into a register.

31	30 29 28 27 26 25 24 23	22 21	20 19 18 17 16 15 14 13 12 11 10 9 8 7 6 5	4 3 2 1 0
sf	1 0 1 0 0 1 0 1	hw	imm	rd
0		0 0	0 0 0 0 0 0 0 0 0 0 1 1 1 1 0 1 1	1 0 0 1 1

Figure 12-7: The instruction for moving a positive constant: `mov w19, 123`

Figure 12-8 shows the instruction for moving a negative constant into a register.

31	30 29 28 27 26 25 24 23	22 21	20 19 18 17 16 15 14 13 12 11 10 9 8 7 6 5	4 3 2 1 0
sf	0 0 1 0 0 1 0 1	hw	imm	rd
0		0 0	0 0 0 0 0 0 0 0 0 1 1 1 1 0 1 0	1 0 1 0 0

Figure 12-8: The instruction for moving a negative constant: `mov w20, -123`

Although both instructions use the mov mnemonic, in Figure 12-7 bit 30 is 1, and in Figure 12-8 it's 0. The difference is that the first instruction is moving a positive number and the second a negative number. When the constant in a mov instruction is negative, the assembler uses the movn (move with NOT) instruction from Chapter 10.

In Figure 12-7, the constant +123 is encoded as 0x007b, as we would expect, but in Figure 12-8 we see that −123 is encoded as 0x007a, which is +122 in decimal.

You learned in Chapter 3 that in the two's complement notation, the negative of a number can be computed by taking the complement of the number and adding 1. In other words, −123 is the complement of +122 in two's complement notation. The mov instruction in Figure 12-8 computes the NOT of the value in the imm field and sign-extends it to the size of the destination register before storing the result there. So, this instruction uses the 0x007a to store 0xffffff85 in the w20 register, as shown in the debugger:

```
Breakpoint 1, main () at add_consts.s:24
24              str      w22, [sp, z]          // Store sum
(gdb) i r w19 w20 w21 w22
w19             0x7b                  123
w20             0xffffff85            4294967173
w21             0x0                   0
w22             0x1c8                 456
```

In both instructions, the constant has to fit within the 16-bit immediate value. The range for positive numbers is 0 to +65,535, and for negative numbers it's −1 to −65,536.

Performing Arithmetic

Let's look at the instruction for adding a constant to a value in a register, shown in Figure 12-9.

```
31 30 29 28 27 26 25 24 23 22 21 20 19 18 17 16 15 14 13 12 11 10 9 8 7 6 5 4 3 2 1 0
sf 0  0  1  0  0  0  1  0 sh           imm                      rs        rd
1                         0  1 0 0 0 0 1 0 1 1 0 0 0   0 0 0 0 0   0 0 0 0 0
```

Figure 12-9: The instruction for adding a constant to a value: add w22, w21, 456

This instruction adds the 12-bit imm value to the value in rs and stores the result in the rd register. When the shift bit, sh, is 1, the imm value is shifted left 12 bits before performing the addition. The shift option allows us to add a 24-bit constant in two add operations. The first will add the low-order 12 bits and the second the high-order 12 bits.

Comparing Figure 12-9 with Figure 12-5, you can see another example of an alias. If imm is 0 and one of rd or rs is 31, this add instruction is the same as a mov to or from the sp register.

Computing Addresses

Now, let's look at the instruction that loads the address of the printf format string into the x0 register, as shown in Figure 12-10.

31	30	29	28	27	26	25	24	23	22	21	20	19	18	17	16	15	14	13	12	11	10	9	8	7	6	5	4	3	2	1	0
0	b:lo	1	0	0	0	0					b_offset:hi																		rd		
	0 0						0	0	0	0	0 0 0 0 0 0 0 0 0 0 0 0 0 0 0 0 0 0 0 0 0																			0	0	0	0	0

Figure 12-10: The instruction to load an address: adr x0, format

You learned in Chapter 11 that this instruction computes the address of format by adding the offset from this instruction to format and the value in pc, then loads the result into x0. The b_offset field in this instruction shows that all 21 bits are 0 (don't forget to include the two low-order bits in the b:lo field). This seems to indicate that the format text string is located at the same place as this instruction, which is clearly not possible. This text string is in the .rodata section. The linker will decide where to locate that section and fill in the b_offset:hi and b:lo fields during the linking process.

Looking at the Details of an Executable File

You can use a program called objdump to look at the code in an executable program file. For example, to dump the contents of the *add_consts* file, you can use the following command:

```
$ objdump -D add_consts
--snip--
0000000000000774 <main>:
 774:   a9827bfd   stp   x29, x30, [sp, #32]!
 778:   910003fd   mov   x29, sp
 77c:   52800f73   mov   w19, #0x7b          // #123
 780:   12800f54   mov   w20, #0xffffff85    // #-123
 784:   0b140275   add   w21, w19, w20
 788:   110722b6   add   w22, w21, #0x1c8
 78c:   b9001ff6   str   w22, [sp, #28]
 790:   b9401fe3   ldr   w3, [sp, #28]
 794:   2a1403e2   mov   w2, w20
 798:   2a1403e2   mov   w2, w20
 79c:   2a1303e1   mov   w1, w19
❶ 7a0:   100005c0   adr   x0, 858 <format>
 7a4:   97ffffab   bl    650 <printf@plt>
 7a8:   2a1f03e0   mov   w0, wzr
 7ac:   a8c27bfd   ldp   x29, x30, [sp, #32]
 7b0:   d65f03c0   ret
 7b4:   d503201f   nop
 7b8:   d503201f   nop
 7bc:   d503201f   nop
--snip--
0000000000000858 <format>:
 858:   2b206925   adds   w5, w9, w0, uxtx #2
 85c:   20692520   .inst  0x20692520 ; undefined
 860:   3534202b   cbnz   w11, 68c64 <__bss_end__+0x57c24>
```

```
864:    203d2036        .inst   0x203d2036 ; undefined
868:    000a6925        .inst   0x000a6925 ; undefined
--snip--
```

The -D option dumps all the sections in the file, assumes that they all contain instructions, and disassembles them as such. I'm showing only the two sections that interest us here.

The first column shows the relative address where each instruction will be loaded into memory. The operating system will decide the base loading address when loading the program.

The second column shows the machine code of the instruction at that address. Note that `objdump` displays the machine code in 32-bit instruction order, not in the little-endian byte order we see in assembly listing files.

The linker has filled in the offset to the `format` text string in the `adr` instruction ❶. Per Figure 12-10, the offset is `000000000000010110100`. Adding this to the relative address of the instruction gives `0x7a4` + `0x0b4` = `0x858`.

The machine code at relative address `0x858` begins with the bytes `0x25`, `0x69`, `0x20`, `0x2b`, which are the code points for the first four characters in the format text string: `%`, `i`, space, and `+`. The assembly listing file, shown in Listing 12-2, displays the bytes in the proper order. Next, I'll show you the two instructions in this program that cause program flow to go someplace other than the next instruction in memory.

Encoding Program Flow Control Instructions

I'll start with the instruction used to call the `printf` function, shown in Figure 12-11.

31 30 29 28 27 26	25 … 0
1 0 0 1 0 1	w_offset
	0 0 0 0 0 0 0 0 0 0 0 0 0 0 0 0 0 0 0 0 0 0 0 0 0 0

Figure 12-11: The function call instruction: `bl printf`

The `bl` instruction copies the address in `pc`, plus 4, to the link register, `x30`. It then shifts `w_offset` 2 bits to the left to give a byte offset, sign-extends it to 64 bits, and adds the result to `pc`. The result is to save the address of the instruction immediately after the `bl` instruction in memory to the link register and then transfer program flow to `w_offset` words from the address of the `bl` instruction. Since `w_offset` is 26 bits wide, the offset in bytes is limited to 28 bits, giving a transfer limit of ±128MB away in memory.

The last instruction we'll look at is `ret`, shown in Figure 12-12.

31 … 10	9 8 7 6 5	4 3 2 1 0
1 1 0 1 0 1 1 0 0 1 0 1 1 1 1 1 0 0 0 0 0 0	rs	0 0 0 0 0
	1 1 1 1 0	

Figure 12-12: The return from function instruction: `ret`

The ret instruction moves the address from the register specified in the rs field to pc. Although I didn't specify a register in Listing 12-2, the assembler uses x30 by default. We could use another register, but that would be inconsistent with the published standards and likely lead to program bugs.

YOUR TURN

12.1 Enter the program in Listing 12-1 and use the debugger to determine when the adr instruction knows the address of the format text string.

12.2 Experiment with the constants in the program in Listing 12-1 to find the magnitude limits of the constants.

12.3 Modify the program in Listing 12-1 to use 64-bit integers (long int in C). Does this allow you to use larger constants?

12.4 Write a program in C that does the same thing as our assembly language program in Listing 12-1. Does your C program allow you to use larger constants? If so, why?

Now that you know what machine code looks like, we'll look at how an assembler program translates assembly language into machine code. The general algorithm is similar for linking functions together; I'll cover that too.

Translating Assembly into Machine Code

The presentation in this section is meant to be an overview, so it ignores most of the details. My intention is to give you only a rough idea of how an assembler translates the source code into machine language and how a linker connects the different modules that make up an entire program.

The Assembler

The simplest approach for an assembler to translate assembly language into machine code would be to go through the source one line at a time, translating each one in turn. This would work fine, except for situations where an instruction refers to a label on a line after the current line.

To see how the assembler deals with these forward references, I'll make a forward reference to Listing 13-11 in Chapter 13, where we'll be making use of them. Listing 12-3 shows a portion of the assembly listing file from that program.

```
--snip--
33  0024 3F00006B       cmp    w1, w0        // Above or below middle?
34  0028 88000054       b.hi   tails         // Above -> tails
35  002c 00000010       adr    x0, heads_msg // Below -> heads message
36  0030 00000094       bl     puts          // Print message
37  0034 03000014       b      continue      // Skip else part
38                tails:
```

```
39 0038 00000010          adr    x0, tails_msg         // Tails message page address
--snip--
```

Listing 12-3: Part of the listing file for the program in Listing 13-11 from Chapter 13

I'll cover the details in Chapter 13, but this section of code compares the values in registers w0 and w1. If the value in w1 is higher, the b.hi instruction causes the program flow to branch to the address labeled tails.

Figure 12-13 shows the machine code that the assembler produced for the b.hi instruction.

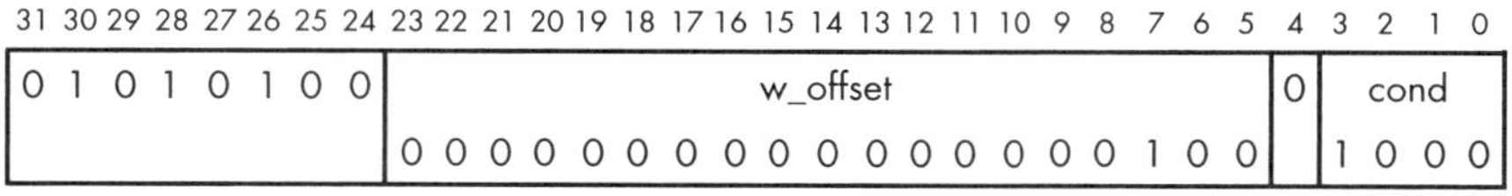

Figure 12-13: A conditional branch: b.hi tails

The tails label is at relative location 0x38, which is 0x10 bytes beyond the b.hi instruction at 0x28. In Figure 12-13, the w_offset is 0x00004, or 0x10 bytes. The question is how the assembler knew the location of the forward reference to the tails label.

A common way to deal with forward references is to use a *two-pass assembler*, which scans the program twice. During the first pass, the assembler creates a *local symbol table*, associating each symbol with a numerical value. Those symbols defined with a .equ directive are entered directly in the table.

For the labeled locations in the code, the assembler needs to determine the location of each label relative to the beginning of the module being assembled and then enter that value and the label in the table. A separate local symbol table is created for each .text and .data segment in the file.

Here's the general algorithm for the first pass of a two-pass assembler, which generates a local symbol table:

```
Let location_counter = 0
do
    Read a line of source code
    if (.equ directive)
        local_symbol_table.symbol = symbol
        local_symbol_table.value = expression value
    else if (line has a label)
        local_symbol_table.symbol = label
        local_symbol_table.value = location_counter
    Determine number_of_bytes required by line when assembled
    location_counter = location_counter + number_of_bytes
while (more lines of source code)
```

Once the local symbol table is created, the assembler does a second pass through the source code file. It uses a built-in *opcode table* to determine the machine code, and when a symbol is used in an instruction, it looks up the value of the symbol in the local symbol table. If it does not find the symbol in the local symbol table, it leaves space in the instruction for a number and records the symbol and its location in the object file.

The general algorithm looks like this:

```
Let location_counter = 0
do
    Read a line of source code
    Find machine code from opcode table
    if (symbol is used in instruction)
        if (symbol found in local_symbol_table)
            Get value of symbol
        else
            Let value = 0
            Write symbol and location_counter to object file
        Add symbol value to instruction
    Write assembled instruction to object file
    Determine number_of_bytes used by the assembled instruction
    location_counter = location_counter + number_of_bytes
while (more lines of source code)
```

As an alternative, we could create a *one-pass assembler*. It would need to maintain a list of the locations of each forward reference and, when the label is found, use the table to go back and fill in the appropriate value.

Again, this is a highly simplified overview of the assembly process that is intended only to show you the general idea of how an assembler works. Chapter 7 in Andrew S. Tanenbaum and Todd Austin's *Structured Computer Organization*, 6th edition (Pearson, 2012), has a section that provides more details about the assembly process. There is a thorough discussion of the design of assembler programs in Chapter 2 of Leland Beck's *System Software: An Introduction to Systems Programming*, 3rd edition (Pearson, 1997).

Most functions will have function calls, which are references to labels in .text segments defined in other files that cannot be resolved by the assembler. The same is true of any labels in .data segments, even if they're defined in the same source code file. I'll show you the program that resolves these references in the next section.

The Linker

The job of the linker is to figure out the relative locations of the labels in a program so it can enter the offset to each label wherever there is a reference to the label. A linker works in much the same way as an assembler, except the basic unit is a block of machine code instead of a line of assembly language. A typical program comprises many object files, each of which often has more than one .text segment and may have .data segments, all of which must be linked together. As with an assembler, two passes can be used to resolve forward references.

An object file created by the assembler includes the size of each segment in the file, together with a list of all the global symbols and where they are used in the segment. During the first pass, the linker reads each object file and creates a *global symbol table* that contains the relative location of each global symbol from the beginning of the program. In the second pass, the linker creates an executable file that includes all the machine code from the object files with the relative location values from the global symbol table plugged into the locations where they are referenced.

This process resolves all the references to names defined in the modules that comprise the program, but it will leave unresolved all references to externally defined names, such as function or variable names that are defined in the C standard library. The linker enters these unresolved references into the *global offset table (GOT)*.

If the external reference is a function call, the linker also enters this information into the *procedure linkage table (PLT)*, along with the location in the machine code where the reference is made. You can see how the linker has done this by looking at how we wrote a call to a C standard library function in Listing 12-1:

```
bl      printf
```

Using the objdump program to look at the contents of the executable file for this program, we see what the linker has added:

```
7a4:    97ffffab        bl      650 <printf@plt>
```

From the encoding of the bl instruction in Figure 12-11, we see that the w_offset is the 26-bit value 0x3ffffab. There are 4 bytes in a word, so this is equal to the 28-bit byte offset of 0xffffeac. Adding the byte offset to the relative address of the instruction gives 0x00007a4 + 0xffffeac = 0x0000650. (Don't forget that these are signed integers, so the carry from this addition is irrelevant.) This is the offset from this bl instruction to where the link to printf is located in the PLT.

When the program runs, the operating system also loads the GOT and the PLT for the program. During execution, if the program accesses an external variable, the operating system loads the library module where the variable is defined and enters its relative address in the GOT. When the program calls one of the functions in the PLT, if the function has not already been loaded, the operating system loads it, inserts its address into the program's GOT, and adjusts the corresponding entry in the PLT accordingly.

I want to reemphasize that, as with the previous discussion of assemblers, this is only a rough overview of how linkers work. If you would like to learn more about linkers, I recommend John R. Levine's *Linkers & Loaders* (Morgan Kaufmann, 1999).

What You've Learned

Machine code   The instruction bit patterns that control the CPU.

Assembly listing   The machine code corresponding to each instruction in a program, optionally generated by the assembler.

Registers   The number of the register is encoded in 5 bits.

Register size   A single bit encodes whether the full 64 bits or the low-order 32 bits is used.

Immediate data   A constant encoded within the instruction.

Address offset   The distance from the referencing instruction to a memory address, which can be encoded within the referencing instruction.

Aliases   The assembler can have more than one name for some instructions, to better show the intent of using the instruction.

Assembler   A program that translates assembly language to machine code and creates a global symbol table.

Linker   A program that resolves cross-references between the segments in the program and creates a procedure linkage table that is used by the operating system.

So far, all our programs have used sequential program flow and called subfunctions. In the next chapter, we'll return to programming and you'll learn about the other two necessary program flow constructs: repetition and two-way branching.

13

CONTROL FLOW CONSTRUCTS

When writing a program in C or assembly language, we specify the order in which each statement or instruction is executed. This order is called the *control flow*. Programming by specifying the control flow is known as *imperative programming*. This is in contrast to *declarative programming*, where we state the logic of the computation and another program figures out the control flow to perform it.

If you have been using make to build your programs, as recommended in Chapter 2, the statements in your makefile are an example of declarative programming. You specify the logic of the results, and the make program figures out the control flow to produce the results.

There are three fundamental control flow constructs: sequence, iteration, and selection. You've already seen sequence in the programs we've written thus far: each instruction, or subfunction, is executed in the order in which it's written. In this chapter, I'll show you how to alter the control flow from the written order to iterate the same block of written instructions or to select between several blocks of written instructions. You'll see how each of these control flow constructs is implemented at the assembly language level. In Chapter 14, I'll cover the details of altering control flow by calling a subfunction.

Branches

A *branch instruction* transfers control flow to the memory location specified by the instruction. There are two types of branches: unconditional and conditional. Both iteration and selection use conditional branches to alter control flow based on a true/false condition. You'll also often use unconditional branches when implementing the iteration and selection flow constructs. We'll start with those and then look at conditional branches.

Unconditional

As you learned in Chapter 9, when an instruction is executed, the CPU automatically increments the program counter, pc, by 4 to hold the address of the next instruction in memory. Instead of adding 4 to the program counter, an unconditional branch instruction changes the program counter to the branch target address, which causes the CPU to continue program execution at the target address.

You already learned about one unconditional branch instruction—ret, which is used to return from functions—in Chapter 10. There are two others, b and br:

b—Branch unconditionally
b *label* branches to the address of *label* within the range of ±128MB from this instruction.

br—Branch register unconditionally
br xs branches to the 64-bit address in xs.

The b instruction is commonly used together with a conditional branch instruction to skip blocks of code or to go back to the beginning of a block of code and execute it again. For the b instruction, the CPU sign-extends the 26-bit word offset between the b instruction and *label* to 64 bits and adds this signed number to pc. The br instruction simply copies the 64 bits in xs to pc.

Although br x30 would seem to have the same effect as ret, the br and ret instructions are not aliases for each other; they are different instructions. The difference is that br tells the CPU that this is probably *not* a function return, while ret tells the CPU that this probably *is* a function return. The details are beyond the scope of this book, but these hints can help the CPU optimize some of the specifics of executing instructions.

Conditional

There are two types of conditional branch instructions. One tests the settings of the condition flags in the rzcv register (see Figure 9-4 in Chapter 9). We need to use another instruction to set the flags before testing them to determine whether to branch or not.

The other type of conditional branch instruction tests the value in a register to determine whether to branch. Instructions in this group do not depend on the condition flags, nor do they change them.

I'll start with the instructions that branch according to the settings of the condition flags:

b.*cond*—Branch conditionally

b.*cond* *label* tests the settings in the nzcv register and branches to *label* if they match *cond*, in the range of ±128MB from this instruction. The possible values for *cond* are given in Table 13-1.

Table 13-1: Allowable Branching Condition Codes

Code	*cond*	Meaning	Condition flags
0000	eq	Equal	Z
0001	ne	Not equal	$\neg Z$
0010	cs or hs	Carry set; unsigned higher or same	C
0011	cc or lo	Carry not set; unsigned lower	$\neg C$
0100	mi	Minus; negative	N
0101	pl	Plus; positive or zero	$\neg N$
0110	vs	Overflow	V
0111	vc	No overflow	$\neg V$
1000	hi	Unsigned higher	$C \wedge \neg Z$
1001	ls	Unsigned lower or same	$\neg(C \wedge \neg Z)$
1010	ge	Signed greater than or equal	$N = V$
1011	lt	Signed less than	$\neg(N = V)$
1100	gt	Signed greater than	$\neg Z \wedge (N = V)$
1101	le	Signed less than or equal	$\neg(\neg Z \wedge (N = V))$
1110	al	Always	Any
1111	nv	Always	Any

You should use the b.*cond* instruction when you want to take one of two branches in your program, depending on the result of another operation. It's important that the b.*cond* instruction immediately follow the instruction whose result is driving the decision to branch. An intervening instruction or function call might change the settings of the condition flags, giving an erroneous basis for the decision.

In addition to this, there are four instructions that branch depending on the value in a general-purpose register:

cbz—Compare and branch if zero

cbz ws, *label* branches to *label* if the value in ws is 0, in the range of ±1MB from this instruction.

cbz xs, *label* branches to *label* if the value in xs is 0, in the range of ±1MB from this instruction.

cbnz—Compare and branch if not zero

`cbnz ws, label` branches to *label* if the value in `ws` is not 0, in the range of ±1MB from this instruction.

`cbnz xs, label` branches to *label* if the value in `xs` is not 0, in the range of ±1MB from this instruction.

tbz—Test bit and branch if zero

`tbz ws, imm, label` branches to *label* if bit number *imm* in `ws` is 0, in the range of ±1MB from this instruction.

`tbz xs, imm, label` branches to *label* if bit number *imm* in `xs` is 0, in the range of ±1MB from this instruction.

tbnz—Test bit and branch if not zero

`tbnz ws, imm, label` branches to *label* if bit number *imm* in `ws` is not 0, in the range of ±1MB from this instruction.

`tbnz xs, imm, label` branches to *label* if bit number *imm* in `xs` is not 0, in the range of ±1MB from this instruction.

NOTE *When using a conditional branch like `b.gt` or `b.le`, it's easy to forget the order of the test: source compared to destination, or destination compared to source. When testing my program, I almost always start by using `gdb` and putting a breakpoint at the conditional branch instruction. When the program breaks, I check the values and use the `si` command to see which way the branch went.*

Now that you know how to control the flow of instruction execution, I'll show you some programming constructs. We'll start with repetition. This can be implemented in two ways: *iteration*, in which the program loops through a block of code repeatedly until a condition is met, and *recursion*, where a function calls itself repeatedly until a condition is met.

I'll cover iteration in the next section and explain how recursion works when I discuss special uses of subfunctions in Chapter 15.

Iteration

Many algorithms use iteration, also known as *looping*. A loop continues the iteration of a block of code until the value(s) of the *loop control variable(s)* meet a *termination condition* that causes the loop to end. With a looping construct, the value(s) of the loop control variable(s) must be changed within the iterated block of instructions.

Processing a text string one character at a time provides a good example of looping. I will use the two system call functions from Figure 2-1 in Chapter 2, `write` and `read`, to illustrate the concepts. That figure shows that `printf` converts data from its memory storage format to a character format and calls the `write` system call function to display the characters on the screen. When reading characters from the keyboard, `scanf` calls the `read` system call function and converts the characters to a memory storage format.

write and read System Call Functions

The write and read system call functions see the screen and keyboard as files. When a program is first launched, the operating system opens three files— *standard input*, *standard output*, and *standard error*—and assigns an integer to each file, which is called the *file descriptor*. The program interacts with each file by using the file descriptor. The C interfaces for calling write and read are specified in the *Portable Operating System Interface (POSIX)* standard, which you can find at *https://pubs.opengroup.org/onlinepubs/9699919799/*.

The general formats for calling these two functions are

```
int write(int fd, char *buf, int n);
```

and

```
int read(int fd, char *buf, int n);
```

where *fd* is the file descriptor, *buf* is the address of the character storage, and *n* is the number of characters to write or read. You can read more details in the man pages for write and read:

```
> man 2 write
> man 2 read
```

Table 13-2 shows the file descriptors I'll use and the device each is normally associated with.

Table 13-2: The File Descriptors for the write and read System Call Functions

Name	Number	Use
STDIN_FILENO	0	Read characters from the keyboard
STDOUT_FILENO	1	Write characters to the screen
STDERR_FILENO	2	Write error messages to the screen

These names are defined in the system header file, *unistd.h*, which is located at */usr/include/unistd.h* on my Raspberry Pi O (note that the location on your system may be different). Now, let's move on to looping constructs.

while Loop

The while loop is a fundamental form of looping. Here is the form in C:

```
initialize loop control variable
while (expression) {
    body
    change loop control variable
}
next statement
```

Before entering the while loop, you need to initialize the loop control variable. At the beginning of the while loop, *expression* is evaluated as a Boolean. If it evaluates to false (0 in C), control flow continues to *next statement*. If *expression* evaluates to true—that is, any nonzero value in C—the statements in *body* are executed, the loop control variable is changed, and control flow continues at the top with the reevaluation of *expression*.

Figure 13-1 shows the control flow of a while loop. Although the loop termination condition can be dependent on more than one variable, I'll use just one here to clarify the discussion.

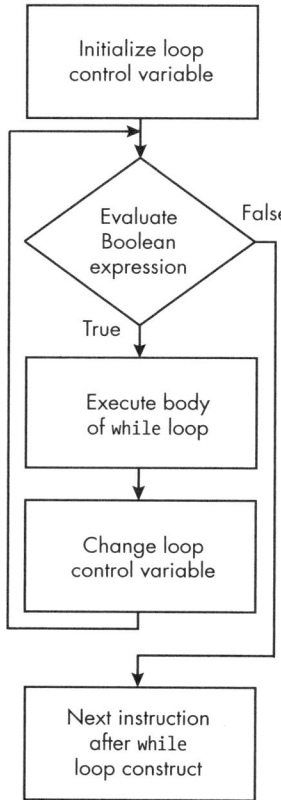

Figure 13-1: The control flow of the while loop

Listing 13-1 shows how to use a while loop to write a text string in the terminal window one character at a time.

hello_world.c   // Write Hello, World! one character at a time.

```
#include <unistd.h>
❶ #define NUL '\x00'

int main(void)
```

```
{
❷ char *message_ptr = "Hello, World!\n";

❸ while (*message_ptr != NUL) {
    ❹ write(STDOUT_FILENO, message_ptr, 1);
    ❺ message_ptr++;
    }

    return 0;
}
```

Listing 13-1: A program to write "Hello, World!" one character at a time

I use the #define directive to give a symbolic name to the NUL character ❶.
The message_ptr variable is defined to be a pointer to a char type and is used
as the loop control variable. It's initialized to point to a text string ❷. As
you'll see when we look at the assembly language for this code, the compiler
will store the text string in a read-only part of memory and store the address
of the first character in that text string in the message_ptr pointer variable.

The while statement first checks to see if the loop control variable,
message_ptr, is pointing to the NUL character ❸; if not, program flow enters
the while loop body and writes the character pointed to by message_ptr to the
screen ❹. The loop control variable is then incremented to point to the next
character in the text string ❺. Program flow returns to the top of the loop,
where the next character is checked to see if it's the NUL character. This loop
terminates when message_ptr points to the NUL character ❸. Testing for this
condition first means the program won't even enter the body of the while
loop if the string is empty, as message_ptr will only point to a NUL character.
This is a subtle but important point about while loops: the code in the body
is never executed if the termination condition is already met.

For Listing 13-1, the compiler generated the assembly language shown
in Listing 13-2.

hello_world.s
```
        .arch armv8-a
        .file   "hello_world.c"
        .text
❶ .section        .rodata
        .align  3
.LC0:
        .string "Hello, World!\n"
        .text
        .align  2
        .global main
        .type   main, %function
main:
        stp     x29, x30, [sp, -32]!
        mov     x29, sp
❷ adrp    x0, .LC0
        add     x0, x0, :lo12:.LC0
```

```
            str     x0, [sp, 24]        /// message_ptr variable
      ❸ b           .L2                 /// Go to check
.L3:
            mov     x2, 1               /// One character
            ldr     x1, [sp, 24]        /// Address in message_ptr
            mov     w0, 1               /// STDOUT_FILENO
            bl      write
            ldr     x0, [sp, 24]
            add     x0, x0, 1
            str     x0, [sp, 24]        /// message_ptr++;
.L2:
            ldr     x0, [sp, 24]
            ldrb    w0, [x0]            /// Current char
      ❹ cmp         w0, 0               /// NUL?
      ❺ bne         .L3                 /// No, back to top
            mov     w0, 0
            ldp     x29, x30, [sp], 32
            ret
            .size   main, .-main
            .ident  "GCC: (Debian 10.2.1-6) 10.2.1 20210110"
            .section        .note.GNU-stack,"",@progbits
```

Listing 13-2: The compiler-generated assembly language for the function in Listing 13-1

The assembly language shows that the text string is stored in the .rodata section ❶. Then, message_ptr is initialized to contain the address of the beginning of the text string ❷.

Although this assembly language seems to be testing for the termination condition at the end of the loop ❹, it follows the logical flow shown in Figure 13-1. It first branches down to .L2 ❸, where the test is made for the terminating condition, before branching up to .L3 to start execution of the body of the while loop ❺. You might notice that the compiler used a bne instruction. This is the same as b.ne; the . character is optional when writing the conditional branch instructions.

There is a new instruction, cmp ❹, in this code:

cmp—Compare

> cmp *reg, imm* subtracts *imm* from the value in *reg* and sets the condition flags accordingly. The result of the subtraction is discarded.
>
> cmp *reg1, reg2* subtracts the value in *reg2* from the value in *reg1* and sets the condition flags accordingly. The result of the subtraction is discarded.

A cmp instruction immediately followed by a conditional branch instruction is commonly used to make decisions in a program.

For comparison with what the compiler did, we'll follow the while loop pattern in my assembly language version, shown in Listing 13-3.

```
hello_world.s   // Write Hello, World! one character at a time.
                .arch armv8-a
        // Useful names
                .equ    NUL, 0
                .equ    STDOUT, 1
        // Stack frame
                .equ    save19, 16
                .equ    FRAME, 32
        // Constant data
                .section  .rodata
        message:
                .string "Hello, World!\n"
        // Code
                .text
                .align  2
                .global main
                .type   main, %function
        main:
                stp     fp, lr, [sp, -FRAME]! // Create stack frame
                mov     fp, sp              // Set our frame pointer
                str     x19, [sp, save19]   // Save for caller
                adr     x19, message        // Address of message
        loop:
                ldrb    w0, [x19]           // Load character
             ❶ cmp     w0, NUL             // End of string?
                b.eq    done                // Yes
                mov     w2, 1               // No, one char
                mov     x1, x19             // Address of char
                mov     x0, STDOUT          // Write on screen
                bl      write
                add     x19, x19, 1         // Increment pointer
                b       loop                //   and continue
        done:
                mov     w0, wzr             // Return 0
                ldr     x19, [sp, save 19]  // Restore reg
                ldp     fp, lr, [sp], FRAME // Delete stack frame
                ret
```

Listing 13-3: An assembly language program to write Hello, World! one character at a time

We could have used a cbz instruction in our condition check instead of the cmp and b.eq sequence ❶, but I think the use of NUL here is clearer. This solution will also work for any terminating character.

My assembly language solution is less efficient than what the compiler generated (Listing 13-2), because the b instruction is executed in addition to the conditional b.eq instruction with each iteration of the loop. The slight increase in execution time is usually worth the code readability improvement.

A while loop works well when a *sentinel value*, which is a unique value that marks the end of a data sequence, is used as the termination condition. For example, the while loop in Listings 13-1 and 13-3 works for any length of text string and continues writing one character at a time to the screen until it reaches the sentinel value, a NUL character. C has another looping construct, the for loop, that many programmers find to be more natural for some algorithms; we'll look at that next.

for Loop

Although their C syntax differs, the looping constructs while and for are semantically equivalent. The syntactical difference is that the *for loop* allows you to group all three control elements—loop control variable initialization, checking, and changing—within the parentheses. The general form of a for loop in C is as follows:

```
for (initialize loop control variable; expression; change loop control variable) {
    body
}
next statement
```

Placing all the control elements within the parentheses is not required. In fact, we could also write a for loop as follows:

```
initialize loop control variable
for (;expression;) {
    body
    change loop control variable
}
next statement
```

Note that the for loop syntax does require the inclusion of both semicolons in the parentheses.

In Listing 13-4, I have rewritten the program from Listing 13-1 using a for loop.

hello_world_for.c
```
// Write Hello, World! one character at a time.

#include <unistd.h>
#define NUL '\x00'

int main(void)
{
    char *message_ptr;

    for (message_ptr = "Hello, Worlc!\n"; *message_ptr != NUL; message_ptr++) {
        write(STDOUT_FILENO, message_ptr, 1);
    }
```

```
        return 0;
}
```

Listing 13-4: A program to write Hello, World! using a for loop

NOTE   *Since the for statement in this program controls only one C statement, you really don't need the curly brackets around that statement. I usually include them anyway, because if I later modify the program and add another statement, I often forget that I then need the curly brackets.*

You may wonder if either looping construct is better than the other. Here's where your knowledge of assembly language becomes useful. When I used gcc to generate the assembly language for Listing 13-4, I got the same assembly language code I did for the while loop version in Listing 13-1. Since the assembly language for the for loop is shown in Listing 13-2, I won't repeat it here.

The conclusion we can reach from this comparison of a for loop with a while loop is that you should use the high-level language looping construct that feels natural for the problem you're solving. It's usually a subjective choice.

A for loop is often used for a *count-controlled loop*, in which the number of iterations is known before the loop is started. You'll see an example of this usage in a moment, when we look at the selection constructs. First, though, let's look at the third looping construct in C. This provides a different behavior: whereas the while loop and for loop constructs will skip the body of the loop if the termination conditions are met by the initial value of the loop control variable, it will always execute the loop body at least once.

do-while Loop

In some situations, your algorithm needs to execute the body of the loop at least once. In these cases, the *do-while loop* may be more natural. It has the following general form:

```
do {
    body
    change loop control variable
} while (expression)
next statement
```

In the do-while looping construct, the value of the expression is computed at the end of the loop body. Looping continues until this evaluation results in a Boolean false.

In Listing 13-5, I have rewritten the Hello, World! program using a do-while loop.

hello_world_do.c
```
// Write Hello, World! one character at a time.

#include <unistd.h>
```

```
#define NUL '\x00'

int main(void)
{
    char *message_ptr = "Hello, World!\n";

    do {
        write(STDOUT_FILENO, message_ptr, 1);
        message_ptr++;
    } while (*message_ptr != NUL);

    return 0;
}
```

Listing 13-5: A program to write Hello, World! using a do-while loop

NOTE   *This program has a potential bug! The* do-while *loop construct will always execute the body of the loop at least once. Consider an empty text string, which is a single byte containing the* NUL *character. A* do-while *loop writes the* NUL *character to the screen (which does nothing) and then checks the next byte in memory, which could be anything. If this byte is not a* NUL *character, the do-while loop will continue to execute, writing whatever characters this and the following bytes represent, until it reaches a* NUL *character. The behavior of the program could be different each time it's run, so the error may not show up in your testing.*

We can use the assembly language generated by gcc, which is shown in Listing 13-6, to illustrate the difference between the do-while construct and the while and for constructs.

hello_world_do.s
```
        .arch armv8-a
        .file   "hello_world_do.c"
        .text
        .section        .rodata
        .align  3
.LC0:
        .string "Hello, World!\n"
        .text
        .align  2
        .global main
        .type   main, %function
main:
        stp     x29, x30, [sp, -32]!
        mov     x29, sp
        adrp    x0, .LC0
        add     x0, x0, :lo12:.LC0
        str     x0, [sp, 24]       /// message_ptr variable
❶ .L2:
        mov     x2, 1              /// One character
```

```
        ldr     x1, [sp, 24]        /// Address in message_ptr
        mov     w0, 1               /// STDOUT_FILENO
        bl      write
        ldr     x0, [sp, 24]
        add     x0, x0, 1
        str     x0, [sp, 24]        /// message_ptr++;
        ldr     x0, [sp, 24]
        ldrb    w0, [x0]            /// Current char
❷ cmp     w0, 0               /// NUL?
        bne     .L2                 /// No, back to top
        mov     w0, 0
        ldp     x29, x30, [sp], 32
        ret
        .size   main, .-main
        .ident  "GCC: (Debian 10.2.1-6) 10.2.1 20210110"
        .section        .note.GNU-stack,"",@progbits
```

Listing 13-6: The compiler-generated assembly language for the function in Listing 13-5

If you compare the assembly language shown in Listing 13-6 with that in Listing 13-2, which shows the assembly language generated for both the while and for loops, you'll see that the only difference is that the do-while loop doesn't branch down to perform the loop control check ❷ before executing the loop for the first time ❶. The do-while construct might seem more efficient, but in the assembly language, the only saving is a single branch the first time the loop is executed.

Next, we'll look at how to select whether to execute a block of code.

YOUR TURN

13.1   Enter the three C programs in Listings 13-1, 13-4, and 13-5, and use the compiler to generate the assembly language for each of them. Compare the assembly language for the three looping constructs. Compilers change with version changes, so you should look at what your version of the compiler does.

13.2   Write a program in assembly language that:
        (a)   Prompts the user to enter some text
        (b)   Uses the read system call function to read the entered text
        (c)   Echoes the user's entered text in the terminal window
        You will need to allocate space on the stack for storing the characters entered by the user.

Conditionals

Another common flow construct is selection, where we determine whether to execute a block of code. I'll start with the simplest case, determining whether to execute a single block based on a Boolean conditional statement, then I'll show you how to use a Boolean conditional statement to select one of two blocks. I'll end the chapter by discussing ways to select between several blocks based on an integral value.

if

The general form of an *if conditional* in C is as follows:

```
if (expression) {
    block
}
next statement
```

The *expression* is evaluated as a Boolean. If it evaluates to false, or 0 in C, control flow continues to *next statement*. If *expression* evaluates to true (a nonzero value in C), the statements in *block* are executed, and control flow continues to *next statement*.

Listing 13-7 gives an example of an if statement that simulates flipping a coin 10 times and showing when it comes up heads.

coin_flips1.c
```
// Flip a coin, show heads.

#include <stdio.h>
#include <stdlib.h>
#define N_TIMES 10

int main()
{
    register int random_number;
    register int i;

❶  for (i = 0; i < N_TIMES; i++) {
❷      random_number = random();
❸      if (random_number < RAND_MAX/2) {
❹          puts("heads");
        }
    }

    return 0;
}
```

Listing 13-7: A program to flip a coin and show when it comes up heads

This program uses a count-controlled for loop to simulate flipping a coin 10 times ❶. The simulation involves calling the random function in the C standard library ❷. If the random number is in the lower half of all possible values from the random function ❸, we call that "heads." To display this result we use the puts function in the C standard library, which prints a simple text string to the screen with an appended newline character ❹. For Listing 13-7, the compiler generated the assembly language shown in Listing 13-8.

```
coin_flips1.s        .arch armv8-a
                     .file    "coin_flips1.c"
                     .text
                     .section       .rodata
                     .align  3
              .LC0:
                     .string "heads"
                     .text
                     .align  2
                     .global main
                     .type   main, %function
              main:
                     stp     x29, x30, [sp, -32]!
                     mov     x29, sp
                     stp     x19, x20, [sp, 16]  /// Use for i and random_number
                     mov     w19, 0
                     b       .L2
              .L4:
                     bl      random
                     mov     w20, w0             /// Random number
                     mov     w0, 1073741822      /// RAND_MAX/2
                     cmp     w20, w0
               ❶ bgt     .L3                 /// Skip message
                     adrp    x0, .LC0
                     add     x0, x0, :lo12:.LC0
                     bl      puts
          ❷ .L3:
                     add     w19, w19, 1         /// i++;
              .L2:
                     cmp     w19, 9
                     ble     .L4                 /// Continue if <= 9
                     mov     w0, 0
                     ldp     x19, x20, [sp, 16]  /// Restore regs for caller
                     ldp     x29, x30, [sp], 32
                     ret
                     .size   main, .-main
                     .ident  "GCC: (Debian 10.2.1-6) 10.2.1 20210110"
                     .section       .note.GNU-stack,"",@progbits
```

Listing 13-8: The compiler-generated assembly language for the function in Listing 13-7

The if statement is implemented with a simple conditional branch. If the condition—in this case, bgt, for branch if greater than ❶—is true, the program flow branches over the block of code that is controlled by the if statement ❷. Next, I'll show you how to select between two different blocks of code.

if-then-else

The general form of an *if-then-else conditional* in C is as follows (C does not use a then keyword):

```
if (expression) {
    then block
} else {
    else block
}
next statement
```

The *expression* is evaluated as a Boolean. If *expression* evaluates to true, the statements in *then block* are executed and control flow branches to *next statement*. If it evaluates to false (0 in C), control flow branches to *else block* and then continues to *next statement*.

Figure 13-2 shows the control flow of the if-then-else conditional.

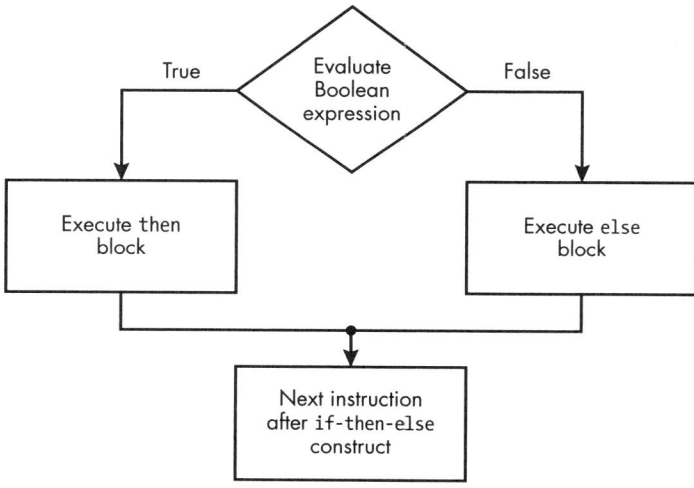

Figure 13-2: The control flow of an if-then-else *conditional*

The coin-flipping program in Listing 13-7 isn't user-friendly because the user doesn't know the total number of times the coin was flipped. We can improve the program by using an if-then-else conditional to print a message stating when the coin came up tails, as shown in Listing 13-9.

coin_flips2.c   // Flip a coin, showing heads or tails.

```
#include <stdio.h>
#include <stdlib.h>
#define N_TIMES 10

int main()
{
```

```
        register int random_number;
        register int i;

        for (i = 0; i < N_TIMES; i++) {
            random_number = random();
            if (random_number < RAND_MAX/2) {
                puts("heads");
            } else {
                puts("tails");
            }
        }

        return 0;
    }
```

Listing 13-9: A program to flip a coin and declare it heads or tails

Listing 13-10 shows the assembly language the compiler generates for Listing 13-9.

coin_flips2.s
```
        .arch armv8-a
        .file   "coin_flips2.c"
        .text
        .section        .rodata
        .align  3
.LC0:
        .string "heads"
        .align  3
.LC1:
        .string "tails"
        .text
        .align  2
        .global main
        .type   main, %function
main:
        stp     x29, x30, [sp, -32]!
        mov     x29, sp
        stp     x19, x20, [sp, 16]
        mov     w19, 0
        b       .L2
.L5:
        bl      random
        mov     w20, w0
        mov     w0, 1073741822
        cmp     w20, w0
        bgt     .L3             /// Go to else block
        adrp    x0, .LC0        /// Then block
        add     x0, x0, :lo12:.LC0
        bl      puts
```

```
        ❶ b       .L4                 /// Branch over else block
    .L3:
          adrp    x0, .LC1            /// Else block
          add     x0, x0, :lo12:.LC1
          bl      puts
❷ .L4:
          add     w19, w19, 1         /// Next statement
    .L2:

          cmp     w19, 9
          ble     .L5
          mov     w0, 0
          ldp     x19, x20, [sp, 16]
          ldp     x29, x30, [sp], 32
          ret
          .size   main, .-main
          .ident  "GCC: (Debian 10.2.1-6) 10.2.1 20210110"
          .section        .note.GNU-stack,"",@progbits
```

Listing 13-10: The compiler-generated assembly language for the function in Listing 13-9

The assembly language shows that we need an unconditional branch
at the end of the then block ❶ to branch over the else block ❷.

My assembly language design of the coin-flipping program differs
slightly, as shown in Listing 13-11.

```
coin_flips2.s  // Flip a coin, showing heads or tails.
               .arch armv8-a
        // Useful names
               .equ    N_TIMES, 10         // Number of flips
               .equ    RAND_MID, 1073741822  // RAND_MAX/2
        // Stack frame
               .equ    save19, 28
               .equ    FRAME, 32
        // Constant data
               .section  .rodata
        heads_msg:
               .string "heads"
        tails_msg:
               .string "tails"
        // Code
               .text
               .align  2
               .global main
               .type   main, %function
        main:
               stp     fp, lr, [sp, -FRAME]! // Create stack frame
               mov     fp, sp                // Set our frame pointer
               str     w19, [sp, save19]     // Save for i local var
               mov     w19, wzr              // i = 0
```

```
loop:
        mov     w0, N_TIMES         // Total number of times
        cmp     w19, w0            // Is i at end?
        b.hs    done               // Yes
        bl      random             // No, get random number
        mov     w1, RAND_MID       // Halfway
  ❶ cmp     w1, w0             // Above or below middle?
        b.hi    tails              // Above -> tails
        adr     x0, heads_msg      // Below -> heads message
        bl      puts               // Print message
        b       continue           // Skip else part
tails:
        adr     x0, tails_msg      // Tails message address
        bl      puts               // Print message
continue:
        add     w19, w19, 1        // Increment i
        b       loop               //   and continue loop
done:
        mov     w0, wzr            // Return 0
        ldr     w19, [sp, save19]  // Restore reg
        ldp     fp, lr, [sp], FRAME // Delete stack frame
        ret                        // Back to caller
```

Listing 13-11: An assembly language design for the coin-flipping program

The random function returns a random number in the w0 register. I leave it there for comparison with the halfway point, which I've loaded into the w1 register ❶. The w0 and w1 registers don't need to be saved in a function. The compiler used w20 for the random_number variable, which does need to be saved.

When deciding which registers to use for variables in a function, it's important that you check the rules in Table 11-3 in Chapter 11. That table says that a function must preserve the value in x19 for the calling function. You can probably see the importance of having agreed-upon rules here. Not only must our function return to the calling function with its value in x19 preserved, but we can assume that the functions that our function calls also preserve our value in x19. So, it's safe to assume that the value remains the same through a function call.

I won't go into the details here, but if you need to select one of several blocks of code to execute, you can use the else-if statement in a *ladder construct*. The general form is as follows:

```
if (expression_1) {
    block_1
} else if (expression_2)  {
    block_2
}
⋮
```

```
    } else if (expression_n-1) {
        block_n-1
    } else {
        block_n
    }
    next statement
```

The if-then-else selection is based on a Boolean evaluation of the controlling expression, but as you'll see in the next section, there are algorithms in which the selection is based on a discrete value, which is used to select one of several cases.

switch

C provides a *switch conditional*, where control flow branches to a place in a list of code blocks depending on the value of a selector. The general form of the switch is as follows:

```
switch (selector) {
    case selector_1:
        block_1
    case selector_2:
        block_2
        ⋮
    case selector_n:
        block_n
    default:
        default block
}
next statement
```

The *selector* can be any expression that evaluates to an integer. Each selector_1, selector_2, ..., selector_n must be an integer constant. The switch will branch to the case whose selector_1, selector_2, ..., selector_n is equal to the *selector* evaluation. If *selector* does not evaluate to any of the selector_1, selector_2, ..., selector_n integers, the switch branches to default. After executing the corresponding block_1, block_2, ..., block_n, program flow continues through the remaining blocks of code. A break statement at any place in the switch will exit the switch at that point and branch down to *next statement*.

Listing 13-12 shows how to use a switch statement in C.

switch.c
```
// Select one of three or default.

#include <stdio.h>
#define N_TIMES 10

int main(void)
{
```

```
        register int selector;
        register int i;

        for (i = 1; i <= N_TIMES; i++) {
            selector = i;
            switch (selector) {
                case 1:
                    puts("i = 1");
                ❶ break;
                case 2:
                    puts("i = 2");
                    break;
                case 3:
                    puts("i = 3");
                    break;
                default:
                    puts("i > 3");
            }
        }

        return 0;
}
```

Listing 13-12: A switch statement

I want this program to execute only the case corresponding to the value of i. To prevent it from executing the following cases in the switch, I end each block with a break statement, which causes an exit from the switch ❶.

Listing 13-13 shows how the compiler implemented this switch.

switch.s
```
        .arch armv8-a
        .file   "switch.c"
        .text
        .section        .rodata
        .align  3
.LC0:
        .string "i = 1"
        .align  3
.LC1:
        .string "i = 2"
        .align  3
.LC2:
        .string "i = 3"
        .align  3
.LC3:
        .string "i > 3"
        .text
        .align  2
        .global main
```

```
                .type   main, %function
        main:
                stp     x29, x30, [sp, -32]!
                mov     x29, sp
                mov     w0, 1
                str     w0, [sp, 28]
                b       .L2
❶ .L8:                                       /// Branch logic to decide
                ldr     w0, [sp, 28]         ///   which block to execute
                cmp     w0, 3
                beq     .L3
                ldr     w0, [sp, 28]
                cmp     w0, 3
                bgt     .L4
                ldr     w0, [sp, 28]
                cmp     w0, 1
                beq     .L5
                ldr     w0, [sp, 28]
                cmp     w0, 2
                beq     .L6
                b       .L4
❷ .L5:                                       /// Blocks to select from
                adrp    x0, .LC0
                add     x0, x0, :lo12:.LC0
                bl      puts
                b       .L7
        .L6:
                adrp    x0, .LC1
                add     x0, x0, :lo12:.LC1
                bl      puts
                b       .L7
        .L3:
                adrp    x0, .LC2
                add     x0, x0, :lo12:.LC2
                bl      puts
                b       .L7
        .L4:
                adrp    x0, .LC3
                add     x0, x0, :lo12:.LC3
                bl      puts
        .L7:
                ldr     w0, [sp, 28]
                add     w0, w0, 1
                str     w0, [sp, 28]
        .L2:
                ldr     w0, [sp, 28]
                cmp     w0, 10
```

```
ble     .L8
mov     w0, 0
ldp     x29, x30, [sp], 32
ret
.size   main, .-main
.ident  "GCC: (Debian 10.2.1-6) 10.2.1 20210110"
.section        .note.GNU-stack,"",@progbits
```

Listing 13-13: Compiler-generated assembly language for the function in Listing 13-12

In Listing 13-13, the compiler creates two parts for the switch. The first part is the logic to decide which block of code to execute ❶. Depending on the value of the selector, this will transfer program flow to the correct block in the second part ❷.

Now, let's look at another way to implement a switch: a *branch table*, also called a *jump table*. A branch table is a table of the block addresses that we need to select from. We need to design an algorithm that will select the correct address in the table, based on the value of the selector, and then branch to that address.

Listing 13-14 shows one way to do this for our current example.

```
switch.s  // Select one of three or default.
          .arch armv8-a
          // Useful names
                .equ    N_TIMES, 10         // Number of loops
                .equ    DEFAULT, 4          // Default case
          // Stack frame
                .equ    save1920, 16
                .equ    FRAME, 32
          // Constant data
                .section   .rodata
          one_msg:
                .string "i = 1"
          two_msg:
                .string "i = 2"
          three_msg:
                .string "i = 3"
          over_msg:
                .string "i > 3"
          // Branch table
              ❶ .align  3
          br_table:
              ❷ .quad   one                 // Addresses where messages
                .quad   two                 //   are printed
                .quad   three
                .quad   default
          // Program code
                .text
                .align  2
```

```
        .global main
        .type   main, %function
main:
        stp     fp, lr, [sp, -FRAME]! // Create stack frame
        mov     fp, sp               // Set our frame pointer
    ❸ stp     x19, x20, [sp, save1920]  // Save for caller
        mov     x19, 1               // i = 1
        mov     x20, DEFAULT         // Default case
loop:
        cmp     x19, N_TIMES         // Is i at end?
        b.hi    done                 // Yes, leave loop
    ❹ adr     x0, br_table         // Address of branch table
        cmp     x19, x20             // Default case?
    ❺ csel    x1, x19, x20, lo     // Low, use i
    ❻ sub     x1, x1, 1            // Relative to first table entry
    ❼ add     x0, x0, x1, lsl 3    // Add address offset in table
    ❽ ldr     x0, [x0]             // Load address from table
        br      x0                   //   and branch there
one:
        adr     x0, one_msg          // = 1
        bl      puts                 // Write to screen
        b       continue
two:
        adr     x0, two_msg          // = 2
        bl      puts                 // Write to screen
        b       continue
three:
        adr     x0, three_msg        // = 3
        bl      puts                 // Write to screen
        b       continue
default:
        adr     x0, over_msg         // > 3
        bl      puts                 // Write to screen
continue:
        add     x19, x19, 1          // Increment i
        b       loop                 //   and continue loop
done:
        mov     w0, wzr              // Return 0
        ldp     x19, x20, [sp, save1920]  // Restore reg
        ldp     fp, lr, [sp], FRAME  // Delete stack frame
        ret                          // Back to caller
```

Listing 13-14: An assembly language design for using a branch table

Each entry in the branch table is the address of the code block to execute for the corresponding value of the selector variable. The .quad assembler directive tells the assembler to allocate 8 bytes of memory and initialize it to the value of the operand ❷. We're using it to store the address of each of the code blocks our algorithm will select from. Since the items in our branch table are 64-bit addresses, we need to align the beginning of the table at a 64-bit address boundary ❶.

Our algorithm uses x19 and x20 as local variables, and the procedure call standard states that we need to save their contents for the calling function (see Table 11-3 in Chapter 11) ❸. We can also assume that their contents will be preserved by the functions we call from this function.

We need to determine which block address to load from the branch table. We start with the address of the beginning of the table ❹. Then, we compare the current value of i, in x19, with the number of the default case. If the value of i is lower than the default case, we'll use the csel instruction to move that value into x1. If it's the same or higher, the csel instruction moves the number of the default case in x20 to x1 ❹. Now that we have the case number in x1, we need to subtract 1 to get the offset in the table from the first item in the table ❻.

Next, we need to convert the case offset to an address offset so we can add it to the address of the beginning of the branch table. Each item in the branch table is 8 bytes wide. We use an option of the add instruction to shift the value of our offset, in x1, 3 bits to the left ❼. This multiplies the offset by 8 before adding it to the beginning address of the branch table, in x0.

Now, x0 contains the address in the branch table of the item we want. We replace the address of the item with the item itself, which is the address of the block to execute ❽.

The csel instruction can be useful for a simple if-then-else construct when you're selecting between two values in registers. It takes this form:

csel—Conditional select

csel *reg1, reg2, reg3, cond* tests the settings in the nzcv register and moves *reg2* to *reg1* if *cond* is true or moves *reg3* to *reg1* if *cond* is false.

You now know two ways to implement a switch construct. It's difficult to say whether a branch table is more efficient than an if-else ladder. For a large number of cases, an if-else ladder may require many tests before reaching the correct case to select. The efficiency also depends on things such as cache usage and the internal CPU design, and it can vary between CPU implementations that use the same instruction set. Any differences between the two techniques will probably be insignificant, so you should choose the one that seems to better match the problem you're solving.

YOUR TURN

13.3 Change the assembly language program in Listing 13-11 so that it sees the lowest one-fourth and the highest one-fourth of the random numbers (0 to RAND_MAX/4 and 3*RAND_MAX/4 to RAND_MAX) as heads. It will see the middle half of the random numbers (RAND_MAX/4 to 3*RAND_MAX/4) as tails.

(continued)

13.4 Remove the break statements in the program in Listing 13-12. How does this change the behavior of the program? Generate the assembly language from your changed program and compare it to that in Listing 13-13.

13.5 Change the program in Listing 13-14 so that it uses if conditionals instead of the csel instruction.

13.6 Rewrite the program in Listing 13-14 so that it uses a ladder of if-else conditionals instead of a switch.

What You've Learned

Unconditional branch   Changes the program counter to alter the control flow.

Conditional branch   Evaluates Boolean combinations of the status flags in the nzcv register and alters control flow if the combination evaluates to true.

while loop   Checks for a Boolean condition and then iterates a block of code until the condition becomes false.

for loop   Checks for a Boolean condition and then iterates a block of code until the condition becomes false.

do-while loop   Executes a block of code once and iterates it until a Boolean condition becomes false.

if conditional   Checks for a Boolean condition and then executes a block of code if the condition is true.

if-then-else conditional   Checks for a Boolean condition and then executes one of two blocks of code, depending on whether the condition is true or false.

switch conditional   Evaluates an expression and then branches to a location in a list of blocks of code, depending on the integer value of the expression.

Now that you know about control flow constructs and the main function, we'll move on to discuss how to write your own subfunctions. In the next chapter, you'll learn how to pass arguments and how to access those arguments in the subfunction.

14

INSIDE SUBFUNCTIONS

Good engineering practice generally includes breaking problems down into functionally distinct subproblems. In software, this approach leads to programs with many functions, each of which solves a subproblem.

The main advantage of this *divide and conquer* approach is that it's usually easier to solve a small subproblem than the overall problem. Another advantage is that previous solutions to subproblems are often reusable, as we have demonstrated by using functions from the C standard library. We can also save development time by having several people work on different parts of the overall problem simultaneously.

When breaking down a problem like this, it's important to coordinate the many partial solutions so that they work together to provide a correct overall solution. In software, this translates to making sure the data interface between a calling function and a called function works correctly. To ensure correct operation of the interface, it must be explicitly specified. In this chapter, I'll show you how to do that. I'll first show you how to place data items in a global location so that all the functions in the program can have direct access to them. Then I'll cover restricting the passage of data items as arguments to a function, which gives us better control over the data the function works with.

In the previous chapters, you learned how to pass arguments to a function in registers. In this chapter, you'll learn how to store these arguments in memory so the registers can be reused inside the called function. You'll also learn how to pass more arguments to a function than can be done with the eight registers specified in Table 11-3 in Chapter 11.

Finally, I'll discuss in more detail the creation of variables within a function. I'll cover variables that exist only when program flow is in the function, as well as variables that stay in memory for the duration of the program but are accessible only within their defining function.

Before we get into the inner workings of functions, however, let's take a look at some of the rules that govern the use of variable names in C.

Scope of Variable Names in C

Scope refers to the places in our code where a variable's name is *visible*, meaning we can use that name. This is not a book on C, so I won't cover all the rules of where variable names can be used in a program, but I'll explain enough to help you understand the basic concepts.

In C, a *declaration* of a variable introduces its name and data type into the current scope. A *definition* of a variable is a declaration that also allocates memory for the variable. A variable can be defined in only one place in a program, but as you'll see in "Global Variables" on page 271, it might be declared in more than one scope.

Variables that are defined inside a function definition are called *local variables*, and names declared in a function's parameter list are called *formal parameters*. Both local variables and formal parameters have *function scope*: their scope extends from the point of declaration to the end of the function.

A *block* in C is a group of C statements enclosed in a matched pair of curly brackets, {}. The scope of variables defined inside a block extends from the point of definition to the end of that block, including any enclosed blocks. This is *block scope*.

A *function prototype* is only a declaration of the function, not its definition. It includes the name of the function, the data types of any parameters passed to the function, and the return data type. The parameters don't need to be named in the prototype, but doing so provides some documentation within the prototype itself. The scope of a parameter name in a prototype declaration is limited to its own prototype. This limit allows us to use the same names in different function prototypes. For example, the C standard library includes functions for computing sine and cosine, whose prototypes are as follows:

```
double sin(double x);
double cos(double x);
```

We can use both function prototypes in the same function without having to use different names for the parameters.

Before looking at the final kind of scope, file scope, I'll give you a brief overview of the reasons for passing arguments to a function.

Overview of Passing Arguments

Input and output are relative to our point of view. As you read through this section, be careful to distinguish between data input from and data output to a calling function and data input from and data output to a user of the program. In this chapter, we're looking at inputs to a function that come from and outputs that go to other functions in the program. We'll look at program inputs from and outputs to I/O devices in Chapter 20.

To illustrate the difference, consider this C program statement (from Listing 2-1 in Chapter 2), which is used to input an integer from the keyboard, an I/O device:

```
scanf("%x", &an_int);
```

The scanf function has one data input from the main function: the address of the formatting text string, "%x". The scanf function reads user data that is input from the keyboard and outputs data, an unsigned integer, to the an_int variable in the main function.

Functions can interact with the data in other parts of the program in four ways:

Direct   Data that is global to the program can be directly accessed from any function in the program.

Input   The data comes from another part of the program and is used by the function, but the original copy is not modified.

Output   The function provides new data to another part of the program.

Update   The function modifies a data item that is held by another part of the program. The new value is based on the value before the function was called.

All four interactions can be performed if the called function also knows the location of the data item, but this exposes the original copy of the data and allows it to be changed even if it's intended to be used only as input to the called function.

We can output data from a function by placing the output in a globally known location, such as a register or a globally known address. We can also pass the called function the address of the place to store the output. Updates require the called function to know the address of the data being updated.

To see how this works, we'll start by looking at how global variables are created and how they are accessed in a subfunction.

Global Variables

Global variables are defined outside any functions and have *file scope*, which means they can be accessed from the point of their definition to the end of the file. Global variables can also be accessed from another file by declaring them with the extern modifier. Using extern only introduces the name and data type of the variable into the scope of the declaration, without allocating memory for it.

Listing 14-1 shows how to define global variables.

sum_ints_global.c
```
// Add two integers using global variables.

#include <stdio.h>
#include "add_two_global.h"

❶ int x = 123, y = 456, z;    // Defire global variables

int main(void)
{
    add_two();
    printf("%i + %i = %i\n", x, y, z);

    return 0;
}
```

Listing 14-1: A main function that uses three global variables

Placing the definitions of the variables x, y, and z outside the function body makes them global ❶. The first two variables are initialized, but not the third. I'll show you how the compiler treats the difference.

This main function calls the add_two function, which will add x and y and store the sum in z. Listing 14-2 shows the assembly language produced by the compiler for this main function.

sum_ints_global.s
```
         .arch armv8-a
         .file   "sum_ints_global.c"
❶       .text
         .global x
❷       .data                      /// Data segment
         .align  2
         .type   x, %object
         .size   x, 4
x:
❸       .word   123                /// Initialize
         .global y
         .align  2
         .type   y, %object
         .size   y, 4
y:
         .word   456
         .global z
❹       .bss                       /// .bss section
         .align  2
         .type   z, %object
```

```
    ❺ .size    z, 4
z:
    ❻ .zero    4                    /// Could use .skip
      .section        .rodata
      .align  3
.LC0:
      .string "%i + %i = %i\n"
      .text
      .align  2
      .global main
      .type   main, %function
main:
      stp     x29, x30, [sp, -16]!
      mov     x29, sp
      bl      add_two
    ❼ adrp    x0, x                /// Address defined
      add     x0, x0, :lo12:x   ///   in this file
      ldr     w1, [x0]
      adrp    x0, y
      add     x0, x0, :lo12:y
      ldr     w2, [x0]
      adrp    x0, z
      add     x0, x0, :lo12:z
      ldr     w0, [x0]
      mov     w3, w0
      adrp    x0, .LC0
      add     x0, x0, :lo12:.LC0
      bl      printf
      mov     w0, 0
      ldp     x29, x30, [sp], 16
      ret
      .size   main, .-main
      .ident  "GCC: (Debian 12.2.0-14) 12.2.0"
      .section        .note.GNU-stack,"",@progbits
```

Listing 14-2: The compiler-generated assembly language for the function in Listing 14-1

I don't know why the compiler added the first .text directive ❶, but it's not needed. Its effect is immediately overridden by the .data assembler directive, which switches us to the data segment ❷.

The .word directive allocates a word (4 bytes) of memory and initializes it to the value of the argument, which is the integer 123 here ❸. The .bss assembler directive then switches us to a *block starting symbol* section, which will be located in the data segment when the program is loaded into memory for execution ❹. Each label defined in a .bss section will name the start of an uninitialized block of memory. Only the size of each labeled block is stored in the program's executable file, thus making the file smaller.

The Linux operating system initializes all the bytes in memory in a `.bss` section to 0 when the program is loaded, but your algorithm should not depend on the variables there being 0 unless they are explicitly set to 0 in your source code.

The `.size` assembler directive associates a label with a number of bytes in its block ❺. The z label is for a 4-byte variable in this program. Although z is not initialized in our C code, and the `.bss` segment will be set to 0 when the program is loaded, the compiler has used the `.zero` assembler directive, which specifies 4 bytes of memory, each set to 0 here ❻. The `.skip` directive would have the same effect as a `.zero` directive in a `.bss` section. Since we are in a `.bss` segment, the assembler does not store the 4 zero bytes in the object file.

The variables are defined in this file, so the compiler uses the adrp/add two-instruction sequence to load their addresses ❼.

Next, let's look at add_two. First, we need a header file for the function. This is shown in Listing 14-3.

---

add_two_global.h   `// Add two global integers.`

❶ `#ifndef ADD_TWO_GLOBAL_H`
❷ `#define ADD_TWO_GLOBAL_H`
❸ `void add_two(void);`
   `#endif`

Listing 14-3: The header file for the add_two function using global variables.

Header files are used to declare a function prototype, which can be declared only once in a C source code file ❸. A header file can include other header files, some of which could include the original header file, leading to a function prototype being declared more than once. To guard against this, we define an identifier that is a stylized version of the header file's name ❷.

We start with an `#ifndef` assembler directive to check if this identifier has already been defined ❶. If not, the contents of the file up to the end of the `#endif` directive are included, defining the filename identifier and declaring the function prototype. The check for the filename identifier in any subsequent inclusions of this header file will then show that the identifier has been defined, so the preprocessor will skip down to the `#endif` and avoid declaring the function prototype again.

Listing 14-4 shows the definition of the add_two function using global variables.

---

add_two_global.c   `// Add two global integers.`

❶ `#include "add_two_global.h"`

❷ `extern int x, y, z;`

   `void add_two(void)`
   `{`

```
    z = x + y;
}
```

Listing 14-4: The add_two function using global variables

The header file for a function should be included in the file where the function is defined to make sure the function prototype in the header file matches the definition ❶. The global variables are defined in only one place, but they need to be declared in any other file that uses them ❷.

Listing 14-5 shows the assembly language generated by the compiler for the add_two function.

add_two_global.s
```
        .arch armv8-a
        .file   "add_two_global.c"
        .text
        .align  2
        .global add_two
        .type   add_two, %function
add_two:
    ❶ adrp    x0, :got:x              /// Global offset table page
    ❷ ldr     x0, [x0, :got_lo12:x]   /// Address of x
        ldr     w1, [x0]
        adrp    x0, :got:y
        ldr     x0, [x0, :got_lo12:y]
        ldr     w0, [x0]
        add     w1, w1, w0
        adrp    x0, :got:z
        ldr     x0, [x0, :got_lo12:z]
        str     w1, [x0]
    ❸ nop
        ret
        .size   add_two, .-add_two
        .ident  "GCC: (Debian 12.2.0-14) 12.2.0"
        .section        .note.GNU-stack,"",@progbits
```

Listing 14-5: The compiler-generated assembly language for the function in Listing 14-4

The add_two function declares the x, y, and z variables with an extern storage class specifier so it can access them, but it needs to use a different technique to load the addresses because they are defined in another file. The loader stores the addresses of the global variables in the global offset table (GOT), introduced in "The Linker" on page 239, when the program is loaded into memory for execution. The :got: operand modifier tells the loader to use the GOT containing the address of the variable when filling in the page offset from the adrp instruction ❶.

The ldr instruction here is using the page address of the GOT, in x0, for its base address ❷. The :got_lo12: operand modifier tells the loader to use the low-order 12 bits of the offset to where the variable's address is stored in the GOT, thus overwriting the page address of the GOT with the variable's address in x0.

Listing 14-5 also contains a new instruction, the nop (pronounced "no-op") ❸. It has no effect on the algorithm. The manual says it's used for instruction alignment purposes:

nop—No operation

nop adds 4 to the program counter with no other effect.

Although global variables are simple to work with in small programs, managing them is unwieldy in large programs. You need to keep track of exactly what each function in the program is doing with the global variables. Managing variables is much easier if you define them within a function and pass only what is needed to each subfunction. In the next section, I'll show you how to maintain control over what gets passed to and from a subfunction.

Explicitly Passing Arguments

When we restrict each function to using only those variables it needs, it's much easier to isolate the inner workings of a function from other functions. This is a principle called *information hiding*. It means that you, the programmer, need to deal with only those variables and constants that a subfunction needs to do its specific job. Of course, most subfunctions will need to interact with some of the variables in their calling functions in one way or another. In this section, we'll look at how a function uses the arguments explicitly passed to it to accept input, produce output, or update a variable.

When a value serves only as input to the called function, we can pass a copy of the value to the called function. This is called *passing by value*. Passing by value prevents the called function from changing the value in the calling function.

Receiving output from the called function is a bit more complex. One way to accomplish this is to use a *return value*, which in our environment is placed in the w0 register. Using the w0 register assumes the return value is an int. This technique is used in most of the example programs in this book. The main function almost always returns a 0 to the function in the operating system that called it. There are other rules for returning larger values, which we won't go into in this book.

The other techniques for the calling function to receive an output from the called function require that the calling function pass the called function the address of the place to store the output. This can be implemented in higher-level languages as either *pass by pointer* or *pass by reference*. The difference is that with pass by pointer, the program can change the pointer to point to another object, while with pass by reference, the program cannot change the pointer. C and C++ both support pass by pointer, but only C++ supports pass by reference. These are the same at the assembly language level; the address of the place to store the output is passed to the called function. The difference is enforced by the high-level language.

Next, you'll learn how C controls access to its local variables.

In C

In this section, I'll write the same program as in Listings 14-1, 14-3, and 14-4, but this time I'll define the variables as local variables in the main function and pass them as arguments to the subfunction. Listing 14-6 shows the new version of the main function.

sum_ints.c
```
// Add two integers using local variables.

#include <stdio.h>
#include "add_two.h"

int main(void)
{
❶ int x = 123, y = 456, z;

❷ add_two(&z, x, y);
    printf("%i + %i = %i\n", x, y, z);

    return 0;
}
```

Listing 14-6: A main function that uses three local variables

Defining the variables inside the body of the function ❶ makes them visible only to this function. The add_two function will store its result at the address we pass in as the first argument. We use the C address operator, &, to get the address of the z variable, giving &z ❷. The values of the x and y variables are inputs to the add_two function, so we pass copies of these variables.

Listing 14-7 shows the header file for the add_two function.

add_two.h
```
// Add two integers and output the sum.

#ifndef ADD_TWO_H
#define ADD_TWO_H
void add_two(int *a, int b, int c);
#endif
```

Listing 14-7: The header file for the add_two function using local variables

Listing 14-8 shows the definition of the add_two function.

add_two.c
```
// Add two integers and output the sum.

#include "add_two.h"

void add_two(int *a, int b, int c)
{
    int sum;
```

```
    sum = b + c;
❶  *a = sum;
}
```

Listing 14-8: The add_two function using local variables

The first parameter in the argument list, a, is a pointer to an int. This means that a holds the address where we need to store the value of sum. To dereference a, we use the C *dereference operator*, *, giving *a ❶. This stores the result of the computation at the address passed in a.

In Assembly Language

Listing 14-9 shows the assembly language generated by the compiler for the main function in Listing 14-6.

---

sum_ints.s

```
        .arch armv8-a
        .file    "sum_ints.c"
        .text
        .section        .rodata
        .align  3
.LC0:
        .string "%i + %i = %i\n"
        .text
        .align  2
        .global main
        .type   main, %function
main:
❶  stp     x29, x30, [sp, -32]!
    mov     x29, sp
    mov     w0, 123
❷  str     w0, [sp, 28]        /// x = 123;
    mov     w0, 456
    str     w0, [sp, 24]        /// y = 456;
❸  add     x0, sp, 20          /// Address of z
❹  ldr     w2, [sp, 24]        /// Load y and x
    ldr     w1, [sp, 28]
    bl      add_two
    ldr     w0, [sp, 20]
    mov     w3, w0
    ldr     w2, [sp, 24]
    ldr     w1, [sp, 28]
    adrp    x0, .LC0
    add     x0, x0, :lo12:.LC0
    bl      printf
    mov     w0, 0
    ldp     x29, x30, [sp], 32
    ret
```

```
.size   main, .-main
.ident  "GCC: (Debian 12.2.0-14) 12.2.0"
.section        .note.GNU-stack,"",@progbits
```

Listing 14-9: The compiler-generated assembly language for the function in Listing 14-6

All three variables are automatic local variables, so the compiler allocates space for them in the stack frame ❶. Initialized automatic local variables are newly created each time the function is called, so they need to be actively initialized ❷.

We pass the address of our z variable to the add_two function so it can store its output there ❸, and we send copies of the values in the x and y variables as inputs to the function ❹.

Listing 14-10 shows the compiler-generated assembly language for the add_two function.

add_two.s
```
        .arch armv8-a
        .file   "add_two.c"
        .text
        .align  2
        .global add_two
        .type   add_two, %function
add_two:
❶ sub     sp, sp, #32
❷ str     x0, [sp, 8]      /// Address for output
   str     w1, [sp, 4]      /// Value of first input
   str     w2, [sp]         /// Value of second input
   ldr     w1, [sp, 4]
   ldr     w0, [sp]
   add     w0, w1, w0
   str     w0, [sp, 28]     /// Store sum locally
   ldr     x0, [sp, 8]
   ldr     w1, [sp, 28]     /// Load sum
   str     w1, [x0]         /// Store for caller
   nop
   add     sp, sp, 32
   ret
        .size   add_two, .-add_two
        .ident  "GCC: (Debian 12.2.0-14) 12.2.0"
        .section        .note.GNU-stack,"",@progbits
```

Listing 14-10: The compiler-generated assembly language for the function in Listing 14-8

The first thing you might notice about this function is that it does not save the contents of the link register, lr, and frame pointer, fp ❶. These two addresses make up the *frame record*. The address in lr provides the link back to the place where this function was called, while fp provides a link back to the frame record of the calling function. This chain of frame records can be useful in certain error situations, but I won't get into the details in this book.

The AArch64 procedure call standard states that a small function that doesn't call a function does not need a frame record, which explains why the compiler has omitted it. A function that does not call any functions is often called a *leaf function*.

This function simply allocates a 32-byte stack frame, where it stores the three items that were passed to it ❷. You can probably tell this is not needed in this very simple function, but it might be in more complex functions. Figure 14-1 gives a pictorial view of add_two's stack frame.

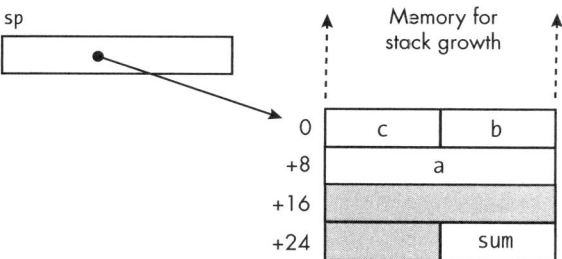

Figure 14-1: The stack frame for the add_two function in Listing 14-10

The values at c and b are inputs to this function, and a is the address where the output from the function will be stored.

Listing 14-11 shows how I would probably write the add_two function in assembly language.

```
add_two.s   // Add two integers and output the sum.
            // Calling sequence:
            //     x0 <- address of output
            //     w1 <- integer
            //     w2 <- integer
            //     Returns 0
                  .arch armv8-a
            // Stack frame
              ❶ .equ    save1920, 16
                .equ    FRAME, 32
            // Code
                  .text
                  .align  2
                  .global add_two
                  .type   add_two, %function
            add_two:
                  stp     fp, lr, [sp, -FRAME]!    // Create stack frame
                  mov     fp, sp                   // Set our frame pointer
              ❷ stp     x19, x20, [sp, save1920] // Save for local vars

                  mov     x20, x0                  // For output
              ❸ add     w19, w2, w1              // Compute sum
                  str     w19, [x20]               // Output sum
```

```
        mov     w0, wzr                  // Return 0
❹ ldp     x19, x20, [sp, save1920]   // Restore reg
   ldp     fp, lr, [sp], FRAME       // Delete stack frame
   ret                              // Back to caller
```

Listing 14-11: The add_two function written in assembly language

A stack frame is not required for this small leaf function, but I have created one here to show how to save registers for the calling function so we can use them as local variables. We first need to specify a location in the stack frame ❶. This leads to the stack frame shown in Figure 14-2.

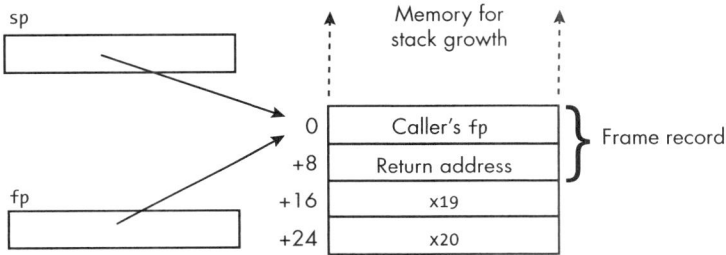

Figure 14-2: The stack frame for the add_two function in Listing 14-11

Although the algorithm uses only the low-order word of the x19 register, we need to save the entire 64 bits because our algorithm might change the high-order 32 bits ❷. In fact, the add instruction here will zero the high-order 32 bits of x19 ❸. Don't forget that we need to restore the saved registers before undoing our stack frame ❹.

Comparing the stack frame for my assembly language version of the add_two function with the stack frame created by the compiler for the C version in Figure 14-1, notice that I've created a frame record at the top of my stack frame. I've then saved the x19 and x20 registers so I can use them for the computations in the function. If I later change my assembly language add_two function such that it calls another function, I don't need to change its stack frame because it already has a frame record, and the standard says that the called function must preserve the values in the x19 and 20 registers for the calling function.

In the next section, you'll see how the stack comes to our rescue when we want to pass more than the eight arguments we can pass in registers.

With More Than Eight Arguments

Most functions take fewer than the eight arguments we can pass in registers, but sometimes a calling function needs to pass more than eight arguments to another function. In these cases, the arguments beyond the first eight are passed on the call stack. They are placed on the stack before the call to the function. I'll use the program in Listings 14-12, 14-14, and 14-15 to show you how this works.

sum11ints.c // Sum the integers 1 to 11.

```c
#include <stdio.h>
#include "add_eleven.h"

int main(void)
{
    int total;
    int a = 1;
    int b = 2;
    int c = 3;
    int d = 4;
    int e = 5;
    int f = 6;
    int g = 7;
    int h = 8;
    int i = 9;
    int j = 10;
    int k = 11;

    total = add_eleven(a, b, c, d, e, f, g, h, i, j, k);
    printf("The sum is %i\n", total);

    return 0;
}
```

Listing 14-12: A program passing more than eight arguments to a subfunction

This main function creates 11 integer variables and initializes them to the values 1 through 11. It then calls the add_eleven function to compute the sum of the 11 numbers and prints the result.

Listing 14-13 shows the assembly language generated by the compiler for the main function in Listing 14-12.

sum11ints.s

```
        .arch armv8-a
        .file   "sum11ints.c"
        .text
        .section        .rodata
        .align  3
.LC0:
        .string "The sum is %i\n"
        .text
        .align  2
        .global main
        .type   main, %function
main:
     ❶  sub     sp, sp, #96         /// Local vars and args
        stp     x29, x30, [sp, 32]  /// Store caller fp and lr
```

```
       add     x29, sp, 32          /// Point fp to caller's fp
       mov     w0, 1                /// Store values in local vars
       str     w0, [sp, 92]
       mov     w0, 2
       str     w0, [sp, 88]
       mov     w0, 3
       str     w0, [sp, 84]
       mov     w0, 4
       str     w0, [sp, 80]
       mov     w0, 5
       str     w0, [sp, 76]
       mov     w0, 6
       str     w0, [sp, 72]
       mov     w0, 7
       str     w0, [sp, 68]
       mov     w0, 8
       str     w0, [sp, 64]
       mov     w0, 9
       str     w0, [sp, 60]
       mov     w0, 10
       str     w0, [sp, 56]
       mov     w0, 11
       str     w0, [sp, 52]
       ldr     w0, [sp, 52]         /// Store args on the stack
   ❷  str     w0, [sp, 16]
       ldr     w0, [sp, 56]
       str     w0, [sp, 8]
       ldr     w0, [sp, 60]
       str     w0, [sp]
   ❸  ldr     w7, [sp, 64]         /// Load args into regs
       ldr     w6, [sp, 68]
       ldr     w5, [sp, 72]
       ldr     w4, [sp, 76]
       ldr     w3, [sp, 80]
       ldr     w2, [sp, 84]
       ldr     w1, [sp, 88]
       ldr     w0, [sp, 92]
       bl      add_eleven
       str     w0, [sp, 48]
       ldr     w1, [sp, 48]
       adrp    x0, .LC0
       add     x0, x0, :lo12:.LC0
       bl      printf
       mov     w0, 0
       ldp     x29, x30, [sp, 32]
       add     sp, sp, 96
       ret
```

```
        .size   main, .-main
        .ident  "GCC: (Debian 12.2.0-14) 12.2.0"
        .section        .note.GNU-stack,"",@progbits
```

Listing 14-13: The compiler-generated assembly language for the function in Listing 14-12

When this function creates its stack frame, it allocates memory on the stack for the additional arguments it needs to pass on the stack ❶. Before calling the add_eleven function, it works from right to left in the argument list. Since it can pass only eight arguments in registers, it needs to store the three excess arguments on the stack ❷. These arguments are stored at the top of our stack frame, where the AArch64 procedure call standard specifies the called function should expect them. Figure 14-3 shows the state of the stack at this point.

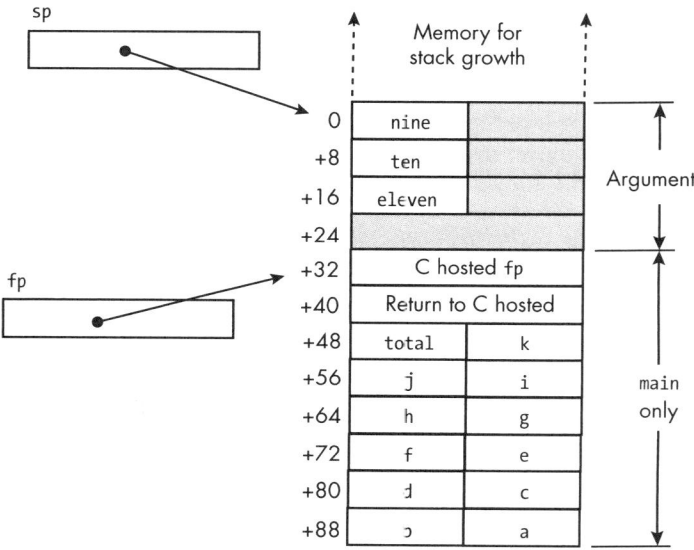

Figure 14-3: The stack frame for the main function in Listing 14-12, just before calling add_eleven

Figure 14-3 shows that the stack pointer is pointing to the arguments that are being passed to add_eleven on the stack. The names in the arguments area in this figure, nine, ten, and eleven, are the corresponding parameter names used by the add_eleven function. The procedure call standard allows both main and add_eleven to access stack memory in the arguments area, but argument passing can only take place from caller to callee—that is, from main to add_eleven in this example.

Although we're passing 4-byte ints, the AArch64 procedure call standard states that we must use 8 bytes for each stack argument, the same number of bytes as a register argument. Following this rule ensures you can use your assembly language functions with C functions. In Figure 14-3, the compiler has stored the ninth, tenth, and eleventh arguments in the low-order

4 bytes of each argument slot on the stack. (Don't forget that our memory order is little-endian.)

With our stack frame set up for calling the add_eleven function, we now store the remaining eight arguments in registers ❸.

Let's look at how the add_eleven function retrieves the arguments from the stack. I'll start with the header file for the function, in Listing 14-14.

add_eleven.h
```
// Add 11 integers and return the sum.

#ifndef ADD_ELEVEN_H
#define ADD_ELEVEN_H
int add_eleven(int one, int two, int three, int four, int five, int six,
               int seven, int eight, int nine, int ten, int eleven);
#endif
```

Listing 14-14: The header file for the add_eleven function

The add_eleven function is defined in Listing 14-15.

add_eleven.c
```
// Add 11 integers and return the sum.

#include <stdio.h>
#include "add_eleven.h"

int add_eleven(int one, int two, int three, int four, int five, int six,
               int seven, int eight, int nine, int ten, int eleven)
{
    int sum = one + two + three + four + five + six
            + seven + eight + nine + ten + eleven;
    printf("Added them\n");

    return sum;
}
```

Listing 14-15: A function that receives more than eight arguments from a calling function

Listing 14-16 shows the assembly language generated by the compiler for the add_eleven function in Listing 14-15.

add_eleven.s
```
        .arch armv8-a
        .file   "add_eleven.c"
        .text
        .section        .rodata
        .align  3
.LC0:
        .string "Added them"
        .text
        .align  2
        .global add_eleven
        .type   add_eleven, %function
```

```
add_eleven:
        stp     x29, x30, [sp, -64]!
        mov     x29, sp
❶ str     w0, [sp, 44]              /// Save register arguments locally
        str     w1, [sp, 40]
        str     w2, [sp, 36]
        str     w3, [sp, 32]
        str     w4, [sp, 28]
        str     w5, [sp, 24]
        str     w6, [sp, 20]
        str     w7, [sp, 16]
        ldr     w1, [sp, 44]              /// Add first 8 inputs
        ldr     w0, [sp, 40]
        add     w1, w1, w0
        ldr     w0, [sp, 36]
        add     w1, w1, w0
        ldr     w0, [sp, 32]
        add     w1, w1, w0
        ldr     w0, [sp, 28]
        add     w1, w1, w0
        ldr     w0, [sp, 24]
        add     w1, w1, w0
        ldr     w0, [sp, 20]
        add     w1, w1, w0
        ldr     w0, [sp, 16]
        add     w1, w1, w0
❷ ldr     w0, [sp, 64]              /// Add inputs 9-11 from the stack
        add     w1, w1, w0
        ldr     w0, [sp, 72]
        add     w0, w1, w0
        ldr     w1, [sp, 80]
        add     w0, w1, w0
        str     w0, [sp, 60]
        adrp    x0, .LC0
        add     x0, x0, :lo12:.LC0
        bl      puts
        ldr     w0, [sp, 60]
        ldp     x29, x30, [sp], 64
        ret
        .size   add_eleven, .-add_eleven
        .ident  "GCC: (Debian 12.2.0-14) 12.2.0"
        .section        .note.GNU-stack,"",@progbits
```

Listing 14-16: The compiler-generated assembly language for the function in Listing 14-15

After creating a stack frame, the compiler saves the arguments that were passed in registers, because the call to another function might change their contents ❶. It does this near the beginning of the function so it doesn't have to keep track of which ones have been saved when compiling the C statements in the function.

After loading each of these eight arguments from the stack and summing them, the function adds the remaining three arguments that are in the calling function's stack frame ❷.

Figure 14-4 shows the stack frames belonging to the main and add_eleven functions.

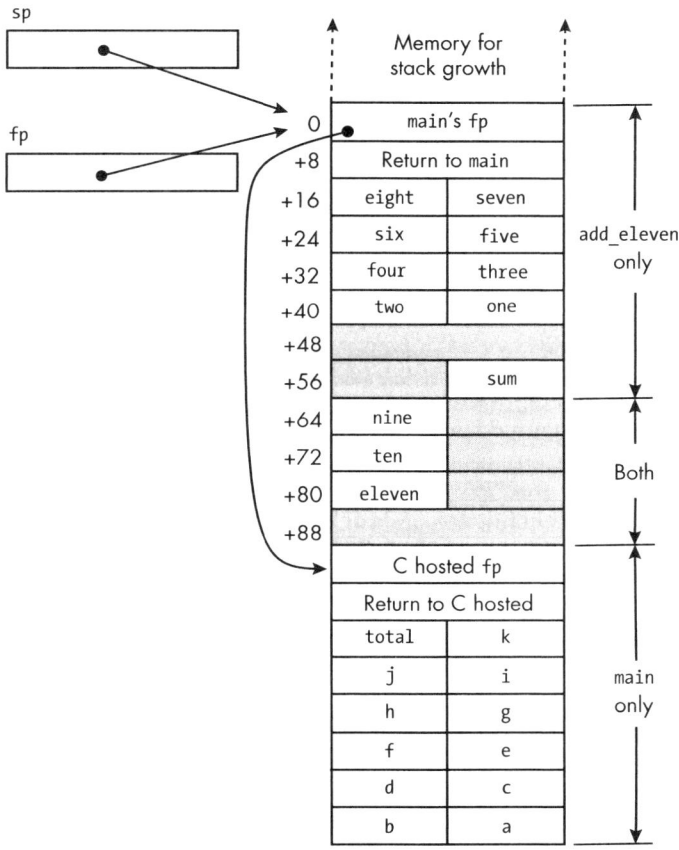

Figure 14-4: The stack frames after the add_eleven function has been called and has created its stack frame

I mentioned on page 279 that the frame pointer points to the frame record, which points to the calling function's frame record, and so forth. Figure 14-4 shows this chain back to main's frame record.

I've shown only the offsets from sp that should be used by add_eleven. This function knows that sp was pointing to three 32-bit arguments before it subtracted 64 from sp, so the first argument on the stack is now +64 from sp.

The procedure call standard allows the add_eleven function to store and load items to and from the area labeled "add_eleven only" in Figure 14-4. It allows the add_eleven function to use items in the stack area labeled "Both," but it does not allow a called function to pass items back to the calling function in this area. The add_eleven function is not allowed to access the stack area labeled "main only."

The main function can store and load items to and from the area labeled "main only" in Figure 14-4, but it is allowed only to store items to the stack area labeled "Both."

Stack Frame Discipline

It's essential that you follow the register usage and argument passing disciplines precisely when writing in assembly language. Any deviation can cause errors that are difficult to debug.

Figure 14-5 shows the overall pattern for a stack frame.

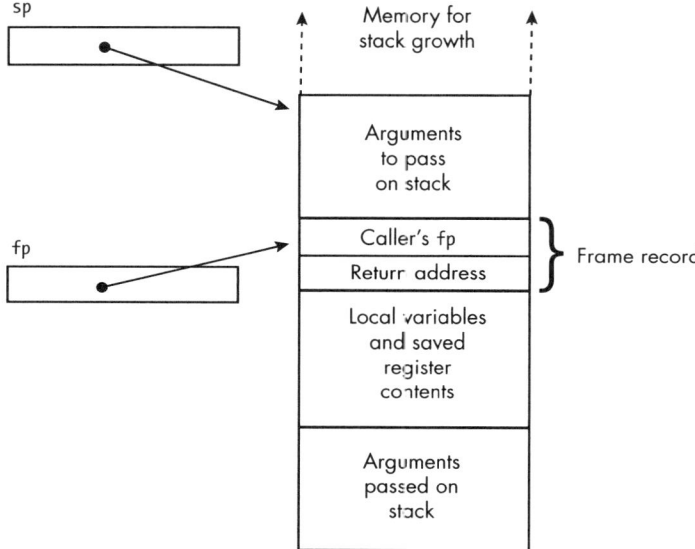

Figure 14-5: A stack frame

A stack frame doesn't always include all the parts in Figure 14-5. If the function never passes more than eight arguments to the functions it calls, the top box doesn't exist. In this case, sp and fp both point to the frame record.

Some functions may not have any local variables or saved register contents. If it's a leaf function, we don't even need a frame record.

If no more than eight arguments are passed to the function, then the bottom box in this diagram does not exist. The bottom box is the only area of the stack frame that both the current function and its calling function have access to.

Let's write the sum11ints program in assembly language. Unless it's a very simple function, I start my designs by drawing a diagram of the stack frame for each function, similar to Figures 14-3 and 14-4. Then I use .equ directives to give symbolic names to the locations on the stack that I need to access in my code.

Listing 14-17 shows how we can do this for the main function in our sum11ints program.

sum11ints.s
```
// Sum the integers 1 to 11.
        .arch armv8-a
// Stack frame
❶ .equ    arg9, 0
    .equ    arg10, 8
    .equ    arg11, 16
    .equ    frame_record, 32
    .equ    total, 48
    .equ    k, 52
    .equ    j, 56
    .equ    i, 60
    .equ    h, 64
    .equ    g, 68
    .equ    f, 72
    .equ    e, 76
    .equ    d, 80
    .equ    c, 84
    .equ    b, 88
    .equ    a, 92
    .equ    FRAME, 96
// Constant data
        .section  .rodata
        .align  3
format:
        .string "The sum is %i\n"
        .text
        .align  2
        .global main
        .type   main, %function
main:
❷ sub     sp, sp, FRAME            // Allocate our stack frame
    stp     fp, lr, [sp, frame_record] // Create frame record
    add     fp, sp, frame_record    // Set our frame pointer
    mov     w0, 1                   // Store values in local vars
❸ str     w0, [sp, a]
    mov     w0, 2
    str     w0, [sp, b]
    mov     w0, 3
    str     w0, [sp, c]
    mov     w0, 4
    str     w0, [sp, d]
    mov     w0, 5
    str     w0, [sp, e]
    mov     w0, 6
    str     w0, [sp, f]
```

```
        mov     w0, 7
        str     w0, [sp, g]
        mov     w0, 8
        str     w0, [sp, h]
        mov     w0, 9
        str     w0, [sp, i]
        mov     w0, 10
        str     w0, [sp, j]
        mov     w0, 11
        str     w0, [sp, k]
        ldr     w0, [sp, k]                    // Store args 9-11
        str     w0, [sp, arg11]                //    on the stack
        ldr     w0, [sp, j]
        str     w0, [sp, arg10]
        ldr     w0, [sp, i]
        str     w0, [sp, arg9]
        ldr     w7, [sp, h]                    // Load args 1-8
        ldr     w6, [sp, g]                    //    in regs 0-7
        ldr     w5, [sp, f]
        ldr     w4, [sp, e]
        ldr     w3, [sp, d]
        ldr     w2, [sp, c]
        ldr     w1, [sp, b]
        ldr     w0, [sp, a]
        bl      add_eleven                     // Add all
        str     w0, [sp, total]                // Store returned sum
        ldr     w1, [sp, total]                // Argument to printf
        adr     x0, format                     // Format string
        bl      printf                         // Print result

        mov     w0, wzr                        // Return 0
        ldp     fp, lr, [sp, frame_record]     // Restore fp and lr
        add     sp, sp, FRAME                  // Delete stack frame
        ret                                    // Back to caller
```

Listing 14-17: The sum11ints main function written in assembly language

The list of .equ directives gives a good view of what our stack frame looks like ❶. Using the symbolic names for our variables makes it easy to read the assembly language code, because we don't have to remember the numerical offset of each item on the stack ❸.

The algorithm for the function prologue needs to take into account that main will be passing arguments on the stack. We start by allocating space for our stack frame ❷. Then, we create the frame record after the area for passing arguments on the stack. This is easy once we have created our .equ view of the stack frame.

Next, we'll write the `add_eleven` function in assembly language, using the diagram in Figure 14-4 to set the values of the `.equ` directives. The assembly language is shown in Listing 14-18.

```
add_eleven.s    // Add 11 integers and return the sum.
                // Calling sequence:
                //      w0 through w7 <- 8 integers
                //      [sp] <- integer
                //      [sp+8] <- integer
                //      [sp+16] <- integer
                //      Returns sum
                        .arch armv8-a
                // Stack frame
                        .equ    eight, 16
                        .equ    seven, 20
                        .equ    six, 24
                        .equ    five, 28
                        .equ    four, 32
                        .equ    three, 36
                        .equ    two, 40
                        .equ    one, 44
                        .equ    sum, 60
                ❶ .equ    FRAME, 64          // End of our frame
                        .equ    nine, 64          // Stack args
                        .equ    ten, 72
                        .equ    eleven, 80
                // Constant data
                        .section  .rodata
                        .align  3
                msg:
                        .string "Added them"
                        .text
                        .align  2
                        .global add_eleven
                        .type   add_eleven, %function
                add_eleven:
                ❷ stp     fp, lr, [sp, -FRAME]! // Create stack frame
                        mov     fp, sp                 // Set our frame pointer

                        str     w0, [sp, one]      // Save register args
                        str     w1, [sp, two]
                        str     w2, [sp, three]
                        str     w3, [sp, four]
                        str     w4, [sp, five]
                        str     w5, [sp, six]
                        str     w6, [sp, seven]
                        str     w7, [sp, eight]
```

```
        ldr     w1, [sp, one]           // Load args
        ldr     w0, [sp, two]
        add     w1, w1, w0              //    and sum them
        ldr     w0, [sp, three]
        add     w1, w1, w0
        ldr     w0, [sp, four]
        add     w1, w1, w0
        ldr     w0, [sp, five]
        add     w1, w1, w0
        ldr     w0, [sp, six]
        add     w1, w1, w0
        ldr     w0, [sp, seven]
        add     w1, w1, w0
        ldr     w0, [sp, eight]
        add     w1, w1, w0
        ldr     w0, [sp, nine]
        add     w1, w1, w0
        ldr     w0, [sp, ten]
        add     w1, w1, w0
        ldr     w0, [sp, eleven]
        add     w1, w1, w0
        str     w1, [sp, sum]           // Store sum
        adr     x0, msg                 // Tell user we're done
        bl      puts

        ldr     w0, [sp, sum]           // Return the sum
        ldp     fp, lr, [sp], FRAME     // Delete stack frame
        ret                             // Back to caller
```

Listing 14-18: The add_eleven function written in assembly language

We need to be careful to distinguish between the part of our stack frame being used only by this function and the arguments that were passed in by the calling function. Naming this boundary with a .equ directive ❶ makes it easy to create our stack frame ❷. As with the main function in Listing 14-17, the .equ directive names also make it easier to read the assembly language.

The values in automatic local variables will be lost when exiting a function. There are times when you want the information provided by a local variable to be hidden, but you also want the content of the variable to remain the same between subsequent calls to the function. We'll look next at how this can be done.

YOUR TURN

14.1   Show that the assembly language add_eleven function in
        Listing 14-18 works with the C main function in Listing 14-12.

14.2 Show that initializing the sum variable in Listing 14-15 is the same as doing the addition separately, like in Listing 14-8.

14.3 Write a program in assembly language that sums all the integers between two integers entered by the user.

14.4 Write the three functions write_char, write_str, and read_str in assembly language. You'll use these functions in exercises later in the book. Here are the specifications for each:

(a) write_char writes one character in the terminal window using the write system call. It takes one argument and returns 0.

(b) write_str writes text in the terminal window using the write system call. It takes one argument and returns the number of characters written.

(c) read_str reads characters from the keyboard using the read system call and stores them in memory as a C-style text string, without the return character. It takes two arguments: a pointer to the memory location to store the text and the maximum number of characters to store. If the number of characters entered exceeds the maximum, it reads the remaining input but does not store it. It returns the number of characters entered, less the NUL terminating character.

Test the functions with the following C main function. Don't forget to write the C header files for your assembly language functions.

```c
// Prompt user to enter text and echo it.

#include "write_char.h"
#include "write_str.h"
#include "read_str.h"
#define MAX 5
#define BUFF_SZ MAX+1    // Make room for NUL

int main(void)
{
    char text[BUFF_SZ];

    write_str("Enter some text: ");
    read_str(text, MAX);
    write_str("You entered: ");
    write_str(text);
    write_char('\n');

    return 0;
}
```

Hint: Use a small number for MAX when testing your read_str function.

Static Local Variables

As discussed in Chapter 11, automatic local variables are created in a function's prologue and get deleted in the function's epilogue. This means the value stored in an automatic local variable will be lost in subsequent calls to the function. But in some cases, we might want to keep the value of a variable between function calls while still providing the information-hiding advantage of a local variable. For example, we might have a function that is called from several other functions and want to maintain a count of how many times it's called. We could use a global variable, but a global variable doesn't provide the information-hiding properties of a local variable.

Instead, we can use a *static local variable*. Like an automatic local variable, a static local variable has local scope; however, like a global variable, it remains in memory throughout the lifetime of the entire program.

In C

I'll explain where static local variables are created in memory using the program in Listings 14-19, 14-20, and 14-21. These listings illustrate the differences between the visibility and persistence of an automatic local variable, a static local variable, and a global variable.

var_life.c
```
// Compare the scope and lifetime of automatic, static, and global variables.

#include <stdio.h>
#include "add_const.h"
#define INIT_X 12
#define INIT_Y 34
#define INIT_Z 56

int z = INIT_Z;

int main(void)
{
    int x = INIT_X;
    int y = INIT_Y;

    printf("             automatic   static   global\n");
    printf("                  x         y        z\n");
    printf("In main:%12i %8i %8i\n", x, y, z);
    add_const();
    add_const();
    printf("In main:%12i %8i %8i\n", x, y, z);
    return 0;
}
```

Listing 14-19: A program to compare automatic local, static local, and global variables

This main function defines three int variables: the global variable z and the automatic local variables x and y.

Listing 14-20 shows the header file for the add_const function, which adds a constant value to an automatic local variable, a static local variable, and the global variable defined in main.

add_const.h   `// Add a constant to an automatic local variable, a static local variable,`

```
// and a global variable.

#ifndef ADD_CONST_H
#define ADD_CONST_H
void add_const(void);
#endif
```

Listing 14-20: The header file for the add_const function

Listing 14-21 is the definition of the add_const function.

add_const.c   `// Add a constant to an automatic local variable, a static local variable,`

```
// and a global variable.

#include <stdio.h>
#include "add_const.h"
#define INIT_X 78
#define INIT_Y 90
#define ADDITION 1000

void add_const(void)
{
    int x = INIT_X;         // Every call
  ❶ static int y = INIT_Y;  // First call only
  ❷ extern int z;           // Global

    x += ADDITION;          // Add to each
    y += ADDITION;
    z += ADDITION;

    printf("In add_const:%7i %8i %8i\n", x, y, z);
}
```

Listing 14-21: A function to add a constant value to three variables

The add_const function defines two local variables, x and y. The y variable is specified to be static ❶. This means it will be initialized to INIT_Y only the first time add_const is called. (If you don't give an initial value to a static local variable, the compiler will initialize it to 0, but I recommend explicitly initializing it to 0 if that is your intention.) Any changes to y by add_const will persist through this call and all subsequent calls to the function. The z variable is declared with the extern modifier ❷ to show that it's defined elsewhere in the program.

The add_const function adds a constant value to each of the three variables declared in the function. The printf statement shows the values of the x and y local variables defined in add_const and the z global variable defined in main each time add_const is called.

Executing this program gives the following output:

```
              automatic    static    global
                      x         y         z
In main:             12        34        56
In add_const:      1078      1090      1056
In add_const: ❶ 1078   ❷ 2090      2056
In main:             12        34  ❸ 2056
```

As you can see, the x in main is different from the x in add_const. Each time main calls add_const, the x in add_const is initialized to 78 and the function adds 1,000 to it ❶. This shows that a new x is automatically created each time add_const is called.

You can also see that the y in main is different from the y in add_const, but the behavior of the x and y variables in add_const is not the same. The first time add_const is called, it initializes its y variable to 90 and adds 1,000 to it. However, the result of this first call to add_const persists. The second call to add_const does not cause its y to be initialized again; the function simply adds 1,000 to the existing value in the static y ❷.

Although there are two xs and two ys in this program, there is only one z, which is defined in main. The output of the program shows that main gives z its initial value, 56, and add_const adds 1,000 to this each time the function is called ❸.

In Assembly Language

Listing 14-22 shows the compiler-generated assembly language for the main function of the var_life program.

var_life.s

```
        .arch armv8-a
        .file   "var_life.c"
        .text
    ❶   .global z
        .data
        .align  2
        .type   z, %object
        .size   z, 4
z:
        .word   56                  /// One instance of z
        .section        .rodata
        .align  3
.LC0:
        .string "            automatic    static    global"
        .align  3
.LC1:
        .string "                    x         y         z"
        .align  3
```

```
.LC2:
        .string "In main:%12i %8i %8i\n"
        .text
        .align  2
        .global main
        .type   main, %function
main:
        stp     x29, x30, [sp, -32]!
        mov     x29, sp
        mov     w0, 12
        str     w0, [sp, 28]        /// main's x
        mov     w0, 34
❷     str     w0, [sp, 24]        /// main's y
        adrp    x0, .LC0
        add     x0, x0, :lo12:.LC0
        bl      puts
        adrp    x0, .LC1
        add     x0, x0, :lo12:.LC1
        bl      puts
        adrp    x0, z
        add     x0, x0, :lo12:z
        ldr     w0, [x0]
        mov     w3, w0
        ldr     w2, [sp, 24]
        ldr     w1, [sp, 28]
        adrp    x0, .LC2
        add     x0, x0, :lo12:.LC2
        bl      printf
        bl      add_const
        bl      add_const
        adrp    x0, z
        add     x0, x0, :lo12:z
        ldr     w0, [x0]
        mov     w3, w0
        ldr     w2, [sp, 24]
        ldr     w1, [sp, 28]
        adrp    x0, .LC2
        add     x0, x0, :lo12:.LC2
        bl      printf
        mov     w0, 0
        ldp     x29, x30, [sp], 32
        ret
        .size   main, .-main
        .ident  "GCC: (Debian 12.2.0-14) 12.2.0"
        .section        .note.GNU-stack,"",@progbits
```

Listing 14-22: The compiler-generated assembly language for the function in Listing 14-19

Most of this code should look familiar to you. The one instance of z in this program is defined as a global in main, and the compiler uses our name to label the variable ❶. main's y is created on the stack ❷.

Let's look at the assembly language the compiler generated for the add_const function, shown in Listing 14-23.

add_const.s

```
            .arch armv8-a
            .file   "add_const.c"
            .text}
            .section        .rodata
            .align  3
.LC0:
            .string "In add_const:%7i %8i %8i\n"
            .text
            .align  2
            .global add_const
            .type   add_const, %function
add_const:
            stp     x29, x30, [sp, -32]!
            mov     x29, sp
            mov     w0, 78
❶   str     w0, [sp, 28]
            ldr     w0, [sp, 28]
            add     w0, w0, 1000
            str     w0, [sp, 28]            /// add_const's x
❷   adrp    x0, y.0
            add     x0, x0, :lo12:y.0      /// add_const's y
            ldr     w0, [x0]
            add     w1, w0, 1000
            adrp    x0, y.0
            add     x0, x0, :lo12:y.0
            str     w1, [x0]
❸   adrp    x0, :got:z             /// Global z
            ldr     x0, [x0, :got_lo12:z]
            ldr     w0, [x0]
            add     w1, w0, 1000
            adrp    x0, :got:z
            ldr     x0, [x0, :got_lo12:z]
            str     w1, [x0]
            adrp    x0, y.0
            add     x0, x0, :lo12:y.0
            ldr     w1, [x0]
            adrp    x0, :got:z
            ldr     x0, [x0, :got_lo12:z]
            ldr     w0, [x0]
            mov     w3, w0
            mov     w2, w1
```

```
        ldr     w1, [sp, 28]
        adrp    x0, .LC0
        add     x0, x0, :lo12:.LC0
        bl      printf
        nop
        ldp     x29, x30, [sp], 32
        ret
        .size   add_const, .-add_const
❹ .data
        .align  2
        .type   y.0, %object
        .size   y.0, 4
y.0:
❺ .word     90
        .ident  "GCC: (Debian 12.2.0-14) 12.2.0"
        .section        .note.GNU-stack,"",@progbits
```

Listing 14-23: The compiler-generated assembly language for the add_const function in Listing 14-21

The compiler allocated the x variable in the stack frame, so it knows the amount of the offset from the stack pointer ❶. As you learned in "Global Variables" on page 271, add_const needs to retrieve the address of the global variable z from the GOT ❸.

The compiler treats the static local variable y a little differently than a global variable. It has changed our name to y.0 ❷. This embellishment of our given name for the variable is called *name decoration* or *name mangling*. I prefer calling it decoration because it adds to our given name.

A static local variable cannot exist in the stack frame. Like the global variable z defined in the main function (see Listing 14-22), the static local variable y is allocated in the .data section ❹. It's labeled with its decorated name and initialized with a .word assembler directive ❺. We get the address of our y variable using its decorated name ❷.

The compiler needs to decorate names to satisfy the rules of C while also producing a valid assembly language file. As you might recall from the first section of this chapter (page 270), the scope of a variable name in C extends only to the end of the block where it's defined. That means we can use the same name to define another static variable in a different block that is not enclosed within the first one. But both variables result in labels in the assembly language, where they have file scope. The C compiler needs to distinguish between the two labels because the assembler requires that each label be unique within a file. It does this by decorating our static local variable names.

When writing in assembly language, we can use more meaningful names to distinguish variables, making the code easier to read. Listings 14-24 and 14-25 show how I would write this program in assembly language.

```
var_life.s  // Compare the scope and lifetime of automatic, static, and global variables.
            .arch armv8-a
```

```
// Useful names
        .equ    INIT_X, 12
        .equ    INIT_Y, 34
        .equ    INIT_Z, 56
// Stack frame
        .equ    x, 24
        .equ    y, 28
        .equ    FRAME, 32
// Code
        .global z
        .data
        .align  2
        .type   z, %object
        .size   z, 4
z:
        .word   INIT_Z
        .section  .rodata
heading0:
        .string "            automatic   static    global"
heading1:
        .string "                    x         y         z"
msg:
        .string "In main:%12i %8i %8i\n"
        .text
        .align  2
        .global main
        .type   main, %function
main:
        stp     fp, lr, [sp, -FRAME]!   // Create stack frame
        mov     fp, sp                  // Set frame pointer

        mov     w0, INIT_X
        str     w0, [sp, x]             // x = INIT_X;
        mov     w0, INIT_Y
        str     w0, [sp, y]             // y = INIT_Y;
        adr     x0, heading0            // Print two-line header
        bl      puts
        adr     x0, heading1
        bl      puts

   ❶ adr     x0, z
        ldr     w3, [x0]                // Global z
        ldr     w2, [sp, y]             // Local y
        ldr     w1, [sp, x]             // Local x
        adr     x0, msg                 // Show values
        bl      printf
```

```
        bl      add_const               // Add constants
        bl      add_const               //   twice

        adr     x0, z                   // Repeat display
        ldr     w3, [x0]
        ldr     w2, [sp, y]
        ldr     w1, [sp, x]
        adr     x0, msg
        bl      printf

        mov     w0, wzr                 // Return 0
        ldp     fp, lr, [sp], FRAME     // Delete stack frame
        ret                             // Back to caller
```

Listing 14-24: An assembly language program to compare automatic local, static local, and global variables

My assembly language `main` function is very similar to what the compiler did in Listing 14-22, but I used more meaningful names. Programs that use only terminal I/O tend to be very small, so I assumed that z will be within ±1MB of the instruction and used the `adr` instruction to load its address ❶. The linker should warn us if this is not true, in which case we would need to use the `adrp`/`add` instruction sequence to load the address of z.

Listing 14-25 shows how I would write add_const in assembly language.

```
add_const.s  // Add a constant to an automatic local variable, a static local variable,
             // and a global variable.
                     .arch armv8-a
             // Useful names
                     .equ    INIT_X, 78
                     .equ    INIT_Y, 90
                     .equ    ADDITION, 1000
             // Stack frame
                     .equ    x, 28
                     .equ    FRAME, 32
             // Code
                     .data
                     .align  2
                     .type   y, %object
                     .size   y, 4
❶ y:
                     .word   INIT_Y
                     .section  .rodata
             msg:
                     .string "In add_const:%7i %8i %8i\n"
                     .text
                     .align  2
                     .global add_const
                     .type   add_const, %function
```

```
add_const:
        stp     fp, lr, [sp, -FRAME]!    // Create stack frame
        mov     fp, sp                   // Set frame pointer

        mov     w0, INIT_X
        add     w0, w0, ADDITION         // Add constant
        str     w0, [sp, x]              // x += ADDITION
❷ adr     x0, y
        ldr     w1, [x0]                 // Load our y
        add     w1, w1, ADDITION         // Add constant
        str     w1, [x0]                 // y += ADDITION
        adrp    x0, :got:z               // z page number
        ldr     x0, [x0, :got_lo12:z]    // z address
        ldr     w1, [x0]                 // Load z
        add     w1, w1, ADDITION         // Add constant
        str     w1, [x0]                 // z += ADDITION

        adrp    x0, :got:z               // z page number
        ldr     x0, [x0, :got_lo12:z]    // z address
        ldr     w3, [x0]                 // Load global z
        adr     x0, y
        ldr     w2, [x0]                 // Load our y
        ldr     w1, [sp, x]              // Load our x
        adr     x0, msg                  // Show current values
        bl      printf

        mov     w0, wzr                  // Return 0
        ldp     fp, lr, [sp], FRAME      // Delete stack frame
        ret                              // Back to caller
```

Listing 14-25: An assembly language function to add a constant value to three variables

I have not decorated the name of the y variable ❶. As we saw earlier, the compiler decorates the names of static local variables to prevent a duplication of labels in the compiler-generated assembly language if we use the same static local name in another function in the same C source file. But writing in assembly language gives us more flexibility in choosing our label names. If we use y to label another memory location in the same file with the add_const function, the assembler will tell us about the error.

As with the z variable in the main function, I assume the y static variable will be close to the instructions that access it ❷.

Next, I'll give a brief summary of program memory characteristics.

Program Memory Characteristics

You learned about the different memory segments when we started programming in assembly language in Chapter 10. Table 14-1 summarizes the memory characteristics of some of the most common components of a program, as well as which segment they are placed in.

Table 14-1: The Memory Characteristics of Common Program Components

Component	Memory segment	Access	Lifetime
Automatic local variable	Stack	Read and write	Function
Constant	Text	Read only	Program
Instruction	Text	Read only	Program
Static local variable	Data	Read and write	Program
Global variable	Data	Read and write	Program

Table 14-2 summarizes some of the more common assembler directives used to control where program components go in memory.

Table 14-2: Some Common Assembler Memory Directives

Directive	Memory segment	Effect
`.text`	Text	Instructions follow
`.rodata`	Text	Constant data follows
`.string "string"`, ...	Text	Arrays of characters, each terminated by NUL
`.ascii "string"`, ...	Text	Arrays of characters
`.asciz "string"`, ...	Text	Arrays of characters, each terminated by NUL
`.bss`	Data	Following data memory is initialized to zero
`.data`	Data	Variable data follows
`.byte expression`, ...	Data	Initialize memory, 1 byte for each *expression*
`.hword expression`, ...	Data	Initialize memory, 2 bytes for each *expression*
`.word expression`, ...	Data	Initialize memory, 4 bytes for each *expression*
`.quad expression`, ...	Data	Initialize memory, 8 bytes for each *expression*

The `.string`, `.ascii`, and `.asciz` directives can allocate more than one text string, each separated by a comma. The `.string` and `.asciz` directives add a NUL character to the end of the text string, while `.ascii` does not.

The `.byte`, `.hword`, `.word`, and `.quad` directives can apply to zero or more *expression*s, each of which must evaluate to an integral value. Multiple-byte values are stored in little-endian order. If there is no *expression*, no memory is allocated.

This is only a summary of these directives. For additional details, consult the info page for as.

YOUR TURN

14.5 Modify the program in Listings 14-24 and 14-25 so that the add_const function prints the number of times it has been called.

14.6 Duplicate the add_const function in the file in Listing 14-21, naming the second copy add_const2. Modify the header file in Listing 14-20 accordingly. Modify the main function in Listing 14-19 so it calls both functions twice. How does this affect the name decorating in the add_const and add_const2 functions?

What You've Learned

Global variables   Persist throughout the entire life of the program (global scope).

Automatic local variables   Created in their function when the function is called and deleted when the function is exited (function scope).

Static local variables   Initialized in the first call to their function. Their value, including any changes, persists between subsequent calls to the function (function scope).

Passing arguments   The first eight arguments are passed in registers. Any additional arguments are passed on the stack.

Pass by value   A copy of the value is passed.

Pass by pointer   The address of the variable is passed. The address can be changed in the called function.

Pass by reference   The address of the variable is passed. The address cannot be changed in the called function.

Stack frame   An area on the stack where a function's frame record, local variables, saved register contents, and arguments to the function can be stored.

Frame pointer   A register containing the address of the frame record in the stack frame.

Frame record   Two addresses: the calling function's frame pointer and the return address to the calling function.

Now that you've learned about the inner workings of functions, I'll show you a couple of specialized uses of subfunctions in the next chapter.

15

SPECIAL USES OF SUBFUNCTIONS

As you learned in Chapter 14, the most common use of a subfunction is to break a problem into smaller, easier-to-solve subproblems. This is the foundation of *recursion*, the subject of the first half of this chapter.

After I cover recursion, I'll show you another use of subfunctions: directly accessing hardware features in assembly language that may not be easily accessible in a higher-level language.

Recursion

Many computer solutions involve repetitive actions. You learned how to use iteration—while, for, and do-while loops—to perform repetitive actions in Chapter 13. While iteration can be used to solve any repetitive problem, some solutions are described more succinctly using recursion.

A *recursive algorithm* is an algorithm that calls itself to compute a simpler case of the problem and uses that result to compute the more complex case at hand. The recursive calls continue until the simpler case reaches a *base case*, which is a case that is easily computed by itself. At this point, the recursive algorithm returns the base case value to the next more complex case, where the value is used in that computation. This return/compute process continues, performing increasingly complex computations along the way, until we arrive at the solution for the original case.

Let's look at an example. In mathematics, we denote the factorial operation on positive integers with an !, which can be defined recursively:

$$n! = n \times (n - 1)!$$
$$0! = 1$$

The first equation shows that $n!$ is defined by computing a simpler case of itself, $(n - 1)!$. This computation is performed repetitively until we reach the base case of $n = 0$. Then we work our way back out, computing each $n!$ along the way.

For comparison, the iterative definition of the factorial operation is:

$$n! = n \times (n - 1) \times (n - 2) \times \ldots \times 1$$
$$0! = 1$$

Although both forms of defining the factorial operation involve the same number of computations, the recursive form is more concise and perhaps more intuitive to some people.

Listings 15-1 to 15-3 show a program that uses a function, factorial, to compute 3!. You'll see the reason for using a small, fixed value when we use gdb to examine the behavior of the program.

three_factorial.c

```
// Compute 3 factorial.

#include <stdio.h>
#include "factorial.h"

int main(void)
{
    unsigned int x = 3;
    unsigned int y;

    y = factorial(x);
    printf("%u! = %u\n", x, y);

    return 0;
}
```

Listing 15-1: A program to compute 3!

The mathematical factorial function is defined for nonnegative integers, so we use unsigned ints.

There is nothing remarkable about the header file for the factorial function, shown in Listing 15-2.

factorial.h `// Return n factorial.`

```
#ifndef FACTORIAL_H
#define FACTORIAL_H
unsigned int factorial(unsigned int n);
#endif
```

Listing 15-2: The header file for the function to compute n*!*

Listing 15-3 shows that the factorial function calls itself to perform a simpler computation, $(n - 1)!$, so it can easily compute $n!$.

factorial.c `// Return n factorial.`

```
#include "factorial.h"

unsigned int factorial(unsigned int n)
{
    unsigned int current = 1;    // Assume base case

 ❶ if (n != 0) {
     ❷ current = n * factorial(n - 1);
    }
    return current;
}
```

Listing 15-3: A function to compute n*!*

The factorial function first checks for the base case of $n = 0$ ❶. If we're at the base case, the current result is 1. If we're not at the base case, the factorial function calls the factorial function to compute $(n - 1)!$ and multiplies the result by n to get $n!$ ❷.

The assembly language for the main function is unremarkable, but let's look at what the compiler generated for the factorial function, shown in Listing 15-4.

factorial.s
```
        .arch armv8-a
        .file   "factorial.c"
        .text
        .align  2
        .global factorial
        .type   factorial, %function
factorial:
        stp     x29, x30, [sp, -48]!
        mov     x29, sp
 ❶ str     w0, [sp, 28]
        mov     w0, 1
        str     w0, [sp, 44]
        ldr     w0, [sp, 28]
```

```
  ❷ cmp     w0, 0                /// Check for base case
    beq     .L2
    ldr     w0, [sp, 28]
    sub     w0, w0, #1           /// n - 1
  ❸ bl      factorial            /// Recursive call
    mov     w1, w0
    ldr     w0, [sp, 28]
  ❹ mul     w0, w0, w1           /// n * (n - 1)!
    str     w0, [sp, 44]
.L2:
    ldr     w0, [sp, 44]
    ldp     x29, x30, [sp], 48
    ret
    .size   factorial, .-factorial
    .ident  "GCC: Debian 12.2.0-14) 12.2.0"
    .section        .note.GNU-stack,"",@progbits
```

Listing 15-4: The compiler-generated assembly language for the function in Listing 15-3

The algorithm used in the factorial function is a simple if construct, which you learned about in Chapter 13 ❷. The important part of a recursive function is that we need to save any arguments passed to it in registers so these registers can be reused to pass arguments in the recursive call to the function.

For example, the factorial function takes one argument, n, which is passed in the w0 register. From Table 11-3 in Chapter 11, we know that we don't need to save the content of x0 in our function, but we need to use the w0 portion of x0 for the recursive call with the new value, (n - 1) ❸. And when the recursive call returns, we need the original value of n to compute n * (n - 1)!. The compiler has allocated space in the stack frame for saving n ❶.

We haven't discussed the mul instruction yet. As you might guess, the mul instruction in Listing 15-4 multiplies the integer in w0 by the one in w1, leaving the product in w0 ❹. The details of multiplication instructions are somewhat complex. I'll cover them in Chapter 16.

We can simplify the factorial function a little by writing it directly in assembly language. Let's start by designing our stack frame, as shown in Figure 15-1.

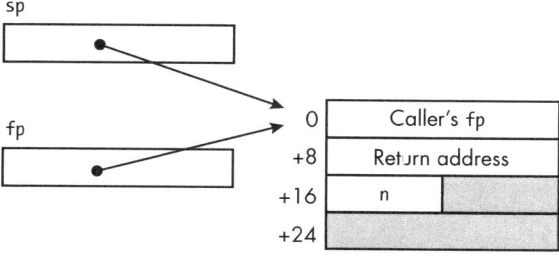

Figure 15-1: The stack frame design for the factorial function

Listing 15-5 shows our assembly language version.

factorial.s
```
// Compute n factorial.
// Calling sequence:
//    w0 <- n
//    Returns n!
        .arch armv8-a
// Stack frame
        .equ    n, 16
❶ .equ    FRAME, 32
// Code
        .text
        .align  2
        .global factorial
        .type   factorial, %function
factorial:
        stp     fp, lr, [sp, -FRAME]!  // Create stack frame
        mov     fp, sp                 // Set our frame pointer

        str     w0, [sp, n]            // Save n
        mov     w1, w0                 //    and make a copy
        mov     w0, 1                  // Assume base case, 0! = 1
❷ cbz     w1, base_case          // Check for base case
        sub     w0, w1, 1              // No,
        bl      factorial              //    compute (n - 1)!
        ldr     w1, [sp, n]            // Get n
❸ mul     w0, w0, w1             // n * (n - 1)!
base_case:
        ldp     fp, lr, [sp], FRAME    // Delete stack frame
        ret                            // Back to caller
```

Listing 15-5: A function to compute n!

There are a few key differences to note here. First, I don't know why the compiler allocated 48 bytes for the stack frame (see Listing 15-4), but we only need 32 bytes ❶. Second, we're using a local variable for the input n. The compiler uses a local variable for the result of the computation n * (n - 1)!, but we're leaving it in the w0 register ❸. Third, we use the cbz instruction instead of the cmp/beq pair the compiler used ❷.

Recursive algorithms can be simple and elegant, but they make heavy use of the stack. I used our assembly language version of factorial (and the C header file in Listing 15-2) with the main function of Listing 15-1 and ran the program under gdb so we can take a look at the stack usage:

```
(gdb) l factorial
11          .text
12          .align  2
13          .global factorial
14          .type   factorial, %function
```

```
15      factorial:
16              stp     fp, lr, [sp, -FRAME]!   // Create stack frame
17              mov     fp, sp                  // Set our frame pointer
18
19              str     w0, [sp, n]             // Save n
20              mov     w1, w0                  //   and make a copy
(gdb)
21              mov     w0, 1                   // Assume base case, 0! = 1
22              cbz     w1, base_case           // Check for base case
23              sub     w0, w1, 1               // No,
❶ 24            bl      factorial               //   compute (n - 1)!
25              ldr     w1, [sp, n]             // Get n
26              mul     w0, w0, w1              // n * (n - 1)!
❷ 27    base_case:
28              ldp     fp, lr, [sp], FRAME     // Delete stack frame
29              ret                             // Back to caller
(gdb) b 24
Breakpoint 1 at 0x7cc: file factorial.s, line 24.
(gdb) b 27
Breakpoint 2 at 0x7d8: file factorial.s, line 28.
```

I set two breakpoints, one at the recursive call to factorial ❶ and the other at the point where the function's algorithm ends ❷. Each time the program breaks back into gdb, we'll look at the input value to this call to factorial, the input value we're passing to the next call to factorial, pc, and the stack frame for each call to factorial:

```
(gdb) r
Starting program: /home/bob/chapter_15/factorial_asm/three_factorial

Breakpoint 1, factorial () at factorial.s:24
24              bl      factorial               // Compute (n - 1)!
(gdb) i r x0 x1 sp pc
x0              0x2                     2
x1              0x3                     3
sp              0x7ffffef40            0x7ffffef40
pc              0x55555507cc           0x55555507cc <factorial+28>
(gdb) x/4gx 0x7ffffef40
0x7ffffef40:    0x0000007ffffef60   ❶ 0x000000555555078c
0x7ffffef50:❷ 0x0000005500000003      0x0000000000000000
```

The main function called the factorial function with 3 as the input, which is saved on the stack ❷. When viewing this display, remember that the input is a 32-bit int. Each item on the stack is 64 bits wide, so this int is stored in the low-order 32 bits of this stack location. Looking at the 32 bytes of the stack frame, we see the return address back to main ❶.

We're now ready to call factorial with the input (3 - 1) = 2 in register w0. When we continue running the program, it will break at the same place in factorial because the function calls itself before returning to main:

```
(gdb) c
Continuing.

Breakpoint 1, factorial () at factorial.s:24
24              bl      factorial           // Compute (n - 1)!
(gdb) i r x0 x1 sp pc
x0              0x1                 1
x1              0x2                 2
sp            ❶ 0x7fffffef20       0x7fffffef20
pc              0x55555507cc        0x55555507cc <factorial+28>
(gdb) x/8gx 0x7fffffef20
0x7fffffef20:   0x0000007fffffef40   ❷ 0x000000555555507d0
0x7fffffef30: ❸ 0x0000007f00000002     0x000000555555081c
0x7fffffef40:   0x0000007fffffef60      0x000000555555078c
0x7fffffef50:   0x0000005500000003      0x0000000000000000
```

The factorial function has added another 32-byte stack frame onto the stack ❶. The input to this call to factorial, 2, has been saved in this new stack frame ❸.

The program counter, pc, shows that the bl factorial instruction is located at 0x55555507cc. All instructions in the A64 architecture are 32 bits wide, so all recursive calls to the factorial function will return to location 0x55555507cc + 0x4 = 0x55555507d0 in the function. This is the return address stored in the frame record ❷.

If we enter c (continue) two more times, we finally reach the point where the program flow leaves the fourth call to factorial, breaking at the second breakpoint:

```
(gdb) c
Continuing.

Breakpoint 2, base_case () at factorial.s:28
28              ldp     fp, lr, [sp], FRAME   // Delete stack frame
(gdb) i r x0 x1 sp pc
x0              0x1                 1
x1              0x0                 0
sp              0x7fffffeee0        0x7fffffeee0
pc              0x55555507d8        0x55555507d8 <base_case>
(gdb) x/16gx 0x7fffffeee0
0x7fffffeee0:   0x0000007fffffef00      0x000000555555507d0
0x7fffffeef0: ❶ 0x0000000000000000      0x0000000000000000
0x7fffffef00:   0x0000007fffffef20      0x000000555555507d0
```

```
0x7ffffef10:    0x0000007f00000001    0x0000000000000000
0x7ffffef20:    0x0000007ffffffef40   0x00000055555507d0
0x7ffffef30:    0x0000007f00000002    0x000000555555081c
0x7ffffef40:    0x0000007ffffffef60   0x000000555555078c
0x7ffffef50:    0x0000005500000003    0x0000000000000000
```

This view shows that each time factorial was called, it created a new stack frame. It also shows where the input to each call of factorial has been saved on the stack, the last one being 0 ❶. Since this is the base case, the program flow went directly to the end of the function.

The return address stored in the frame records of the top three stack frames is 0x00000055555507d0. When each recursive call to factorial returns, it returns to the instruction immediately following the bl factorial instruction in the factorial function itself. When we continue execution of the program, it again breaks at our second breakpoint:

```
(gdb) c
Continuing.

Breakpoint 2, base_case () at factorial.s:28
28              ldp     fp, lr, [sp], FRAME    // Delete stack frame
(gdb) i r x0 x1 sp pc
x0              0x1                    1
x1              0x1                    1
sp              0x7ffffef00            0x7ffffef00
pc              0x55555507d8           0x55555507d8 <base_case>
(gdb) x/12gx 0x7ffffef00
0x7ffffef00:    0x0000007ffffffef20   0x00000055555507d0
0x7ffffef10:    0x0000007f00000001    0x0000000000000000
0x7ffffef20:    0x0000007ffffffef40   0x00000055555507d0
0x7ffffef30:    0x0000007f00000002    0x000000555555081c
0x7ffffef40:    0x0000007ffffffef60   0x000000555555078c
0x7ffffef50:    0x0000005500000003    0x0000000000000000
```

Comparing this display with the previous display, we can see that the top frame record—the one created when factorial was called with the base case of 0 as input—has been removed from the stack.

When we continue, the program breaks again at the second breakpoint before returning from this invocation of factorial:

```
(gdb) c
Continuing.

Breakpoint 2, base_case () at factorial.s:28
28              ldp     fp, lr, [sp], FRAME    // Delete stack frame
```

Using the continue command (c) once more takes us back to the original call to factorial from main:

```
(gdb) c
Continuing.

Breakpoint 2, base_case () at factorial.s:28
28              ldp    fp, lr, [sp], FRAME   // Delete stack frame
(gdb) i r x0 x1 sp pc
x0              0x6                6
x1              0x3                3
sp              0x7fffffef40       0x7fffffef40
pc              0x55555507d8       0x55555507d8 <base_case>
(gdb) x/4gx 0x7fffffef40
0x7fffffef40:   0x0000007fffffef60   ❶ 0x000000555555078c
0x7fffffef50:   0x0000005500000003     0x0000000000000000
```

The return address in the frame record is back in main ❶. When we continue, main prints the result for us:

```
(gdb) c
Continuing.
3! = 6
[Inferior 1 (process 2310) exited normally]
(gdb)
```

The debugger has also printed some information about the process for us. We're still in gdb and need to quit that.

Looking back at the stack display when the program is at the base case (page 311), notice that each call to the recursive function creates another stack frame. We used a small number in this example, but computing the factorial of a large number would use a lot of stack space. And since there is a call to a function in each repetition, recursive algorithms can be time-consuming.

Every recursive solution has an equivalent iterative solution, which is usually more efficient, both in time and in stack usage. For example, the iterative algorithm to compute the factorial of an integer (see page 306) is simple, so an iterative solution might be preferable. However, many problems (such as some sorting algorithms) lend themselves more naturally to a recursive solution. For such problems, the increased simplicity of the code is often worth the cost of recursion.

We would typically write a recursive function in a higher-level language, but I used assembly language here so you can gain an understanding of how recursion works. Next, I'll show you how to use assembly language to access hardware features that might not be directly accessible in the high-level language you're using.

Accessing CPU Features in Assembly Language

In Chapter 14, it may have seemed a bit silly to create a whole subfunction
just to add two integers for the sum_ints program (see Listing 14-8), which
can be done with a single instruction. But as you learned in Chapter 3, even
simple addition can produce carry or overflow.

The add and sub instructions you learned about in Chapter 11 have no
effect on the condition flags, but the A64 architecture includes variants of
add and sub, adds and subs, that will set the condition flags in the nzcv register
according to the result of the operation.

C and C++ don't provide a way to check the overflow or carry flags in
the nzcv register. In this section, I'll show you two ways to use assembly language in C programs to indicate when there is overflow from addition: we
can write a separate function in assembly language that is callable from our
C code, or we can embed assembly language directly within our C code.

Writing a Separate Function

I'll start by rewriting the sum_ints program from Chapter 14 in C so that it
warns the user if the addition produces overflow. I'll check for overflow in
the subfunction add_two, and I'll pass the result back to the main function using the return mechanism.

Listing 15-6 shows the modified main function that checks the return
value from the add_two function for overflow.

---

sum_ints.c   `// Add two integers and show if there is overflow.`

```
#include <stdio.h>
#include "add_two.h"

int main(void)
{
    int x, y, z, overflow;

    printf("Enter an integer: ");
    scanf("%i", &x);
```

```
    printf("Enter an integer: ");
    scanf("%i", &y);
    overflow = add_two(&z, x, y);
    printf("%i + %i = %i\n", x, y, z);
    if (overflow)
        printf("** Overflow occurred **\n");

    return 0;
}
```

Listing 15-6: A program to add two integers and show if there is overflow

Next, I'll rewrite the add_two function such that it returns 0 if there is no overflow and 1 if there is overflow (recall that in C, zero is logically false and a nonzero value is true). I'll assign this result to the variable overflow in main.

Listing 15-7 shows the header file for the new add_two function.

add_two.h
```
// Add two integers and return 1 for overflow, 0 for no overflow.

#ifndef ADD_TWO_H
#define ADD_TWO_H
int add_two(int *a, int b, int c);
#endif
```

Listing 15-7: The header file for the add_two function

The only change in the function declaration is returning an int instead of void. We need to add a check for overflow in the definition of the add_two function, as shown in Listing 15-8.

add_two.c
```
// Add two integers and return 1 for overflow, 0 for no overflow.

#include "add_two.h"

int add_two(int *a, int b, int c)
{
    int sum;
    int overflow = 0;    // Assume no overflow

    sum = b + c;
❶  if (((b > 0) && (c > 0) && (sum < 0)) ||
            ((b < 0) && (c < 0) && (sum > 0))) {
        overflow = 1;
    }
    *a = sum;

    return overflow;
}
```

Listing 15-8: A function to add two integers and return an overflow indication

You learned in Chapter 3 that if adding two integers of the same sign gives a result of the opposite sign, you have overflow, so we use this logic as the check for overflow ❶.

Listing 15-9 shows the assembly language generated by the compiler from this C source.

add_two.s

```
          .arch armv8-a
          .file   "add_two.c"
          .text
          .align  2
          .global add_two
          .type   add_two, %function
add_two:
          sub     sp, sp, #32
          str     x0, [sp, 12]    /// a
          str     w1, [sp, 8]     /// b
          str     w2, [sp]        /// c
          str     wzr, [sp, 28]   /// overflow = 0;
          ldr     w1, [sp, 12]
          ldr     w0, [sp, 8]
          add     w0, w1, w0
          str     w0, [sp, 24]
❶ ldr     w0, [sp, 12]    /// Start overflow check
          cmp     w0, 0
          ble     .L2
          ldr     w0, [sp, 8]
          cmp     w0, 0
          ble     .L2
          ldr     w0, [sp, 24]
          cmp     w0, 0
          blt     .L3
.L2:
          ldr     w0, [sp, 12]
          cmp     w0, 0
          bge     .L4
          ldr     w0, [sp, 8]
          cmp     w0, 0
          bge     .L4
          ldr     w0, [sp, 24]
          cmp     w0, 0
          ble     .L4
.L3:
          mov     w0, 1
          str     w0, [sp, 28]    /// overflow = 1;
.L4:
          ldr     x0, [sp]
          ldr     w1, [sp, 24]
```

```
        str     w1, [x0]
        ldr     w0, [sp, 28]
        add     sp, sp, 32
        ret
        .size   addTwo, .-addTwo
        .ident  "GCC: Debian 12.2.0-14) 12.2.0"
        .section        .note.GNU-stack,"",@progbits
```

Listing 15-9: The compiler-generated assembly language for the add_two function in Listing 15-8

As you can see, it takes about 20 instructions to check for overflow in C ❶. In Listing 15-10, I rewrite the add_two function in assembly language so I can use the adds instruction for the addition operation and then detect overflow from the condition flags in the nzcv register.

add_two.s
```
// Add two integers and output the sum; return overflow T or F.
// Calling sequence:
//     x0 <- address a, for output
//     w1 <- integer b
//     w2 <- integer c
//     Returns 1 for overflow, 0 for no overflow
        .arch armv8-a
// Code
        .text
        .align  2
        .global add_two
        .type   add_two, %function
add_two:
        adds    w1, w1, w2      // Add and set condition flags
        str     w1, [x0]        // Store output
❶ cinc    w0, wzr, vs      // Overflow flag
        ret                     // Back to caller
```

Listing 15-10: The add_two function with overflow detection in assembly language

I didn't create a stack frame for this very simple leaf function because it is unlikely we would ever modify this function to call another function.

I used the cinc instruction ❶ to read the overflow flag in the nzcv register and load the w0 register with either a 0 or a 1, depending on whether the overflow flag is 0 or 1:

cinc—Conditional increment

cinc wd, ws, *cond* moves the value in ws to wd, adding 1 to the value if *cond* is true.

cinc xd, xs, *cond* moves the value in xs to xd, adding 1 to the value if *cond* is true.

The possible values for *cond* are given in Table 13-1 in Chapter 13.

Using the assembly language version of add_two in Listing 15-10 with the main function in Listing 15-6 shows one of the reasons for writing a subfunction in assembly language. It allows us to access a feature of the CPU, the V flag in the nzcv register, that is not accessible in C, the higher-level language we're using. Writing in assembly language allows us to ensure that there are no intervening instructions that might change the flags between the operation (addition, in this example) and the flag check.

This example also illustrates a common use of the return value. Inputs and outputs are often passed in the argument list, with supplemental information about the computation carried in the return value.

That said, calling a function to simply add two numbers is inefficient. In the next section, we'll look at a common extension to C that allows us to insert assembly language directly in our C code.

Using Inline Assembly Language

Like many C compilers, gcc includes an extension to the standard C language that allows us to embed assembly language in our C code, usually called *inline assembly*. Doing so can be complex. We'll look at a simple case here. You can read the details at *https://gcc.gnu.org/onlinedocs/gcc/Using -Assembly-Language-with-C.html*, or you can use the info gcc command and select **C Extensions ▶ Using Assembly Language with C ▶ Extended Asm**.

The gcc compiler uses the following general form for embedding assembly language in C, which starts with the asm keyword:

```
asm asm-qualifiers (assembly language statements
                 : output operands
                 : input operands
                 : clobbers);
```

The *asm-qualifiers* are used to help the compiler optimize the C code, a topic that is beyond the scope of this book. We're not asking the compiler to optimize our C code, so we won't use *asm-qualifiers*.

The *output operands* are the C variables that could be changed by the *assembly language statements*, thus acting as outputs from the *assembly language statements*. The *input operands* refer to the C variables that are used by the *assembly language statements* but are not changed, thus acting as inputs to the *assembly language statements*. The *clobbers* are the registers that get explicitly changed by the *assembly language statements*, thus telling the compiler about the possible changes in these registers.

In Listing 15-11, I use inline assembly language to check for overflow in the addition.

```
sim_ints.c   // Add two integers and show if there is overflow.

#include <stdio.h>

int main(void)
```

```
{
    int x, y, z, overflow;

    printf("Enter an integer: ");
    scanf("%i", &x);
    printf("Enter an integer: ");
    scanf("%i", &y);

❶   asm ("adds %w0, %w2, %w3\n"
        "cinc %w1, wzr, vs"
❷       : "=r" (z), "=r" (overflow)
❸       : "r" (x), "r" (y));

    printf("%i + %i = %i\n", x, y, z);
    if (overflow)
        printf("** Overflow occurred **\n");

    return 0;
}
```

Listing 15-11: A program to add two integers and show if there's overflow

The first thing to note about the code here is that it's important to place the adds instruction in assembly language so we can check for overflow immediately after the instruction is executed ❶. If we were to do the addition in C, the compiler would use the add instruction, as in Listing 15-9, which does not set the condition flags.

There is a template for each assembly language instruction as a text string enclosed in quotes ❶. The operands for each instruction are numbered according to their relative position on the *output:input* operand list, starting from 0. I preface the variable numbers with w in the assembly language template to tell the compiler that these are word (32-bit) values. Remember that assembly language code is line-oriented, so it's important to place a newline character, \n, at the end of each assembly language statement. The newline is not needed at the end of the last assembly language statement.

NOTE   *Be careful not to confuse operand numbers with register numbers. %w0 is the 32-bit value of the first operand on our* output:input *operand list, and w0 is the low-order 32 bits of the x0 register.*

The syntax for each output or input operand is:

`"constraint" (C variable name)`

In our program, z is in position 0 and overflow is in position 1 ❷; x is in position 2 and y is in position 3 ❸.

The *constraint* tells the compiler what kind of operand it can use in the assembly language template. For example, "m" means the compiler should use a memory location and "r" means it should use a register. Prefixing the kind with = tells the compiler that our assembly language stores a value there. The "=r" (z) constraint thus tells the compiler that it needs to use a register for the %w0 operand, that our assembly language will store a value in that register, and to store the value in that register in the C variable z ❷. The "r" (x) constraint tells the compiler to use a register for the value in the C variable x, but our assembly language does not change the value in that register ❸.

Be aware that when you use inline assembly language, the compiler could generate assembly language for your C code that does not work well with your assembly language. It's a good idea to generate the assembly language for the entire function (using the -S compiler option) and read it carefully to make sure the function is doing what you intend. We'll do this in Listing 15-12.

sum_ints.s

```
        .arch armv8-a
        .file   "sum_ints.c"
        .text
        .section        .rodata
        .align  3
.LC0:
        .string "Enter an integer: "
        .align  3
.LC1:
        .string "%i"
        .align  3
.LC2:
        .string "%i + %i = %i\n"
        .align  3
.LC3:
        .string "** Overflow occurred **"
        .text
        .align  2
        .global main
        .type   main, %function
main:
        stp     x29, x30, [sp, -32]!
        mov     x29, sp
        adrp    x0, .LC0
        add     x0, x0, :lo12:.LC0
        bl      printf
        add     x0, sp, 20
        mov     x1, x0
        adrp    x0, .LC1
        add     x0, x0, :lo12:.LC1
        bl      __isoc99_scanf
        adrp    x0, .LC0
```

```
        add     x0, x0, :lo12:.LC0
        bl      printf
        add     x0, sp, 16
        mov     x1, x0
        adrp    x0, .LC1
        add     x0, x0, :lo12:.LC1
        bl      __isoc99_scanf
❶ ldr     w0, [sp, 20]    /// w0 <- x
        ldr     w1, [sp, 16]    /// w1 <- y
#APP
// 14 "sumInts.c" 1
        adds w1, w0, w1
csinc w0, wzr, wzr, vc
// 0 "" 2
#NO_APP
❷ str     w1, [sp, 28]    /// z <- result of addition
        str     w0, [sp, 24]    /// overflow <- overflow flag
        ldr     w0, [sp, 20]
        ldr     w1, [sp, 16]
        ldr     w3, [sp, 28]
        mov     w2, w1
        mov     w1, w0
        adrp    x0, .LC2
        add     x0, x0, :lo12:.LC2
        bl      printf
        ldr     w0, [sp, 24]
        cmp     w0, 0
        beq     .L2
        adrp    x0, .LC3
        add     x0, x0, :lo12:.LC3
        bl      puts
.L2:
        mov     w0, 0
        ldp     x29, x30, [sp], 32
        ret
        .size   main, .-main
        .ident  "GCC: Debian 12.2.0-14) 12.2.0"
        .section        .note.GNU-stack,"",@progbits
```

Listing 15-12: The compiler-generated code for inline assembly

We told the compiler that the assembly language we've inserted uses registers for the inputs ("r"), so it loads the values from the C variables into registers ❶. Similarly, we specified that we're using registers for the outputs in our assembly language ("=r"), and the compiler stores the values from the registers into the C variables ❷.

If you think inline assembly looks tricky, you're right. The C language standard lists inline assembly as a common extension to the language but points out that extensions are not part of the standard. This means that using inline assembly in C code may not work if you use a different compiler, even on the same computer. In most cases, if I need to use assembly language, I use a separate function, as we did in Listing 15-10, which is portable between compilers.

YOUR TURN

15.2 Modify the C program in Listings 15-6, 15-7, and 15-8 to use unsigned ints and tell the user when the addition produces carry. It will declare the variables as follows:

```
unsigned int x = 0, y = 0, z;
```

The formatting code for reading and printing the values of the unsigned ints is %u. Here's an example:

```
scanf("%u", &x);
```

15.3 Modify the program in Listing 15-11 to use unsigned ints and tell the user when the addition produces carry.

15.4 Modify the program in Listing 15-11 to use register ints for the z and overflow variables. How does this change the compiler-generated assembly language?

What You've Learned

Recursion   Allows for simple and elegant solutions to some problems, but uses a lot of stack space.

Accessing hardware features   Most programming languages do not allow direct access to all the hardware features in a computer. Using an assembly language subfunction or inline assembly language may be the best solution.

Inline assembly   Allows us to embed assembly language in our C code frame pointer and the return address to the calling function.

Now that you know some common ways to use functions in a program, we'll move on to multiplication, division, and logic operations. In the next chapter, you'll learn how to convert a string of numerals in ASCII code to the integer they represent.

16

BITWISE LOGIC, MULTIPLICATION, AND DIVISION INSTRUCTIONS

Now that you've learned about program organization, let's turn our attention to computation. I'll start by explaining the logic operators, which can be used to change individual bits in a value using a technique called *masking*.

Then I'll move on to shift operations, which provide a way to multiply or divide by powers of two. In the last two sections of this chapter, I'll cover arithmetic multiplication and division of integers.

Bitmasking

It's often better to think of data items as patterns of bits rather than numerical entities. For example, if you look back at Table 2-5 in Chapter 2, you'll see that the only difference between uppercase and lowercase alphabetic characters in ASCII is bit number 5, which is 1 for lowercase and 0 for uppercase. The ASCII code for m, for instance, is 0x6d, and for M, it's 0x4d. If you wanted to write a function that changed the case of a string of alphabetic characters from lowercase to uppercase, you could view this as a numerical difference of 32. You would need to determine the current case of the character and then decide whether to change it by subtracting 32.

But there's a faster way. We can change bit patterns by using logical bitwise operations and a mask, or bitmask. A *mask* is a specific pattern of bits that can be used to make specified bits in a variable either 1 or 0, or to invert them. For example, to make sure an alphabetic character is uppercase, we need to ensure its bit number 5 is 0, giving the mask 11011111 = 0xdf. Then, using the previous example of m, 0x6d ∧ 0xdf = 0x4d, which is M. If the character is already uppercase, then 0x4d ∧ 0xdf = 0x4d, leaving it as uppercase. This solution avoids checking for the case before the conversion.

We can use similar logic for other operations. To make a bit 1, place a 1 in the appropriate bit position in the mask and use the bitwise OR operation. To produce a 0 in a bit position, place a 0 in that position and a 1 in each of the other bit positions in the mask and then use the bitwise AND operation. You can invert bits by placing a 1 in each bit position you want to invert and a 0 in all other positions and using the bitwise XOR operation.

Bitmasking in C

The program in Listings 16-1 to 16-3 shows how to use a mask to convert all lowercase alphabetic characters in a text string to uppercase.

uppercase.c `// Make an alphabetic text string uppercase.`

```
#include <stdio.h>
#include "to_upper.h"
#include "write_str.h"
#include "write_char.h"
#include "read_str.h"
❶ #define MAX 50
❷ #define ARRAY_SZ MAX+1

int main(void)
{
    char my_string[ARRAY_SZ];

    write_str("Enter up to 50 alphabetic characters: ");
❸   read_str(my_string, MAX);

    to_upper(my_string, my_string);
    write_str("All upper: ");
    write_str(my_string);
    write_char('\n');

    return 0;
}
```

Listing 16-1: A program to make an alphabetic text string uppercase

This program, and many that follow in the book, uses the read_str, write_char, and write_str functions that you were asked to write in "Your Turn" exercise 14.4 on page 293. If you want to, you can instead use the gets, putchar, and puts functions, respectively, in the C standard library, but you'll need to make the appropriate changes in the book's functions that call them because their behavior is a little different.

In Listing 16-1, we use #define to give a symbolic name to the maximum number of characters allowed ❶. The char array needs to have one more element to allow for the terminating NUL character ❷. The two instances of #define allow us to easily change the length in one place and make sure that the char array is the correct length and the correct value gets passed to the read_str function.

You learned in Chapter 14 that when an argument's name is used to pass a variable to a function, it's passed by value; a copy of the variable's value is passed to the called function. If we wanted to pass the address of the variable, we would need to use the & (address of) operator. C treats array names differently. When the name of an argument is an array, C uses pass by pointer; the address of the beginning of the array is passed to the function instead of a copy of all the values in the array. So, we *do not* use the & operator when passing an array as an argument to a function ❸. You'll learn more about how arrays are implemented in Chapter 17.

Nothing else is new in this main function, so we'll move on to the to_upper subfunction. Listing 16-2 shows the header file for this function.

to_upper.h
```
// Convert alphabetic letters in a C string to uppercase.

#ifndef TO_UPPER_H
#define TO_UPPER_H
int to_upper(char *dest_ptr, char *src_ptr);
#endif
```

Listing 16-2: The header file for the to_upper function

The first argument, src_ptr, is the address of the text string to be converted, and the second argument, dest_ptr, is the address where the result of the conversion will be stored. In Listing 16-1, we passed the same array as both the source and destination arrays, so to_upper will replace the characters stored in the array with the new values.

Listing 16-3 gives the definition of to_upper.

to_upper.c
```
// Convert alphabetic letters in a C string to uppercase.

   #include "to_upper.h"
❶ #define UPMASK 0xdf
   #define NUL '\0'

   int to_upper(char *dest_ptr, char *src_ptr)
```

```
{
    int count = 0;
    while (*src_ptr != NUL) {
     ❷ *dest_ptr = *src_ptr & UPMASK;
        src_ptr++;
        dest_ptr++;
        count++;
    }
 ❸ *dest_ptr = *src_ptr;   // Include NUL

    return count;
}
```

Listing 16-3: A function to convert lowercase alphabetic characters to uppercase

To make sure bit 5 is 0, we use a mask that has a 0 in bit position 5 and 1s elsewhere ❶. While the current character is not the NUL character, we perform a bitwise AND with the character in the source array, which masks out bit 5 and allows all the other bits to remain the same in the result ❷. The result of this AND operation is stored in the destination array. Don't forget to include the NUL character from the input text string ❸! Forgetting to do so is a programming error that won't show up in testing if the byte in memory following where the output is stored happens to be 0x00 (the NUL character). If you change the length of the input text string, the next byte in memory may not be 0x00. This error might therefore show up in a seemingly random way.

Although this function returns a count of the number of characters processed, our main function does nothing with the value. A calling function doesn't need to use a returned value, but I usually include a counting algorithm in functions like this for debugging purposes.

Listing 16-4 shows the assembly language the compiler generates for the to_upper function.

to_upper.s
```
            .arch armv8-a
            .file   "to_upper.c"
            .text
            .align  2
            .global to_upper
            .type   to_upper, %function
to_upper:
            sub     sp, sp, #32
            str     x0, [sp, 8]      /// Save destination address
            str     x1, [sp]        /// Save source address
            str     wzr, [sp, 28]   /// count = 0;
            b       .L2
.L3:
            ldr     x0, [sp, 8]
            ldrb    w0, [x0]
         ❶ and     w0, w0, -33     ///! -33 = 0xffffffdf
            and     w1, w0, 255     ///! 255 = 0x000000ff
```

```
            ldr     x0, [sp]
            strb    w1, [x0]
            ldr     x0, [sp, 8]
            add     x0, x0, 1
            str     x0, [sp, 8]
            ldr     x0, [sp]
            add     x0, x0, 1
            str     x0, [sp]
            ldr     w0, [sp, 28]
            add     w0, w0, 1
            str     w0, [sp, 28]
    .L2:
            ldr     x0, [sp, 8]
            ldrb    w0, [x0]
            cmp     w0, 0
            bne     .L3
 ❷  ldr     x0, [sp, 8]         /// Copy NUL char
            ldrb    w1, [x0]
            ldr     x0, [sp]
            strb    w1, [x0]
            ldr     w0, [sp, 28]
            add     sp, sp, 32
            ret
            .size   to_upper, .-to_upper
            .ident  "GCC: (Debian 12.2.0-14) 12.2.0"
            .section        .note.GNU-stack,"",@progbits
```

Listing 16-4: The compiler-generated assembly language for the function in Listing 16-3

You might notice that our compiler structures while loops such that it is unnecessary to copy the NUL character after the loop terminates ❷. But we still need to write correct C code, because another compiler might use a different structure for while loops.

After loading the current character from the source char array, the first and instruction masks the word in w0 with -33 = 0xffffffdf, which leaves bit 5 equal to 0, thus making sure the character is uppercase ❶. The second and instruction uses the 0x000000ff mask to leave us with an 8-bit char in w0.

Treating the characters as bit patterns rather than as numerical values allows us to convert lowercase characters to uppercase while leaving uppercase characters unchanged, without using an if statement to first test the case of the character.

You might be wondering why the compiler used two and instructions instead of simply using 0xdf as the mask with one and instruction. To answer this question, let's look at the basic logic instructions in more detail.

Basic Logic Instructions

Logic instructions work bitwise—that is, they operate on the individual bits in the corresponding bit positions of the two operands. The three basic logic instructions are for the AND, OR, or XOR operations. The A64 instruction set includes two versions for each operation. The shifted register versions allow you to shift one of the source operands before applying the operation. The immediate data versions allow only certain bit patterns, which I'll explain after describing the instructions:

and—AND shifted register

and `wd, ws1, ws2{, shft amnt}` performs a bitwise AND between the values in `ws1` and `ws2` and stores the result in `wd`. The value from `ws2` can be shifted 0 to 31 bits before the AND operation using the `shft amnt` option.

and `xd, xs1, xs2{, shft amnt}` performs a bitwise AND between the values in `xs1` and `xs2` and stores the result in `xd`. The value from `xs2` can be shifted 0 to 63 bits before the AND operation using the `shft amnt` option.

and—AND immediate

and `wd, ws, imm` performs a bitwise AND between the 32-bit pattern of `imm` and the value in `ws` and stores the result in `wd`.

and `xd, xs, imm` performs a bitwise AND between the 64-bit pattern of `imm` and the value in `xs` and stores the result in `xd`.

orr—Inclusive OR shifted register

orr `wd, ws1, ws2{, shft amnt}` performs a bitwise OR between the values in `ws1` and `ws2` and stores the result in `wd`. The value from `ws2` can be shifted 0 to 31 bits before the OR operation using the `shft amnt` option.

orr `xd, xs1, xs2{, shft amnt}` performs a bitwise OR between the values in `xs1` and `xs2` and stores the result in `xd`. The value from `xs2` can be shifted 0 to 63 bits before the OR operation using the `shft amnt` option.

orr—Inclusive OR immediate

orr `wd, ws, imm` performs a bitwise OR between the 32-bit pattern of `imm` and the value in `ws` and stores the result in `wd`.

orr `xd, xs, imm` performs a bitwise OR between the 64-bit pattern of `imm` and the value in `xs` and stores the result in `xd`.

eor—Exclusive OR shifted register

eor `wd, ws1, ws2{, shft amnt}` performs a bitwise XOR between the values in `ws1` and `ws2` and stores the result in `wd`. The value from `ws2` can be shifted 0 to 31 bits before the XOR operation using the `shft amnt` option.

eor `xd, xs1, xs2{, shft amnt}` performs a bitwise XOR between the values in `xs1` and `xs2` and stores the result in `xd`. The value from `xs2` can be shifted 0 to 63 bits before the XOR operation using the `shft amnt` option.

eor—Exclusive OR immediate

eor `wd, ws, imm` performs a bitwise XOR between the 32-bit pattern of `imm` and the value in `ws` and stores the result in `wd`.

eor `xd, xs, imm` performs a bitwise XOR between the 64-bit pattern of `imm` and the value in `xs` and stores the result in `xd`.

Table 16-1 lists the allowable values for the *shft* option.

Table 16-1: Allowable Values for *shft* in Shifted Register Logic Instructions

shft	Effect
lsl	Logical shift left
lsr	Logical shift right
asr	Arithmetic shift right
ror	Rotate right

A logical shift fills the vacated bits with 0s. An arithmetic shift fills the vacated bits with copies of the high-order bit of the value being shifted. A right rotation shifts all the bits to the right, moving the low-order bits to the high-order positions. The 32-bit versions of these logic instructions do not change the 32 high-order bits in the destination register, so a shift or rotation of a ws register applies only to the low-order 32 bits of the corresponding xs register.

You learned in Chapter 12 that the *imm* values in these logic instructions cannot be 32 or 64 bits. To see how these three instructions encode the *imm* value, let's take a look at the machine code for the first and instruction in Listing 16-4, shown in Figure 16-1.

31 30 29 28 27 26 25 24 23 22	21	20 19 18 17 16	15 14 13 12 11 10	9 8 7 6 5	4 3 2 1 0
sf 0 0 1 0 0 1 0 0	N	immr	imms	rs	rd
0	0	0 1 1 0 1 0	0 1 1 1 1 0	0 0 0 0 0	0 0 0 0 0

Figure 16-1: The machine code for the and w0, w0, -33 instruction in Listing 16-4

The 0 in the N field specifies a 32-bit operation. A 1 would specify a 64-bit operation.

The imms field specifies two numbers: the number of bits in a repeating pattern and the number of consecutive 1s in the pattern. I'll use Table 16-2 to explain how this works.

Table 16-2: Encoding imms Values in Immediate Logic Instructions

N	imms	Pattern size (bits)	Number of 1s
0	11110x	2	1
0	1110xx	4	1–3
0	110xxx	8	1–7
0	10xxxx	16	1–15
0	0xxxxx	32	1–31
1	xxxxxx	64	1–63

For the rows with 0 in the N column, the location of the first 0 in the imms column (reading from the left) specifies the number of bits in the pattern. The 1 in the N column specifies a 64-bit pattern.

In each row, the binary number in the x positions plus 1 specifies the number of consecutive 1s in the pattern, starting from the right-hand side. For example, if N is 0 and imms is 110010, this specifies an 8-bit pattern with three consecutive 1s. This would result in the 32-bit mask 0x07070707.

The 6-bit number in the immr field of the and instruction that's shown in Figure 16-1 specifies the number of right rotations to be applied to the mask before the logical operation.

The mask specified in this instruction starts with a 32-bit pattern with 31 consecutive 1s, 0x7fffffff, that occurs only once. This pattern then gets rotated 26 bits to the right to give 0xffffffdf for the mask that is used in the AND operation.

Next, I'll show you a way to write this program directly in assembly language.

Bitmasking in Assembly Language

We'll use the same masking algorithm in our assembly language version, but we'll use identifiers that make it easier to see what's going on. Listing 16-5 shows the main function written in assembly language.

```
uppercase.s  // Make an alphabetic text string uppercase.
             .arch armv8-a
             // Useful constant
             .equ    MAX,50                      // Character limit
             // Stack frame
             .equ    the_string, 16
           ❶ .equ    FRAME, 80                   // Allows >51 bytes
             // Code
             .text
             .section  .rodata
             .align  3
     prompt:
             .string "Enter up to 50 alphabetic characters: "
     result:
             .string "All upper: "
             .text
             .align  2
             .global main
             .type   main, %function
     main:
             stp     fp, lr, [sp, -FRAME]! // Create stack frame
             mov     fp, sp                      // Set our frame pointer
             adr     x0, prompt                  // Prompt message
             bl      write_str                   // Ask for input
```

```
        add     x0, sp, the_string   // Place to store string
        mov     w1, MAX              // Limit number of input chars
        bl      read_str             // Get from keyboard

        add     x1, sp, the_string   // Address of string
❷ mov     x0, x1               // Replace the string
        bl      to_upper             // Do conversion

        adr     x0, result           // Show result
        bl      write_str
        add     x0, sp, the_string   // Converted string
        bl      write_str
        mov     w0, '\n'             // Nice formatting
        bl      write_char

        mov     w0, 0                // Return 0
        ldp     x29, x30, [sp], FRAME // Delete stack frame
        ret
```

Listing 16-5: A program to make a text string uppercase

We have allocated 50 bytes on the stack for our character array. Adding 16 bytes to save sp and fp takes us to a frame size of at least 66 bytes. To keep the stack pointer properly aligned on a 16-byte boundary, we allocate 80 bytes for the stack frame ❶.

We pass the address of our char array to the to_upper function as both the source and the destination, so it will replace the original values in the array with the new ones ❷.

I'll use the same masking algorithm as the compiler to write to_upper in assembly language, but I'll structure the function differently. Listing 16-6 shows the code.

to_upper.s
```
// Convert alphabetic letters in a C string to uppercase.
// Calling sequence:
//     x0 <- pointer to result
//     x1 <- pointer to string to convert
//     Return number of characters converted.
        .arch armv8-a
// Useful constant
❶ .equ    UPMASK, 0xdf
// Program code
        .text
        .align  2
        .global to_upper
        .type   to_upper, %function
to_upper:
        mov     w2, wzr              // counter = 0
```

```
loop:
    ❷ ldrb    w3, [x1]          // Load character
      cbz     w3, done          // All done if NUL char
    ❸ movz    w4, UPMASK        // If not, do masking
      and     w3, w3, w4        // Mask to upper
      strb    w3, [x0]          // Store result
      add     x0, x0, 1         // Increment destination pointer,
      add     x1, x1, 1         //    source pointer,
      add     w2, w2, 1         //    and counter,
      b       loop              //    and continue
done:
      strb    w3, [x0]          // Terminating NUL got us here
      mov     w0, w2            // Return count
      ret                       // Back to caller
```

Listing 16-6: A program to convert text to uppercase

We're using registers w2, w3, and w4 for our local variables instead of placing them in our stack frame. The standard says we don't need to save the contents of these registers for the calling function.

The ldrb instruction loads a character into a w register ❷. We need to use a 32-bit mask to match the width of the register. The correct mask for this algorithm is 0x000000df ❶. The compiler uses two masks to achieve the correct result:

```
and    w3, w3, -33
and    w3, w3, 255
```

The ldrb instruction zeros the 24 high-order bits in the register, so we could use only the first instruction. But this might confuse a person maintaining this code, since the algorithm works with bit patterns, not integers, and writing the instruction as

```
and    w3, w3, 0xffffffdf
```

could be even more confusing.

Our use of the movz instruction to load the correct mask into a register clearly shows our intent ❸. Then, we use the register form of the and instruction to mask out the lowercase bit in the character. In the next section, I'll show you ways to shift bits to multiply or divide a value by powers of two.

YOUR TURN

16.1 Write a program in assembly language that converts all alphabetic characters to lowercase.

16.2 Write a program in assembly language that changes the case of all alphabetic characters to the opposite case.

Shifting Bits

It's sometimes useful to be able to shift all the bits in a variable to the left
or to the right. If the variable is an integer, shifting all the bits one position
to the left effectively multiplies the integer by two, and shifting them one
position to the right effectively divides it by two. Using left/right shifts to do
multiplication/division by powers of two is very efficient.

In C

I'll cover shifts by showing you a program that reads an integer entered in
hexadecimal from the keyboard and stores it as a `long int`. The program
reads up to eight hexadecimal characters, 0, 1, . . . , f, each in 8-bit ASCII code
and representing a 4-bit integer: 0, 1, . . . , 15.

Listing 16-7 shows the `main` function for this program.

convert_hex.c
```
// Get a hex number from the user and store it as an int.

#include <stdio.h>
#include "write_str.h"
#include "read_str.h"
#include "hex_to_int.h"

#define MAX 8
#define ARRAY_SZ MAX+1

int main()
{
    char the_string[ARRAY_SZ];
    int the_int;

    write_str("Enter up to 8 hex characters: ");
    read_str(the_string, MAX);

    hex_to_int(&the_int, the_string);
    printf("0x%x = %i\n", the_int, the_int);
    return 0;
}
```

Listing 16-7: A program to convert hexadecimal input to an `int`

In "Your Turn" exercise 14.4 on page 293, you designed the read_str function to limit the number of characters it will store in the char array passed to it. If the user enters more than eight characters, read_str will terminate the string with a NUL character and discard the excess characters.

Listing 16-8 shows the header file for the hex_to_int function.

```
// Convert a hex character string to an int.
// Return number of characters.

#ifndef HEX_TO_INT_H
#define HEX_TO_INT_H
int hex_to_int(int *int_ptr, char *string_ptr);
#endif
```

Listing 16-8: The header file for the hex_to_int function

The header file declares the hex_to_int function, which takes two pointers. The char pointer is the input, and the long int pointer is the location for the primary output. The hex_to_int function also returns an int that gives the number of characters it converted.

Listing 16-9 shows the definition of the hex_to_int function.

```
// Convert a hex character string to an int.
// Return number of characters.

#include "hex_to_int.h"
#define GAP 0x07
#define INTPART 0x0f  // Also works for lowercase
#define NUL '\0'

int hex_to_int(int *int_ptr, char *string_ptr)
{
    char current;
    int result;
    int count;

    count = 0;
❶   result = 0;
    current = *string_ptr;
    while (current != NUL) {
❷       if (current > '9') {
            current -= GAP;
        }
❸       current = current & INTPART;
❹       result = result << 4;
❺       result |= current;
        string_ptr++;
        count++;
```

```
        current = *string_ptr;
    }

    *int_ptr = result;
    return count;
}
```

Listing 16-9: The hex_to_int function in C

Our program first sets the 32-bit output to 0 ❶. Then, starting with the most significant hexadecimal character (the first one entered by the user), the program converts each 8-bit ASCII code to its corresponding 4-bit integer.

Looking at Tables 2-4 and 2-5 in Chapter 2, we see that the ASCII codes for the numeric characters range from 0x30 to 0x39, and for the lowercase alphabetic characters, they range from 0x61 to 0x66. Subtracting this 0x27 gap from the alphabetic characters gives us the bit patterns 0x30, 0x31, . . . , 0x39, 0x3a, . . . , 0x3f for the characters entered ❷. Of course, the user may enter uppercase alphabetic characters, which range from 0x41 to 0x46. Subtracting 0x27 then gives us 0x30, 0x31, . . . , 0x39, 0x1a, . . . , 0x1f. Each hexadecimal character represents 4 bits, and if we look at the low-order 4 bits after subtracting 0x27, they are the same whether the user enters lowercase or uppercase alphabetic characters. We can convert the character code to a 4-bit integer by masking off the upper 4 bits with the bit pattern 0x0f using &, the C bitwise AND operator ❸.

Next, we shift all the bits in the accumulated value 4 bits to the left to make room for the next 4 bits represented by the hexadecimal character ❹. The left shift leaves 0s in the four least significant bit positions, so we can copy the 4 bits in current into these positions using |, the bitwise OR operator ❺.

The type of the current variable is char, and the type of result is int. In C, the width of a narrower value will automatically be extended to match the width of a wider value for arithmetic and logic operations ❺.

Let's look at the assembly language the compiler generates for the hex_to_int function, shown in Listing 16-10.

hex_to_int.s

```
        .arch armv8-a
        .file   "hex_to_int.c"
        .text
        .align  2
        .global hex_to_int
        .type   hex_to_int, %function
hex_to_int:
        sub     sp, sp, #32
        str     x0, [sp, 8]
        str     x1, [sp]
        str     wzr, [sp, 20]
        str     wzr, [sp, 24]
```

```
        ldr     x0, [sp]
        ldrb    w0, [x0]
        strb    w0, [sp, 31]
        b       .L2
.L4:
        ldrb    w0, [sp, 31]
        cmp     w0, 57          /// > '9'?
        bls     .L3
        ldrb    w0, [sp, 31]    /// Yes
        sub     w0, w0, #7      /// Remove gap
        strb    w0, [sp, 31]
.L3:
  ❶ ldrb       w0, [sp, 31]
  ❷ and        w0, w0, 15      /// Leave only 4 bits
        strb    w0, [sp, 31]
        ldr     w0, [sp, 24]
  ❸ lsl        w0, w0, 4       /// Room for 4 bits
        str     w0, [sp, 24]
        ldrb    w0, [sp, 31]
        ldr     w1, [sp, 24]
        orr     w0, w1, w0      /// Copy new 4 bits
        str     w0, [sp, 24]
        ldr     x0, [sp]
        add     x0, x0, 1
        str     x0, [sp]
        ldr     w0, [sp, 20]
        add     w0, w0, 1
        str     w0, [sp, 20]
        ldr     x0, [sp]
        ldrb    w0, [x0]
        strb    w0, [sp, 31]
.L2:
        ldrb    w0, [sp, 31]
        cmp     w0, 0           /// NUL
        bne     .L4
        ldr     x0, [sp, 8]
        ldr     w1, [sp, 24]
        str     w1, [x0]
        ldr     w0, [sp, 20]
        add     sp, sp, 32
        ret
        .size   hex_to_int, .-hex_to_int
        .ident  "GCC: (Debian 12.2.0-14) 12.2.0"
        .section        .note.GNU-stack,"",@progbits
```

Listing 16-10: The compiler-generated assembly language for the C function in Listing 16-9

The compiler uses the ldrb instruction to load characters into a w register ❶. This sets bits 8 through 31 to 0, effectively typecasting the 8-bit char to a 32-bit int. This would have occurred even without our explicit typecasting in the C code in Listing 16-9, but the explicit typecasting more clearly shows our intent and doesn't affect the efficiency of our code.

The mask in this algorithm is four sequential 1s, so the immediate data form of the and instruction can be used ❷.

We see a new instruction here, lsl ❸. As you can probably guess, this instruction shifts the value in x0 4 bits to the left and loads the result into x1. Let's look at some common shift instructions:

lsl—Logically shift left immediate

    lsl wd, ws, amnt shifts the value in ws by amnt bits to the left, with 0s in the vacated bits, and loads the result into wd.

    lsl xd, xs, amnt shifts the value in xs by amnt bits to the left, with 0s in the vacated bits, and loads the result into xd.

lsr—Logically shift right immediate

    lsr wd, ws, amnt shifts the value in ws by amnt bits to the right, with 0s in the vacated bits, and loads the result into wd.

    lsr xd, xs, amnt shifts the value in xs by amnt bits to the right, with 0s in the vacated bits, and loads the result into xd.

asr—Arithmetic shift right immediate

    asr wd, ws, amnt shifts the value in ws by amnt bits to the right, copying the highest-order bit into the vacated bits, and loads the result into wd.

    asr xd, xs, amnt shifts the value in xs by amnt bits to the right, copying the highest-order bit into the vacated bits, and loads the result into xd.

ror—Rotate right immediate

    ror wd, ws, amnt shifts the value in ws by amnt bits to the right, copying the low-order bits into the vacated high-order bits, and loads the result into wd.

    ror xd, xs, amnt shifts the value in xs by amnt bits to the right, copying the low-order bits into the vacated high-order bits, and loads the result into xd.

Next, I'll take a similar approach to writing the hexadecimal-to-integer conversion program in assembly language as I did for the earlier case conversion C program.

In Assembly Language

I'll start the design for our convert_hex program with a diagram of the stack frame for the main function, shown in Figure 16-2.

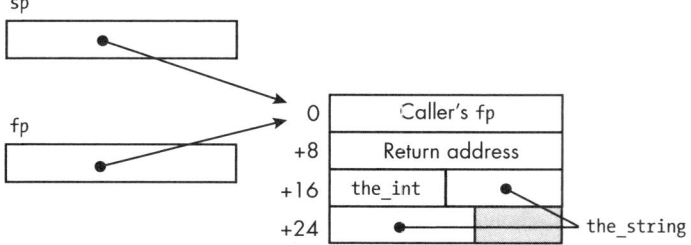

Figure 16-2: The stack frame for the convert_hex program

With this diagram, the assembly language design of the main function is straightforward, as shown in Listing 16-11.

```
convert_hex.s  // Get a hex number from the user and store it as an int.
               .arch armv8-a
               // Useful constant
               .equ    MAX, 8
               // Stack frame
               .equ    the_int, 16
               .equ    the_string, 20
           ❶ .equ    FRAME, 32
               // Code
               .text
               .section  .rodata
               .align  3
        prompt:
               .string "Enter up to 8 hex characters: "
        format:
               .string "0x%x = %i\n"
               .text
               .align  2
               .global main
               .type   main, %function
        main:
               stp     fp, lr, [sp, -FRAME]! // Create stack frame
               mov     fp, sp                // Our frame pointer

               adr     x0, prompt            // Prompt message
               bl      write_str             // Ask for input

               add     x0, sp, the_string    // Place to store string
               mov     w1, MAX               // Limit number of input chars
               bl      read_str              // Get from keyboard

               add     x1, sp, the_string    // Address of string
               add     x0, sp, the_int       // Place to store int
```

```
            bl      hex_to_int              // Do conversion

            ldr     w2, [sp, the_int]       // Load int
            ldr     w1, [sp, the_int]       // printf shows this copy in hex
            adr     x0, format              // Format string
            bl      printf

            mov     w0, 0                   // Return 0
            ldp     x29, x30, [sp], FRAME   // Delete stack frame
            ret
```

Listing 16-11: The assembly language main function for converting a hex value to an int

There is nothing new in this main function. In addition to the 16 bytes for saving the fp and lr registers and 4 bytes for the int, we need to allocate 9 bytes in our stack frame for the hexadecimal text string, giving a frame size of at least 29 bytes. The frame size must be a multiple of 16 to keep the stack pointer properly aligned, so we use 32 ❶.

We'll use registers for the variables in our assembly language version of hex_to_int. Our stack frame will be simple, so we won't need a diagram to design it. Figure 16-12 shows our function.

hex_to_int.s
```
// Convert a hex character string to an int.
// Calling sequence:
//     x0 <- pointer to int result
//     x1 <- pointer to hex character string to convert
//     Return number of characters converted.
        .arch armv8-a
// Useful constants
        .equ    INTPART, 0x0f           // Also works for lowercase
        .equ    GAP, 0x07               // Between numerals and alpha
// Program code
        .text
        .align  2
        .global hex_to_int
        .type   hex_to_int, %function
hex_to_int:
        mov     w2, wzr                 // result = 0
        mov     w3, wzr                 // counter = 0
convert:
        ldrb    w4, [x1]                // Load character
        cbz     w4, done                // NUL character?
        cmp     w4, '9                  // Numeral?
        b.ls    no_gap                  // Yes
        sub     w4, w4, GAP             // No, remove gap
no_gap:
        and     w4, w4, INTPART         // 4-bit integer
        lsl     w2, w2, 4               // Make room for it
```

```
          orr    w2, w2, w4            // Insert new 4-bit integer
          add    x1, x1, 1            // Increment source pointer
          add    w3, w3, 1            //   and counter
          b      convert             //   and continue
done:
          str    w2, [x0]            // Output result
          mov    w0, w3              // Return count
          ret                        // Back to caller
```

Listing 16-12: The assembly language version of the hex_to_int function

Shifts are good for multiplying and dividing by powers of two, but we also need to be able to multiply and divide by other numbers. We'll look at multiplying and dividing by arbitrary integers in the next two sections, deferring consideration of fractional and floating-point values until Chapter 19.

YOUR TURN

16.4 Modify the C main function in Listing 16-7 so it displays the number of hexadecimal characters converted. Use the assembly language hex_to_int function in Listing 16-12 for the conversion.

16.5 Write a program in assembly language that converts octal input to a long int.

Multiplication

In this section, I'll cover multiplication by integers that are not powers of two. It can be done using loops, but most general-purpose CPUs include multiply instructions.

In C

Let's modify the C program in Listings 16-7 to 16-9 to convert decimal number text strings into unsigned integers. When converting from hexadecimal text strings, we shifted the accumulated value 4 bits to the left, thus multiplying it by 16. We'll use the same algorithm for converting decimal text strings, but this time we'll multiply by 10 instead of 16.

Listings 16-13 to 16-15 show the C program.

---

convert_dec.c `// Get a decimal number from the user and store it as an int.`

```
#include <stdio.h>
#include "write_str.h"
#include "read_str.h"
#include "dec_to_int.h"
```

```
❶ #define MAX 11
  #define ARRAY_SZ MAX+1

  int main(void)
  {
      char the_string[ARRAY_SZ];
      int the_int;

      write_str("Enter an integer: ");
      read_str(the_string, MAX);

      dec_to_int(&the_int, the_string);
      printf("\"%s\" is stored as 0x%x\n", the_string, the_int);

      return 0;
  }
```

Listing 16-13: A program to convert decimal input to an int

This main function is very similar to the one for converting hexadecimal input to an int, but the maximum number of characters in an int is 10. We need to set MAX to 11 characters to allow for the possible + or − sign preceding the integer ❶.

Listing 16-14 shows the header file for the dec_to_int function.

hex_to_int.h
```
// Convert a decimal character string to an int.
// Return number of decimal characters.

#ifndef DEC_TO_INT_H
#define DEC_TO_INT_H
int dec_to_int(int *int_ptr, char *string_ptr);
#endif
```

Listing 16-14: The header file for the dec_to_int function

The header file declares the dec_to_int function, which takes two pointers: the char pointer is the input, and the int pointer is the location for the primary output. The dec_to_int function also returns an int that gives the number of characters it converted.

Listing 16-15 shows the definition of the dec_to_int function.

dec_to_int.c
```
// Convert a decimal character string to an unsigned int.
// Return number of characters.

#include <stdio.h>
#include <stdbool.h>
#include "dec_to_int.h"
#define INTMASK 0x0f
#define RADIX 10
#define NUL '\0'
```

```
❶ int dec_to_int(int *int_ptr, char *string_ptr)
{
    bool negative = false;      // Assume positive
    int result = 0;
    int count = 0;

❷   if (*string_ptr == '-') {
        negative = true;
        string_ptr++;
❸   } else if (*string_ptr == '+') {
        string_ptr++;
    }

    while (*string_ptr != NUL) {
❹       result = RADIX * result;
❺       result += (int)(*string_ptr & INTMASK);
        string_ptr++;
        count++;
    }

    if (negative) {
        result = -result;
    }
    *int_ptr = result;
    return count;
}
```

Listing 16-15: The dec_to_int function in C

The first thing we need to do is check for a possible + or − sign preceding the number. If there's a − sign, we set the negative flag to true ❷. It's typical for users to enter positive numbers without a + sign, but we still need to increment the pointer to the first numerical character in the string if there is one ❸.

The RADIX constant is not a power of two, so we can't do multiplication with a simple left shift ❹.

The string_ptr variable points to a char ❶. The char is being masked and added to result, which is an int. Most compilers will promote a char value when it's assigned to an int variable, but I prefer to explicitly typecast the value ❺.

Let's look at how the compiler does the multiplication by 10. This is shown in Listing 16-16.

dec_to_int.s
```
        .arch armv8-a
        .file   "dec_to_int.c"
        .text
        .align  2
```

```
        .global  dec_to_int
        .type    dec_to_int, %function
dec_to_int:
        sub      sp, sp, #32
        str      x0, [sp, 8]      /// Save int_ptr
        str      x1, [sp]         /// Save string_ptr
        strb     wzr, [sp, 31]    /// negative = false;
        str      wzr, [sp, 24]    /// result = 0;
        str      wzr, [sp, 20]    /// count = 0;
        ldr      x0, [sp]
        ldrb     w0, [x0]
        cmp      w0, 45
        bne      .L2
        mov      w0, 1
        strb     w0, [sp, 31]
        ldr      x0, [sp]
        add      x0, x0, 1
        str      x0, [sp]
        b        .L4
.L2:
        ldr      x0, [sp]
        ldrb     w0, [x0]
        cmp      w0, 43
        bne      .L4
        ldr      x0, [sp]
        add      x0, x0, 1
        str      x0, [sp]
        b        .L4
.L5:
        ldr      w1, [sp, 24]
        mov      w0, w1
❶ lsl       w0, w0, 2        /// 4 * result
        add      w0, w0, w1       /// (4 * result) + result
        lsl      w0, w0, 1        /// 2 * ((4 * result) + result)
        str      w0, [sp, 24]     /// result = 10 * result;
        ldr      x0, [sp]
        ldrb     w0, [x0]
        and      w0, w0, 15
        ldr      w1, [sp, 24]
        add      w0, w1, w0
        str      w0, [sp, 24]
        ldr      x0, [sp]
        add      x0, x0, 1
        str      x0, [sp]
        ldr      w0, [sp, 20]
        add      w0, w0, 1
        str      w0, [sp, 20]
```

```
.L4:
        ldr     x0, [sp]
        ldrb    w0, [x0]
        cmp     w0, 0
        bne     .L5
        ldrb    w0, [sp, 31]      /// Check negative flag
        cmp     w0, 0
        beq     .L6
        ldr     w0, [sp, 24]
❷   neg     w0, w0
        str     w0, [sp, 24]
.L6:
        ldr     x0, [sp, 8]
        ldr     w1, [sp, 24]
        str     w1, [x0]
        ldr     w0, [sp, 20]
        add     sp, sp, 32
        ret
        .size   dec_to_int, .-dec_to_int
        .ident  "GCC: (Debian 12.2.0-14) 12.2.0"
        .section        .note.GNU-stack,"",@progbits
```

Listing 16-16: The compiler-generated assembly language for the dec_to_int function in Listing 16-15

The multiplication instruction usually takes longer for the CPU to execute, so the compiler used a combination of shifting and adding to multiply result by 10 ❶. This four-instruction sequence is equivalent to the following C statement:

```
result = 2 * ((4 * result) + result);
```

The two multiplications in this statement are by powers of two, so they are done by simple left shifts.

Notice that the arithmetic in this conversion algorithm is unsigned. We checked for a – sign at the beginning of the number string, and we negate the converted result at the end if there was a – sign ❷.

Using shifts and adds to multiply is limited. To see how the multiplication instructions work, we'll use one to rewrite our decimal conversion program in assembly language.

In Assembly Language

The A64 architecture has over a dozen variations of multiply instructions. I'll show you only a few of them in this book; you can read about the others in the manual.

Figure 16-3 shows the stack frame design for our assembly language version of the main function of the program to convert a decimal text string to an int.

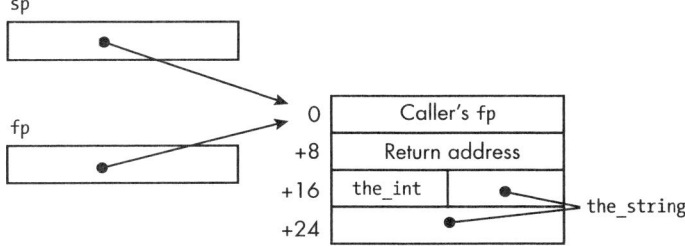

Figure 16-3: The stack frame for the convert_dec program

Our assembly language version of the main function is similar to the C version; it's shown in Listing 16-17.

convert_dec.s

```
// Get a decimal number from the user and store it as an int.
        .arch armv8-a
// Useful constant
        .equ    MAX, 12              // Character storage limit
// Stack frame
        .equ    the_int, 16
        .equ    the_string, 20
        .equ    FRAME, 32
// Code
        .text
        .section  .rodata
        .align  3
prompt:
        .string "Enter an integer: "
        .align  3
format:
        .string "\"%s\" is stored as 0x%x\n"
        .text
        .align  2
        .global main
        .type   main, %function
main:
        stp     fp, lr, [sp, -FRAME]! // Create stack frame
        mov     fp, sp                // Our frame pointer
        adr     x0, prompt            // Prompt message
        bl      write_str             // Ask for input

        mov     w1, MAX               // Limit number of input chars
        add     x0, sp, the_string    // Place to store string
        bl      read_str              // Get from keyboard

        add     x1, sp, the_string    // Address of string
        add     x0, sp, the_int       // Place to store the int
        bl      dec_to_int            // Do conversion
```

```
        ldr     w2, [sp, the_int]      // Load the int
        add     x1, sp, the_string     // Input text string
        adr     x0, format             // Format message
        bl      printf                 // Show results
        mov     w0, wzr                // Return 0
        ldp     x29, x30, [sp], FRAME  // Delete stack frame
        ret
```

Listing 16-17: A program to convert decimal values to ints in assembly language

Listing 16-18 shows our assembly language version of dec_to_int.

dec_to_int.s
```
// Convert a decimal text string to an int.
// Calling sequence:
//    x0 <- place to store int
//    x1 <- pointer to string
//    Return number of characters.
        .arch armv8-a
// Useful constants
        .equ    RADIX,10
        .equ    INTMASK,0x0f
// Program code
        .text
        .align  2
        .global dec_to_int
        .type   dec_to_int, %function
dec_to_int:
        mov     w2, wzr                // count = 0
        mov     w3, wzr                // result = 0
        mov     w4, wzr                // negative = false
        mov     w5, RADIX              // Handy to have in reg

        ldrb    w6, [x1]               // Load first character
        cmp     w6, '-                 // Minus sign?
        b.ne    check_pos              // No, check for plus sign
        mov     x4, 1                  // Yes, negative = true
        add     x1, x1, 1              // Increment string pointer
        b       convert                //   and convert numerals
check_pos:
        cmp     w6, '+                 // Plus sign?
        b.ne    convert                // No, convert numerals
        add     x1, x1, 1              // Yes, skip over it

convert:
        ldrb    w6, [x1]               // Load character
        cbz     w6, check_sign         // NUL char?
        and     w6, w6, INTMASK        // No, mask to integer
❶ mul     w3, w3, w5             // result * RADIX
```

```
            add     w3, w3, w6          // Add new integer
            add     w2, w2, 1           // count++
            add     x1, x1, 1           // string_ptr++
            b       convert             //   and continue
check_sign:
            cbz     w4, positive        // Check negative flag
            neg     w3, w3              // Negate if flag is true
positive:
            str     w3, [x0]            // Output result
            mov     w0, w2              // Return count
            ret                         // Back to caller
```

Listing 16-18: The dec_to_int function in assembly language

Instead of using a shift-and-add algorithm to multiply by 10, we're using the mul instruction ❶. Let's look at some variations of this instruction:

mul—Multiply register

> mul w*d*, w*s1*, w*s2* multiplies the values in w*s1* and w*s2* and stores the result in w*d*.

> mul x*d*, x*s1*, x*s2* multiplies the values in x*s1* and x*s2* and stores the result in x*d*.

When multiplying two n-bit integers, the product can be up to $2n$ bits wide. Without offering a formal proof here, you can probably be convinced by considering the largest 3-bit number, 111. Add 1 to get 1000. From 1000 * 1000 = 1000000, we can conclude that 111 * 111 <= 111111. More precisely, 111 * 111 = 110001.

If the result of the mul instruction exceeds the width of the destination register, the high-order bits are lost. For example, if w2 contains 0xcccccccc and w1 contains 0x00000002, then mul w0, w1, w2 will give 0x0000000099999998 in the x0 register. The correct result is 0x0000000199999998 if we're treating these values as unsigned integers and 0xffffffff99999998 if we're treating these values as signed. But when an instruction writes to the w portion of a register, the high-order 32 bits of that register are set to 0. Thus, the mul instruction yields an incorrect result if the product of two 32-bit integers is not within the range $0 \leq product \leq 4{,}294{,}967{,}295$ if we're using unsigned integers and $-2{,}147{,}483{,}648 \leq product \leq +2{,}147{,}483{,}647$ if we're using signed integers.

To deal with this size problem, the A64 architecture includes two multiplication instructions that use a 64-bit destination register for the case when the result of multiplying two 32-bit numbers exceeds the range of 32 bits:

umull—Unsigned multiply long

> umull x*d*, w*s1*, w*s2* multiplies the values in w*s1* and w*s2* and loads the result in x*d*. If the magnitude of the result doesn't take up the full 64 bits of x*d*, the unoccupied high-order bits are filled with 0s.

smull—Signed multiply long

> smull x*d*, w*s1*, w*s2* multiplies the values in w*s1* and w*s2* and loads the result in x*d*. If the magnitude of the result doesn't take up the full 64 bits

of xd, the unoccupied high-order bits are each filled with a copy of the highest-order bit of the result, thus providing sign extension.

Continuing with our example, if w2 contains 0xcccccccc and w1 contains 0x00000002, then umull x0, w1, w2 will give 0x0000000199999998 in x0 and smull x0, w1, w2 will give 0xffffffff99999998.

If we're using 64-bit long ints and cannot prove that the result of the multiplication can never exceed 64 bits, the A64 architecture includes two multiplication instructions that will give the high-order 64 bits when multiplying two 64-bit numbers:

umulh—Unsigned multiply high

umulh xd, xs1, xs2 multiplies the values in xs1 and xs2 and loads the high-order 64 bits of the result into xd with zero extension.

smulh—Signed multiply high

smulh xd, xs1, xs2 multiplies the values in xs1 and xs2 and loads the high-order 64 bits of the result into xd with sign extension.

Thus, the multiplication of two 64-bit integers requires two instructions. We would use the following two instructions if we were treating two integers in x0 and x1 as unsigned:

```
mul     x3, x0, x1
umulh   x2, x0, x1
```

And we would use the following two instructions if we were treating two integers in x0 and x1 as signed:

```
mul     x3, x0, x1
smulh   x2, x0, x1
```

In both cases, the result is a 128-bit integer with the high-order 64 bits in register x2 and the low-order 64 bits in x3.

The multiply instructions don't affect the condition flags in the nzcv register. We need to carefully analyze our algorithms for all possible values and use the appropriate instructions.

Next, I'll cover division, the inverse of multiplication.

YOUR TURN

16.6   Write a dec_to_uint function in assembly language that converts an unsigned decimal number from its text string format to its unsigned int format.

16.7   I asserted that the C statement result = 2 * ((4 * result) + result); is equivalent to the result = RADIX * result; statement in Listing 16-15. Make that change in Listing 16-15 and compare the compiler-generated assembly language with that in Listing 16-16.

Division

When multiplying two *n*-bit numbers, we were concerned about the result being $2n$ bits wide. In division, the quotient will never be wider than the dividend, but division takes much longer than multiplication. In this section, you'll learn about an algorithm that can speed up division when the divisor is a constant. Integer division can give a remainder, which may also need to be computed.

I'll start with a C function that converts an int to the numerical text string it represents, the inverse of the earlier dec_to_int function.

In C

Our main function will read an integer from the user, subtract 123 from it, and show the result. Our subfunction, int_to_dec, will use a division algorithm to convert a 32-bit int to the text string that represents it so that the main function can display the result. Listings 16-19 through 16-21 show the complete program.

---

sub_123.c // Read an int from the user, subtract 123, and display the result.

```c
#include "write_str.h"
#include "write_char.h"
#include "read_str.h"
#include "dec_to_int.h"
#include "int_to_dec.h"
#define MAX 11
#define ARRAY_SZ MAX+1

int main(void)
{
    char the_string[ARRAY_SZ];
    int the_int;

    write_str("Enter an integer: ");
    read_str(the_string, MAX);

    dec_to_int(&the_int, the_string);
    the_int -= 123;
    int_to_dec(the_string, the_int);

    write_str("The result is: ");
    write_str(the_string);
    write_char('\n');

    return 0;
}
```

Listing 16-19: A program to subtract 123 from an int

The main function for this program is quite simple. We use the assembly language version of dec_to_int in Listing 16-18 to convert the user's input to an int. We then subtract 123 from the int, convert the resulting number to its text string representation, and display the result.

Listing 16-20 shows the header file for the int_to_dec function.

int_to_dec.h
```
// Convert an int to its decimal text string representation.
// Return number of characters.

#ifndef INT_TO_DEC_H
#define INT_TO_DEC_H
int int_to_dec(char *dec_string, int the_int);
#endif
```

Listing 16-20: The header file for the int_to_dec function

The header file declares the int_to_dec function. The int is the input, and the char pointer is the location for the primary output. The int_to_dec function also returns an int that gives the number of characters in the output string.

Listing 16-21 shows the definition of the int_to_dec function.

int_to_dec.c
```
// Convert an int to its decimal text string representation.
// Return number of characters.

#include "int_to_dec.h"
#define ARRAY_SZ 12
#define ASCII 0x30
#define RADIX 10
#define NUL '\0'

int int_to_dec(char *dec_string, int the_int)
{
    char reverse[ARRAY_SZ];
    char digit;
    char *_ptr;
    unsigned int working;
    int count = 0;

❶   if (the_int < 0) {
        the_int = -the_int;
        *dec_string = '-';
        count++;
        decString++;
    }
    ptr = reverse;                        // Point to local char array
❷   *ptr = NUL;                           // Start with termination char
❸   working = (unsigned int)the_int;      // Use unsigned arithmetic
```

```
    do {
        ptr++;
    ❹ digit = (char)(working % RADIX);
        *ptr = ASCII | digit;
        working = working / RADIX;
    } while (working > 0);

    count = 0;
    if (negative) {
        *dec_string = '-';
        count++;
        dec_string++;
    }
❺ do {                                  // Reverse string
        *dec_string = *ptr;
        count++;
        dec_string++;
        ptr--;
    ❻ } while (*ptr != NUL);
    *dec_string = *ptr;                  // Copy termination char

    return count;
}
```

Listing 16-21: The int_to_dec function in C

The algorithm we're using to find the characters that represent the int in decimal involves the repeated integer division of the int by 10. The % operator computes the remainder from the division ❹. For positive integers, the remainder will be a 32-bit int in the range 0 through 9, or 0x00000000 through 0x00000009, which is the value of the lowest-order decimal digit.

However, for negative integers, the remainder will be an int in the range 0 through −9, or 0x00000000 through 0xfffffff7. The negative values in this range require a different algorithm to convert them to their corresponding ASCII numeric character. The solution we're using here is to negate an input negative integer, prepend the resulting text string with a − sign, and convert the positive result ❶.

This works for all but one 32-bit negative number: −2,147,483,648. There is no 32-bit +2,147,483,648 in two's complement format; negating −2,147,483,648 gives −2,147,483,648. Our solution is to convert the negated int to an unsigned int ❸. This doesn't change the bit pattern of the value, 0x80000000, but it tells the compiler to use unsigned % and / operations. So, for 2,147,483,648, the working % RADIX operation will give us 0x00000008.

We convert the unsigned int from the % operation to a char with (char), the *cast operator* ❹. The parentheses are part of the syntax for a cast operator. Then, we use a bitwise OR operation to convert the char to its corresponding numeric character in ASCII code.

Be careful when using a cast operator to convert the type of a value. We're converting from a 32-bit value to an 8-bit one, which may cause a loss of information. In this case, we know the information will be encoded in 4 bits, so the conversion is safe.

Since this algorithm works from right to left, the characters are stored in reverse order. So, we need to reverse the order of the text string for the calling function ❺. Storing the NUL character first ❷ provides a way to know when the entire text string has been completely copied in reverse order ❻.

Next, we'll look at the assembly language generated by the compiler, shown in Listing 16-22.

int_to_dec.s
```
          .arch armv8-a
          .file   "int_to_dec.c"
          .text
          .align  2
          .global int_to_dec
          .type   int_to_dec, %function
int_to_dec:
          sub     sp, sp, #48
          str     x0, [sp, 8]
          str     w1, [sp, 4]
          str     wzr, [sp, 32]
          ldr     w0, [sp, 4]
          cmp     w0, 0             /// Check for negative
          bge     .L2
          ldr     w0, [sp, 4]
          neg     w0, w0
          str     w0, [sp, 4]
          ldr     x0, [sp, 8]
          mov     w1, 45
          strb    w1, [x0]
          ldr     w0, [sp, 32]
          add     w0, w0, 1
          str     w0, [sp, 32]
          ldr     x0, [sp, 8]
          add     x0, x0, 1
          str     x0, [sp, 8]
.L2:
          add     x0, sp, 16
          str     x0, [sp, 40]      /// ptr
          ldr     x0, [sp, 40]
          strb    wzr, [x0]         /// *ptr = NUL;
          ldr     w0, [sp, 4]
          str     w0, [sp, 36]      /// working = the_int;
.L3:
          ldr     x0, [sp, 40]
          add     x0, x0, 1
```

```
        str     x0, [sp, 40]
        ldr     w2, [sp, 36]
❶ mov     w0, 52429              /// 0xcccd
        movk    w0, 0xcccc, lsl 16  /// 0xcccccccd
❷ umull   x0, w2, w0             /// Multiply by 0.1
        lsr     x0, x0, 32          /// Divide by 2^35
        lsr     w1, w0, 3
        mov     w0, w1
❸ lsl     w0, w0, 2
        add     w0, w0, w1
        lsl     w0, w0, 1
❹ sub     w1, w2, w0             /// working % RADIX;
        mov     w0, w1
        strb    w0, [sp, 31]
        ldrb    w0, [sp, 31]
❺ orr     w0, w0, 48             /// Convert to ASCII
        and     w1, w0, 255
        ldr     x0, [sp, 40]
        strb    w1, [x0]           /// *ptr = ASCII | digit;
        ldr     w1, [sp, 36]
❻ mov     w0, 52429
        movk    w0, 0xcccc, lsl 16
        umull   x0, w1, w0
        lsr     x0, x0, 32
        lsr     w0, w0, 3
        str     w0, [sp, 36]       /// working = working / RADIX;
        ldr     w0, [sp, 36]
        cmp     w0, 0
        bne     .L3
.L4:
        ldr     x0, [sp, 40]
        ldrb    w1, [x0]
        ldr     x0, [sp, 8]
        strb    w1, [x0]
        ldr     w0, [sp, 32]
        add     w0, w0, 1
        str     w0, [sp, 32]
        ldr     x0, [sp, 8]
        add     x0, x0, 1
        str     x0, [sp, 8]
        ldr     x0, [sp, 40]
        sub     x0, x0, #1
        str     x0, [sp, 40]
        ldr     x0, [sp, 40]
        ldrb    w0, [x0]
        cmp     w0, 0
        bne     .L4
```

```
        ldr     x0, [sp, 40]
        ldrb    w1, [x0]
        ldr     x0, [sp, 8]
        strb    w1, [x0]
        ldr     w0, [sp, 32]
        add     sp, sp, 48
        ret
        .size   int_to_dec, .-int_to_dec
        .ident  "GCC: (Debian 12.2.0-14) 12.2.0"
        .section        .note.GNU-stack,"",@progbits
```

Listing 16-22: The compiler-generated assembly language for the `int_to_dec` function in Listing 16-21

The C algorithm involves division by 10, but the compiler uses a `umull` instruction to perform the remainder (%) operation ❷. This is because division takes much more time than multiplication. Since we're dividing by a constant, the compiler uses the following arithmetic:

$$\frac{x}{10} = \frac{2^n}{10} \times \frac{x}{2^n}$$
$$= \frac{\frac{2^n}{10} \times x}{2^n}$$

The compiler uses $n = 35$, giving the constant $2^{35}/10 = 3{,}435{,}973{,}836.8$. Rounding this to the nearest integer gives $3{,}435{,}973{,}837 = \text{0xcccccccd}$ ❶. After multiplying the `working` integer by this constant, the algorithm shifts the result 35 bits to the right to divide by 2^{35}.

The compiler then uses the shift-and-add algorithm to multiply this quotient by 10 ❸. Subtracting the result from the original dividend leaves us with the remainder ❹, which is converted to the corresponding ASCII character ❺.

The compiler implements the / operation with the same multiply-and-shift algorithm that it used for the % operation ❻.

Using multiplication and shifts to divide is limited. To see how the division instructions work, we'll use a divide instruction for our assembly language version of the `int_to_dec` function.

In Assembly Language

We didn't look at the compiler-generated assembly language for the `main` function in the C version of our `sub_123` program (Listing 16-19). It's similar to our assembly language version, which is shown in Listing 16-23.

```
sub_123.s    // Subtract 123 from an integer.
             .arch armv8-a
        // Useful constants
             .equ    CONSTANT, 123       // Number to subtract
             .equ    MAX, 11             // Maximum digits
```

❶ ```
// Stack frame
        .equ   the_int, 16
        .equ   the_string, 20
        .equ   FRAME, 32
// Code
        .text
        .section .rodata
        .align 3
prompt:
        .string "Enter an integer: "
message:
        .string "The result is: "
        .text
        .align 2
        .global main
        .type   main, %function
main:
        stp   fp, lr, [sp, -FRAME]! // Create stack frame
        mov   fp, sp   // Our frame pointer

        adr   x0, prompt   // Prompt message
        bl   write_str   // Ask for input
        add   x0, sp, the_string
        mov   w1, MAX
        bl   read_str

        add   x1, sp, the_string   // Input
        add   x0, sp, the_int   // Place for output
        bl   dec_to_int   // Convert to int

        ldr   w1, [sp, the_int]
        sub   w1, w1, CONSTANT   // Subtract our constant
        add   x0, sp, the_string   // Place for output
        bl   int_to_dec   // Convert to text string

        adr   x0, message   // Tell user that
        bl   write_str
        add   x0, sp, the_string   //   this is the result
        bl   write_str
        mov   w0, '\n'
        bl   write_char

        mov   w0, wzr   // Return 0
        ldp   fp, lr, [sp], FRAME   // Delete stack frame
        ret   // Back to caller
```

*Listing 16-23: The assembly language version of the main function for the sub_123 program*
```

There isn't anything new in the main function; we can use the same stack frame design from Figure 16-3 ❶.

Listing 16-24 shows our assembly language version of the int_to_dec function.

int_to_dec.s
```
// Convert an int to its decimal text string representation.
// Calling sequence:
//     x0 <- place to store string
//     w1 <- the int
//     Return number of characters in the string.
        .arch armv8-a
// Useful constants
        .equ    RADIX, 10               // Number base
        .equ    INT2CHAR, 0x30          // ASCII zero
        .equ    MINUS, '-               // Minus sign
❶ // Stack frame
        .equ    reverse, 0
        .equ    FRAME, 16
// Code
        .text
        .align  2
        .global int_to_dec
        .type   int_to_dec, %function
int_to_dec:
        sub     sp, sp, FRAME           // Local string on stack

        cmp     w1, wzr                 // => 0?
        tbz     w1, 31, non_negative    // Yes, go to conversion
        neg     w1, w1                  // No, negate int
        mov     w2, MINUS
        strb    w2, [x0]                // Start with minus sign
        add     x0, x0, 1               // Increment pointer
non_negative:
        add     x3, sp, reverse         // Pointer to local string storage
        strb    wzr, [x3]               // Create end with NUL
        mov     w2, RADIX               // Put in register
do_while:
        add     x3, x3, 1               // Increment local pointer
❷ udiv    w4, w1, w2              // Quotient = dividend / RADIX
❸ msub    w5, w4, w2, w1          // Rem. = dividend - RADIX * quot.
        orr     w5, w5, INT2CHAR        // Convert to ASCII
        strb    w5, [x3]                // Store character
❹ mov     w1, w4                  // Remove remainder
        cbnz    w1, do_while            // Continue if more left

        mov     w6, wzr                 // count = 0
```

```
copy:
        ldrb    w5, [x3]                // Load character
        strb    w5, [x0]                // Store it
        add     x0, x0, 1               // Increment to pointer
        sub     x3, x3, 1               // Decrement from pointer
        add     w6, w6, 1               // Increment counter
        cbnz    w5, copy                // Continue until NUL char
        strb    w5, [x0]                // Store NUL character

        mov     w0, w6                  // Return count
        add     sp, sp, FRAME           // Delete stack frame
        ret                             // Back to caller
```

Listing 16-24: The assembly language version of the int_to_dec function

Since this is a leaf function, we don't need a frame record, but we do need space on the stack for storing the text string locally as we generate it in reverse order ❶.

Rather than using a multiply-and-shift algorithm like the compiler did, we use the udiv instruction to divide by 10 ❷. This gives us the quotient in the w4 register. Then, we use the msub instruction to multiply the quotient (register w4) by RADIX (register w2) and subtract that product from the dividend (register w1), leaving the remainder in register w5 ❸. Since we already have the quotient in register w4, we can use that for the next iteration of this loop ❹.

In Listing 16-24, we see two new instructions: msub and udiv. I'll also describe sdiv here:

msub—Multiply and subtract

msub *wd, ws1, ws2, ws3* multiplies ws1 by ws2, subtracts the value in ws3 from the product, and loads the result in wd.

msub *xd, xs1, xs2, xs3* multiplies xs1 by xs2, subtracts the value in xs3 from the product, and loads the result in xd.

udiv—Unsigned divide

udiv *wd, ws1, ws2* divides ws1 by ws2 and stores the result in wd. It treats all values as unsigned numbers.

udiv *xd, xs1, xs2* divides xs1 by xs2 and stores the result in xd. It treats all values as unsigned numbers.

sdiv—Signed divide

sdiv *wd, ws1, ws2* divides ws1 by ws2 and stores the result in wd. If ws1 and ws2 are of the same sign, the value in wd will be positive. If they are of opposite signs, the value in wd will be negative.

sdiv *xd, xs1, xs2* divides xs1 by xs2 and stores the result in xd. If xs1 and xs2 are of the same sign, the value in xd will be positive. If they are of opposite signs, the value in xd will be negative.

The divide instructions don't affect the condition flags in the nzcv register. They don't even give an error if you divide by zero; they load 0 into the destination register. You need to carefully analyze your algorithms for all possible values to make sure you never divide by zero.

YOUR TURN

16.8 Write the two functions put_int and get_int in assembly language. The put_int function takes one argument, a 32-bit signed integer, and displays it on the screen. The get_int function returns a 32-bit signed integer, which it reads from keyboard input. Write a main function in C to test put_int and get_int. We'll be using put_int and get_int in subsequent chapters for displaying and reading integers.

16.9 Write the two functions put_uint and get_uint in assembly language. The put_uint function takes one argument, a 32-bit unsigned integer, and displays it on the screen. The get_uint function returns a 32-bit unsigned integer, which it reads from keyboard input. Use the dec_to_uint function from exercise 16.6 on page 348, and write the function uint_to_dec. Write a main function in C to test put_uint and get_uint. We'll be using put_uint and get_uint in subsequent chapters for displaying and reading integers.

16.10 Write a program in assembly language that allows a user to enter two signed decimal integers. The program will add, subtract, multiply, and divide the two integers. It will display the sum, difference, product, quotient, and remainder resulting from these operations.

What You've Learned

Bitmasking We can use bitwise logic instructions to directly change bit patterns in variables.

Bit shifting Bits in variables can be shifted left or right, effectively multiplying or dividing by multiples of 2.

Multiplication The multiply instructions allow us to perform signed or unsigned multiplication. Multiplying large 64-bit values requires two instructions for the 128-bit result.

Faster multiplication When multiplying by a constant, a combination of adding and shifting can be faster than a multiply instruction.

Division The divide instructions allow us to perform signed or unsigned division.

Faster division When dividing by a constant, a combination of multiplying and shifting can be faster than a divide instruction.

Converting numbers between binary storage and character display
Arithmetic operations are easier when numbers are stored in the binary system, but keyboard input and screen display use the corresponding character format.

We've now covered ways to organize program flow and perform arithmetic or logic operations on data items. In the next chapter, we'll explore two of the most fundamental ways to organize data: arrays and records.

17

DATA STRUCTURES

An essential part of programming is determining how best to organize data. In this chapter, we'll cover two of the most fundamental ways of organizing data: arrays, which can be used for grouping data items of the same data type; and records, which can be used for grouping data items of different data types.

These ways of organizing data determine how we access the individual data items. Both require two addressing items to locate a data item. Since the data items in an array are all of the same type, we can access an individual data item if we know the name of the array and the index number of the item. Accessing an individual data item in a record requires the name of the record and the name of the data item in the record.

Arrays

An *array* is a collection of data elements of the same data type, arranged in a sequence. We can access a single element in an array using the name of the array together with an *index value*, which specifies the number of the element relative to the beginning of the array. We have used char arrays in previous chapters to store ASCII characters as text strings. Each element in the array was the same type, a char, which is 1 byte. In our earlier applications, we were accessing each character in order, so we started with a pointer to the first char and simply incremented it by 1 to access each subsequent char. We didn't need an index to locate each char within the text string array.

In this chapter, we'll look at int arrays, which use 4 bytes for each data element in the array. If we started with a pointer to the first element, we'd need to increment it by 4 to access each subsequent element; it's much easier to use the array index number to access each individual element. You'll see how the index number is converted to an address offset to access an array element relative to the beginning of the array. You'll also see that C passes arrays to other functions differently from other data items.

In C

We define an array in C by stating the element data type, giving the array a name, and specifying the number of elements in the array. Let's start with the example in Listing 17-1.

fill_array.c
```
// Allocate an int array, store (2 * element number)
// in each element, and print the array contents.

#include "twice_index.h"
#include "display_array.h"
#define N 10

int main(void)
{
    int my_array[N];

    twice_index(my_array, N);
    display_array(my_array, N);

    return 0;
}
```

Listing 17-1: A program to store ints in an array and display them

This main function calls the twice_index function, which sets each element in the array to twice its index. For example, twice_index stores the int 8 in array element number 4. The main function then calls display_array, which prints the contents of the entire array in the terminal window.

You first encountered arrays in Chapter 2, when learning about C-style strings. Those strings used a sentinel value, NUL, to mark the end of the array. The array we're using here doesn't have a sentinel value, so we need to pass the number of elements in the array to each function that processes it.

One thing you might notice about the arguments we're passing to the functions is that it appears the array is being passed by value, since we give only its name in the argument list. But twice_index stores values in the array, so it needs to know where the array is located in memory.

Usually, a programmer passes an input value to a function by value. But if the input consists of a large number of data items, copying them all into registers and onto the stack would be very inefficient; it makes more sense to pass by pointer. Arrays almost always have many data items, so the designers of the C language decided to always pass them by pointer. When you give the name of the array as an argument to a function call, C will pass the address of the first element of the array; thus, twice_index can output data to the array.

To see this explicitly, let's look at the compiler-generated assembly language for this main function, as shown in Listing 17-2.

fill_array.s

```
        .arch armv8-a
        .file    "fill_array.c"
        .text
        .align  2
        .global main
        .type   main, %function
main:
❶ stp    x29, x30, [sp, -64]!
   mov    x29, sp
❷ add    x0, sp, 24              /// Address of array
   mov    w1, 10
   bl     twice_index
❸ add    x0, sp, 24
   mov    w1, 10
   bl     display_array
   mov    w0, 0
   ldp    x29, x30, [sp], 64
   ret
        .size   main, .-main
        .ident  "GCC: (Debian 12.2.0-14) 12.2.0"
        .section        .note.GNU-stack,"",@progbits
```

Listing 17-2: The compiler-generated assembly language for the function in Listing 17-1

The entire int array is allocated in main's stack frame ❶. In assembly language, the address of the array is passed both to the twice_index function ❷ and to the display_array function ❸. The elements of the array are inputs to the display_array function, so it does not need to know the address of the array, but it's much more efficient to pass the address of the entire array than a copy of each of the array elements.

Next, we'll look at the function to store the ints in the array, twice_index. Listing 17-3 shows its header file.

twice_index.h

```
// Store (2 * element number) in each array element.

#ifndef TWICE_INDEX_H
#define TWICE_INDEX_H
```

```
void twice_index(int the_array[], int n_elements);
#endif
```

Listing 17-3: The header file for the twice_index *function*

This prototype statement shows how we use the [] syntax to indicate that the argument to a function is an array. As described previously, we need to provide the number of elements in the array as a separate argument.

The definition of the twice_index function is given in Listing 17-4.

twice_index.c
```
// Store (2 * element number) in each array element.

#include "twice_index.h"

void twice_index(int the_array[], int n_elements)
{
    int i;

    for (i = 0; i < n_elements; i++) {
        the_array[i] = 2 * i;
    }
}
```

Listing 17-4: A function to store twice the index number in each element of an array

The number of iterations is known when this loop starts, so we use a for loop to process the array. The compiler generated the assembly language shown in Listing 17-5 for the twice_index function.

twice_index.s
```
        .arch armv8-a
        .file   "twice_index.c"
        .text
        .align  2
        .global twice_index
        .type   twice_index, %function
twice_index:
        sub     sp, sp, #32
        str     x0, [sp, 8]     //! Address of the_array
        str     w1, [sp, 4]     //! n_elements
        str     wzr, [sp, 28]   //! i = 0;
        b       .L2
.L3:
        ldrsw   x0, [sp, 28]
      ❶ lsl     x0, x0, 2       //! Each element is 4 bytes
        ldr     x1, [sp, 8]
      ❷ add     x0, x1, x0      //! Address of ith element
        ldr     w1, [sp, 28]
        lsl     w1, w1, 1       //! 2 * i;
        str     w1, [x0]
        ldr     w0, [sp, 28]
```

```
        add    w0, w0, 1          /// i++;
        str    w0, [sp, 28]
.L2:
        ldr    w1, [sp, 28]
        ldr    w0, [sp, 4]
        cmp    w1, w0
        blt    .L3
        nop
        nop
        add    sp, sp, 32
        ret
        .size    twice_index, .-twice_index
        .ident   "GCC: (Debian 12.2.0-14) 12.2.0"
        .section        .note.GNU-stack,"",@progbits
```

Listing 17-5: The compiler-generated assembly language for the function in Listing 17-4

To access an array element, the compiler computes the offset of the element from the beginning of the array and then adds that offset to the address of the beginning. This is an array of ints, so each element is 4 bytes. The compiler shifts the array index, i, 2 bits to the left to multiply it by 4 ❶. Adding 4 * i to the address of the beginning of the array gives the address of the array element ❷.

Next, we'll look at the display_array function used to display the contents of the array. Listing 17-6 shows the header file for this function.

display_array.h
```
// Print the int array contents.

#ifndef DISPLAY_ARRAY_H
#define DISPLAY_ARRAY_H
void display_array(int the_array[], int n_elements);
#endif
```

Listing 17-6: The header file for the `display_array` function

As with the twice_index function, we use the [] syntax to indicate that the argument to the display_array function is an array. We also need to provide the number of elements in the array as a separate argument. The function definition is given in Listing 17-7.

display_array.c
```
// Print the int array contents.

#include "display_array.h"
#include "write_str.h"
#include "write_char.h"
#include "put_int.h"
void display_array(int the_array[], int n_elements)
{
    int i;
```

```
        for (i = 0; i < n_elements; i++) {
            write_str("my_array[");
            put_int(i);
            write_str("] = ");
            put_int(the_array[i]);
            write_char('\n');
        }
}
```

Listing 17-7: A function to display ints in an array

To display the integers, we're using the put_int function that you wrote in "Your Turn" exercise 16.8 on page 358. Listing 17-8 shows the compiler-generated assembly language for this function.

display_array.s

```
            .arch armv8-a
            .file    "display_array.c"
            .text
            .section      .rodata
            .align  3
            .LC0:
            .string "my_array["
            .align  3
.LC1:
            .string "] = "
            .text
            .align  2
            .global display_array
            .type   display_array, %function
display_array:
            stp     x29, x30, [sp, -48]!
            mov     x29, sp
   ❶ str     x0, [sp, 24]      ///! Address of the_array
            str     w1, [sp, 20]      ///! n_elements
            str     wzr, [sp, 44]     ///! i = 0;
            b       .L2
.L3:
            adrp    x0, .LC0
            add     x0, x0, :lo12:.LC0
            bl      write_str
            ldr     w0, [sp, 44]
            bl      put_int
            adrp    x0, .LC1
            add     x0, x0, :lo12:.LC1
            bl      write_str
            ldrsw   x0, [sp, 44]
   ❷ lsl     x0, x0, 2         ///! Each element is 4 bytes
   ❸ ldr     x1, [sp, 24]      ///! Address of array
            add     x0, x1, x0        ///! Address of ith element
```

```
        ldr     w0, [x0]
        bl      put_int
        mov     w0, 10          /// '\n' character
        bl      write_char
        ldr     w0, [sp, 44]
        add     w0, w0, 1       /// i++;
        str     w0, [sp, 44]
.L2:
        ldr     w1, [sp, 44]
        ldr     w0, [sp, 20]
        cmp     w1, w0
        blt     .L3
        nop
        nop
        ldp     x29, x30, [sp], 48
        ret
        .size   display_array, .-display_array
        .ident  "GCC: (Debian 12.2.0-14) 12.2.0"
        .section        .note.GNU-stack,"",@progbits
```

Listing 17-8: The compiler-generated assembly language for the function in Listing 17-7

Although the array is an input to the display_array function, C passes the address of the array to the called function ❶ ❸. As in the twice_index function, the compiler multiplies the index by 4 to get the offset of each int in the array ❷. Next, I'll demonstrate a different way to index the array elements when writing this program directly in assembly language.

In Assembly Language

Our approach to the fill_array program will be similar to the compiler's, but we'll use instructions that are a little more intuitive. Listing 17-9 shows our main function.

fill_array.s
```
// Allocate an int array, store (2 * element number)
// in each element, and print array contents.
        .arch armv8-a
// Useful constant
        .equ    N, 10                   // Array length
// Stack frame
        .equ    my_array, 16
        .equ    FRAME, 64
// Code
        .text
        .align  2
        .global main
        .type   main, %function
main:
        stp     fp, lr, [sp, -FRAME]!   // Create stack frame
```

```
        mov     fp, sp                  // Set our frame pointer

        mov     w1, N                   // Length of array
        add     x0, sp, my_array        // Address of array
        bl      twice_index             // Fill the array

        mov     w1, N                   // Number of elements
        add     x0, sp, my_array        // Address of array
        bl      display_array           // Print array contents

        mov     w0, wzr                 // Return 0
        ldp     fp, lr, [sp], FRAME     // Delete stack frame
        ret
```

Listing 17-9: The assembly language program to store ints in an array and display them

This is similar to what the compiler generated in Listing 17-2, except that we use more meaningful names. However, we'll use a different way to compute the address of each array element in our twice_index function, as shown in Listing 17-10.

twice_index.s
```
// Store (2 * element number) in each array element.
// Calling sequence:
//     x0 <- address of array
//     w1 <- number of array elements
//     Return 0.
        .arch armv8-a
// Code
        .text
        .align  2
        .global twice_index
        .type   twice_index, %function
twice_index:
        mov     w2, wzr                 // i = 0
loop:
        add     w3, w2, w2              // 2 * i
❶ str     w3, [x0, w2, uxtw 2]         // Current element address
        add     w2, w2, 1               // i++
        cmp     w2, w1                  // At end?
        b.lt    loop                    // No, continue filling

        mov     w0, wzr                 // Yes, return 0
        ret
```

Listing 17-10: The assembly language function to store twice the index number in each element of an array

We're using a variant of the str instruction that uses a register to hold the offset from the base register instead of a constant ❶. In our case, the index is in a 32-bit register, w2, so the value needs to be extended to 64 bits before adding it to the address in the base register, x0. Since each element in the array is 4 bytes, the index value needs to be multiplied by 4 to give an address offset.

Let's look at the load and store instructions that use a register to hold the offset from a base register:

ldr—Load register, base register–relative, register offset

ldr *wd, [xb, wo, xtnd{ amnt}]* loads *wd* with the 32-bit value at the memory location obtained by adding the address in *xb* and the value in *wo*, optionally shifted left 2 bits, extended to 64 bits.

ldr *wd, [xb, xo{, xtnd{ amnt}}]* loads *wd* with the 32-bit value at the memory location obtained by adding the address in *xb* and the value in *xo*, optionally shifted left 2 bits.

ldr *xd, [xb, wo, xtnd{ amnt}]* loads *xd* with the 64-bit value at the memory location obtained by adding the address in *xb* and the value in *wo*, optionally shifted left 3 bits, extended to 64 bits.

ldr *xd, [xb, xo{, xtnd{ amnt}}]* loads *xd* with the 64-bit value at the memory location obtained by adding the address in *xb* and the value in *xo*, optionally shifted left 3 bits.

str—Store register, base register–relative, register offset

str *ws, [xb, wo, xtnd{ amnt}]* stores the 32-bit value in *ws* in the memory location obtained by adding the address in *xb* and the value in *wo*, optionally shifted left 2 bits, extended to 64 bits.

str *ws, [xb, xo{, xtnd{ amnt}}]* stores the 32-bit value in *ws* in the memory location obtained by adding the address in *xb* and the value in *xo*, optionally shifted left 2 bits.

str *xs, [xb, wo, xtnd{ amnt}]* stores the 64-bit value in *xs* in the memory location obtained by adding the address in *xb* and the value in *wo*, optionally shifted left 3 bits, extended to 64 bits.

str *xs, [xb, xo{, xtnd{ amnt}}]* stores the 64-bit value in *xs* in the memory location obtained by adding the address in *xb* and the value in *xo*, optionally shifted left 3 bits.

Table 17-1 lists the allowable values for the *xtnd* option for the ldr and str instructions.

Table 17-1: Allowable Values for *xtnd* in ldr and str Instructions

xtnd	**Effect**
uxtw	Unsigned extension of word, optional left shift
lsl	Left shift
sxtw	Signed extension of word, optional left shift
sxtx	Left shift

A 32-bit offset, wo, must be extended to 64 bits to be added to the address in the base register, xb. The sxtx option exists for syntactic symmetry; it has the same effect as lsl.

Allowable values for *amnt* are 0 or 2 for wd and ws registers, and 0 or 3 for xd and xs registers. This allows us to multiply the value in the offset register, wo or xo, by the number of bytes in the data element we are loading or storing. This makes it easy for us to convert an array index number into an array element address offset, as we saw in Listing 17-10 ❶.

Listing 17-11 shows the function for displaying the contents of the array.

display_array.s
```
// Display ints in an array.
// Calling sequence:
//      x0 <- address of array
//      w1 <- number of array elements
        .arch armv8-a
// Stack frame
        .equ    save1920, 16
        .equ    save21, 32
        .equ    FRAME, 48
// Code
        .section  .rodata
        .align  3
msg1:
        .string "my_array["
msg2:
        .string "] = "
        .text
        .align  2
        .global display_array
        .type   display_array, %function
display_array:
    ❶ stp      fp, lr, [sp, -FRAME]!     // Create stack frame
        mov      fp, sp                   // Set our frame pointer
        stp      x19, x20, [sp, save1920] // Save regs
        str      x21, [sp, save21]

        mov      x19, x0                  // Array address
        mov      w20, w1                  // Array size
        mov      w21, wzr                 // Array index
loop:
        adr      x0, msg1                 // Start line
        bl       write_str
        mov      w0, w21                  // Index
        bl       put_int
        adr      x0, msg2                 // More text on line
```

```
        bl      write_str
        ldr     w0, [x19, w21, uxtw 2]      // Current element
        bl      put_int
        mov     w0, '\n'                    // Finish line
        bl      write_char
        add     w21, w21, 1                 // Increment index
        cmp     w21, w20                    // At end?
        b.lt    loop                        // No, continue

        mov     w0, wzr                     // Return 0
        ldp     x19, x20, [sp, save1920]    // Restore regs
        ldr     x21, [sp, save21]
        ldp     fp, lr, [sp], FRAME         // Delete stack frame
        ret
```

Listing 17-11: The assembly language function to display ints in an array

This function uses the same basic algorithm as the twice_index function, but it calls other functions, so we need to create a stack record ❶. We also need to save the x19, x20, and x21 registers for the calling function.

Arrays are used to group data items of the same type. In the next section, we'll look at how to group items of different data types.

YOUR TURN

17.1   Change the twice_index and display_array functions to use pass by pointer (int *the_array) instead of pass by array (int the_array[]). Compare the compiler-generated assembly language with that shown in Listings 17-2, 17-5, and 17-8.

17.2   Modify the program in Listings 17-9 to 17-11 to store 16 times the index number in each element of the array.

Records

A *record* (or *structure*) allows a programmer to group several data items of possibly different data types together into a new programmer-defined data type. The location of each individual data item in a record is called a *field* or *element*. You may also see a field called a *member*, especially in object-oriented programming. I'll cover C++ objects in the next chapter.

Since the fields in a record can have different sizes, accessing them is a bit more complex than accessing the data items in an array. I'll first describe how this is done in C, and then we'll look at how records are passed to other functions.

In C

Let's start by looking at a program that defines a record, stores data in each of its fields, and then displays the values, as shown in Listing 17-12.

fill_record.c

```
// Allocate a record and assign a value to each field.

#include <stdio.h>

int main(void)
{
    struct {
    ❶ char a;
        int i;
        char b;
        int j;
        char c;
    ❷ } x;

    ❸ x.a = 'a';
       x.i = 12;
       x.b = 'b';
       x.j = 34;
       x.c = 'c';

       printf("x: %c, %i, %c, %i, %c\n", x.a, x.i,
               x.b, x.j, x.c);
       return 0;
}
```

Listing 17-12: A program to store data in a record

We use the struct keyword to declare a record in C. The fields of the record are declared using the usual C syntax: a data type followed by the field name ❶. The entire sequence, starting with the struct keyword through the ending } bracket, defines a new data type ❷. We define a record variable by following this data type with a name for the variable. The individual fields of a record are accessed with the dot operator followed by the field name ❸.

We can learn how the record is stored in memory by looking at the assembly language the compiler generates for this function, which is shown in Listing 17-13.

fill_record.s

```
        .arch armv8-a
        .file   "fill_record.c"
        .text
        .section        .rodata
        .align  3
.LC0:
        .string "x: %c, %i, %c, %i, %c\n"
```

```
        .text
        .align  2
        .global main
        .type   main, %function
main:
        stp     x29, x30, [sp, -48]!
        mov     x29, sp
        mov     w0, 97
❶ strb        w0, [sp, 24]     /// x.a = 'a';
        mov     w0, 12
❷ str         w0, [sp, 28]     /// x.i = 12;
        mov     w0, 98
        strb    w0, [sp, 32]     /// x.b = 'b';
        mov     w0, 34
        str     w0, [sp, 36]     /// x.j = 34;
        mov     w0, 99
        strb    w0, [sp, 40]     /// x.c = 'c';
        ldrb    w0, [sp, 24]
        mov     w6, w0
        ldr     w0, [sp, 28]
        ldrb    w1, [sp, 32]
        mov     w3, w1
        ldr     w1, [sp, 36]
        ldrb    w2, [sp, 40]
        mov     w5, w2
        mov     w4, w1
        mov     w2, w0
        mov     w1, w6
        adrp    x0, .LC0
        add     x0, x0, :lo12:.LC0
        bl      printf
        mov     w0, 0
        ldp     x29, x30, [sp], 48
        ret
        .size   main, .-main
        .ident  "GCC: (Debian 12.2.0-14) 12.2.0"
        .section        .note.GNU-stack,"",@progbits
```

Listing 17-13: The compiler-generated assembly language for the main function in Listing 17-12

Like other local variables, the record is allocated in the function's stack frame. The individual fields in the record are accessed by offsets from the stack pointer ❶. Figure 17-1 shows the stack frame used by the compiler for this main function.

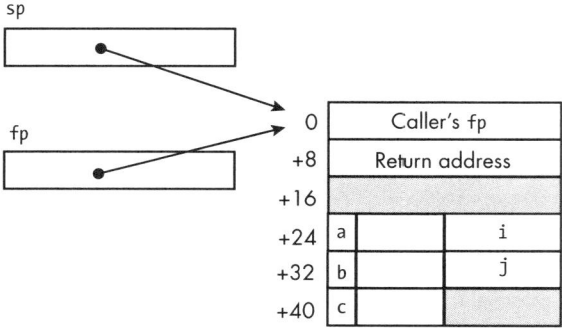

Figure 17-1: The stack frame for fields in a record

You learned in Chapter 12 that the ldr and str instructions encode the word offset (see the discussion following Figures 12-1 and 12-2), so the i and j fields must each be aligned to a 4-byte word boundary ❷. Each of the a, b, and c fields is placed in the low-order bytes of the words at the offsets 24, 32, and 40, respectively.

The struct occupies 20 bytes in the stack frame. The blank areas you see in Figure 17-1 are unused bytes in the struct. The gray areas are unused bytes in the stack frame.

Passing a record to another function raises additional issues. As you have seen, we need to specify the type of data we're passing, but a record can have many fields, each of which can have a different data type. Next, you'll see how C solves this problem.

Defining the fields every time we define another instance of a record is cumbersome. C allows us to define our own struct types using a *structure tag* (or simply *tag*), which serves as a synonym for the field definitions. This is not only useful for defining multiple records of the same field composition but also necessary for passing records to other functions.

For example, we defined the struct variable x in Listing 17-12 as follows:

```
struct {
    char a;
    int i;
    char b;
    int j;
    char c;
} x;
```

Instead, we can create a tag for the fields in the struct, like this:

```
struct chars_and_ints {
    char a;
    int i;
    char b;
    int j;
    char c;
};
```

Now that we have created a name for our programmer-defined data type, struct `chars_and_ints`, we can define its variables in the usual way:

```
struct chars_and_ints x;
```

We'll start by declaring our new struct data type in a separate header file, as shown in Listing 17-14.

my_record.h
```
// Declare a record.

#ifndef MY_RECORD_H
#define MY_RECORD_H
struct chars_and_ints {
    char a;
    int i;
    char b;
    int j;
    char c;
};
#endif
```

Listing 17-14: A record tag

We include this header file in any file where we want to define a struct `chars_and_ints` variable or function parameter.

Listing 17-15 shows how we can use `chars_and_ints` to define two records in a function.

fill_records.c
```
// Allocate two records, assign a value to each field
// in each record, and display the contents.

#include "my_record.h"
#include "load_record.h"
#include "display_record.h"

int main(void)
{
❶ struct chars_and_ints x;
   struct chars_and_ints y;

❷ load_record(&x, 'a', 12, 'b', 34, 'c');
   load_record(&y, 'd', 56, 'e', 78, 'f');

❸ display_record(x);
   display_record(y);

   return 0;
}
```

Listing 17-15: A program to load data into two records and display their contents

The struct C keyword and our tag specify the data type of the record variables we're defining ❶. Since the load_record function outputs data values to the record, we need to pass the address of the record ❷. The record is an input to the display_record function, so we use pass by value to pass a copy of the record ❸.

The compiler-generated assembly language for the main function in Listing 17-16 shows the differences between passing a record by pointer to load_record and passing by value to display_record.

fill_records.s

```
        .arch armv8-a
        .file   "fill_records.c"
        .text
        .align  2
        .global main
        .type   main, %function
main:
❶ stp     x29, x30, [sp, -96]!
   mov     x29, sp
❷ add     x0, sp, 72      /// Pass by pointer
   mov     w5, 99
   mov     w4, 34
   mov     w3, 98
   mov     w2, 12
   mov     w1, 97
   bl      load_record
   add     x0, sp, 48
   mov     w5, 102
   mov     w4, 78
   mov     w3, 101
   mov     w2, 56
   mov     w1, 100
   bl      load_record
❸ add     x2, sp, 16      /// Point to temporary place
   add     x3, sp, 72      ///   and copy record there
   ldp     x0, x1, [x3]
   stp     x0, x1, [x2]
   ldr     w0, [x3, 16]
   str     w0, [x2, 16]
❹ add     x0, sp, 16
   bl      display_record  /// Pass temp place by pointer
   add     x2, sp, 16
   add     x3, sp, 48
   ldp     x0, x1, [x3]
   stp     x0, x1, [x2]
   ldr     w0, [x3, 16]
   str     w0, [x2, 16]
   add     x0, sp, 16
   bl      display_record
```

```
        mov     w0, 0
        ldp     x29, x30, [sp], 96
        ret
        .size   main, .-main
        .ident  "GCC: (Debian 12.2.0-14) 12.2.0"
        .section        .note.GNU-stack,"",@progbits
```

Listing 17-16: The compiler-generated assembly language for the main function
in Listing 17-15

The load_record function will output data to the struct, so it's passed by
pointer ❷. As we saw in Listing 17-2, C uses pass by pointer when we pass
the name of an array to a function even when it's an input, because arrays
are typically large. Records can also be large, but this is less common than
with arrays, so C uses pass by value when we pass the name of a struct to a
function. However, the procedure call standard states that if a struct is over
16 bytes, it must be copied to memory and the copy passed by pointer.

Figure 17-1 shows that the size of our struct is 20 bytes. The compiler
has allocated extra memory in the stack frame for this copy ❶. Our main
function makes a copy of the struct ❸ and passes a pointer to the copy as
an input to the load_record function ❹.

Let's look at the load_record function, whose header file is shown in
Listing 17-17.

load_record.h
```
// Load a record with data.

#ifndef LOAD_RECORD_H
#define LOAD_RECORD_H
#include "my_record.h"
int load_record(struct chars_and_ints *a_record, char x, int y, char z);
#endif
```

Listing 17-17: The header file for the function to load data into a record

Listing 17-18 shows the definition of the load_record function.

load_record.c
```
// Load a record with data.

#include "load_record.h"

void load_record(struct chars_and_ints *a_record, char v, int w,
                 char x, int y, char z)
{
❶   (*a_record).a = v;
❷   a_record->b = x;        // Equivalent syntax
    a_record->c = z;
    a_record->i = w;
    a_record->j = y;
}
```

Listing 17-18: A function to load data into a record

The parentheses are required to dereference the a_record pointer variable before the field selection because the field selection operator (.) has a higher precedence than the dereference operator (*) in C ❶. Without them, *a_record.a means *(a_record.a). Pointers to records are so common that C provides the equivalent -> syntax to dereference the record pointer first and then select a field ❷.

Listing 17-19 shows the assembly language the compiler generated for our load_record function.

```
        .arch armv8-a
        .file   "load_record.c"
        .text
        .align  2
        .global load_record
        .type   load_record, %function
load_record:
❶ sub     sp, sp, #32
    str     x0, [sp, 24]    /// a_record address
    strb    w1, [sp, 23]    /// v
    str     w2, [sp, 16]    /// w
    strb    w3, [sp, 22]    /// x
    str     w4, [sp, 12]    /// y
    strb    w5, [sp, 21]    /// z
    ldr     x0, [sp, 24]    /// Load a_record address
    ldrb    w1, [sp, 23]    /// Load v
    strb    w1, [x0]        /// Store in record field
❷ ldr     x0, [sp, 24]    /// Load a_record address
    ldrb    w1, [sp, 22]    /// Load x
    strb    w1, [x0, 8]     /// Store in record field
    ldr     x0, [sp, 24]
    ldrb    w1, [sp, 21]
    strb    w1, [x0, 16]
    ldr     x0, [sp, 24]    /// Load a_record address
    ldr     w1, [sp, 16]    /// Load w
    str     w1, [x0, 4]     /// Store in record field
    ldr     x0, [sp, 24]
    ldr     w1, [sp, 12]
    str     w1, [x0, 12]
    nop
    add     sp, sp, 32
    ret
    .size   load_record, .-load_record
    .ident  "GCC: (Debian 12.2.0-14) 12.2.0"
    .section        .note.GNU-stack,"",@progbits
```

Listing 17-19: The compiler-generated assembly language for the function in Listing 17-18

This is a leaf function, so we don't need a frame record, but the compiler created a stack frame for saving the arguments to the function ❶. The address of the struct is retrieved before accessing each field ❷.

Now, let's look at the display_record function, whose header file is shown in Listing 17-20.

display_record.h

```
// Display the contents of a record.

#ifndef DISPLAY_RECORD_H
#define DISPLAY_RECORD_H
#include "a_record.h"
void display_record(struct chars_and_ints a_record);
#endif
```

Listing 17-20: The header file for the function to display data in a record

Listing 17-21 shows the definition of the display_record function.

display_record.c

```
// Display the contents of a record.

#include <stdio.h>
#include "display_record.h"

void display_record(struct chars_and_ints a_record)
{
    printf("%c, %i, %c, %i, %c\n", a_record.a, a_record.i, a_record.b,
        a_record.j, a_record.c);
}
```

Listing 17-21: A function to display data in a record

Listing 17-22 shows the compiler-generated assembly language for the display_record function.

display_record.s

```
        .arch armv8-a
        .file   "display_record.c"
        .text
        .section        .rodata
        .align  3
.LC0:
        .string "%c, %i, %c, %i, %c\n"
        .text
        .align  2
        .global display_record
        .type   display_record, %function
display_record:
        stp     x29, x30, [sp, -32]!
        mov     x29, sp
        str     x19, [sp, 16]
❶     mov     x19, x0          /// Pointer to caller's copy
```

```
        ldrb    w0, [x19]
        mov     w6, w0
        ldr     w0, [x19, 4]
        ldrb    w1, [x19, 8]
        mov     w3, w1
        ldr     w1, [x19, 12]
        ldrb    w2, [x19, 16]
❷ mov     w5, w2              /// Arguments to printf
        mov     w4, w1
        mov     w2, w0
        mov     w1, w6
        adrp    x0, .LC0
        add     x0, x0, :lo12:.LC0
        bl      printf
        nop
        ldr     x19, [sp, 16]
        ldp     x29, x30, [sp], 32
        ret
        .size   display_record, .-display_record
        .ident  "GCC: (Debian 12.2.0-14) 12.2.0"
        .section        .note.GNU-stack,"",@progbits
```

Listing 17-22: The compiler-generated assembly language for the function in Listing 17-21

The compiler uses x19 as a pointer to the caller's copy of the struct ❶.
After retrieving the values in each field of the record, it loads them in the
proper registers for passing to the printf function ❷.

You've seen how to pass by value structs that are larger than 16 bytes.
Next, let's look at passing records of less than 16 bytes. We'll do this by
rearranging the fields of the record and using assembly language.

In Assembly Language

Although it's seldom an issue, we can rearrange the fields in our record to
make it a bit smaller. Figure 17-2 shows how we'll place both records in the
main function's stack frame and where their fields are.

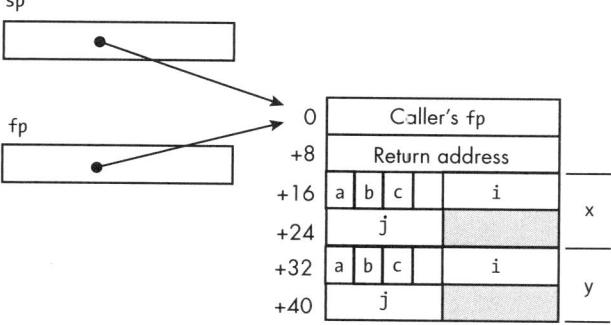

Figure 17-2: Two records in the stack frame

Using this diagram of the stack frame, we can design the `main` function as shown in Listing 17-23.

fill_records.s
```
// Allocate two records, assign a value to each field
// in each record, and display the contents.
            .arch armv8-a
// Stack frame
            .equ    x, 16
❶         .equ    y, 32
            .equ    FRAME, 48
// Code
            .text
            .align  2
            .global main
            .type   main, %function
main:
            stp     fp, lr, [sp, -FRAME]!    // Create stack frame
            mov     fp, sp                   // Set our frame pointer

            mov     w5, 'c'                  // Data to load
            mov     w4, 34
            mov     w3, 'b'
            mov     w2, 12
            mov     w1, 'a'
            add     x0, sp, x                // Address of first record
            bl      load_record              // Load values

            mov     w5, 'f'                  // Data to load
            mov     w4, 78
            mov     w3, 'e'
            mov     w2, 56
            mov     w1, 'd'
            add     x0, sp, y                // Address of second record
            bl      load_record              // Load values

❷         ldr     x0, [sp, x]              // First 8 bytes of x
            ldr     w1, [sp, x+8]            // Last 4 bytes of x
            bl      display_record           // Display x

❸         ldr     x0, [sp, y]              // First 8 bytes of y
            ldr     w1, [sp, y+8]            // Last 4 bytes of y
            bl      display_record           // Display y

            mov     w0, wzr                  // Return 0
            ldp     fp, lr, [sp], FRAME      // Delete stack frame
            ret
```

Listing 17-23: The assembly language program to load and display two records

In Figure 17-2, the record is 12 bytes long. The procedure call standard states that records less than 16 bytes long should be passed in registers. We load the entire 12 bytes of a record, including the unused memory gaps between the fields, into registers x0 and w1 to pass to display_record ❷.

The ldr instruction requires that the offset be a multiple of the number of bytes in the destination register. When we designed the stack frame in Figure 17-2, we placed the start of the y record on a doubleword boundary ❶ so we can pass the first 8 bytes of the record in the x0 register ❸.

Using the diagram of our stack frame in Figure 17-2, we'll place the .equ directives for the record field offsets in a file called *my_record.s*, as shown in Listing 17-24.

my_record.s
```
// Assembly language declaration of a record.
// This record takes 12 bytes.
        .equ    a, 0
        .equ    b, 1
        .equ    c, 2
        .equ    i, 4
        .equ    j, 8
```

Listing 17-24: The field offsets for a record

We can include the *my_record.s* file in any assembly language file that uses the field names to ensure consistency. Let's look at how this works in the load_record function in Listing 17-25.

load_record.s
```
// Load the fields of my_record.s.
// Calling sequence:
//     x0 <- address of record
//     w1 <- char a
//     w2 <- int x
//     w3 <- char b
//     w4 <- int y
//     w5 <- char c
//     Returns 0
        .arch armv8-a
❶ .include  "my_record.s"   // Field offsets
// Code
        .text
        .align  2
        .global load_record
        .type   load_record, %function
load_record:
        strb    w1, [x0, a]      // First char
        str     w2, [x0, i]      // First int
        strb    w3, [x0, b]      // Second char
```

```
        str     w4, [x0, j]         // Second int
        strb    w5, [x0, c]         // Third char

        mov     w0, wzr             // Return 0
        ret
```

Listing 17-25: The assembly language function to load data into a record

The algorithm of this function is very simple. You can see a new assembly directive here, `.include` ❶. The argument to this directive is a filename in quotes. The text in that file is inserted at this location. The `.equ` values in *my_record.s* give the offsets to the fields in the record.

The procedure call standard says that when records of less than 16 bytes are passed in registers, we need to make a copy of the record in the called function. This differs from passing larger records by value, where the copy of the record is made in the calling function, with a pointer to the copy passed to the called function. We'll place `display_record`'s copy in its stack frame, as shown in Figure 17-3.

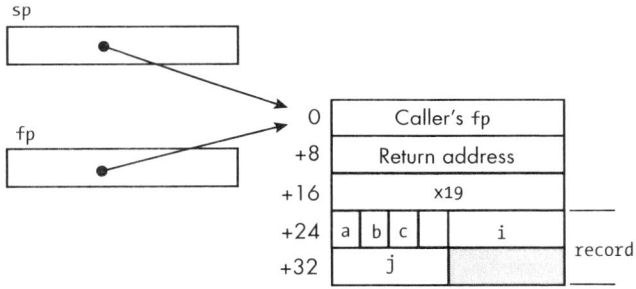

Figure 17-3: The saved x19 register and record in a stack frame

Listing 17-26 shows the resulting `display_record` function design.

display_record.s
```
// Display the fields of my_record.s.
//      x0 <- first 8 bytes of record contents
//      w1 <- remaining 4 bytes of record contents
        .arch armv8-a
        .include  "my_record.s"       // Field offsets
// Stack frame
        .equ    save19, 16
        .equ    record, 24
        .equ    FRAME, 48
// Code
        .section  .rodata
        .align  3
separator:
        .string ", "
```

```
            .text
            .align  2
            .global display_record
            .type   display_record, %function
display_record:
            stp     fp, lr, [sp, -FRAME]! // Create stack frame
            mov     fp, sp               // Set our frame pointer
❶ str     x19, [sp, save19]    // Save reg

            add     x19, sp, record      // Point to our copy
❷ str     x0, [x19]            // Make a copy of record
            str     w1, [x19, 8]

            ldrb    w0, [x19, a]         // First char
            bl      write_char           // Display
            adr     x0, separator        // Field separation
            bl      write_str
            ldr     w0, [x19, i]         // First int
            bl      put_int              // Display
            adr     x0, separator        // Field separation
            bl      write_str
            ldrb    w0, [x19, b]         // Second char
            bl      write_char           // Display
            adr     x0, separator        // Field separation
            bl      write_str
            ldr     w0, [x19, j]         // Second int
            bl      put_int              // Display
            adr     x0, separator        // Field separation
            bl      write_str
            ldrb    w0, [x19, c]         // Third char
            bl      write_char           // Display
            mov     w0, '\n'             // Newline
            bl      write_char

            mov     w0, wzr              // Return 0
            ldr     x19, [sp, save19]    // Restore reg
            ldp     fp, lr, [sp], FRAME  // Delete stack frame
            ret
```

Listing 17-26: The assembly language function to display data in a record

The procedure call standard states that a called function needs to preserve the value in x19. We save its contents in our stack frame so we can use the register to point to our local copy of the record ❶. We then store the 12 bytes in the record, 8 in x0 and 4 in w1, in the memory in our stack frame to create our local copy of the record ❷.

17.3   Change the order of the fields in Listing 17-12 to group the char
       fields together, followed by the int fields. Recompile the program
       in Listings 17-15, 17-17, 17-18, 17-20, and 17-21. Compare the
       assembly language generated by the compiler with what you see in
       Listings 17-16, 17-19, and 17-22.

What You've Learned

Arrays   Collections of data items of the same data type, stored contiguously in memory.

Processing arrays   The CPU has an addressing mode for accessing an array element using an index value.

Passing arrays   In C, arrays are passed by pointer rather than by value.

Records   Collections of data items, possibly of different data types, stored together in memory, possibly with padding for address alignment purposes.

Accessing record fields   The address with offset addressing mode can be used to access a record field.

Passing records   It's often more efficient to pass a record by pointer, even when it's an input.

In the next chapter, I'll show you how C++ uses records to implement the object-oriented programming paradigm.

18

OBJECT-ORIENTED PROGRAMMING

So far in this book, I have been using the procedural programming paradigm (described in "Exploring Data Formats with C" on page 23). In this chapter, I'll introduce how object-oriented programming is implemented at the assembly language level in C++.

In object-oriented programming, we can create *objects*, each of which is an instance of a class. A class has a set of *attributes*, the data items that define the state of the object, and *methods* that can query or change the attributes of an object of the class. A software solution typically consists of constructing objects and then programming the sending of messages to the objects, which use the methods to act on the attributes.

I'll use C++, an object-oriented extension of C, to illustrate some of these concepts. You'll learn how a record can be used to store the attributes of an object and how methods are implemented as functions associated with the record.

Many other features of C++ are important for creating good object-oriented programming solutions, but I won't go into them in this book. If you're new to C++, Josh Lospinoso's *C++ Crash Course* (No Starch Press, 2019) would be a good place to start. If you want to dig into the design of

C++ after learning how to use it, I recommend *A Tour of C++*, 3rd edition, by Bjarne Stroustrup, the creator of C++ (Addison-Wesley Professional, 2022). A good online resource for using C++ is the C++ Core Guidelines at *https://isocpp.github.io/CppCoreGuidelines/CppCoreGuidelines*. It's kept up to date by Bjarne Stroustrup and Herb Sutter.

Let's start with a very simple C++ class and then look at some assembly language generated by the C++ compiler.

Objects in C++

C++ allows us to create *classes*, which are like blueprints for creating objects. A C++ class is very much like a C record, but in addition to the *data members* that define the attributes of the object, it can include functions as members of the class. In C++, we send a message to an object telling it to perform a method by calling a class *member function*.

C++ specifies six special member functions that are used to create and delete objects. I'll only cover the two most commonly used ones in this book: the constructor and the destructor. The *constructor* function is used to create an instance of an object, which is called *instantiation*. The job of a constructor is to allocate the necessary memory resources and place the object in a known state before sending messages to it.

The C++ compiler generates the code to call our constructor function automatically at the point where we instantiate an object. A constructor function has the same name as the class. It cannot have a return value—not even void. The *default constructor* does not take any arguments. We can also write constructors that take arguments, and a class can have more than one constructor.

The job of a *destructor* function is to release any resources that were allocated by a constructor, thus deleting the object. For example, a constructor might allocate memory from the heap (described in Chapter 10), which the destructor would deallocate. There can be only one destructor function, which has the same name as the class, preceded by the ~ (tilde) character. The destructor cannot have a return value and takes no arguments. The C++ compiler will generate the code to call the destructor automatically when program flow leaves the scope of the object.

To demonstrate these concepts, we'll look at a simple Fraction class whose attributes are two ints: a numerator and a denominator. We'll include a constructor, a destructor, and some member functions to work with our Fraction objects. If we don't supply constructor or destructor member functions, the C++ compiler will supply appropriate code to perform the construction and destruction of an object; we'll explore what this means in "Writing a Constructor and Destructor via the Compiler" on page 399.

We'll start with the declaration of our Fraction class, which we'll place in a header file so it can be included in any file that uses the class, as shown in Listing 18-1.

```
#ifndef FRACTION_H
#define FRACTION_H
class Fraction {
```
❶ `public:`
```
    Fraction();             // Default constructor
    ~Fraction();            // Destructor
    void get();             // Get user's values
    void display();         // Display fraction
    void add_integer(int x); // Add x to fraction
```
❷ `private:`
```
    int numerator;
    int denominator;
};
#endif
```

Listing 18-1: The C++ Fraction class

The overall syntax of a class declaration is similar to a record declaration in C, but it adds the capability to include the methods of the class as member functions. Access to members of a class can be *private*, *protected*, or *public*. We'll look only at basic public and private access control here and leave the more complex access control concepts to books on C++.

We declare the member functions to be public ❶. This means they can be used from outside the class to send messages to objects of this class. They provide an interface to the object.

We place the data members in the private part of the class declaration ❷. This means only member functions can access them directly, thus giving the member functions control over numerator and denominator, the attributes of our Fraction class. Code outside this class can access them only through the public interface.

Access to a class is private by default. If we listed the attributes before the public area, we wouldn't need to use the private keyword, but I like to list the public interface of a class first.

The struct keyword can also be used to declare a C++ class, as shown in Listing 18-2.

```
#ifndef FRACTION_H
#define FRACTION_H
struct Fraction {
public:
    Fraction();             // Default constructor
    ~Fraction();            // Destructor
    void get();             // Get user's values
    void display();         // Display fraction
```

```
        void add_integer(int x);  // Add x to fraction
private:
    int numerator;
    int denominator;
};
#endif
```

Listing 18-2: The C++ Fraction struct

The default access scope for a C++ struct is public, but I like to be explicit. The private declaration is required for the private scope.

Although class and struct are the same except for the default access scope, I prefer using the class keyword because it emphasizes that there is more to it than a simple record. However, this is a personal choice. Next, we'll look at how to create objects and how to send messages to them.

Creating an Object

I'll illustrate how to create an object and send messages to it using a simple program that allows the user to enter the numerator and denominator values of a fraction and then adds 1 to the fraction. This program is shown in Listing 18-3.

inc_fraction.cpp
```
// Get a fraction from the user and add 1.

#include "fraction.h"

int main(void)
{
❶ Fraction my_fraction;

❷ my_fraction.display();
    my_fraction.get();
    my_fraction.add_integer(1);
    my_fraction.display();

    return 0;
}
```

Listing 18-3: A program to add 1 to a fraction

We instantiate an object by using the class name and providing a name for the object ❶, just like when defining a variable. The dot operator (.) is used to send a message to a method in the class ❷, which calls the respective member function in the class the object belongs to. This program displays the state of the fraction before getting user input values and then again after adding 1 to the user's fraction.

Next, we'll look at the assembly language generated by the C++ compiler to implement the main function in Listing 18-3. The C++ compiler in our environment is called g++.

I used the following command to generate the assembly language in Listing 18-4:

```
$ g++ -S -Wall -O0 -fno-unwind-tables -fno-asynchronous-unwind-tables
    -fno-exceptions inc_fraction.cpp
```

This is the same as the command we've been using for C code, except I've added the -fno-exceptions option. C++ provides an *exception* mechanism for dealing with detected runtime errors. The compiler provides the information for this feature through assembler directives, which would tend to obscure the discussion here of how objects are implemented. Using the -fno-exceptions option turns off this feature.

inc_fraction.s

```
        .arch armv8-a
        .file   "inc_fraction.cpp"
        .text
        .align  2
        .global main
        .type   main, %function
main:
❶ stp      x29, x30, [sp, -48]!
    mov     x29, sp
    str     x19, [sp, 16]
❷ add      x0, sp, 40
❸ bl       _ZN8FractionC1Ev        /// Construct my_fraction
    add     x0, sp, 40
❹ bl       _ZN8Fraction7displayEv
    add     x0, sp, 40
    bl      _ZN8Fraction3getEv
    add     x0, sp, 40
    mov     w1, 1
❺ bl       _ZN8Fraction11add_integerEi
    add     x0, sp, 40
    bl      _ZN8Fraction7displayEv
    mov     w19, 0
    add     x0, sp, 40
❻ bl       _ZN8FractionD1Ev        /// Destruct my_fraction
    mov     w0, w19
    ldr     x19, [sp, 16]
    ldp     x29, x30, [sp], 48
    ret
    .size   main, .-main
    .ident  "GCC: (Debian 10.2.1-6) 10.2.1 20210110"
    .section        .note.GNU-stack,"",@progbits
```

Listing 18-4: The compiler-generated assembly language for the main function in Listing 18-3

The first thing to note is that my_fraction (❶ in Listing 18-3) is an automatic local variable, so memory space is allocated on the stack for this

Fraction object in the main function's prologue ❶. The address of this memory area is passed to the constructor function, _ZN8FractionC1Ev, which will initialize the object ❷.

The C++ compiler has decorated the name of our constructor function Fraction, declared in Listing 18-1, to be _ZN8FractionC1Ev ❸. You learned about the C compiler decorating the names of static local variables in Chapter 15. The purpose there was to distinguish between different static local variables with the same name in different functions defined in the same file.

C++ uses name decorating to associate member functions with their class. Looking at the calls to the class member functions in Listing 18-4, you can see that they all begin with _ZN8Fraction. Since function names are global in scope, including the class name allows us to define other classes in the program that have the same names for member functions. For example, we might have more than one class in a program that has a display member function. Name decorating identifies each display member function with the class it belongs to ❹.

C++ name decorating also allows *function overloading*, which is the ability to have more than one class member function with the same name but that differ in the number of arguments and their types. In Listing 18-4, the decorated _ZN8Fraction11add_integerEi, which is our add_integer member function, ends with an appended i; this shows that the function takes a single int argument ❺. Including the number and types of the arguments in the name decorating differentiates overloaded functions. You'll get a chance to overload the default constructor in "Your Turn" exercise 18.1 on page 406.

There is no standard for how name decorating is done, so each compiler may do it differently. This means that all C++ code in a program must be compiled and linked using compatible compilers and linkers.

Look at the instruction just before each call to a member function ❷. The address of the object is passed as the first argument to each of them. This is an *implicit argument* that doesn't show up in the C++ code. You'll see how to access this address in a member function when we look inside the member functions in the following section.

Although it doesn't show in the C++ code that we write, the compiler generates a call to our destructor function at the point where program flow leaves the scope of the object ❻. In some more advanced programming techniques, we would call the destructor explicitly, but we won't cover them in the book. Most of the time, we let the compiler decide when to call the destructor.

Next, we'll look at the constructor and destructor and the other member functions of this Fraction class.

Defining Class Member Functions

Although it's common to put each C function definition in its own file, C++ source files are commonly organized to include all the function definitions in a class. Listing 18-5 shows the definitions of the member functions for our Fraction class.

fraction.cpp // A simple Fraction class

```cpp
#include "fraction.h"
#include <iostream>
```
❶ `using namespace std;`

❷
```cpp
Fraction::Fraction()
{
```
❸
```cpp
  numerator = 0;
    denominator = 1;
}

Fraction::~Fraction() {}
// Nothing to do for this object

void Fraction::get()
{
```
❹ `cout << "Enter numerator: ";`
❺ `cin >> numerator;`
```cpp

    cout << "Enter denominator: ";
    cin >> denominator;

    if (denominator == 0) {
        cout << "WARNING: Setting 0 denominator to 1\n";
        denominator = 1;
    }
}

void Fraction::display()
{
    cout << numerator << '/' << denominator << '\n';
}

void Fraction::add_integer(int x)
{
    numerator += x * denominator;
}
```

Listing 18-5: The member function definitions for our Fraction class

C++ adds some scoping rules to the C scoping rules you learned about in Chapter 14. Even though the member functions declared in Listing 18-1 are public, they have *class scope*, meaning their names need to be associated with the class. The compiler does this by decorating the names when it uses them, but we need to use the *scope resolution operator* (::) to make this association when defining the member functions outside the class scope ❷.

One of the primary purposes of a constructor is to initialize the object. We'll set our Fraction object to 0/1 ❸, a reasonable initial value for a fraction.

The C++ standard library provides objects for writing to the screen and reading from the keyboard. The cout object in the ostream class writes a character stream to standard output, which is typically connected to the screen ❹. It uses the *insertion operator* (<<) and converts the data to the appropriate character string. The cin object in the istream class reads a character stream from standard input, which is typically connected to the keyboard ❺. It uses the *extraction operator* (>>) and converts the character string to the appropriate data type for the variable it's reading into.

In addition to its class scope, C++ allows us to collect names of things into a *namespace scope*. The iostream header file places the cout and cin objects in the std namespace. We need to specify this namespace when using these objects ❶.

Next, we'll look at the compiler-generated assembly language for these member functions. To simplify the discussion, we'll look at each function in the file separately, in Listings 18-6 through 18-11. As we go through them, keep in mind that this is one file, so the labels are visible across all six of the listings.

The beginning of the *fraction.s* file, shown in Listing 18-6, is code that allocates memory used by functions in the C++ I/O library for the cin and cout I/O objects. Our inclusion of the iostream header file in Listing 18-5 tells the compiler to insert this code.

fraction.s(a)

```
        .arch armv8-a
        .file   "fraction.cpp"
        .text
        .section        .rodata     /// For operating system
        .align  3
        .type   _ZStL19piecewise_construct, %object
        .size   _ZStL19piecewise_construct, 1
_ZStL19piecewise_construct:
        .zero   1
    ❶ .local   _ZStL8__ioinit
    ❷ .comm    _ZStL8__ioinit,1,8
```

Listing 18-6: A byte used by the cin and cout I/O objects

The .local assembler directive limits the _ZStL8__ioinit label to this object ❶. The .comm directive allocates 1 byte in memory, which is aligned to an 8-byte address and labeled _ZStL8__ioinit ❷. If there are other .comm directives with the same label in our program, they will share the same memory. This memory is for use by the cin and cout I/O objects; the details of its usage are beyond the scope of this book.

Listing 18-7 shows the second part of the file, the constructor for our Fraction object.

fraction.s(b)

```
        .text
        .align  2
```

```
        .global _ZN8FractionC2Ev
        .type   _ZN8FractionC2Ev, %function
_ZN8FractionC2Ev:
        sub     sp, sp, #16
❶ str     x0, [sp, 8]        /// Save this pointer
        ldr     x0, [sp, 8]
❷ str     wzr, [x0]          /// numerator = 0;
        ldr     x0, [sp, 8]
        mov     w1, 1
❸ str     w1, [x0, 4]        /// denominator = 1;
        nop
        add     sp, sp, 16
        ret
        .size   _ZN8FractionC2Ev, .-_ZN8FractionC2Ev
        .global _ZN8FractionC1Ev
        .set    _ZN8FractionC1Ev,_ZN8FractionC2Ev
```

Listing 18-7: The compiler-generated assembly language for the constructor in Listing 18-5

Our constructor initializes the numerator ❷ and denominator ❸ data members in the Fraction object located in our stack frame. Back in Listing 18-4, you saw that the first argument to each member function is the address of the object that the member function is operating on. But looking at the class declaration in Listing 18-1, this address doesn't show up in the member function's parameter list. It's called the *hidden parameter*.

If a member function is accessing another object in the same class as the object it was called from, it needs to be able to distinguish between the two objects. Although it doesn't show up in the parameter list, C++ uses the name this for the hidden parameter, which is a pointer variable that contains the address of the object that called the member function ❶.

The compiler assumes that our member functions are working with the object at the address in the this pointer variable, so we usually don't need to use it. But some situations require that we explicitly use the pointer. For example, we might write a Fraction constructor that allows us to specify the initialization values like this:

```
Fraction::Fraction(int numerator, int denominator) {
    this->numerator = numerator;
    this->denominator = denominator;
}
```

The parameter names have precedence over the member names, so we had to disambiguate with the this pointer.

Now that you know where the Fraction object's data members are located within the object, you can see in Figure 18-1 how the object is stored in main's stack frame.

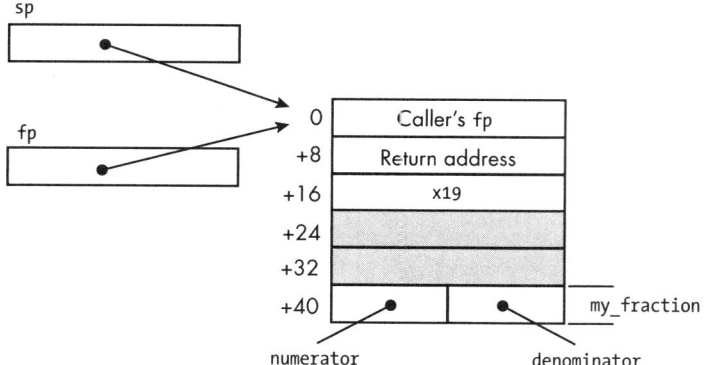

Figure 18-1: The my_fraction *object in* main's *stack frame*

I don't know why the compiler included 16 bytes in this stack frame that are not used in the program.

The constructor is followed by the destructor, shown in Listing 18-8.

fraction.s(c)

```
        .align  2
        .global _ZN8FractionD2Ev
        .type   _ZN8FractionD2Ev, %function
_ZN8FractionD2Ev:
        sub     sp, sp, #16
        str     x0, [sp, 8]
        nop
        add     sp, sp, 16
        ret
        .size   _ZN8FractionD2Ev, .-_ZN8FractionD2Ev
        .global _ZN8FractionD1Ev
        .set    _ZN8FractionD1Ev,_ZN8FractionD2Ev
```

Listing 18-8: The compiler-generated assembly language for the destructor in Listing 18-5

There is nothing for the destructor to do in this simple class. Earlier, in Listing 18-4, you saw that the memory for the object was allocated in the stack frame by the main function's prologue, not by the constructor. Similarly, the object's memory is deleted from the stack in main's epilogue code, after the call to the destructor. Some constructors allocate memory from the heap, in which case the destructor should release that memory.

The assembly language for the destructor is followed by that for the member functions. Listing 18-9 shows the assembly language for the get member function.

fraction.s(d)

```
        .section        .rodata
        .align  3
.LC0:
        .string "Enter numerator: "
        .align  3
```

```
        .LC1:
                .string "Enter denominator: "
                .align  3
        .LC2:
                .string "WARNING: Setting 0 denominator to 1"
                .text
                .align  2
                .global _ZN8Fraction3getEv
                .type   _ZN8Fraction3getEv, %function
_ZN8Fraction3getEv:
                stp     x29, x30, [sp, -32]!
                mov     x29, sp
                str     x0, [sp, 24]
                adrp    x0, .LC0
                add     x1, x0, :lo12:.LC0
        ❶ adrp    x0, :got:_ZSt4cout          /// From global library
                ldr     x0, [x0, #:got_lo12:_ZSt4cout]
                bl      _ZStlsISt11char_traitsIcEERSt13basic_ostreamIcT_ES5_PKc
                ldr     x0, [sp, 24]
                mov     x1, x0
        ❷ adrp    x0, :got:_ZSt3cin           /// From global library
                ldr     x0, [x0, #:got_lo12:_ZSt3cin]
                bl      _ZNSirsERi
                adrp    x0, .LC1
                add     x1, x0, :lo12:.LC1
                adrp    x0, :got:_ZSt4cout
                ldr     x0, [x0, #:got_lo12:_ZSt4cout]
                bl      _ZStlsISt11char_traitsIcEERSt13basic_ostreamIcT_ES5_PKc
                ldr     x0, [sp, 24]
                add     x0, x0, 4
                mov     x1, x0
                adrp    x0, :got:_ZSt3cin
                ldr     x0, [x0, #:got_lo12:_ZSt3cin]
                bl      _ZNSirsERi
                ldr     x0, [sp, 24]
                ldr     w0, [x0, 4]
                cmp     w0, 0                       /// Check for 0 denominator
                bne     .L5
                adrp    x0, .LC2
                add     x1, x0, :lo12:.LC2
                adrp    x0, :got:_ZSt4cout
                ldr     x0, [x0, #:got_lo12:_ZSt4cout]
                bl      _ZStlsISt11char_traitsIcEERSt13basic_ostreamIcT_ES5_PKc
                ldr     x0, [sp, 24]
                mov     w1, 1
                str     w1, [x0, 4]
```

```
.L5:
        nop
        ldp     x29, x30, [sp], 32
        ret
        .size   _ZN8Fraction3getEv, .-_ZN8Fraction3getEv
```

Listing 18-9: The compiler-generated assembly language for get in Listing 18-5

When the program is loaded into memory, the location of the cout object is loaded into our global offset table (GOT) ❶. The location of the cin object is also loaded into our GOT ❷.

Next, we'll look at the display member function, shown in Listing 18-10.

fraction.s(e)

```
        .align  2
        .global _ZN8Fraction7displayEv
        .type   _ZN8Fraction7displayEv, %function
_ZN8Fraction7displayEv:
        stp     x29, x30, [sp, -32]!
        mov     x29, sp
        str     x0, [sp, 24]
        ldr     x0, [sp, 24]
        ldr     w0, [x0]
        mov     w1, w0
        adrp    x0, :got:_ZSt4cout
        ldr     x0, [x0, #:got_lo12:_ZSt4cout]
❶      bl      _ZNSolsEi
        mov     w1, 47          /// '/' character
❷      bl      _ZStlsISt11char_traitsIcEERSt13basic_ostreamIcT_ES5_c
        mov     x2, x0
        ldr     x0, [sp, 24]
        ldr     w0, [x0, 4]
        mov     w1, w0
        mov     x0, x2
        bl      _ZNSolsEi
        mov     w1, 10          /// '/n' character
        bl      _ZStlsISt11char_traitsIcEERSt13basic_ostreamIcT_ES5_c
        nop
        ldp     x29, x30, [sp], 32
        ret
        .size   _ZN8Fraction7displayEv, .-_ZN8Fraction7displayEv
```

Listing 18-10: The compiler-generated assembly language for display in Listing 18-5

In our C++ code (see Listing 18-5), we chain insertions to the cout object. The compiler matches the data item type with the ostream class member function it calls. The first value is an int ❶, the second a char ❷, and so forth.

Listing 18-11 shows the compiler-generated assembly language for the add_integer member function.

fraction.s(f)

```
        .align  2
        .global _ZN8Fraction11add_integerEi
        .type   _ZN8Fraction11add_integerEi, %function
_ZN8Fraction11add_integerEi:
        sub     sp, sp, #16
❶       str     x0, [sp, 8]
        str     w1, [sp, 4]
        ldr     x0, [sp, 8]
        ldr     w1, [x0]
        ldr     x0, [sp, 8]
        ldr     w2, [x0, 4]
        ldr     w0, [sp, 4]
        mul     w0, w2, w0
        add     w1, w1, w0
        ldr     x0, [sp, 8]
        str     w1, [x0]
        nop
        add     sp, sp, 16
        ret
        .size   _ZN8Fraction11add_integerEi, .-_ZN8Fraction11add_integerEi
```

Listing 18-11: The compiler-generated assembly language for add_integer in Listing 18-5

The this pointer variable is created in this function's stack frame ❶. This is a leaf function, so the compiler doesn't generate a frame record in the stack frame.

If you use the g++ compiler to generate the assembly language yourself, you'll see two other functions, _Z41__static_initialization_and_destruction_0ii and _GLOBAL__sub_I__ZN8FractionC2Ev. The operating system calls these functions when the program is loaded to set up the cout and cin I/O streams. The details are beyond the scope of this book, so I won't show them here.

The purpose of a constructor is to allocate any system resources an object needs and to initialize the object. The destructor then releases the resources allocated by the constructor. In the next section, you'll see that the compiler can automatically generate a constructor and a destructor for simple objects such as in our Fraction class.

Writing a Constructor and Destructor via the Compiler

Initialization of objects in C++ is complex, because there are many ways to do it. The previous section covered the most basic way. Now, I'll show you some simple C++ syntax that tells the compiler to figure out how to do the initialization itself.

Recommendation C.45 in the C++ Core Guidelines (see *https://isocpp .github.io/CppCoreGuidelines/CppCoreGuidelines#Rc-default* states: "Don't define a default constructor that only initializes data members; use in-class member initializers instead."

Listing 18-12 shows how we can rewrite our Fraction class to tell the compiler to generate a constructor and destructor for us.

fraction_dflt.h // A simple Fraction class

```
#ifndef FRACTION_DFLT_H
#define FRACTION_DFLT_H
class Fraction {
public:
❶ Fraction() = default;       // Tell compiler to generate default
   ~Fraction() = default;      //    constructor and destructor
   void get();                 // Get user's values
   void display();             // Display fraction
   void add_integer(int x);    // Add x to fraction
private:
❷ int numerator {};
   int denominator {1};
};
#endif
```

Listing 18-12: The C++ Fraction class specifying the default constructor and destructor

The C++11 standard published in September 2011 added *explicitly defaulted functions*, which are specified with the = default notation ❶. The standard says that the compiler must generate the function body and place it inline if possible.

Following the recommendation of the C++ Core Guidelines, I've used *in-class member initializers* in Listing 18-12 to specify the initialization values for the data members ❷. The initial value for the data member is specified in curly brackets, {}; an empty set of curly brackets tells the compiler to use 0. C++ also allows the following syntaxes, using an equal sign for data member initialization:

```
int numerator = 0;
int numerator = {};
```

I like the plain curly brackets initialization syntax because it conveys the message that the actual assignment to the variable doesn't take place until an object is instantiated, as you'll see shortly. The differences are covered in Josh Lospinoso's book, cited at the beginning of this chapter.

Since we have told the compiler to create a default constructor and destructor, we can eliminate these functions from our member function definition file, as shown in Listing 18-13.

fraction_dflt.cpp // A simple Fraction class

```
#include "fraction_dflt.h"
#include <iostream>
```

```
using namespace std;

void Fraction::get()
{
    cout << "Enter numerator: ";
    cin >> numerator;

    cout << "Enter denominator: ";
    cin >> denominator;

    if (denominator == 0) {
        cout << "WARNING: Setting 0 denominator to 1\n";
        denominator = 1;
    }
}

void Fraction::display()
{
    cout << numerator << '/' << denominator << '\n';
}

void Fraction::add_integer(int x)
{
    numerator += x * denominator;
}
```

Listing 18-13: The C++ Fraction class with a compiler-generated constructor and destructor

Listing 18-14 shows the main function for this program.

inc_fraction
_dflt.cpp
```
// Get a fraction from the user and add 1.

❶ #include "fraction_dflt.h"

int main(void)
{
    Fraction my_fraction;

    my_fraction.display();
    my_fraction.get();
    my_fraction.add_integer(1);
    my_fraction.display();

    return 0;
}
```

Listing 18-14: A program to add 1 to a fraction

This is the same `main` function as in Listing 18-3, except that we're using the *fraction_dflt.h* header file from Listing 18-12 to match the member function definitions in Listing 18-13 ❶.

This header file tells the compiler that it needs to write the constructor and destructor for us, as shown in Listing 18-15.

inc_fraction_dflt.s

```
        .arch armv8-a
        .file   "inc_fraction_dflt.cpp"
        .text
        .align  2
        .global main
        .type   main, %function
main:
❶ stp     x29, x30, [sp, -32]!
    mov     x29, sp
❷ str     wzr, [sp, 24]           /// int numerator {};
    mov     w0, 1
    str     w0, [sp, 28]           /// int denominator {1};
    add     x0, sp, 24
    bl      _ZN8Fraction7displayEv
    add     x0, sp, 24
    bl      _ZN8Fraction3getEv
    add     x0, sp, 24
    mov     w1, 1
    bl      _ZN8Fraction11add_integerEi
    add     x0, sp, 24
    bl      _ZN8Fraction7displayEv
    mov     w0, 0
    ldp     x29, x30, [sp], 32
    ret
        .size   main, .-main
        .ident  "GCC: (Debian 10.2.1-6) 10.2.1 20210110"
        .section        .note.GNU-stack,"",@progbits
```

Listing 18-15: The compiler-generated assembly language from Listing 18-14, showing the default constructor and destructor specified in Listing 18-12

Comparing this with Listing 18-4, you can see that the compiler has allocated 16 fewer bytes in the stack frame for the Fraction object than when we provided a constructor member function ❶. It then places the initialization of the data members inline instead of calling a function to do it ❷.

The default constructor takes no arguments, but we might want to pass some arguments to a constructor at the point of instantiating an object. C++ allows us to have multiple constructors, as long as their parameter lists differ. You'll see how this works in the next section.

Overloading the Default Constructor in C++

Function overloading is when two or more functions in a class have the same name but differ in their parameter list or return type. To demonstrate, we'll overload our default constructor, which takes no arguments, with one that takes a single `int` argument that allows us to specify the value of the numerator when instantiating a `Fraction` object. Listing 18-16 shows our new class.

---

fraction_2.h `// The Fraction class with two constructors`

```
#ifndef FRACTION_2_H
#define FRACTION_2_H
class Fraction {
public:
    Fraction() = default;      // Tell compiler to generate default
  ❶ Fraction(int n) : numerator{n} {}; // Allow setting numerator

    ~Fraction() = default;
    void get();               // Get user's values
    void display();           // Display fraction
    void add_integer(int x);  // Add x to fraction
private:
  ❷ int numerator {123};       // Weird values so we can see
    int denominator {456};    //   what the compiler is doing
};
#endif
```

Listing 18-16: Adding a second constructor to the Fraction class

The second constructor differs from the default only in its parameter list ❶. We're using the C++ syntax that tells the compiler how to use the parameter to initialize the `numerator` data member.

I'm using weird in-class member initialization values to make it easier for you to see what the assembly language is doing to initialize our object ❷.

Let's modify our `main` function to add another `Fraction` object that uses our overloaded constructor, as shown in Listing 18-17.

---

inc_fractions.cpp `// Get two fractions from the user and increment each by 1.`

```
#include "fraction_2.h"

int main(void)
{
    Fraction x;
    x.display();
    x.get();
    x.add_integer(1);
    x.display();
```

```
❶ Fraction y(78);
   y.display();
   y.get();
   y.add_integer(1);
   y.display();

   return 0;
}
```

Listing 18-17: A program to add 1 to two fractions that use different constructors

For the second Fraction object, we're passing 78 to the constructor as the initial value numerator ❶.

Listing 18-18 shows how the compiler implements this second constructor in assembly language.

inc_fractions.s

```
        .arch armv8-a
        .file   "inc_fractions.cpp"
        .text
❶ .section .text._ZN8FractionC2Ei,"axG",@progbits,_ZN8FractionC5Ei,comdat
        .align  2
❷ .weak   _ZN8FractionC2Ei     /// Define label once
        .type   _ZN8FractionC2Ei, %function
❸ _ZN8FractionC2Ei:
        sub     sp, sp, #16
        str     x0, [sp, 8]
        str     w1, [sp, 4]        /// Save n
        ldr     x0, [sp, 8]
❹ ldr     w1, [sp, 4]
        str     w1, [x0]          /// Initialize numerator
        ldr     x0, [sp, 8]
❺ mov     w1, 456           /// Initialize denominator
        str     w1, [x0, 4]
        nop
        add     sp, sp, 16
        ret
        .size   _ZN8FractionC2Ei, .-_ZN8FractionC2Ei
        .weak   _ZN8FractionC1Ei
        .set    _ZN8FractionC1Ei,_ZN8FractionC2Ei
        .text
        .align  2
        .global main
        .type   main, %function
main:
        stp     x29, x30, [sp, -32]!
        mov     x29, sp
        mov     w0, 123
        str     w0, [sp, 24]
```

```
        mov     w0, 456
        str     w0, [sp, 28]
        add     x0, sp, 24
        bl      _ZN8Fraction7displayEv
        add     x0, sp, 24
        bl      _ZN8Fraction3getEv
        add     x0, sp, 24
        mov     w1, 1
        bl      _ZN8Fraction11add_integerEi
        add     x0, sp, 24
        bl      _ZN8Fraction7displayEv
        add     x0, sp, 16
❻ mov     w1, 78              /// Constant supplied in main
        bl      _ZN8FractionC1Ei
        add     x0, sp, 16
        bl      _ZN8Fraction7displayEv
        add     x0, sp, 16
        bl      _ZN8Fraction3getEv
        add     x0, sp, 16
        mov     w1, 1
        bl      _ZN8Fraction11add_integerEi
        add     x0, sp, 16
        bl      _ZN8Fraction7displayEv
        mov     w0, 0
        ldp     x29, x30, [sp], 32
        ret
        .size   main, .-main
        .ident  "GCC: (Debian 10.2.1-6) 10.2.1 20210110"
        .section        .note.GNU-stack,"",@progbits
```

Listing 18-18: The compiler-generated assembly language for the function in Listing 18-17

The compiler generates a separate function for our constructor, which takes an argument ❸. The compiler places this constructor in a special section, marked comdat, where it can be called from functions in other files that use this same constructor to instantiate a Fraction object ❶. The .weak assembler directive tells the compiler to generate this label only once in this file ❷. Although we're passing an explicit integer to the constructor in our main function ❻, the separate function is more efficient if we're instantiating several Fraction objects with variables whose values aren't known until the program is running.

The argument passed to the _ZN8FractionC2Ei constructor is used to initialize the numerator attribute of our Fraction object ❹. Our default in-class value is used to initialize the denominator attribute ❺.

Since the compiler wrote this constructor for us, we only need to change #include "fraction_dflt.h" to #include "fraction_2.h" in the file that defines our other member functions, Listing 18-13. I won't repeat that listing here.

It doesn't really make sense to write an object-oriented program in assembly language. We could invent a name decoration scheme for all our functions, but we would still be using the procedural programming paradigm to call them, not the object-oriented paradigm. However, there are situations in which we may wish to call functions written in assembly language. We'll look at how to do this in the next section.

YOUR TURN

18.1 Add another constructor to the C++ program in Listings 18-1, 18-3, and 18-5 that takes two integer arguments to initialize Fraction. Add an object that uses your second constructor. For example, Fraction y(1,2); would create the Fraction object initialized to 1/2. Modify the main function to display this second Fraction object, get a new value for it, add an integer to the second object, and display it again.

18.2 Write a program in C++ that prompts the user to enter a numerator and a denominator and then instantiates a Fraction object using the user's values. Display the new object, add 1 to it, and display the new state of the object.

Calling Assembly Language Functions in C++

To show you how to call assembly language functions in C++, I'll change our Fraction member functions to use our assembly language functions write_str, write_char, put_int, and get_int for writing to the screen and reading from the keyboard. Listing 18-19 shows the changes we need to make in the definitions of our member functions.

fraction_asm.cpp
```
// A simple Fraction class

#include "fraction_dflt.h"
// Use the following C functions.
❶ extern "C" {
    #include "write_str.h"
    #include "write_char.h"
    #include "get_int.h"
    #include "put_int.h"
}
// Use char arrays because write_str is a C function.
char num_msg[] = "Enter numerator: ";
char den_msg[] = "Enter denominator: ";

void Fraction::get()
{
    write_str(num_msg);
    numerator = get_int();
    write_str(den_msg);
```

```
        denominator = get_int();
}

void Fraction::display()
{
    put_int(numerator);
    write_char('/');
    put_int(denominator);
    write_char('\n');
}

void Fraction::add_integer(int x)
{
    numerator += x * denominator;
}
```

Listing 18-19: Calling assembly language functions in the Fraction class

The extern "C" tells the C++ compiler that the items in these header files have C linkage, so the compiler doesn't decorate their names ❶.

Listing 18-20 shows how this affects the get member function.

fraction_asm.s

```
        .arch armv8-a
        .file   "fraction_asm.cpp"
        .text
        .global num_msg
        .data
        .align  3
        .type   num_msg, %object
        .size   num_msg, 18
num_msg:
        .string "Enter numerator: "
        .global den_msg
        .align  3
        .type   den_msg, %object
        .size   den_msg, 20
den_msg:
        .string "Enter denominator: "
        .text
        .align  2
        .global _ZN8Fraction3getEv
        .type   _ZN8Fraction3getEv, %function
_ZN8Fraction3getEv:
        stp     x29, x30, [sp, -32]!
        mov     x29, sp
        str     x0, [sp, 24]
        adrp    x0, num_msg
        add     x0, x0, :lo12:num_msg
❶ bl     write_str
```

```
        bl      get_int
        mov     w1, w0
        ldr     x0, [sp, 24]
        str     w1, [x0]
        adrp    x0, den_msg
        add     x0, x0, :lo12:den_msg
        bl      write_str
        bl      get_int
        mov     w1, w0
        ldr     x0, [sp, 24]
        str     w1, [x0, 4]
        nop
        ldp     x29, x30, [sp], 32
        ret
        .size   _ZN8Fraction3getEv, .-_ZN8Fraction3getEv
--snip--
```

Listing 18-20: The compiler-generated assembly language for get in Listing 18-19

The assembly language functions are called by the names we've given them, without any decoration ❶. If you use g++ to generate the assembly language for the display member function, you'll see similar results for the put_int and write_char function calls.

What You've Learned

Class   The declaration of the data members that define the state of an object, along with any member functions used to access these data members.

Objects in C++   A named area of memory that contains the data members declared in a class.

Methods or member functions   The member functions declared in a class can be called to access the state of an object of the same class.

Name decoration   The compiler creates member function names that include the function name, the class it belongs to, and the number and types of any arguments to the function.

Constructor   A member function used to initialize an object.

Destructor   A member function used to clean up resources that are no longer needed.

This chapter has been a brief introduction to the way C++ implements basic object-oriented programming features.

Now that you've learned several techniques for organizing data in programs, I'll turn back to how data is stored in binary. So far in this book, I've used only integral values in our programs. In the next chapter, you'll see how fractional values are represented in memory and learn about some of the CPU instructions to manipulate them.

19

FRACTIONAL NUMBERS

We have been using only integral values—integers and characters—in our programs so far. In this chapter, we'll look at how computers represent fractional numbers. You'll learn about two ways to represent fractional values: fixed point and floating point.

I'll start with fixed-point numbers, to show you how fractional values are represented in binary. As you will see, using some of the bits for the fractional part of a number reduces the number of bits left for the integer part, thus reducing the range of numbers we can represent. Including a fractional part only allows us to divide that range into smaller portions.

This limitation on the range will lead us to a discussion of floating-point numbers, which allow for a much larger range but introduce other limitations. I'll show you the format and properties of floating-point representation and then discuss the most common floating-point binary standard, IEEE 754. I'll end the chapter with a brief look at how floating-point numbers are processed in the A64 architecture.

Fractional Values in Binary

Let's start by looking at the mathematics of fractional values. Recall from Chapter 2 that a decimal integer, N, is expressed in binary as

$$N = d_{n-1} \times 2^{n-1} + d_{n-2} \times 2^{n-2} + \ldots + d_1 \times 2^1 + d_0 \times 2^0$$

where each $d_i = 0$ or 1.

We can extend this to include a fractional part, F, such that

$$
\begin{aligned}
N.F \quad &= d_{n-1} \times 2^{n-1} + d_{n-2} \times 2^{n-2} + \ldots \\
&\quad + d_0 \times 2^0 + d_{-1} \times 2^{-1} + d_{-2} \times 2^{-2} + \ldots \\
&= d_{n-1}d_{n-2} \ldots d_0.d_{-1}d_{-2} \ldots
\end{aligned}
$$

where each $d_i = 0$ or 1. Note the *binary point* between d_0 and d_{-1} on the right-hand side of this equation. All the terms to the right of the binary point are inverse powers of two, so this portion of the number sums to a fractional value. Like the decimal point on the left-hand side, the binary point separates the fractional part from the integral part of the number. Here's an example:

$$
\begin{aligned}
1.6875_{10} \quad &= 1.0_{10} + 0.5_{10} + 0.125_{10} + 0.0625_{10} \\
&= 1 \times 2^0 + 1 \times 2^{-1} + 0 \times 2^{-2} + 1 \times 2^{-3} + 1 \times 2^{-4} \\
&= 1.1011_2
\end{aligned}
$$

Although any integer can be represented as a sum of powers of two, an exact representation of fractional values in binary is limited to sums of *inverse* powers of two. For example, consider an 8-bit representation of the fractional value 0.9. From the equalities

$$
\begin{aligned}
0.11100110_2 \quad &= 0.89843750_{10} \\
0.11100111_2 \quad &= 0.90234375_{10}
\end{aligned}
$$

we get the following:

$$0.11100110_2 < 0.9_{10} < 0.11100111_2$$

In fact,

$$0.9_{10} = 0.11100\overline{1100}_2$$

where $\overline{1100}$ means this bit pattern repeats indefinitely.

To round a fractional value to the nearest value, check the bits to the right of the rounding place. If the next bit to the right is 0, drop all the bits to the right of the bit position where you're rounding. If the next bit to the right is 1 and any of the bits following it are 1, add 1 to the bit position where you're rounding.

If the next bit to the right is 1 and all the bits following it are 0, use the *ties-to-even* rule. If the bit you're rounding to is 0, simply drop all the bits to the right of your rounding place. If the bit you're rounding to is 1, add 1 to it and drop all the bits to the right of your rounding place.

Let's round 0.9 to 8 bits. Earlier, you saw that the ninth bit to the right of the binary point is 0, so we drop all the bits to the right of the eighth bit position. Thus, we use

$$0.9_{10} \approx 0.11100110_2$$

which gives a rounding error as follows:

$$
\begin{aligned}
0.9_{10} - 0.11100110_2 &= 0.9_{10} - 0.8984375_{10} \\
&= 0.0015625_{10}
\end{aligned}
$$

The AArch64 architecture supports other floating-point rounding algorithms. These are discussed in the *Arm Architecture Reference Manual for A-Profile Architecture*, available at *https://developer.arm.com/documentation/ddi0487/latest*.

We typically write numbers in decimal, with a decimal point in a fixed location in the number to separate the fractional part from the integer part. Let's see how this works in binary.

Fixed-Point Numbers

A *fixed-point number* is essentially a scaled integer representation in which the scaling is shown by the location of the *radix point*, which separates the fractional part of a number from the integral part. We call it the *decimal point* in decimal numbers and the *binary point* in binary numbers. English-speaking countries commonly use a period; other regions typically use a comma.

For example, $1{,}234.5_{10}$ represents $12{,}345_{10}$ scaled by $1/10$, and the binary 10011010010.1_2 is 100110100101_2 scaled by a factor of $1/2$. When performing computations with fixed-point numbers, you need to be mindful of the location of the radix point.

In the first part of this section, we'll look at scaling numbers with a fractional part that is an inverse power of two, in which case the fractional part can be represented exactly. Then, we'll look at scaling fractional numbers in decimal to avoid the rounding errors described earlier.

When the Fractional Part Is a Sum of Inverse Powers of Two

I'll start with a program that adds two measurements that are specified to the nearest sixteenth. An example would be measuring a length in inches. The fractional parts of inches are often specified in inverse powers of two $(1/2, 1/4, 1/8,$ and so forth), which can be represented exactly in the binary system.

Our program uses lengths to the nearest sixteenth, so we'll multiply each value by 16 to give us an integral number of sixteenths. The program will first read the integer part of a length from the keyboard and then read the number of sixteenths. Listing 19-1 shows how we scale the integer part of the number and then add in the fractional part as they're read from the keyboard.

```
get_length.s  // Get a length in inches and 1/16s.
              // Calling sequence:
              //    Return the fixed-point number.
                    .arch armv8-a
              // Stack frame
                    .equ    save19, 16
                    .equ    FRAME, 32
              // Constant data
                    .section  .rodata
                    .align  3
              prompt:
                    .string "Enter length (inches and 1/16s)\n"
              inches:
                    .string "          Inches: "
              fraction:
                    .string "      Sixteenths: "
              // Code
                    .text
                    .align  2
                    .global get_length
                    .type   get_length, %function
              get_length:
                    stp     fp, lr, [sp, -FRAME]! // Create stack frame
                    mov     fp, sp                // Set our frame pointer
                    str     x19, [sp, save19]     // For local var

                    adr     x0, prompt            // Ask for length
                    bl      write_str
                    adr     x0, inches            // Ask for integer
                    bl      write_str
          ❶ bl      get_uint              // Integer part
          ❷ lsl     w19, w0, 4            // 4 bits for fraction

                    adr     x0, fraction          // Ask for fraction
                    bl      write_str
                    bl      get_uint              // Fractional part
                    add     w0, w0, w19           // Add integer part

                    ldr     x19, [sp, save19]     // Restore for caller
                    ldp     fp, lr, [sp], FRAME   // Delete stack frame
                    ret                           // Back to caller
```

Listing 19-1: A function to read a number in inches and sixteenths of an inch from the keyboard

We allocate 32 bits for both the number of inches and the number of sixteenths of an inch, each to be read as integers from the keyboard. Notice that we're using the get_uint function to read each unsigned int ❶. You were asked to write this function in "Your Turn" exercise 16.9 on page 358.

We shift the integral part 4 bits to the left to multiply it by 16 ❷. After adding the fractional part, we have the total number of sixteenths in our value. For example, 5 9/16 would be stored as the integer $5 \times 16 + 9 = 89$.

The scaling leaves 28 bits for the integral part. This limits the range of our numbers to be 0 to 268,435,455 15/16. This is 16 times less than the 0 to 4,294,967,295 range of a 32-bit unsigned integer, but the resolution is to the nearest 1/16.

Our function to display these measurements, shown in Listing 19-2, displays both the integral and fractional parts.

display_length.s
```
// Display a length to the nearest sixteenth.
        .arch armv8-a
// Calling sequence:
//     w0[31-4] <- integer part
//     w0[3-0]  <- fractional part
//     Return 0
// Useful constants
  ❶ .equ    FOUR_BITS, 0xf        // For fraction
// Stack frame
        .equ    save19, 16
        .equ    FRAME, 32
// Constant data
        .section  .rodata
        .align  3
sixteenths:
        .string "/16"
// Code
        .text
        .align  2
        .global display_length
        .type   display_length, %function
display_length:
        stp     fp, lr, [sp, -FRAME]! // Create stack frame
        mov     fp, sp                 // Set our frame pointer
        str     x19, [sp, save19]      // For local var

        mov     w19, w0                // Save input
  ❷ lsr     w0, w19, 4             // Integer part
        bl      put_uint

        mov     w0, ' '                // Some formatting
        bl      write_char

  ❸ and     w0, w19, FOUR_BITS     // Mask off integer
        bl      put_uint               // Fractional part
```

```
    ❹ adr      x0, sixteenths       // More formatting
      bl       write_str

      mov      w0, wzr              // Return 0
      ldr      x19, [sp, save19]    // Restore for caller
      ldp      fp, lr, [sp], FRAME  // Delete stack frame
      ret                           // Back to caller
```

Listing 19-2: A function to display a number to the nearest sixteenth

We shift the number 4 bits to the right so we can display the integral part as an integer ❷. Using a 4-bit mask ❶, we mask off the integral part and display the fractional part as another integer ❸. We add some text to show that this second integer is the fractional part ❹.

Listing 19-3 shows a main function that adds two numbers to the nearest sixteenth.

```
add_lengths.s  // Add 2 lengths, fixed-point, to nearest sixteenth.
               .arch armv8-a
       // Stack frame
               .equ    save1920, 16
               .equ    FRAME, 32
       // Constant data
               .section  .rodata
               .align  3
       sum_msg:
               .string "Sum = "
       // Code
               .text
               .align  2
               .global main
               .type   main, %function
       main:
               stp      fp, lr, [sp, -FRAME]!  // Create stack frame
               mov      fp, sp                 // Set our frame pointer
               stp      x19, x20, [sp, save1920] // For local vars

               bl       get_length
               mov      w19, w0                // First number
               bl       get_length
               mov      w20, w0                // Second number

               adr      x0, sum_msg            // Some formatting
               bl       write_str
            ❶ add      w0, w20, w19           // Add lengths
               bl       display_length         // Show result
```

```
        mov     w0, '\n'                    // Finish formatting
        bl      write_char

        mov     w0, wzr                     // Return 0
        ldp     x19, x20, [sp, save1920]    // Restore for caller
        ldp     fp, lr, [sp], FRAME         // Delete stack frame
        ret                                 // Back to caller
```

Listing 19-3: A program to add two lengths to the nearest sixteenth

If you look at the equation for representing fractional values in binary on page 410, you can probably convince yourself that the integer add instruction will work for the entire number, including the fractional part ❶.

Let's think about how we've handled the fractional part in our fixed-point format here. When we read the integer part from the keyboard, we shifted it four bit positions to the left to multiply by 16. This left room to add the number of sixteenths of the fractional part to this int. We effectively created a 32-bit number with the binary point between the fifth and fourth bits (bits 4 and 3). This works because the fractional part is a sum of inverse powers of two.

This example works nicely with binary numbers, but we mostly use decimal numbers in computations. As you saw earlier in this chapter, most fractional decimal numbers can't be converted to a finite number of bits and need to be rounded. In the next section, I'll discuss how to avoid rounding errors when representing fractional decimal numbers in binary.

When the Fractional Part Is in Decimal

I'll use a program that adds two US dollar values to the nearest cent as an example of using fractional values in decimal. As with the measurement adding program in Listings 19-1 to 19-3, we'll start with the function to read money values from the keyboard, get_money, shown in Listing 19-4.

get_money.s
```
// Get dollars and cents from the keyboard.
// Calling sequence:
//      Return integer amount as cents.
        .arch armv8-a
// Stack frame
        .equ    save19, 16
        .equ    FRAME, 32
// Constant data
        .section  .rodata
        .align  3
prompt:
        .string "Enter amount (use same sign for dollars and cents)\n"
dollars:
        .string "   Dollars: "
```

```
cents:
        .string "       Cents: "
// Code
        .text
        .align  2
        .global get_money
        .type   get_money, %function
get_money:
        stp     fp, lr, [sp, -FRAME]! // Create stack frame
        mov     fp, sp                // Set our frame pointer
        str     x19, [sp, save19]     // For local var

        adr     x0, prompt            // Ask for amount
        bl      write_str
        adr     x0, dollars           // Ask for dollars
        bl      write_str
        bl      get_int               // Dollars
❶ mov       w1, 100               // 100 cents per dollar
        mul     w19, w0, w1           // Scale

        adr     x0, cents             // Ask for cents
        bl      write_str
        bl      get_int               // Cents
❷ add       w0, w0, w19           // Add scaled dollars

        ldr     x19, [sp, save19]     // Restore for caller
        ldp     fp, lr, [sp], FRAME   // Delete stack frame
        ret                           // Back to caller
```

Listing 19-4: A function to read dollars and cents from the keyboard

Our money values are specified to the nearest cent here, so we multiply dollars—the integer part—by 100 ❶. Then we add cents—the fractional part— to give our scaled int ❷.

When storing decimal fractions, the integer and fractional parts are not separated into bit fields as in our previous example. For example, $1.10 would be stored as 110 = 0x0000006e and $2.10 as 210 = 0x000000d2. Because we use 32-bit signed integers in this program, the range of a money value is $-\$21{,}473{,}836.48 \leq money\_amount \leq +\$21{,}473{,}836.47$.

Displaying dollars and cents will require a different algorithm from displaying lengths in sixteenths, as shown in Listing 19-5.

display_money.s
```
// Display dollars and cents.
        .arch armv8-a
// Calling sequence:
//   w0 <- value in cents
//   Return 0
```

```
// Stack frame
        .equ    save1920, 16
        .equ    FRAME, 32
// Constant data
        .section  .rodata
        .align  3
// Code
        .text
        .align  2
        .global display_money
        .type   display_money, %function
display_money:
        stp     fp, lr, [sp, -FRAME]!    // Create stack frame
        mov     fp, sp                   // Set our frame pointer
        stp     x19, x20, [sp, save1920] // For local vars

        mov     w1, 100                  // 100 cents per dollar
 ❶ sdiv    w20, w0, w1                   // Dollars
        msub    w19, w20, w1, w0         // Leaving cents

        mov     w0, '$'                  // Some formatting
        bl      write_char
        mov     w0, w20                  // Dollars
        bl      put_int

        mov     w0, '.'                  // Some formatting
        bl      write_char
        cmp     w19, wzr                 // Negative?
 ❷ cneg    w19, w19, mi                  // Make nonnegative
 ❸ cmp     w19, 10                       // Check for single digit
        b.hs    no_zero                  // Two digits
        mov     w0, '0'                  // One digit needs leading '0'
        bl      write_char
no_zero:
        mov     w0, w19                  // Cents
        bl      put_int

        mov     w0, wzr                  // Return 0
        ldp     x19, x29, [sp, save1920] // Restore for caller
        ldp     fp, lr, [sp], FRAME      // Delete stack frame
        ret                              // Back to caller
```

Listing 19-5: A function to display dollars and cents

Shifting won't allow us to divide by 100, so we use the signed divide instruction, sdiv, to get the dollars ❶. The remainder from this division will be
the number of cents.

Our computation of the remainder will have the same sign as the integer part. The negative sign will show when we display the dollars, but we don't want to repeat it for the cents, so we negate the value for cents before displaying it ❷. We check whether the number of cents is less than 10, and if so, we make the first digit to the right of the decimal point a 0 ❸.

We see a new instruction here. cneg:

cneg—Conditional negate

cneg wd, ws, cond loads the negated value of the 32-bit value in ws into wd if cond is true. If it's not true, ws is loaded into wd.

cneg xd, xs, cond loads the negated value of the 64-bit value in xs into xd if cond is true. If it's not true, xs is loaded into xd.

The possible conditions, cond, can be any of the condition flags listed in Table 13-1 on page 245 except for al and nv.

Our main function for this program, shown in Listing 19-6, will get two dollar amounts entered from the keyboard, add them, and display their sum.

add_money.s
```
// Add two dollar values.
        .arch armv8-a
// Stack frame
        .equ    save1920, 16
        .equ    FRAME, 32
// Constant data
        .section  .rodata
        .align  3
sum_msg:
        .string "Sum = "
// Code
        .text
        .align  2
        .global main
        .type   main, %function
main:
        stp     fp, lr, [sp, -FRAME]!     // Create stack frame
        mov     fp, sp                    // Set our frame pointer
        stp     x19, x20, [sp, save1920]  // For local vars

        bl      get_money
        mov     w19, w0                   // First number
        bl      get_money
        mov     w20, w0                   // Second number

        adr     x0, sum_msg               // Some formatting
        bl      write_str
  ❶     add     w0, w19, w20              // Add values
        bl      display_money             // Show result
        mov     w0, '\n'                  // Finish formatting
```

```
        bl      write_char

        mov     w0, wzr                 // Return 0
        ldp     x19, x20, [sp, save1920]  // Restore for caller
        ldp     fp, lr, [sp], FRAME       // Delete stack frame
        ret                             // Back to caller
```

Listing 19-6: A program to add two dollar values

Our scaling of the integer part has converted dollars to cents, so a simple add instruction computes the sum for us ❶. Our display_money function will sort out the dollars and cents in this sum.

This solution works well for many numbers, but we commonly use scientific notation for writing very large and very small numbers. In the next sections, you'll see how the scientific notation has led to another way to store fractional values.

YOUR TURN

19.1   Enter the program in Listings 19-1 to 19-3. Using the gdb debugger, examine the numbers stored in the w19 and w20 registers in main. Identify the integral and fractional parts.

19.2   Enter the program in Listings 19-4 to 19-6. Using the gdb debugger, examine the numbers stored in the w19 and w20 registers in main. Identify the integral and fractional parts.

19.3   Enter the program in Listings 19-4 to 19-6. Run the program, using $21,474,836.47 for one amount and $0.01 for the other. What total does the program give? Why?

19.4   Write a program in assembly language that allows a user to enter a start time and the amount of time a task takes, then computes the finish time. Use a 24-hour clock with resolution to the nearest second.

Floating-Point Numbers

Floating-point numbers allow for a much larger range than fixed-point numbers. However, it's important to understand that floating-point numbers are not *real numbers*. Real numbers include the continuum of all numbers from $-\infty$ to $+\infty$. You already know that we have a finite number of bits to work with in a computer, so there is a limit on the largest values that can be represented. But the problem is worse than simply a limit on the magnitude.

As you will see in this section, floating-point numbers comprise a small subset of real numbers. There are significant gaps between adjacent floating-point numbers. These gaps can produce several types of errors, as detailed in "Floating-Point Arithmetic Errors" on page 425. To make matters worse, these errors can occur in intermediate results, where they are difficult to debug.

Floating-Point Representation

Floating-point representation is based on scientific notation. In floating-point representation, we have a sign and two numbers to completely specify a value: a *significand* and an *exponent*. A decimal floating-point number is written as a significand times 10 raised to an exponent. For example, consider these two numbers:

$$0.0010123 \quad = 1.0123 \times 10^{-3}$$
$$-456.78 \quad = -4.56783 \times 10^{2}$$

In the floating-point representation, the number is *normalized* such that only one digit appears to the left of the decimal point and the exponent of 10 is adjusted accordingly. If we agree that each number is normalized and that we are working in base 10, then each floating-point number is completely specified by three items: the significand, exponent, and sign. In the previous two examples:

$$10,123, -3, \text{ and } + \text{ represent } +1.0123 \times 10^{-3}$$
$$45,678, +2, \text{ and } - \text{ represent } -4.5678 \times 10^{+2}$$

The advantage of using floating-point representation is that, for a given number of digits, we can represent a larger range of values.

Let's look at how floating-point numbers are stored in a computer.

IEEE 754 Floating-Point Standard

The most commonly used standard for storing floating-point numbers is IEEE 754 (*https://standards.ieee.org/standard/754-2019.html*). Figure 19-1 shows the general pattern.

S	Exponent	Significand

Figure 19-1: The general pattern for storing IEEE 754 floating-point numbers

The A64 architecture supports four variants of this format for storing floating-point numbers: two 16-bit, one 32-bit, and one 64-bit. Of these, the 16-bit half-precision, 32-bit single-precision, and 64-bit double-precision formats follow the IEEE 754 standard. The *BF16* format (also called *BFloat16*) is the same as the IEEE 754 single-precision format but with a truncated significand. This reduces memory storage requirements while preserving the dynamic range of the 32-bit format, but at the expense of precision. This trade-off is useful in some machine learning algorithms. The A64 architecture includes instructions to operate on BF16 data, but we won't use them in this book. These formats are shown in Figure 19-2.

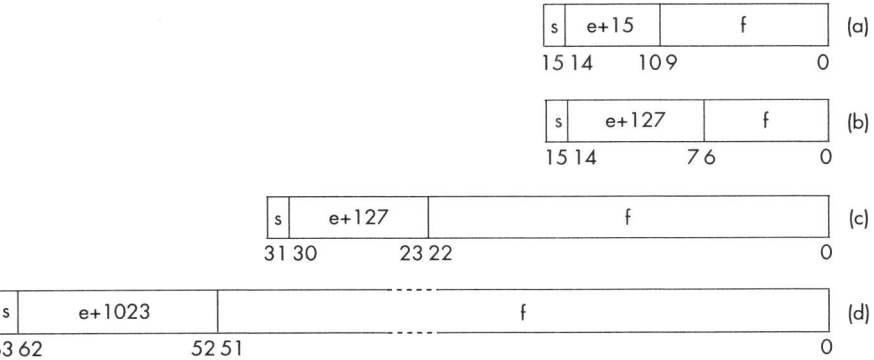

Figure 19-2: The formats for (a) half-precision, (b) BF16, (c) single-precision, and (d) double-precision floating point

Values in the formats shown in Figure 19-2 represent a floating-point number, N, stored in the normalized form:

$$N = (-1)^s \times 1.f \times 2^e$$

The first bit, s, is the sign bit, 0 for positive and 1 for negative. As in decimal scientific notation, the exponent is adjusted such that there is only one nonzero digit to the left of the binary point. In binary, though, this digit is always 1, giving $1.f$ as the significand. Since it's always 1, the integer part (1) is not stored. It's called the *hidden bit*. Only the fractional part of the significand, f, is stored.

The formats need to allow for negative exponents. Your first thought might be to use two's complement. However, the IEEE standard was developed in the 1970s, when floating-point computations took a lot of CPU time. Many algorithms in programs depend upon only the comparison of two numbers, and the computer scientists of the day realized that a format that allowed integer comparison instructions would result in faster execution times. So, they decided to add an amount, called a *bias*, to the exponent before storing it, such that the most negative allowable exponent would be stored as 0. The result, a *biased exponent*, can then be stored as an `unsigned int`. In Figure 19-2, the bias is 15 for the half-precision IEEE format, 127 for the single-precision IEEE and BF16 formats, and 1,023 for the double-precision IEEE format.

The hidden bit scheme presents a problem: there is no way to represent 0. To address this and other issues, the IEEE 754 standard has several special cases:

Zero value　All the biased exponent bits and fraction bits are 0, allowing for both −0 and +0. This preserves the sign of a computation that converges to 0.

Denormalized　If the value to be represented is smaller than can be represented with all the biased exponent bits being 0, meaning that e has the most negative value possible, the hidden bit is no longer assumed. In this case, the amount of bias is reduced by 1.

Infinity   Infinity is represented by setting all the biased exponent bits to 1 and all the fraction bits to 0. This allows the sign bit to designate both $+\infty$ and $-\infty$, allowing us to still compare numbers that are out of range.

Not a number (NaN)   If the biased exponent bits are all 1 but the fraction bits are not all 0, this represents a value that is in error. This might be used to indicate that a floating-point variable doesn't yet have a value. NaN should be treated as a program error.

An example of an operation that gives infinity is dividing a nonzero value by 0. An example that produces NaN is an operation that has an undefined result, such as dividing 0 by 0.

Next, I'll discuss the A64 hardware used to work with floating-point numbers.

Floating-Point Hardware

Table 9-1 in Chapter 9 shows that the A64 architecture includes a register file that has 32 128-bit registers for floating-point or vector computations, the *SIMD&FP* registers.

The A64 architecture includes vector instructions that can operate on multiple data items in an SIMD&FP register simultaneously. This is a computing method called *single-instruction multiple-data (SIMD)*. Data items for these instructions can range from 8 to 64 bits, so a register can hold 2 to 16 data items. There are vector instructions for both integer and floating-point operations.

A vector instruction operates on each data item in a SIMD&FP register independently from all the other data items in the register. These instructions are useful for algorithms that do things like process arrays. One vector instruction can operate on several array elements in parallel, resulting in considerable speed gains. Such algorithms are common in multimedia and scientific applications.

The A64 architecture also includes scalar floating-point instructions that operate on a single floating-point data item in the low-order bits of the SIMD&FP registers.

Programming with SIMD instructions is beyond the scope of this book; we'll consider only scalar floating-point computations here. Figure 19-3 shows the names of the portions of the SIMD&FP registers used for the scalar floating-point instructions.

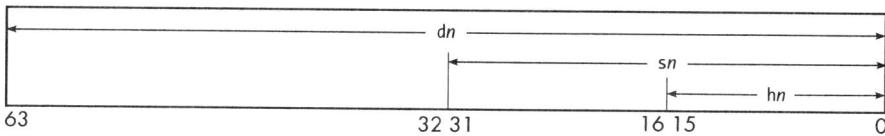

Figure 19-3: The A64 floating-point register names

Listing 19-7 shows how we can use these registers to perform floating-point arithmetic.

add_floats.s
```
// Add two floats.
        .arch armv8-a
// Stack frame
        .equ    x, 16
        .equ    y, 20
        .equ    FRAME, 32
// Constant data
        .section  .rodata
        .align  3
prompt_format:
        .string "Enter number: "
get_format:
        .string "%f"
sum_format:
        .string "%f + %f = %f\n"
// Code
        .text
        .align  2
        .global main
        .type   main, %function
main:
        stp     fp, lr, [sp, FRAME]!  // Create stack frame
        mov     fp, sp

        adr     x0, prompt_format     // Ask for number
        bl      printf
        add     x1, sp, x             // Place for first number
        adr     x0, get_format        // Get it
❶ bl      scanf
        adr     x0, prompt_format     // Ask for number
        bl      printf
        add     x1, sp, y             // Place for second number
        adr     x0, get_format        // Get it
        bl      scanf

❷ ldr     s0, [sp, x]           // Load x
        ldr     s1, [sp, y]           //    and y
❸ fadd    s2, s0, s1            // Sum
        fcvt    d0, s0                // Doubles for printf
        fcvt    d1, s1
        fcvt    d2, s2
        adr     x0, sum_format        // Formatting for printf
        bl      printf
```

```
        mov     w0, wzr              // Return 0
        ldp     fp, lr, [sp], FRAME  // Delete stack frame
        ret
```

Listing 19-7: A program to add two floating-point numbers

We use the scanf function from the C standard library to read a floating-point number from the keyboard ❶. This will store the number in memory in the 32-bit IEEE 754 format. Thus, we don't need a special instruction to load the number into a floating-point register; we can simply use an ldr instruction ❷.

We need to use the floating-point add instruction, fadd, to sum the numbers ❸. I won't list all the floating-point instructions for performing arithmetic, but here are the four basic ones:

fadd—Floating-point add (scalar)

fadd h*d*, h*s1*, h*s2* adds the half-precision floating-point numbers in h*s1* and h*s2* and stores the result in h*d*.

fadd s*d*, s*s1*, s*s2* adds the single-precision floating-point numbers in s*s1* and s*s2* and stores the result in s*d*.

fadd d*d*, d*s1*, d*s2* adds the double-precision floating-point numbers in d*s1* and d*s2* and stores the result in d*d*.

fsub—Floating-point subtract (scalar)

fsub h*d*, h*s1*, h*s2* subtracts the half-precision floating-point number in h*s2* from the one in h*s1* and stores the result in h*d*.

fsub s*d*, s*s1*, s*s2* subtracts the single-precision floating-point number in s*s2* from the one in s*s1* and stores the result in s*d*.

fsub d*d*, d*s1*, d*s2* subtracts the double-precision floating-point number in d*s2* from the one in d*s1* and stores the result in d*d*.

fmul—Floating-point multiply (scalar)

fmul h*d*, h*s1*, h*s2* multiplies the half-precision floating-point numbers in h*s1* and h*s2* and stores the result in h*d*.

fmul s*d*, s*s1*, s*s2* multiplies the single-precision floating-point numbers in s*s1* and s*s2* and stores the result in s*d*.

fmul d*d*, d*s1*, d*s2* multiplies the double-precision floating-point numbers in d*s1* and d*s2* and stores the result in d*d*.

fdiv—Floating-point divide (scalar)

fdiv h*d*, h*s1*, h*s2* divides the half-precision floating-point number in h*s1* by the one in h*s2* and stores the result in h*d*.

fdiv s*d*, s*s1*, s*s2* divides the single-precision floating-point number in s*s1* by the one in s*s2* and stores the result in s*d*.

fdiv d*d*, d*s1*, d*s2* divides the double-precision floating-point number in d*s1* by the one in d*s2* and stores the result in d*d*.

The `printf` function requires that floating-point numbers be passed as doubles, so we use the `fcvt` instruction to convert our `float` values to `doubles`. The `fcvt` instruction converts from the floating-point format of the source register to the floating-point format of the destination register:

`fcvt`—Floating-point convert precision (scalar)

`fcvt` `sd, hs` converts half-precision in `hs` to single-precision in `sd`.

`fcvt` `dd, hs` converts half-precision in `hs` to double-precision in `dd`.

`fcvt` `hd, ss` converts single-precision in `ss` to half-precision in `hd`.

`fcvt` `dd, ss` converts single-precision in `ss` to double-precision in `dd`.

`fcvt` `hd, ds` converts double-precision in `ds` to half-precision in `hd`.

`fcvt` `sd, ds` converts double-precision in `ds` to single-precision in `sd`.

Although we're not using comparisons in this program, here's an example of a floating-point compare instruction:

`fcmp`—Floating-point compare (scalar)

`fcmp` `hs1, hs2` compares the half-precision floating-point number in `hs1` with `hs2` and sets the condition flags in the `nzcv` register accordingly.

`fcmp` `hs, 0.0` compares the half-precision floating-point number in `hs` with 0.0 and sets the condition flags in the `nzcv` register accordingly.

`fcmp` `ss1, ss2` compares the single-precision floating-point number in `ss1` with `ss2` and sets the condition flags in the `nzcv` register accordingly.

`fcmp` `ss, 0.0` compares the single-precision floating-point number in `ss` with 0.0 and sets the condition flags in the `nzcv` register accordingly.

`fcmp` `ds1, ds2` compares the double-precision floating-point number in `ds1` with `ds2` and sets the condition flags in the `nzcv` register accordingly.

`fcmp` `ds, 0.0` compares the double-precision floating-point number in `ds` with 0.0 and sets the condition flags in the `nzcv` register accordingly.

Since the `fcmp` instruction sets the condition flags in the `nzcv` register, we can use the conditional branch instruction described in Chapter 13 with the conditions in Table 13-1 to control program flow based on floating-point values.

As mentioned earlier, floating-point computations can lead to some subtle numerical errors in our programs. I'll cover these in the next section.

Floating-Point Arithmetic Errors

It's easy to think of floating-point numbers as real numbers, but they're not. Most floating-point numbers are rounded approximations of the real numbers they represent. When using floating-point arithmetic, you need to be aware of the effects of rounding on your computations. If you don't pay close attention to the rounding effects, you might not notice the errors that can creep into your computations.

Most of the arithmetic errors I'll discuss here are also possible with fixed-point arithmetic. Probably the most common arithmetic error is *rounding error*, which can occur for two reasons: either the number of bits available for storage is limited or the fractional values cannot be precisely represented in all number bases.

Both of these limitations also apply to fixed-point representation. As you saw earlier in this chapter, you can often scale fixed-point numbers to eliminate the problem with fractional values—but then the number of bits available for storage limits the range of the values.

Floating-point representation reduces the range problem by using an exponent to specify where the integer part begins. However, the significand of a floating-point number is a fraction, which means that most floating-point numbers do not have an exact representation in binary, leading to rounding errors.

One of the biggest problems with floating-point arithmetic is that the CPU instructions can shift the significand of a number, adjusting the exponent accordingly and causing bits to be lost and more rounding errors. With integer arithmetic, any shifting of bits is explicit in the program.

When computing with integers, you need to be aware of errors in the most significant places of the results: carry for unsigned integers and overflow for signed integers. With floating-point numbers, the radix point is adjusted to maintain the integrity of the most significant places. Most errors in floating-point arithmetic are the result of rounding in the low-order places that is needed to fit the value within the allocated number of bits. The errors in floating-point arithmetic are more subtle, but they can have important effects on the accuracy of our programs.

Let's look at the different types of errors that can arise in floating-point computations.

Rounding Error

You saw at the beginning of this chapter that most decimal fractional values do not have exact equivalents in binary, leading to a rounded-off approximation being stored in memory. Running the add_floats program from Listing 19-7 illustrates this problem:

```
$ ./add_floats
Enter number: 123.4
Enter number: 567.8
123.400002 + 567.799988 = 691.199989
```

The numbers the program is using are not the ones I entered, and the fadd instruction didn't add the program's numbers correctly. Before you go back to look for the bugs in Listing 19-7, let's bring in the debugger to see if we can figure out what's happening:

```
--snip--
(gdb) b 43
```

```
Breakpoint 1 at 0x7fc: file add_floats.s, line 43.
(gdb) r
Starting program: /home/bob/add_floats_asm/add_floats
Enter number: 123.4
Enter number: 567.8

Breakpoint 1, main () at add_floats.s:42
43              bl      printf
```

I set a breakpoint at the call to printf and then ran the program, entering the same numbers as earlier. Let's look at the three values that are passed to printf:

```
(gdb) i r d0 d1 d2
d0              {f = 0x7b, u = 0x405ed999a0000000, s = 0x405ed999a0000000}
{f = 123.40000152587891, u = 4638383920075767808, s = 4638383920075767808}
d1              {f = 0x237, u = 0x4081be6660000000, s = 0x4081be6660000000}
{f = 567.79998779296875, u = 4648205637329616896, s = 4648205637329616896}
d2              {f = 0x2b3, u = 0x4085999994000000, s = 0x4085999994000000}
{f = 691.19998931884766, u = 4649291075221979136, s = 4649291075221979136}
(gdb)
```

This display can be a bit confusing. For each floating-pointing register, the values in the first set of brackets are in hexadecimal. The first value (f =) shows the integer part of the number in hexadecimal. For example, the integer part of the value in d0 is 0x7b = 123_{10}, which is the integer part of the number I entered. The next two values (u = and s =) show the bit pattern of the entire number as it's stored. We can use this bit pattern with the format in Figure 19-2(d) to figure out the floating-point number.

The values in the second set of brackets show the number in floating point (f =), as though the bits were interpreted as an unsigned integer (u =) and as a signed integer (s =).

Don't worry if you're still confused by this display. I also find it a bit confusing. The important part is where the display shows the floating-point number that is actually stored in each register: 123.40000152587891 in d0, 567.79998779296875 in d1, and 691.19998931884766 in d2. The printf function rounded each of these numbers to six decimal places when I ran the program. These values reflect the fact that most decimal fractional values do not have an exact binary equivalence.

Absorption

Absorption results from adding or subtracting two numbers of widely different magnitude. The value of the smaller number gets lost in the computation. Let's run our add_floats program under gdb to see how this occurs:

```
--snip--
(gdb) b 39
Breakpoint 1 at 0x7f0: file add_floats.s, line 39.
```

```
(gdb) r
Starting program: /home/bob/add_floats_asm/add_floats
Enter number: 16777215.0
Enter number: 0.1

Breakpoint 1, main () at add_floats.s:39
39              fcvt    d0, s0                // Doubles for printf
(gdb) i r s0 s1 s2
s0              {f = 0xffffff, u = 0x4b7fffff, s = 0x4b7fffff}
{f = 16777215, u = 1266679807, s = 1266679807}
s1              {f = 0x0, u = 0x3dcccccd, s = 0x3dcccccd}
{f = 0.100000001, u = 1036831949, s = 1036831949}
s2              {f = 0xffffff, u = 0x4b7fffff, s = 0x4b7fffff}
{f = 16777215, u = 1266679807, s = 1266679807}
(gdb) c
Continuing.
16777215.000000 + 0.100000 = 16777215.000000
[Inferior 1 (process 2109) exited normally]
(gdb)
```

From the gdb display, we see that the values in the registers are:

```
s0: 0x4b7fffff
s1: 0x3dcccccd
s2: 0x4b7fffff
```

The CPU aligns the binary points of the numbers before performing the addition. The pattern in Figure 19-2(c) shows that the fadd instruction performed the following addition:

```
s0 :     111111111111111111111111.00000000000000000000000000000
s1 : +   000000000000000000000000.00011001100110011001100110011100
s2 :     111111111111111111111111.00000000000000000000000000000
```

Since the significand in single-precision floating point is 24 bits (one is the hidden bit), the number in s2 is rounded to 111111111111111111111111, thus losing everything to the right of the binary point. The number in s1 was absorbed by the much larger number in s0.

Cancellation

Cancellation can occur when subtracting two numbers that differ by a small amount. Since floating-point notation preserves the integrity of the high-order portions, the subtraction will give 0 in the high-order portion of the result. If either of the numbers has been rounded, its low-order portion is not exact, which means the result will be in error.

To demonstrate, we can use our `add_floats` program to subtract by entering a negative number. Here's an example using two close numbers:

```
Enter number: 1677721.5
Enter number: -1677721.4
1677721.500000 + -1677721.375000 = 0.125000
```

From the gdb display, we see that the values in the registers are:

```
s0: 0x4b7fffff
s1: 0x3dcccccd
s2: 0x4b7fffff
```

The relative error in this subtraction is $(0.125 - 0.1) / 0.1 = 0.25 = 25\%$. The second number has been rounded from $-1,677,721.4$ to $-1,677,721.375$, which led to the error in the arithmetic.

Let's look at how these numbers are treated as `floats`:

$$s0: \quad 1.10011001100110011001100 \times 2^{20}$$
$$s1: \quad 1.10011001100110011001011 \times 2^{20}$$
$$s2: \quad 1.00000000000000000000000 \times 2^{-3}$$

Subtraction has caused the high-order 20 bits in s0 and s1 to cancel, leaving only three bits of significance for s2. The rounding error in s1 carries through to cause an error in s2.

Let's use two values that will not give a rounding error:

```
Enter number: 1677721.5
Enter number: -1677721.25
1677721.500000 + -1677721.250000 = 0.250000
```

In this case, the three numbers are stored exactly:

$$s0: \quad 1.10011001100110011001100 \times 2^{20}$$
$$s1: \quad 1.10011001100110011001010 \times 2^{20}$$
$$s2: \quad 1.00000000000000000000000 \times 2^{-2}$$

The subtraction has still caused the high-order 20 bits of s0 and s1 to cancel and left only three bits of significance for s3, but s3 is correct.

Catastrophic cancellation occurs when at least one of the floating-point numbers has a rounding error that causes an error in the difference. If both numbers are stored exactly, we get *benign cancellation*. Both types of cancellation cause a loss of significance in the result.

Associativity

Probably the most insidious effects of floating-point errors are those that cause errors in intermediate results. They can show up in some sets of data but not in others. Errors in intermediate results can even cause floating-point addition not to be associative—that is, there are some values of the floats x, y, and z for which (x + y) + z is not equal to x + (y + z).

Let's write a simple C program to test for associativity, as shown in Listing 19-8.

three_floats.c

```
// Test the associativity of floats.

#include <stdio.h>

int main(void)
{
    float x, y, z, sum1, sum2;

    printf("Enter a number: ");
    scanf("%f", &x);
    printf("Enter a number: ");
    scanf("%f", &y);
    printf("Enter a number: ");
    scanf("%f", &z);

    sum1 = x + y;
    sum1 += z;        // sum1 = (x + y) + z
    sum2 = y + z;
    sum2 += x;        // sum2 = x + (y + z)

    if (sum1 == sum2)
        printf("%f is the same as %f\n", sum1, sum2);
    else
        printf("%f is not the same as %f\n", sum1, sum2);

    return 0;
}
```

Listing 19-8: A program to show that floating-point arithmetic is not associative

We'll start with some simple numbers:

```
$ ./three_floats
Enter a number: 1.0
Enter a number: 2.0
Enter a number: 3.0
6.000000 is the same as 6.000000
$ ./three_floats
Enter a number: 1.1
Enter a number: 1.2
Enter a number: 1.3
3.600000 is not the same as 3.600000
```

It appears that our program has a bug. Let's use gdb to see if we can figure out what's going on here. I set a breakpoint at the sum1 += z statement so we can view the contents of the five variables in this program, then I ran the program:

```
--snip--
(gdb) b 16
Breakpoint 1 at 0x83c: file three_floats.c, line 16.
(gdb) r
Starting program: /home/bob/three_floats/three_floats
Enter a number: 1.1
Enter a number: 1.2
Enter a number: 1.3

Breakpoint 1, main () at three_floats.c:16
16              sum1 += z;      // sum1 = (x + y) + z
```

Next, let's determine the addresses of the variables:

```
(gdb) p &x
$1 = (float *) 0x7fffffef94
(gdb) p &y
$2 = (float *) 0x7fffffef90
(gdb) p &z
$3 = (float *) 0x7fffffef8c
(gdb) p &sum1
$4 = (float *) 0x7fffffef9c
(gdb) p &sum2
$5 = (float *) 0x7fffffef98
```

The variables are stored in five consecutive 32-bit words beginning with z at 0x7fffffef8c. Let's look at these five values, both in floating-point format and in hexadecimal:

```
(gdb) x/5fw 0x7fffffef8c
0x7fffffef8c:   1.29999995    1.20000005    1.10000002    0
0x7fffffef9c:   2.30000019
(gdb) x/5xw 0x7fffffef8c
0x7fffffef8c:   0x3fa66666    0x3f99999a    0x3f8ccccd    0x00000000
0x7fffffef9c:   0x40133334
```

We'll work with the values in hexadecimal to determine what's going on here. Using the IEEE 754 format for single-precision floating point in Figure 19-2(c), we get the following addition:

$$
\begin{array}{rl}
x: & 1.00011001100110011001101 \\
y: & +\ \ 1.0011001100110011001101 \overline{0} \\
\hline
x+y: & 10.01001100110011001100111
\end{array}
$$

Since the format allows only 23 bits for the significand, the CPU will round off the sum to give the following number (remember the ties-to-even rule discussed on page 410):

sum1 :   10.0100110011001100110100

This is the number we saw stored in IEEE 754 format at the address of sum1 (0x7fffffef9c) in our gdb display earlier.

Now we'll execute the current instruction, which adds z to sum1, and look at its new value:

```
(gdb) n
17          sum2 = y + z;
(gdb) x/1fw 0x7fffffef9c
0x7fffffef9c:   3.60000014
(gdb) x/1xw 0x7fffffef9c
0x7fffffef9c:   0x40666667
```

The CPU has performed the following addition:

$$
\begin{array}{rl}
\text{sum1}: & 10.0100110011001100110100 \\
\text{z}: + & 1.0100110011001100110110 \\
\hline
\text{sum1 + z}: & 11.1001100110011001110110
\end{array}
$$

The CPU then rounds off sum1 to give a 23-bit significand:

sum1 :   11.10011001100110011001111

Now, we'll go though the same steps to compute sum2:

```
(gdb) n
18          sum2 += x;      // sum2 = x + (y + z)
(gdb) x/1fw 0x7fffffef98
0x7fffffef98:   2.5
(gdb) x/1xw 0x7fffffef98
0x7fffffef98:   0x40200000
```

The numbers here are the result of the following addition:

$$
\begin{array}{rl}
\text{y}: + & 1.0011001100110011001101 0 \\
\text{z}: + & 1.0100110011001100110011 0 \\
\hline
\text{y + z}: & 10.10000000000000000000000
\end{array}
$$

Rounding off gives:

sum2 :   10.10000000000000000000000

The current statement adds x:

```
(gdb) n
20          if (sum1 == sum2)
(gdb) x/1fw 0x7fffffef98
0x7fffffef98:   3.5999999
(gdb) x/1xw 0x7fffffef98
0x7fffffef98:   0x40666666
```

This performs the addition:

sum2 :	10.1000000000000000000000
x :	1.00011001100110011001101
sum2 + x :	11.10011001100110011001101

The CPU then rounds off sum2 to give a 23-bit significand (again, remember the ties-to-even rule):

sum2 :	11.10011001100110011001100110

Continuing the program to the end gives:

```
(gdb) c
Continuing.
3.600000 is not the same as 3.600000
[Inferior 1 (process 3107) exited normally]
```

The printf function has rounded off the display of sum1 and sum2 so they look equal, but looking inside the program with gdb shows that they are not equal. We conclude that the bug in our program is not in our logic but in our use of floating-point variables.

The difference between the two orders of adding the three floats is very small:

$$0.00000000000000000000001_2 = 3.6000001_{10} - 3.5999999_{10}$$
$$= 0.0000015_{10}$$

However, this small difference could become significant if this is part of a computation that involves multiplying by large numbers.

The main lesson to learn from this example is that floating-point arithmetic is seldom precise.

YOUR TURN

19.5   Modify the C program in Listing 19-8 to use doubles. Does this make floating-point addition associative?

Comments About Numerical Accuracy

Novice programmers often see floating-point numbers as real numbers and thus think they are more accurate than integers. It's true that using integers carries its own set of problems: even adding two large integers can cause overflow. Multiplying integers is even more likely to produce a result that will overflow. And you need to take into account that integer division results in two values, the quotient and the remainder, instead of the one value that floating-point division gives us.

But floating-point numbers are not real numbers. As you've seen in this chapter, floating-point representations extend the range of numerical values but have their own set of potential inaccuracies. Arithmetically accurate results require a thorough analysis of your algorithm. Here are some ideas to consider:

- Try to scale the data such that integer arithmetic can be used.

- Use `doubles` instead of `floats`. This improves accuracy and may actually increase the speed of execution. Most C and C++ library routines take `doubles` as arguments, so the compiler converts `floats` to `doubles` when passing them as arguments, as in the call to `printf` in Listing 19-7.

- Try to arrange the order of computations so that similarly sized numbers are added or subtracted.

- Avoid complex arithmetic statements that may obscure incorrect intermediate results.

- Choose test data that stresses your algorithm. If your program processes fractional values, include data that does not have an exact binary equivalent.

The good news is that with today's 64-bit computers, the range of integers is

$$-9{,}223{,}372{,}036{,}854{,}775{,}808 \le N \le +9{,}223{,}372{,}036{,}854{,}775{,}807$$

and there are libraries available in many programming languages that allow us to use arbitrary-precision arithmetic in our programs. You can find a list of these libraries at *https://en.wikipedia.org/wiki/List_of_arbitrary-precision_arithmetic_software*.

This section has provided an overview of the primary causes of numerical errors when using floating-point numbers. For a more rigorous treatment of the topic, David Goldberg's paper "What Every Computer Scientist Should Know About Floating-Point Arithmetic" (*ACM Computing Surveys*, Vol. 23, No. 1, March 1991) and *https://en.wikipedia.org/wiki/Floating-point_arithmetic* are good starting points. For an example of a programming technique to reduce rounding errors, you can read about the Kahan summation algorithm at *https://en.wikipedia.org/wiki/Kahan_summation_algorithm*.

What You've Learned

Binary representation of fractional values   Fractional values in binary are equal to sums of inverse powers of two.

Fixed point in binary   The binary point is assumed to be in a specific position in the binary representation of the number.

Floating-point numbers are not real numbers   The gap between adjacent floating-point numbers varies according to the exponent.

Floating-point is usually less accurate than fixed-point   Rounding errors are commonly obscured by floating-point format normalization and can accumulate through multiple computations.

IEEE 754   The most common standard for representing floating-point values in a computer program. The integer part is always 1. The exponent specifies the number of bits included in, or excluded from, the integer part.

SIMD and floating-point hardware   Floating-point instructions use a separate register file in the CPU.

So far in this book, I have discussed programs that follow a step-by-step order of execution of instructions. But in some instances, an instruction cannot do anything meaningful with its operands—for example, when we divide by 0. As you saw earlier in this chapter, this can trigger an exception to the intended order of program execution. We may also want to allow outside events, such as using the keyboard, to interrupt the ongoing program execution. After discussing input/output in Chapter 20, I'll cover interrupts and exceptions in Chapter 21.

20

INPUT/OUTPUT

The *I/O subsystem* is what programs use to communicate with the outside world, meaning devices other than the CPU and memory. Most programs read data from one or more input devices, process the data, and then write the results to one or more output devices.

Keyboards and mice are typical input devices; display screens and printers are typical output devices. Although most people don't think of them this way, devices such as magnetic disks, solid-state drives (SSDs), USB sticks, and so forth are also I/O devices.

I'll start this chapter by discussing some of the timing characteristics of I/O devices compared to memory, then I'll cover how this affects the interface between the CPU and I/O devices.

Timing Considerations

Since the CPU accesses memory and I/O devices over the same buses (see Figure 1-1 in Chapter 1), it might seem that a program could access I/O devices in the same way as it accesses memory. That is, you might expect that I/O can be performed by using the ldr and str instructions to transfer bytes of data between the CPU and a specific I/O device. This can be done with many devices, but some particularities must be taken into account to make it work correctly. One of the main issues lies in the timing differences between memory and I/O. Before tackling I/O timing, let's consider memory timing characteristics.

NOTE   *As I've pointed out, the three-bus description given in this book shows the logical interaction between the CPU and I/O devices. Most modern computers employ several types of buses. The way the CPU connects to the various buses is handled in hardware. A programmer generally deals only with the logical view.*

Memory Timing

An important characteristic of memory is that its timing is relatively uniform and not dependent on external events. This means memory timing can be handled by the hardware, so programmers don't need to be concerned about it; we can simply move data to and from memory using CPU instructions.

Two types of RAM are commonly used in computers:

SRAM   Holds its values as long as the power is on. It requires more components to do this, so it is more expensive and physically larger, but access times are very fast.

DRAM   Uses passive components that hold data values for only a few fractions of a second. DRAM includes circuitry that automatically refreshes the data values before the values are completely lost. It is less expensive than SRAM, but also 5 to 10 times slower.

Most of the memory on the Raspberry Pi is DRAM, because it is much less expensive and smaller than SRAM. As each instruction must be fetched from memory, slow memory access limits program execution speed.

Program execution speed is improved by using cache memory systems made from SRAM. The combination of SRAM cache with DRAM main memory works well to ensure minimal time delays when the CPU accesses memory.

It's worth noting here that CPU speeds are still faster than memory speeds (even SRAM). Accessing memory—fetching an instruction, loading data, storing data—is typically the most important factor that slows program execution. There are techniques for improving cache performance, which improves memory access times, but employing such techniques requires a thorough understanding of the CPU and memory configuration of the system you're using, which is beyond the scope of this book.

I/O Device Timing

Almost all I/O devices are much slower than memory. Consider a common input device, the keyboard. Typing at 120 words per minute is equivalent to entering approximately 10 characters per second, or a delay of ~100 ms between each character. A CPU running at 2 GHz can execute approximately

200 million instructions during that time. This is to say nothing of the fact that the time intervals between keystrokes are very inconsistent. Many will be much longer than this.

Even an SSD is slow compared to memory. For example, data can be transferred to and from a typical SSD at about 500MBps. The transfer rate for DDR4 memory (which is commonly used for main memory) is around 20GBps, some 40 times faster.

In addition to being much slower, I/O devices exhibit much more variance in their timing. Some people type very quickly on a keyboard, some very slowly. The required data on a magnetic disk might be just coming up to the read/write head, or it may have just passed by, in which case you'll have to wait for nearly a full revolution of the disk for it to come under the head again.

As pointed out at the beginning of Chapter 9, the Raspberry Pi uses a System on a Chip (SoC), which includes one or more processor cores and many of the controllers for other parts of the computer. Most SoCs based on the ARM architecture use the Advanced Microcontroller Bus Architecture (AMBA), first introduced by Arm in 1997. This architecture specifies several protocols, which are used to select the appropriate speeds for the communications between the CPU and other functional parts in the SoC. The details are beyond the scope of this book, but if you're interested in learning more about AMBA, a good starting point is the free online training videos at *https://www.arm.com/architecture/system-architectures/amba*.

The SoC includes controllers for most of the external I/O interfaces. All Raspberry Pis, except the Raspberry Pi Zero, have a second chip that provides additional external I/O interfaces. The I/O chip on a Raspberry Pi 1, 1+, 2, 3, or 3+ provides Ethernet and USB 2.0 ports, and it communicates with the SoC via USB 2.0. The I/O chip on a Raspberry Pi 4 provides USB 2.0 and USB 3.0 ports, and it communicates with the SoC via a PCI Express (PCI-E) bus.

The Raspberry Pi 5 uses a new I/O controller chip named *RP1* that incorporates most of the controllers for the external I/O interfaces that were previously on the SoC, including USB, MIPI camera and display, Ethernet, and general-purpose input/output (GPIO). Such a device is often called a *southbridge*. The RP1 communicates with the SoC via a PCI-E bus. Moving the slower I/O functionality to a separate chip simplifies the SoC, allowing it to run faster and to focus on computation-intensive tasks.

Next, I'll show you how we access the registers of an I/O device.

Accessing I/O Devices

The CPU works with an I/O device through a *device controller*, the hardware that does the actual work of controlling the I/O device. For example, a keyboard controller detects which key is pressed and converts this to a bit pattern that represents the key. It also detects whether modifier keys, such as SHIFT or CTRL, are pressed and sets the bit pattern accordingly.

The device controller interfaces with the CPU through a set of registers. In general, a device controller provides the following types of I/O registers:

Data   Used to send data to an output device or to read data from an input device

Status   Provides information about the current state of the device, including the controller itself

Control   Allows a program to send commands to the controller to change the settings of the device and the controller

It's common for a device controller interface to have more than one register of the same type, especially control registers and status registers.

Sending data to an output device is very much like storing data in memory: you store the data in a data register on the device controller. Where the output device differs from memory is the timing. As I've already said, a programmer doesn't need to be concerned about the timing when storing data in memory. However, an output device may not be ready to accept new data—it may be working on previously sent data. This is where the status register comes into play. The program needs to check the status register to see if the device controller is ready to accept new data.

Reading data from an input device is like loading data from memory into the CPU: you load the data from a data register on the device controller. Again, the difference from memory is that an input device may not have new data, so the program needs to check the status register of the input device controller to see if it does.

Most I/O devices also need to be told what to do by a control register. For example, after waiting for an output device controller to become ready for new data and then moving the data to a data register, some device controllers require that you tell them to output the data to the actual device. Or, if you want to get data from an input device, some device controllers require that you request them to get an input. You can send commands like these to a control register.

The CPU can access the I/O registers on a device controller in two ways: via memory-mapped I/O and port-mapped I/O. With *memory-mapped I/O*, a range of memory addresses is dedicated to the I/O ports, and each I/O register is mapped to one of the memory addresses in that range. Then, the load and store instructions are used to read from or write to the I/O registers on a device controller.

With *port-mapped I/O*, the I/O device controller registers are assigned addresses in a separate addressing space. The CPU uses special I/O instructions to communicate with the I/O registers.

The AArch64 architecture supports only memory-mapped I/O. The x86 architecture is an example of one that supports both types of I/O.

It'll be easier to understand memory-mapped I/O if we first look at how memory is managed by Linux and most other operating systems when executing a program. Programs run in a *virtual memory* address space, a technique that simulates a large memory with contiguous addressing from 0 to some maximum value. These are the addresses you see when using gdb—for example, the addresses in the sp and pc registers.

Although the AArch64 architecture allows 64-bit addressing, current CPU hardware implementations use only 52 bits for the address. This allows a maximum address of 2^{52} bytes (4 pebibytes) to execute programs in this virtual address space. But a Raspberry Pi has only 1 to 8GiB (or gibibytes) of *physical memory*, the actual RAM installed in the computer, and a program needs to be in physical memory to be executed.

NOTE *We commonly use the metric naming convention for specifying multiple-byte quantities that is based on powers of 10: kilobyte, megabyte, gigabyte, and so forth. The International Electrotechnical Commission (IEC) has also defined a naming convention that is based on powers of two: kibibyte, mebibyte, gibibyte, and so forth. For example, a kilobyte is 1,000 bytes, and a kibibyte is 1,024 bytes. You can read more about the naming conventions at https://en.wikipedia.org/wiki/Byte.*

The operating system manages the placement of programs in physical memory by dividing each program into *pages*. Raspberry Pi OS uses a 4KiB (or kibibyte) page size on most models and a 16KiB page size on the model 5. Physical memory is divided into the same size *page frames*. The page of the program that contains the code currently being executed by the CPU is loaded from the place where it's stored (for example, disk, DVD, USB stick) into a page frame of physical memory.

The operating system maintains a *page table* that shows where the page of the program is currently loaded in physical memory. Figure 20-1 shows the relationship between virtual memory and physical memory using the page table.

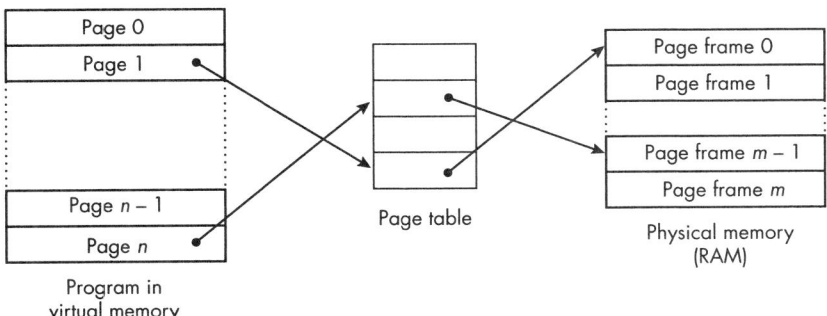

Figure 20-1: The relationship between virtual memory and physical memory

The SoC used on a Raspberry Pi includes a *memory management unit (MMU)*. When the CPU needs to access an item in memory, it uses the virtual address of the item. The MMU uses the virtual address as an index into the page table to locate the page in physical memory and, from there, the item. If the requested page is not currently loaded into physical memory, the MMU generates a *page fault exception*, which calls a function in the operating system to load the page into physical memory and enter its location in the page table. (You'll learn about exceptions in Chapter 21.)

The page table is stored in main memory, so using it requires two memory accesses: one to retrieve the frame number from the page table and another to access the location in main memory. To speed things up, the MMU includes a *translation lookaside buffer (TLB)* in its hardware. The TLB is a small amount of fast memory that contains the most recently used entries from the page table. Like the memory cache you learned about in Chapter 8, the TLB uses the tendency of a program to reference nearby memory addresses over a short period of time to speed up memory accesses. The MMU first looks in the TLB. If the page table entry is there, then only one access of main memory is required.

Similar to how virtual memory is mapped to physical memory, virtual memory addresses can be mapped to the I/O device controller register address space. Having the controller registers associated with virtual memory addresses allows us to use the CPU instructions that access memory to access the I/O device controller registers. One advantage of memory-mapped I/O is that you can usually write the I/O functions in a higher-level language such as C without using inline assembly language.

I/O Programming

Depending on the amount of data they process and the speed with which they process it, I/O devices use different techniques for communicating with the CPU. These differences are reflected in the way a device controller is programmed to perform its functions.

When timing is not important, we can simply use instructions to send a data item to an output device or read a data item from an input device at the point in our program where we wish to output or input it. This works for I/O devices that don't need time to process the binary data being transferred. You'll see an example of this technique later in this chapter, when we program an I/O device to output one of two voltage levels on a single output pin.

Most I/O device controllers require significant time to process input and output data. For example, when we press a key on the keyboard, the keyboard device controller needs to detect which key was pressed and then convert that knowledge into an 8-bit pattern that represents the character we pressed. If our program needs that character, we have to first check the status register of the keyboard device controller to determine if it has completed this process. If the device controller is in a ready state, then we can read data from the device controller.

We do this in our program using a *polling* algorithm. Polling typically involves a loop that iterates, checking the device's status register in each iteration of the loop, until the device is in a ready state. When the device controller is ready, we load the data into a general-purpose CPU register. When programmed I/O uses a polling algorithm, it's often called *polled I/O*.

Similarly, an output device controller might be busy outputting a previous data item. Our program needs to poll the device controller and wait until it's ready to accept new output data.

The downside of polled I/O is that the CPU can be tied up for a long time waiting for the device to become ready. This would probably be acceptable if the CPU were dedicated to running only one program on the system (for example, controlling a microwave oven), but it's not acceptable in the multiprogram environments of modern computing.

We could get more work out of the CPU if we could tell an I/O device to let us know when it was ready for data input or output and use the CPU for something else in the meantime. Many I/O devices include an *interrupt controller* for just this purpose: it can send an interrupt signal to the CPU when the device has completed an operation or is ready to take on another operation.

An interrupt from an external device causes the CPU to call an *interrupt handler*, a function within the operating system that deals with the input or output from the interrupting device. This is usually called *interrupt-driven I/O*. I'll discuss the features of a CPU that allow it to call interrupt handlers in Chapter 21.

In all of these techniques, the CPU initiates the transfer of data to or from the I/O device controller. We call this *programmed I/O*.

I/O devices that transfer large amounts of data at high speed often have the capability of *direct memory access (DMA)*. They have a *DMA controller* that can access main memory directly without the CPU. For example, when reading from a disk, the DMA controller accepts a memory address and a command to read data from the disk. When the DMA controller has read the data from the disk into its own buffer memory, it writes that data directly to main memory. When the DMA data transfer has completed, the controller sends an interrupt to the CPU, thus invoking the disk interrupt handler that notifies the operating system that the data is now available in memory.

Next, we'll look at an output that doesn't even need to be polled: a single pin that we can place at one of two voltages.

Programming a General-Purpose I/O Device

A *general-purpose I/O (GPIO)* is a signal line that can be configured to either input or output 1 bit. They were originally implemented in groups on an integrated circuit chip, with each I/O line of the GPIO circuitry connected to a pin on the chip. These days, GPIO circuits are typically included in SoC designs, where they can be used for lighting an LED, reading a switch, and so forth.

All Raspberry Pi models include GPIOs arranged in groups, still called chips. One of the chips has 28 lines that are connected to pins on a 40-pin *GPIO header* located on the top edge of the Raspberry Pi board that we can use to control external I/O devices. (The original Raspberry Pi 1 has a 26-pin GPIO header connected to 17 GPIO lines.)

In this section, I'll show you how to program a GPIO line to output a single bit that causes its corresponding GPIO header pin to alternate between 0.0 V and +3.3 V. We don't need to poll the GPIO line to see if it's ready for this 1-bit output, because it's always ready. We'll use these voltage alternations to blink an LED.

The correspondences between the 28 GPIO lines and the GPIO header pins for a 40-pin header are shown in Table 20-1.

Table 20-1: Correspondences Between GPIO Lines and Raspberry Pi Header Pins

Signal	Header pins		Signal
+3.3 V power	1	2	+5 V power
GPIO2	3	4	+5 V power
GPIO3	5	6	Ground
GPIO4	7	8	GPIO14
Ground	9	10	GPIO15
GPIO17	11	12	GPIO18
GPIO27	13	14	Ground
GPIO22	15	16	GPIO23
+3.3 V power	17	18	GPIO24
GPIO10	19	20	Ground
GPIO9	21	22	GPIO25
GPIO11	23	24	GPIO8
Ground	25	26	GPIO7
GPIO0	27	28	GPIO1
GPIO5	29	30	Ground
GPIO6	31	32	GPIO12
GPIO13	33	34	Ground
GPIO19	35	36	GPIO16
GPIO26	37	38	GPIO20
Ground	39	40	GPIO21

The pin numbering of the GPIO header assumes we are looking down at the top of the Raspberry Pi, with the header on the right. There are two rows of header pins, with the odd-numbered pins on the left and the even-numbered pins on the right. Notice that the GPIO lines are not in the same numerical order as the GPIO header pins.

You can also see this information online at *https://www.raspberrypi.com/documentation/computers/raspberry-pi.html#gpio-and-the-40-pin-header*, and on the Raspberry Pi the `pinout` command will give you the pin correspondence information.

Much of the Raspberry Pi documentation calls the signal from the GPIO device a GPIO pin. To avoid confusion, I'll use the names *GPIO line* for the signals and *GPIO header pin* for the physical connectors on the GPIO header. As you'll see later in this chapter, this naming convention is consistent with the `gpiod` library, which we'll use for programming the GPIO lines in C. We'll start by connecting our hardware circuit for blinking an LED.

Connecting the Blinking LED Circuit

To follow along with this project, you'll need an LED, a 220 Ω resistor, and several connecting jumper wires. Building the circuit on a breadboard is easier than just putting the components on a desktop or a workbench.

Before you connect anything to the GPIO header pins on your Raspberry Pi, you should shut it down and turn off the power. The pins are close together, and it's easy to accidentally short two of them together, which may damage your Raspberry Pi.

We'll use the circuit shown in Figure 20-2.

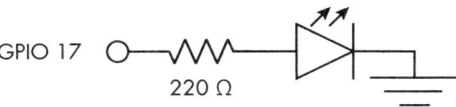

Figure 20-2: The circuit for a blinking LED

You saw the circuit symbol for a resistor in Figure 5-3 in Chapter 5. The triangle with two arrows above it is the circuit symbol for an LED, and the triangular-shaped group of three horizontal lines is the symbol for ground (0.0 V). Using the information in Table 20-1, we'll connect to GPIO17 using pin 11 on the GPIO header and connect to ground using header pin 9.

Make sure you connect the LED correctly. The left-hand side of the LED in this figure is the *anode* and the right-hand side is the *cathode*. The manufacturer of your LED should provide documentation showing which lead is which on the LED.

We'll write a program that alternates the voltage on the GPIO17 pin between +3.3 V and 0.0 V. At +3.3 V, current flows through the resistor and LED, causing the LED to turn on. The 220 Ω resistor is necessary to limit the amount of current flowing through it, as excessive current could destroy the LED. When our program switches the GPIO17 pin to 0.0 V, current no longer flows through the LED, turning it off.

Let's start with a C program to make sure our circuit is connected correctly.

Blinking an LED in C, All Models

Raspberry Pi OS comes with two libraries of functions that allow us to work with the GPIO in high-level languages. The pigpio library provides C and Python functions, and gpiozero provides a simple Python programming interface. You can read about them at *https://abyz.me.uk/rpi/pigpio/* and *https://gpiozero.readthedocs.io/en/stable/*, respectively.

As of this writing, the pigpio library does not work on the Raspberry Pi 5. I installed the gpiod package, which includes some useful command line tools for working with the GPIO. It also installs the libgpiod library, which is the officially supported interface to the GPIO. I have tested this library with C and Python programs on both my Raspberry Pi 3 and my Raspberry Pi 5.

I installed the command line and development tools with the following three commands:

```
$ sudo apt install gpiod
$ sudo apt install libgpiod-dev
$ sudo apt install libgpiod-doc
```

NOTE *At the time of writing, this installs version 1.6.3 of the library and tools. The developers have released version 2.1.1, but it's not yet in the Raspberry Pi OS repository. When the repository is updated, I expect additional utilities to be added, and some of the function names in the library may change. The source code for all versions is available at* https://git.kernel.org/pub/scm/libs/libgpiod/libgpiod.git.

The gpiod package installs six utility programs for working with the GPIO device: gpiodetect, gpiofind, gpioget, gpioinfo, gpiomon, and gpioset. The libgpiod-doc package installs the man pages for each of these utilities, and the libgpiod-dev package installs the interface to the functions in the libgpiod library we'll use to program the GPIO in C.

Other useful tools included with Raspberry Pi OS are pinout and pinctrl. The pinout program has a man page that describes its use. The pinctrl help command shows how to use pinctrl. I used pinctrl to help debug the programs to blink an LED that you'll see here.

We will use functions from the libgpiod library to write a program in C, which is shown in Listing 20-1, to blink an LED for testing the circuit in Figure 20-2. The documentation for our version of the library can be found at *https://www.lane-fu.com/linuxmirror/libgpiod/doc/html/index.html*. If you prefer to use Python, see "Your Turn" exercise 20.2 on page 460.

```c
blink_led.c    // Blink an LED.
               #include <stdio.h>
               #include <unistd.h>
               #include <gpiod.h>

               #define LINE 17        // GPIO line connected to LED
               #define OFF 0          // Pin at 0.0 V
               #define ON 1           // Pin at 3.3 V
               #define BLINKS 5       // Number of blinks
               #define SECONDS 3      // Time between blinks

               int main(void)
               {
               ❶ struct gpiod_chip *chip;
                 struct gpiod_line *line;
                 int i;
                 int error;
```

```
❷ chip = gpiod_chip_open("/dev/gpiochip0");   // On RPi 5 use /dev/gpiochip4
   if(!chip) {
       puts("Cannot open chip");
       return -1;
 }

   line = gpiod_chip_get_line(chip, LINE);
   if(line == NULL) {
       gpiod_chip_close(chip);
       puts("Cannot get GPIO line");
       return -1;
   }
   error = gpiod_line_request_output(line, "example", 0);
   if(error == -1) {
       gpiod_line_release(line);
       gpiod_chip_close(chip);
       puts("Cannot set GPIO output");
       return -1;
   }

   for (i = 0; i < BLINKS; i++) {
    ❸ gpiod_line_set_value(line, ON);
       printf("led on...\n");
       sleep(SECONDS);
       gpiod_line_set_value(line, OFF);
       printf("...led off\n");
       sleep(SECONDS);
   }
   gpiod_line_release(line);
   gpiod_chip_close(chip);

   return 0;
}
```

Listing 20-1: A C program to blink an LED using the GPIO

When compiling this file, we need to explicitly specify the libgpiod library at the end of the command, as shown here:

```
$ gcc -g -Wall -o blink_led blink_led.c -lgpiod
```

Both struct gpiod_chip and struct gpiod_line are declared in the *gpiod.h* header file ❶ as follows:

```
struct gpiod_chip;
struct gpiod_line;
```

This C syntax is a way to define the chip and line pointer variables as holding addresses.

The Raspberry Pi has several GPIO chips. GPIO chip 0 is connected to the GPIO header pins on models 3 and 4; GPIO chip 4 is connected to the GPIO header pins on the Raspberry Pi 5, so you if you're using that model you'll need to change gpiochip0 to gpiochip4 ❷.

Once the GPIO line is configured to be an output, we turn the bit on and off to blink the LED ❸.

Next, let's look at how we can use assembly language to blink the LED.

NOTE *The assembly language code we'll be using is not robust. It's intended to provide an overview of how I/O devices are programmed. If you want to use the GPIO to control external devices, I recommend using the functions in the libgpiod library. It's integrated with the operating system to provide robust functioning of the GPIO.*

Blinking an LED in Assembly Language, Models 3 and 4

The function of each GPIO device line is selected through six 32-bit registers, named GPFSEL0 through GPFSEL5. Three bits are used to select the function of a GPIO device line. Registers GPFSEL0 through GPFSEL4 each select the function of 10 lines, with 2 unused bits. The GPFSEL5 register on model 3 selects the functions of 4 lines, leaving 20 unused bits, and on model 4 the GPFSEL5 register selects the functions of 8 lines, leaving 8 unused bits.

I recommend downloading the datasheet for your Raspberry Pi—the Broadcom BCM2835 SoC datasheet at *https://datasheets.raspberrypi.com/bcm2835/bcm2835-peripherals.pdf* for the model 3 or the Broadcom BCM-2711 SoC datasheet at *https://datasheets.raspberrypi.com/bcm2711/bcm2711-peripherals.pdf* for the model 4—for reference while reading this section. It's not easy to read the datasheets, but going back and forth between the explanation here and the datasheet for your model should help you learn how to read it.

Note that I only tested this program on my Raspberry Pi 3. The datasheet for the Raspberry Pi 4 shows that the GPIO registers are the same as on the model 3, so this code should also work on a model 4.

Listing 20-2 shows our assembly language program to blink an LED.

---

blink_led.s

```
// Blink an LED connected to GPIO line 17 every three seconds.

// Define your RPi model: 0, 1, 2, 3, 4, 5
❶   .equ    RPI_MODEL, 3
// Useful constants
        .equ    N_BLINKS, 5                 // Number of times to blink
        .equ    DELTA_TIME, 3               // Seconds between blinks
        .equ    GPIO_LINE, 17               // Line number
// The following are defined in /usr/include/asm-generic/fcntl.h
// Note that the values are specified in octal.
        .equ    O_RDWR, 00000002            // Open for read/write
        .equ    O_SYNC, 04010000            // Complete writes in hardware
```

```
        // The following are defined in /usr/include/asm-generic/mman-common.h.
                .equ    PROT_READ, 0x1          // Page can be read
                .equ    PROT_WRITE, 0x2         // Page can be written
                .equ    MAP_SHARED, 0x01        // Share changes
        // Beginning address of peripherals
      ❷ .if     (RPI_MODEL == 0) || (RPI_MODEL == 1)
                .equ    PERIPHS, 0x20000000 >> 16 // RPi 0 or 1
           .elseif (RPI_MODEL == 2) || (RPI_MODEL == 3)
                .equ    PERIPHS, 0x3f000000 >> 16 // RPi 2 or 3
           .elseif RPI_MODEL == 4
                .equ    PERIPHS, 0x7e000000 >> 16 // RPi 4
           .else
                .equ    PERIPHS, 0x1f00000000 >> 16    // RPi 5
           .endif
        // Offset to GPIO registers
           .if     RPI_MODEL != 5
                .equ    GPIO_OFFSET, 0x200000       // Other RPi models
           .else
                .equ    GPIO_OFFSET, 0xd0000        // RPi 5
           .endif
        // Amount of memory to map and flags
                .equ    MEM_SIZE, 0x400000          // Enough to include all GPIO regs
      ❸ .equ    OPEN_FLAGS, O_RDWR | O_SYNC    // Open file flags
                .equ    PROT_RDWR, PROT_READ | PROT_WRITE    // Allow read and write
                .equ    NO_ADDR_PREF, 0             // Let OS choose address of mapping

        // Stack frame
                .equ    save1920, 16            // Save regs
                .equ    save21, 32
                .equ    FRAME, 48
        // Constant data
                .section .rodata
                .align  2
        dev_mem:
                .asciz  "/dev/mem"
        err_msg:
                .asciz  "Cannot map I/O memory.\n"
        on_msg:
                .asciz  "led on...\n"
        off_msg:
                .asciz  "...led off\n"

        // Code
                .text
                .align  2
                .global main
                .type   main, %function
```

```
main:
        stp     fp, lr, [sp, -FRAME]!    // Create stack frame
        mov     fp, sp                   // Set our frame pointer
        stp     x19, x20, [sp, save1920] // Save regs
        str     x21, [sp, save21]

// Open /dev/mem for read/write and syncing.
        mov     w1, OPEN_FLAGS & 0xffff   // Move 32-bit flags
        movk    w1, OPEN_FLAGS / 0x10000, lsl 16
        adr     x0, dev_mem              // I/O device memory
   ❹ bl       open
        cmp     w0, -1                   // Check for error
        b.eq    error_return             // End if error
        mov     w19, w0                  // /dev/mem file descriptor

// Map the GPIO registers to a main memory location so we can access them.
        movz    x5, PERIPHS & 0xffff, lsl 16
        movk    x5, PERIPHS / 0x10000, lsl 32
        mov     w4, w19                  // File descriptor
        mov     w3, MAP_SHARED           // Share with other processes
        mov     w2, PROT_RDWR            // Read/write this memory
        mov     w1, MEM_SIZE             // Amount of memory needed
        mov     w0, NO_ADDR_PREF         // Let kernel pick memory
   ❺ bl       mmap
        cmp     x0, -1                   // Check for error
        b.eq    error_return             // w0 also = -1, end function
        mov     x20, x0                  // Save mapped address
        mov     w0, w19                  // /dev/mem file descriptor
        bl      close                    // Close /dev/mem file

// Make the line an output.
        mov     x0, x20                  // Get mapped memory address
        add     x0, x0, GPIO_OFFSET      // Start of GPIO registers
        mov     w1, GPIO_LINE
   ❻ .if     RPI_MODEL != 5
        bl      gpio_line_to_output
     .else
        bl      gpio_5_line_to_output
     .endif
        mov     x21, x0                  // Pointer to register base

// Turn the line on and off.
        mov     x19, N_BLINKS            // Number of times to do it
loop:
        adr     x0, on_msg               // Tell user it's on
        bl      write_str
```

```
        mov     w1, GPIO_LINE           // GPIO line number
        mov     x0, x21                 // Pointer to register base
❼ .if    RPI_MODEL != 5
        bl      gpio_line_set           // Turn LED on
  .else
        bl      gpio_5_line_set         // Turn LED on
  .endif
        mov     w0, DELTA_TIME          // Wait
        bl      sleep

        adr     x0, off_msg             // Tell user it's off
        bl      write_str
        mov     w1, GPIO_LINE           // GPIO line number
        mov     x0, x21                 // Pointer to register base
❽ .if    RPI_MODEL != 5
        bl      gpio_line_clr           // Turn LED off
  .else
        bl      gpio_5_line_clr         // Turn LED off
  .endif
        mov     w0, DELTA_TIME          // Wait
        bl      sleep

        subs    x19, x19, 1             // Decrement loop counter
        b.gt    loop                    // Loop if > 0

        mov     x0, x20                 // Our mapped memory
        mov     w1, MEM_SIZE            // Amount we mapped for GPIO
❾ bl      munmap                        // Unmap it
        mov     w0, wzr                 // Return 0
error_return:
        ldr     x21, [sp, save21]       // Restore regs
        ldp     x19, x20, [sp, save1920]
        ldp     fp, lr, [sp], FRAME     // Delete stack frame
        ret
```

Listing 20-2: An assembly language program to blink an LED using the GPIO

The C program in Listing 20-1 uses library functions provided by the operating system to control the GPIO line. Our assembly language program in Listing 20-2 accesses the GPIO registers directly. The operating system only allows a user with root privileges to do that, so we need to run the program with sudo, like this:

```
$ sudo ./blink_led
```

Linux treats I/O devices as files. They are listed by name in the */dev* directory. The */dev/mem* file is an image of main memory. Addresses in this file represent physical memory addresses. Opening the file with the open system call function gives us access to the I/O device's physical memory ❹. Its man page gives us the prototype for the open function:

```
int open(const char *pathname, int flags);
```

The *pathname* is the full path and name of the file or device to be opened. The man page lists the names of the *flags* that must be passed to the open function to specify how it can be accessed by the calling function.

The numerical value of each flag can be found in the header file at */usr/include/asm-generic/fcntl.h*. The header file is written in C, so we can't use the .include directive to add it into our assembly language source code. I've used the .equ directive to define the flags we need in the open function. The assembler supports arithmetic and logic operations on literal values. We use the OR operator (|) to combine the different flags we need into a single 32-bit integer for the *flags* argument ❸.

The operating system prevents application programs from directly accessing the I/O memory address space. We need to tell the operating system to map the GPIO memory address space into the application memory address space so we can access the GPIO registers in our application.

The I/O peripheral address space begins at different places, depending on the Raspberry Pi model. The GNU assembler has directives that allow us to select which lines of code to include in the assembly. We use the .if directive together with a series of .elseif directives to select the value of PERIPHS according to the model we're using ❷. Using a .if directive with a .else directive selects the correct offset of the GPIO registers from the beginning address of the I/O peripherals. A single .equ directive sets RPI_MODEL to control these *conditional assembly* directives ❶. Don't forget to end each .if construct with a .endif directive.

We use the mmap system call function, specified in the POSIX standard, to map the GPIO registers into application memory ❺. Its man page gives us the prototype for the function:

```
void *mmap(void addr[.length], size_t length, int prot,
        int flags int fd, off_t offset);
```

If *addr* is 0, the operating system chooses the application memory address for the mapping. The *length* is the number of bytes we'll need for all the registers on the device. The mapping will use an integral number of pages. I've chosen 4MB to ensure we include all the I/O registers used for programming the GPIO in all the Raspberry Pi models.

The man page for mmap lists the *prot* values that must be passed to the function to specify how it can be accessed by the calling function. The man page also lists values for the *flags*, which specify how access is treated by the operating system.

The numerical value of each *prot* and *flag* can be found in the header file */usr/include/asm-generic/mman-common.h*. The header file is also written in C, so I have used .equ directives to define the *prot* and *flags* we need in this function.

After calling the open and mmap functions to make the GPIO registers accessible through application memory, we use the close function to release the file descriptor. The GPIO registers remain accessible to our application program.

Now that we can access the I/O registers on the GPIO through application memory addressing, we program our GPIO line to be an output. As you'll see in the next section, the method for doing this is different for the Raspberry Pi 5 ❻. After setting up the GPIO as an output, we enter a loop where we alternately turn the LED on and off. Again, a different method is used for the Raspberry Pi 5 ❼ ❽. We leave the LED in its on or off state for a few seconds using the sleep function from the unistd library.

Although the program will release the application memory we used for the GPIO registers when it ends, it's good practice to call the munmap function to release the memory in your program when it's no longer needed ❾.

Specifying a GPIO line as an output is done with the function shown in Listing 20-3.

gpio_line _to_output.s

```
// Make a GPIO line an output. Assume that GPIO registers
// have been mapped to application memory.
// Calling sequence:
//      x0 <- address of GPIO in mapped memory
//      w1 <- GPIO line number
//      Return address of GPIO.


// Useful constants
        .equ    FIELD_MASK, 0b111   // 3 bits
        .equ    OUTPUT, 1           // Use line for output


// Code
        .text
        .align  2
        .global gpio_line_to_output
        .type   gpio_line_to_output, %function
gpio_line_to_output:
// Determine register and location of line function field.
        mov     w3, 10              // 10 fields per GPFSEL register
❶ udiv     w4, w1, w3              // GPFSEL register number
❷ msub     w5, w4, w3, w1          // Relative FSEL number in register
// Compute address of GPFSEL register and line field in register.
❸ lsl      w4, w4, 2               // Offset to GPFSEL register
        add     x7, x0, x4          // GPFSELn memory address
        ldr     w4, [x7]            // GPFSELn register contents

❹ add      w5, w5, w5, lsl 1       // 3 X relative FSEL number
        mov     w6, FIELD_MASK      // FSEL line field
```

```
        lsl    w6, w6, w5          // Shift to relative FSEL bit position
❺ bic    w4, w4, w6          // Clear current FSEL

        mov    w2, OUTPUT          // Function = output
❻ lsl    w2, w2, w5          // Shift function code to FSEL position
        orr    w4, w4, w2          // Insert function code
        str    w4, [x7]            // Update GPFSEL register

        ret
```

Listing 20-3: Making a GPIO line an output in most Raspberry Pi models

The GPIO has six 32-bit function-select registers, GPFSEL0 through GPFSEL5. Each of these registers is divided into 10 3-bit fields, named FSELn, where $n = 0, 1, \ldots, 57$. Bits 2 through 0 in GPFSEL0 are the FSEL0 field, bits 5 through 3 are the FSEL1 field, and so forth up to bits 23 through 21 in GPFSEL5 for the FSEL57 field. Bits 31 and 30 in GPFSEL0 through GPFSEL4 and bits 31 through 24 in GPFSEL5 are unused. All the lines can be configured as an input, 000, or an output, 001. Some lines can be configured to have other functionalities; FSELn specifies the functionality of GPIO line n.

Dividing the GPIO line number by 10 gives us the number of the GPFSEL register ❶. The remainder from this division gives us the number of the FSEL field in the register ❷. For example, our program uses GPIO line 17, and its function is controlled by the seventh FSEL field in the GPFSEL1 register.

The GPFSEL registers are located at the beginning of the GPIO memory, so multiplying the GPFSEL register number by 4 gives us the memory address offset of the register ❸. Each FSEL field is 3 bits, so we multiply the FSEL number by 3 to get the relative bit position in the GPFSEL register ❹.

We need to make sure we don't change any of the other FSEL fields in the GPFSEL register. After loading a copy of the GPFSEL register into a CPU register, we use a 3-bit mask to clear our FSEL field with the bic instruction ❺:

bic—Bit clear

bic *wd, ws1, ws2*{, *shft amnt*} performs a bitwise AND between *ws1* and *ws2*, optionally shifted *amnt* bits before the AND, storing the result in *wd*. The *shft* can be lsl, lsr, 0 to 31. The default is no shift.

bic *xd, xs1, xs2*{, *shft amnt*} performs a bitwise AND between *xs1* and *xs2*, optionally shifted *amnt* bits before the AND, storing the result in *xd*. The *shft* can be lsl, lsr, asr, or ror. The *amnt* can be 0 to 63. The default is no shift.

Next, we shift our function code to the FSEL field position in the GPFSEL register, use the orr instruction to insert the function code, and update the mapped GPIO memory ❻.

NOTE *Although we have mapped the GPIO registers into application memory addresses, we can't directly examine the contents of these registers with gdb because it uses a different technique for accessing memory addresses than the mmap function. I'll show you another way to examine the register contents in gdb in "Your Turn" exercise 20.3 on page 460.*

Now that we have set up the GPIO line as a 1-bit output device, we can control the voltage it outputs. The line is always ready for us to change the voltage, so we don't need to check its status. We'll use the gpio_line_set function in Listing 20-4 to set the line, which places it at +3.3 V.

gpio_line_set.s
```
// Set a GPIO line. Assume that GPIO registers
// have been mapped to application memory.
// Calling sequence:
//      x0 <- address of GPIO in mapped memory
//      w1 <- line number

// Constants
 ❶ .equ    GPSET0, 0x1c     // GPSET register offset

// Code
        .text
        .align  2
        .global gpio_line_set
        .type   gpio_line_set, %function
gpio_line_set:
        add     x0, x0, GPSET0  // Address of GPSET0 register
        mov     w2, 1           // Need a 1
 ❷ lsl     w2, w2, w1      // Move to specified bit position
        str     w2, [x0]        // Output

        ret
```

Listing 20-4: Setting a GPIO line in most Raspberry Pi models

The GPIO has two 32-bit output-set registers, GPSET0 and GPSET1. The GPSET0 register is located 0x1c bytes from the beginning of GPIO memory ❶. The GPSET1 register immediately follows at 0x20. Bits 31 through 0 in GPSET0 control lines 31 through 0, and bits 21 through 0 in GPSET1 control lines 53 through 32. The GPIO header pins are connected only to GPIO lines 27 through 0, so this function only works with GPSET0.

The GPSET registers are write-only. Unlike the GPFSEL registers, we don't load the contents of a GPSET register; we simply shift a 1 to the bit position corresponding to the line we're using as an output and set the line with a str instruction, placing +3.3 V on the line ❷. Writing a 0 to a bit position has no effect.

When we want to change the output of the line to 0.0 V, we clear the line, as shown in Listing 20-5.

gpio_line_clr.s

```
// Clear GPIO line. Assume that GPIO registers
// have been mapped to application memory.
// Calling sequence:
//        x0 <- address of GPIO in mapped memory
//        w1 <- line number

// Constants
❶ .equ      GPCLR0, 0x28     // GPCLR register offset

// Code
        .text
        .align  2
        .global gpio_line_clr
        .type   gpio_line_clr, %function
gpio_line_clr:
        add     x0, x0, GPCLR0  // Address of GPCLR0 register
        mov     w2, 1           // Need a 1
        lsl     w2, w2, w1      // Move to specified bit position
        str     w2, [x0]        // Output

        ret
```

Listing 20-5: Clearing a GPIO line in most Raspberry Pi models

Like the set registers, the GPIO has two 32-bit output-clear registers, GPCLR0 and GPCLR1. GPCLR0 is located 12 bytes beyond GPSET0 ❶. They are programmed the same way as the GPSET registers, except that storing a 1 in a bit position corresponding to a line that is selected as an output clears the line, placing 0.0 V on the line.

Next, we'll look at blinking an LED on a Raspberry Pi 5, which uses a very different programming interface to the GPIO.

Blinking an LED in Assembly Language, Model 5

The main function in Listing 20-2 is designed to work for the Raspberry Pi 5 if you simply change the RPI_MODEL to 5. The conditional assembly directives will then select the appropriate values and function calls. But the methods for controlling the GPIO are different. Let's see how it's done on the Raspberry Pi 5.

The GPIO circuitry on the Raspberry Pi 5 is on the RP1 chip. The documentation is incomplete as of this writing, but a preliminary draft of *RP1 Peripherals* (November 2023) is available at *https://datasheets.raspberrypi.com/rp1/rp1-peripherals.pdf*.

Setting a GPIO line to be an output on a Raspberry Pi 5 is different from on the other models. Listing 20-6 shows our function to do this.

```
gpio_5_line   // Make a GPIO line an output. Assume that GPIO registers
_to_output.s  // have been mapped to application memory.
              // Calling sequence:
              //       x0 <- address of GPIO in mapped memory
              //       w1 <- GPIO line number
              //       Return address of RIOBase.

              // Constants
                      .equ    RIOBase, 0x10000  // Offset to RIO registers
                      .equ    PADBase, 0x20000  // Offset to PAD registers
                      .equ    SYS_RIO, 5        // Use RIO to control GPIO
                      .equ    PAD_AMPS, 0x10    // 4 mA
                      .equ    RIO_SET, 0x2000   // Set reg offset
                      .equ    RIO_OE, 0x04      // Output enable

              // Code
                      .text
                      .align  2
                      .global gpio_5_line_to_output
                      .type   gpio_5_line_to_output, %function
              gpio_5_line_to_output:
❶ lsl       x2, x1, 3        // 8 x line number
   add       x3, x0, x2       // GPIO_line_number_STATUS
   mov       w2, SYS_RIO      // System registered I/O
❷ str       w2, [x3, 4]      // GPIO_line_number_CTRL

   add       x2, x0, PADBase
   add       x2, x2, 4        // Skip over VOLTAGE_SELECT reg
   lsl       x3, x1, 2        // 4 x line number
   add       x3, x3, x2       // Pad reg address of line number
   mov       w4, PAD_AMPS     // 4 mA
❸ str       w4, [x3]         // Set pad amps

   add       x0, x0, RIOBase
   mov       w2, 1            // A bit
   lsl       w2, w2, w1       // Shift to line location
   add       x3, x0, RIO_SET  // Use RIO set register
❹ str       w2, [x3, RIO_OE] // Make line an output

   ret
```

Listing 20-6: A function to make a GPIO line an output on the Raspberry Pi 5

The Raspberry Pi 5 GPIO device has 28 pairs of registers, which are called GPIO0_STATUS, GPIO0_CTRL, GPIO1_STATUS, GPIO1_CTRL, through GPIO27_STATUS, and GPIO27_CTRL. The address offset of the GPIOn_CTRL register corresponding to GPIO line n is $8 \times n$ ❶. Bits 4 through 0 set the function.

RP1 provides a set of *registered I/O (RIO)* registers to control the GPIO lines. To use the RIO interface, we store the SYS_RIO function in the GPIO control register ❷.

The output circuit of a GPIO line is called a *pad*. We can set the characteristics of the output pad in several ways—for example, to either 2, 4, 8, or 12 mA. We set it to 4 mA for blinking an LED ❸. We complete our setup of the GPIO line by making it an output device ❹.

Now that we have set up the GPIO line as a 1-bit output device, we can control the voltage that it outputs. The RIO interface to the GPIO has four registers for controlling the lines. Table 20-2 shows the offset of each register from the RIO base.

Table 20-2: RIO Register Offsets

Offset	Action
0x0000	Normal read/write
0x1000	XOR on write
0x2000	Bitmask set on write
0x3000	Bitmask clear on write

Bit n in each register corresponds to the GPIOn line. Storing a word to one of these registers causes the action to be taken on the GPIO line(s). Bitmask set or clear means that only the bits that are 1 act on the corresponding GPIO lines. A 0 in a bit position has no effect on the corresponding GPIO line. The separate set and clear registers mean that we don't need to read the contents of a register, make our changes, and write the result back.

A GPIO line configured for output is always ready for us to change the voltage, so we don't need to check its status. We'll use the gpio_5_line_set function in Listing 20-7 to set the line, which places it at +3.3 V.

gpio_5_line_set.s

```
// Set GPIO line. Assume that GPIO registers
// have been mapped to programming memory.
// Calling sequence:
//      x0 <- address of RIOBase in mapped memory
//      w1 <- line number

// Constants
❶ .equ    RIO_SET, 0x2000     // Set reg

// Code
        .text
        .align  2
```

```
            .global gpio_5_line_set
            .type   gpio_5_line_set, %function
    gpio_5_line_set:
            mov     w2, 1              // A bit
        ❷ lsl     w2, w2, w1         // Shift to line location
            add     x0, x0, RIO_SET    // Address of RIO set reg
            str     w2, [x0]           // Line low
            ret
```

Listing 20-7: A function to set a GPIO line on the Raspberry Pi 5

We move a 1 to the bit position corresponding to our line number ❷. Then, we store this word in the RIO set register, which places the GPIO line at the high voltage ❶.

The algorithm to clear a line is the same as the one to set it, as shown in Listing 20-8.

gpio_5_line_clr.s
```
// Clear a GPIO line. Assume that GPIO registers
// have been mapped to programming memory.
// Calling sequence:
//      x0 <- address of RIOBase in mapped memory
//      w1 <- line number

// Constants
    ❶ .equ     RIO_CLR, 0x3000     // Clear reg

// Code
        .text
        .align  2
        .global gpio_5_line_clr
        .type   gpio_5_line_clr, %function
gpio_5_line_clr:
        mov     w2, 1              // A bit
        lsl     w2, w2, w1         // Shift to line location
        add     x0, x0, RIO_CLR    // Address of RIO clear reg
        str     w2, [x0]           // Line low
        ret
```

Listing 20-8: A function to clear a GPIO line on the Raspberry Pi 5

The only difference in the gpio_line_clr function is that we use the RIO clear register to place the GPIO line at the low voltage ❶.

Blinking an LED is a very simple example of performing output. We don't have to check to see if the line is ready for us to turn it on or off; we just send a command to the device. Most I/O isn't this simple. It takes some time to form an image to display on a screen, or to convert a keystroke on a keyboard to a bit pattern.

In the next section, I'll give you a general overview of how our program code deals with these timing issues.

Polled I/O Programming Algorithms

Let's look at some simple polling algorithms that show how we might program a *universal asynchronous receiver/transmitter (UART)* for I/O.

When used as an output device, a UART performs parallel-to-serial conversion to transmit a byte of data 1 bit at a time. As an input device, a UART receives the bits one at a time and performs serial-to-parallel conversion to reassemble the byte that was sent to it. Thus, an 8-bit byte can be transmitted and received using only three wires: transmit, receive, and common. Both the transmitting and receiving UARTs must be set at the same bit rate.

In the idle state, the transmitting UART places the high voltage on the transmission line. When a program outputs a byte to the UART, the transmitting UART first sends a *start bit*; it does this by placing the transmission line at the low voltage for the amount of time it takes to transmit one bit, corresponding to the agreed-upon bit rate.

After the start bit, the transmitter sends the data bits at the agreed-upon bit rate. The UART uses a shift register to shift the byte 1 bit at a time, setting the voltage on the output line accordingly. Most UARTs start with the low-order bit. When the entire byte has been sent, the UART returns the output line to the idle state for at least 1 bit time, thus sending at least one *stop bit*.

Figure 20-3 shows how a UART with typical settings would send the two characters *m* and *n* encoded in ASCII.

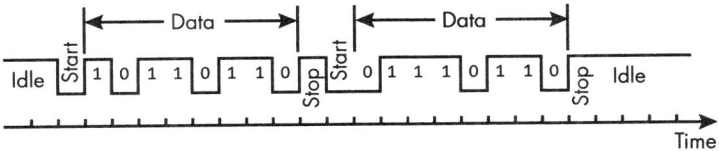

Figure 20-3: A UART output to send the characters m and n

The receiving UART watches the transmission line, looking for a start bit. When it detects a start bit, it uses a shift register to reassemble the individual bits into a byte, which it provides to the receiving program as input.

We'll use the 16550 UART, a common type, for our programming example. The 16550 UART has 13 8-bit registers, shown in Table 20-3.

Table 20-3: The Registers of the 16550 UART

Name	Address	DLAB	Purpose
RHR	000	0	Receiver holding (input byte)
THR	000	0	Transmitter holding (output byte)
IER	001	0	Interrupt enable (set type of interrupt)
ISR	010	x	Interrupt status (show type of interrupt)
FCR	010	x	FIFO control (set FIFO parameters)
LCR	011	x	Line control (set communications format)
MCR	100	x	Modem control (set interface with modem)
LSR	101	x	Line status (show status of data transfers)
MSR	110	0	Modem status (show status of modem)
SCR	111	x	Scratch
DLL	000	1	Divisor latch (low-order byte)
DLM	001	1	Divisor latch (high-order byte)
PSD	101	1	Prescaler division

The addresses in Table 20-3 are address offsets from the UART's base address. You probably noticed that some of the registers have the same offset. The functionality of the register at that offset depends on how our program treats it. For example, if the program loads from offset 000, it's loading from the receiver holding register (RHR). But if the program stores to offset 000, it's storing to the transmitter holding register (THR).

The divisor latch access bit (DLAB) is bit number 7 in the line control register (LCR). When it is set to 1, offset 000 connects to the low-order byte of the 16-bit divisor latch value and offset 001 connects to the high-order byte of the divisor latch value.

The 16550 UART can be programmed for interrupt-driven I/O and direct memory access. It includes 16-byte first in, first out (FIFO) buffers on both the transmitter and the receiver registers. It can also be programmed to control a serial modem.

Older PCs typically connected the UART to a COM port. In past years, COM ports were often used to connect devices such as printers and modems to computers, but most PCs today use USB ports for serial I/O.

The Raspberry Pi has a 16550-like UART with the receiver and transmitter registers connected to GPIO lines. Programming the UART is beyond the scope of this book, but I'll use C to give a general idea of how it's done.

Note that the C functions we'll write in this section are meant only to show the concepts, not to do anything useful. In fact, running them will elicit an error message from the operating system.

I'll assume the UART is installed in a computer that uses memory-mapped I/O so I can show the algorithms in C. To keep things simple, I'll do only polled I/O here, which requires these three functions:

UART_init   Initializes the UART. This includes setting parameters in the hardware, such as the speed and communications protocol.

UART_in   Reads one character that was received by the UART.

UART_out   Writes one character to be transmitted by the UART.

These three functions would allow us to use a UART to receive a character and then transmit that same character, as shown in Listing 20-9.

UART_echo.c
```
// Use a UART to echo a single character.
// WARNING: This code does not run on any known device. It is
// meant to sketch some general I/O concepts only.

#include "UART_functions.h"
#define UART0 (unsigned char *)0xfe200040   // Address of UART

int UART_echo(void)
{
    unsigned char character;

    UART_init(UART0);
    character = UART_in(UART0);
    UART_out(UART0, character);

    return 0;
}
```

Listing 20-9: A function to use a UART to read and write a single character

We'll explore only a few features of the UART. Let's start with a file that provides symbolic names for the registers and some numbers we'll be using in our example program, as shown in Listing 20-10.

UART_def.h
```
// Definitions for a 16550 UART.
// WARNING: This code does not run on any known device. It is
// meant to sketch some general I/O concepts only.
```

```
#ifndef UART_DEFS_H
#define UART_DEFS_H

// Register offsets
#define RHR 0x00     // Receive holding register
#define THR 0x00     // Transmit holding register
#define IER 0x01     // Interrupt enable register
#define FCR 0x02     // FIFO control register
#define LCR 0x03     // Line control register
#define LSR 0x05     // Line status register
#define DLL 0x00     // Divisor latch LSB
#define DLM 0x01     // Divisor latch MSB

// Status bits
#define RxRDY 0x01   // Receiver ready
#define TxRDY 0x20   // Transmitter ready

// Commands
#define NO_FIFO       0x00  // Don't use FIFO
#define NO_INTERRUPT  0x00  // Polling mode
#define MSB_38400     0x00  // 2 bytes used to
#define LSB_38400     0x03  //    set baud 38400
#define N_BITS        0x03  // 8 bits
#define STOP_BIT      0x00  // 1 stop bit
#define NO_PARITY     0x00
❶ #define SET_COM      N_BITS | STOP_BIT | NO_PARITY
❷ #define SET_BAUD     0x80 | SET_COM
#endif
```

Listing 20-10: The definitions for a 16550 UART

The offsets to the registers are at fixed positions relative to the start of the mapped memory address of the UART. These offsets, and the status and control bit settings, are taken from a 16550 datasheet, which you can download at *https://www.ti.com/product/TL16C550D*.

Let's look at how I arrived at the value for the SETCOM control ❶. The communication parameters are set by writing 1 byte to the line status register. There can be 5 to 8 bits in each data frame. The datasheet tells us that setting bits 1 and 0 to 11 will specify 8 bits. Hence, I set NBITS to 0x03. Setting bit 2 to 0 specifies one stop bit, so STOPBIT = 0x00. I don't use parity, which is bit 3, so NOPARITY = 0x00. I combine these constants with the OR operator to create the byte that sets the communication parameters. Of course, we don't really need the two zero values, but specifying them makes our intent explicit.

The unit *baud* is a measure of the speed of communication, defined as the number of symbols per second. A UART uses only two voltage levels for communication, symbolically 0 or 1, or 1 bit. For a UART, the baud rate is equivalent to the number of bits transmitted or received per second. We need to set the DLAB bit to 1 to place our UART in the mode that allows us to set the baud rate ❷.

Next, we need a header file for declaring the functions, as shown in Listing 20-11.

UART_functions.h
```
// Initialize, read, and write functions for an abstract UART.
// WARNING: This code does not run on any known device. It is
// meant to sketch some general I/O concepts only.


#ifndef UART_FUNCTIONS_H
#define UART_FUNCTIONS_H
void UART_init(unsigned char* UART);                     // Initialize UART
unsigned char UART_in(unsigned char* UART);              // Input
void UART_out(unsigned char* UART, unsigned char c);  // Output
#endif
```

Listing 20-11: The UART function declarations

The header file declares the three basic functions for using our UART. I won't cover the more advanced features of a UART in this book.

We'll place the definitions of these three functions in one file, as shown in Listing 20-12, because they would typically be used together.

UART_functions.c
```
// Initialize, read, and write functions for a 16550 UART.
// WARNING: This code does not run on any known device. It is
// meant to sketch some general I/O concepts only.

#include "UART_defs.h"
#include "UART_functions.h"

// UART_init initializes the UART and enables it.
void UART_init(unsigned char* UART)
{
    unsigned char* port = UART;

    *(port+IER) = NO_INTERRUPT;   // No interrupts
    *(port+FCR) = NO_FIFO;        // No FIFO
    *(port+LCR) = SET_BAUD;       // Set frequency mode
    *(port+DLM) = MSB_38400;      // Set to 38400 baud
    *(port+DLL) = LSB_38400;      // 2 regs to set
    *(port+LCR) = SET_COM;        // Communications mode
}

// UART_in waits until the UART has a character and then reads it.
unsigned char UART_in(unsigned char* UART)
{
    unsigned char* port = UART;
    unsigned char character;
```

```
❶ while ((*(port+LSR) & RxRDY) != 0) {
    }
    character = *(port+RHR);
    return character;
}

// UART_out waits until the UART is ready and then writes a character.
void UART_out(unsigned char* UART, unsigned char character)
{
    unsigned char* port = UART;

❷ while ((*(port+LSR) & TxRDY) != 0) {
    }
    *(port+THR) = character;
}
```

Listing 20-12: The UART memory-mapped I/O function definitions in C

The UART_init function sets the various communication parameters for the UART. The purposes of the values I used in this example are explained after Listing 20-10.

The UART_in function waits in a while loop until the RxRDY bit becomes 1, which occurs when the UART has a character ready to read from its receive holding register ❶. The character is read from the receive holding register with an assignment to a local variable.

The UART_out function waits in a while loop until the TxRDY bit becomes 1, which occurs when the UART is ready for us to send a character to the transmit holding register ❷. The character is sent with an assignment to the transmit holding register.

These functions provide an overall view of how a UART is used in a polling mode. I've omitted many details here that are required to ensure robust operation. If you would like to use one of the UARTs on a Raspberry Pi, you can start with the documentation at *https://www.raspberrypi.com/ documentation/computers/raspberry-pi.html#gpio-and-the-40-pin-header*. I recommend accessing the UART through the operating system instead of directly, as we did when blinking an LED earlier in this chapter. I have not used the UARTs on a Raspberry Pi, so I can't vouch for any of them, but tutorials are available online.

What You've Learned

Virtual memory   The memory address space used by a program.

Memory mapping unit (MMU)   A hardware device that uses a map table to convert virtual memory addresses to physical memory addresses.

Translation lookaside buffer (TLB)   Memory in the MMU where the most recently used map table entries are cached.

Memory timing   Memory access is synchronized with the timing of the CPU.

I/O timing   I/O devices are much slower than the CPU and have a wide range of characteristics, so we need to program their access.

Bus timing   Buses are often arranged in a hierarchical manner to better match the differences in timing between various I/O devices.

Port-mapped I/O   With this technique, I/O device registers have their own address space.

Memory-mapped I/O   With this technique, I/O registers are given a portion of the main memory address space.

Programmed I/O   The program transfers data directly from an input device or to an output device at the point where it's needed.

Polled I/O   The program waits in a loop until the I/O device is ready to transfer data.

Interrupt-driven I/O   The I/O device interrupts the CPU when it is ready to transfer data.

Direct memory access   The I/O device can transfer data to and from main memory without using the CPU.

General-purpose I/O (GPIO)   A general-purpose I/O device can be programmed to input or output a single bit of information.

In the next chapter, you'll learn about the CPU features that allow it to maintain control over the I/O hardware and prevent application programs from accessing the hardware without going through the operating system.

21

EXCEPTIONS AND INTERRUPTS

Thus far, we've viewed each application as having exclusive use of the computer. But like most operating systems, Raspberry Pi OS allows multiple applications to run concurrently. It manages the hardware in an interleaved fashion, providing each application, and the operating system itself, with the use of the hardware components it needs at any given time.

There are two issues here. First, for the operating system to carry out its management tasks, it needs to maintain control over the interaction between applications and hardware. It does this by using a system of privilege levels in the CPU that allows the operating system to control a gateway between itself and the applications.

Second, we saw in Chapter 20 that most I/O devices can interrupt the ongoing activity of the CPU when they are ready to provide input or to accept output. The CPU has a mechanism to direct I/O interruptions through this gateway and invoke functions that are under the control of the operating system, thus allowing the operating system to maintain its control over the I/O devices.

In this chapter, I'll start by discussing how the CPU uses privilege levels to enforce its control over the hardware. Then I'll cover what sorts of events can cause a change in the privilege level and how the CPU reacts to such events. I'll end the chapter with a discussion of an instruction that allows applications to traverse the gateway between application and system software to directly call utility functions in the operating system.

A full treatment of this material would require a detailed understanding of the internal structure of the operating system and how to program the specific hardware you're using, which is beyond the scope of this book. The goal here is to provide you with a very general overview.

Application vs. System Software

Software can generally be classified as application software or system software. We use *application software* for most of what we do on a computer, while *system software* manages usage of hardware resources, providing controlled access to the hardware by application software.

The split between system and application software is maintained by a system of *privilege levels*. The operating system executes at a *privileged* level, allowing it to manage most of the hardware resources. Application programs execute at an *unprivileged* level to prevent them from directly accessing much of the hardware. The operating system, being privileged, acts as a supervisor over the use of the computer resources by applications.

This separation of privileges allows the operating system to manage the resources needed to execute several application programs concurrently. For example, we could be running a media application to play music while using an editor application to edit a source file. While waiting for us to press another key, the operating system lets the media application use the CPU. When we press the key, the operating system pauses the media application long enough to read the keystroke and then passes control back to the media application while waiting for the very slow (in CPU time) human to press the next key.

An *exception* is an event that causes the currently executing code stream to be suspended and CPU control to be passed to software running at a privileged level. An *interrupt* is a type of exception event that comes from a device connected to the CPU. Before discussing what can cause an exception and what takes place when one occurs, let's look at the privilege levels.

NOTE *Although the general concepts are the same, the terminology varies, so you need to be mindful when reading the respective manuals. For example, ARM uses* exception *as the more general term, with an* interrupt *being a type of exception. Intel, on the other hand, uses* interrupt *as the more general term, with an* exception *being a type of interrupt.*

Privilege and Exception Levels

The operating system uses *exception levels* in the CPU to enforce privilege levels for the currently executing software. At any given time, the CPU is running at one of four possible exception levels. Table 21-1 shows the levels, from least privileged to most.

Table 21-1: The AArch64 Exception Levels

Level	Usage
EL0	Application programs
EL1	Operating system
EL2	Hypervisor
EL3	Firmware/secure monitor

Application programs execute with the CPU set at the lowest exception level, EL0. The operating system executes at exception level EL1.

A *hypervisor* allows us to run multiple operating systems concurrently on the same computer by coordinating their interactions with the hardware resources. A hypervisor executes at exception level EL2, giving it supervisorial control over the operating systems.

Firmware provides low-level control of device hardware. It's stored in read-only memory and is executed at the highest exception level, EL3. When the Raspberry Pi is first booted up, the CPU starts at EL3 so that it has access to all the hardware.

The AArch64 architecture defines a *secure state* and a *non-secure state*. All the hardware can be accessed in the secure state, while access is limited in the non-secure state. Switching between the two states is controlled by a *secure monitor*, which is software that can be executed only when the exception level is at EL3.

In Chapter 20, you learned that the memory management unit (MMU) uses a page table to map virtual memory addresses to physical memory addresses. The entry in the page table for each virtual memory range includes a 2-bit *access permissions (AP)* field for that memory range. Table 21-2 shows what these permissions are at each CPU exception level.

Table 21-2: The AArch64 Memory Access Permission Levels

AP	EL0 (unprivileged)	EL1/2/3 (privileged)
00	No access	Read/write
01	Read/write	Read/write
10	No access	Read only
11	Read only	Read only

Application programs execute with their instructions and read-only data loaded into virtual memory that has its access permission set to 11. If they have any global variables, those are loaded into virtual memory with access permission set to 01.

The operating system's instructions and read-only data are loaded into virtual memory that has its access permission set to 10, and its global variables exist in virtual memory with access permission set to 00.

You saw an example of dealing with these memory access permissions when programming the GPIO device in Listing 20-2 in Chapter 20. The operating system maps a range of its privileged virtual memory address space to the hardware addresses of the GPIO device registers. We used the mmap system call function to map unprivileged memory in our application program to the operating system's GPIO addressing space so that our application program could access it.

In addition to exception level, the Armv8-A processor has two execution states, AArch32 and AArch64, as discussed in the introduction to Chapter 9. The operating system sets the execution state when it first starts up.

Exceptions provide a way to change the execution state. When an exception takes the CPU to a higher exception level, we can tell the processor to stay at the same execution state or transition to AArch64. When returning from an exception to a lower exception level, we can tell the processor to stay at the same execution state or transition to AArch32. This allows us to run 32-bit applications under our 64-bit Raspberry Pi OS but prevents us from running 64-bit applications under a 32-bit version of Raspberry Pi OS.

In the next sections, you'll see how exceptions allow the use of privileged software.

Exception Events

There are several kinds of events that can cause an exception. One of the most common causes is when an application program (unprivileged) needs a service provided by the operating system (privileged).

An example is when we call the write system call function to display text on the screen. As illustrated in Figure 2-1 in Chapter 2, the write function communicates directly with the operating system, which in turn sends the characters to the screen. It does this with an svc instruction, which causes an exception to occur. You'll see how to use svc later in this chapter.

An exception caused by the svc instruction is a *synchronous exception*, which is when the timing is synchronized with that of the CPU. Other causes of synchronous exceptions include an attempt to execute an instruction that is not valid at the current exception level, an attempt to access a memory address that is out of the range of the current exception level, and a debugger inserting a breakpoint in a program.

An *asynchronous exception* is not related to the timing of the CPU. Asynchronous exceptions, also called *interrupts*, typically come from an I/O device.

An example of an asynchronous exception is when we use the read system call function to get characters from the keyboard. As you saw in Figure 2-1, the read function also communicates directly with the operating system. However, when the read function requests characters from the keyboard, the operating system has no idea when the next key will be pressed.

The operating system notifies the keyboard device controller that it's waiting for a character and places the currently running program in a waiting state. If there's another program ready to run, the operating system gives CPU control to that program. When a user finally presses a key on the keyboard, the keyboard device controller sends an interrupt signal to the CPU, which causes an exception. When the CPU finishes executing the current instruction, it processes the interrupting exception, which typically places the waiting program in a ready state.

Exception processing is done by a piece of code called an *exception handler*. The CPU responds to an exception by executing the handler code. Let's look at how the CPU does this.

CPU Response to an Exception

The processor includes a set of *system registers* that hold the configuration settings for the processor. These include registers that hold data needed for responding to and handling exceptions. Some of the system registers used for exceptions are shown in Table 21-3.

Table 21-3: Some of the System Registers for Handling Exceptions

Name	Register	Usage
currentel	Current exception level	Bits 3 and 2 hold the exception level (00 for EL0, 01 for EL1, 10 for EL2, 11 for EL3)
elr	Exception link	Address of instruction that caused the exception
esr	Exception syndrome	Information about the reasons for the exception
far	Fault address	Address of access that caused the fault
hcr	Hypervisor configuration	Virtualization settings related to EL2
scr	Secure configuration	Secure state settings related to EL3
sctlr	System control	Information about the system
spsr	Saved program status	PSTATE when exception was taken to this exception level
vbar	Vector base address	Exception base address for exception taken to this exception level

These registers are accessible only from software running at a privileged level. There is only one currentel register. The hcr register exists at EL2 and the scr register at EL3. The other system registers in this table have instances at levels EL1, EL2, and EL3.

The current exception level of the CPU is determined by bits 3 and 2 in currentel. The other 62 bits are reserved for possible future use. The content can be loaded into a general-purpose register with the mrs *xd*, currentel instruction executed at a privileged level:

mrs—Move system register

mrs *xd, systemreg* copies the content of a system register, *systemreg*, into *xd*. Valid only at exception levels EL1 and higher.

There is also an msr instruction for storing content in some system registers, but not the currentel register. The content of the 2-bit exception level field in the currentel register can be changed only by an exception.

The exception level can be increased only by an exception event, which can either increase the level or keep it the same, except for an exception event at EL0, which can only increase the level. The only way to decrease the exception level is with the eret instruction, which will either decrease the level or keep it the same:

eret—Exception return

> eret restores PSTATE from the spsr register for the current exception level and loads the address in the elr register for the current exception level into pc.

PSTATE is an abstraction for the bit settings of the system registers that define the current processor state. For example, bits 3 and 2 of the currentel register are included in PSTATE. The condition flags in the nzcv register listed in Table 9-2 in Chapter 9 are also included in PSTATE.

In response to an exception, the CPU performs an operation that is similar to the bl instruction, but there are some significant differences. The most obvious difference is that we specify the address in our program code that the bl instruction branches to, but an exception causes a branch to a block of code in an *exception vector table*.

An exception vector table has 16 entries, arranged in groups of 4, as shown in Table 21-4.

Table 21-4: The Entries in an Exception Vector Table

Offset	Type	Conditions
0x000	Synchronous	From current EL while using EL0's SP
0x080	IRQ	
0x100	FIQ	
0x180	SError	
0x200	Synchronous	From current EL while using current level's SP
0x280	IRQ	
0x300	FIQ	
0x380	SError	
0x400	Synchronous	From lower EL, next lower EL using AArch64
0x480	IRQ	
0x500	FIQ	
0x580	SError	
0x600	Synchronous	From lower EL, next lower EL using AArch32
0x680	IRQ	
0x700	FIQ	
0x780	SError	

Exception levels EL1, EL2, and EL3 each have their own copies of the 2KiB exception vector table shown here. Each of the 16 entries contains the code that handles the type and conditions of the exception corresponding to that entry. The length of each entry, 128 bytes, allows for up to 32 instructions for the exception handler. If more than 32 instructions are needed to handle an exception, a function outside the table can be called from the table entry program code.

Each exception vector table is created when the operating system first starts up. The address of each table is stored in the vector base address register, vbar, for its respective exception level. An exception causes a branch to the first instruction at the beginning of one of these entries, depending on the type of exception and the conditions when the exception occurred.

A synchronous exception comes from the CPU, as covered in the previous section. Of the three types of asynchronous exceptions, an *IRQ* is an interrupt request that usually comes from an I/O device controller. In previous versions of the ARM architecture, an *FIQ* was a fast interrupt request that also came from an I/O device controller but that had a higher priority than an IRQ. Starting with the Armv8-A architecture, an FIQ has the same priority as an IRQ; it simply provides another path for interrupts. How the two paths are used is dependent on the implementation of the architecture.

An *SError* is a system error meant to signal an unexpected event in the memory system. The events that cause an SError exception also vary based on the implementation.

The entry selected for each type of exception is dependent on whether the exception comes from the same exception level or from a lower level. If it's from the current exception level, the selection depends on whether the stack pointer at EL0 or at the current exception level is being used.

If the exception comes from a lower exception level, the entry selected depends on whether the exception level immediately below the level you're going to is executing in AArch32 or AArch64. For example, you might have a 32-bit virtual machine running alongside a 64-bit operating system. Applications in the 32-bit virtual machine run at EL0, and their 32-bit operating system runs at EL1. An exception occurring while in the AArch32 mode that goes to the hypervisor at EL2 would go to one of the entries in the fourth group in Table 21-4. All the handlers in this group would be from the 32-bit virtual machine's operating system. The exception handler in the appropriate entry would execute within the 32-bit operating system.

The CPU's response to an exception is based on the assumption that we want to return to the place where the execution stream was interrupted by the exception and to continue with the CPU in the same state it was in before the exception occurred.

When responding to an exception, the CPU does the following:

1. Saves the contents of PSTATE in the spsr register of the exception level it's going to

2. Stores the address of the last completed instruction in the elr register

3. For synchronous and system error exceptions, writes the cause to the esr register of the exception level it's going to

4. For address-related synchronous exceptions, writes the cause to the far register of the exception level it's going to

5. Updates PSTATE to the new exception level

6. Loads into pc the address of the appropriate entry in the exception vector table

It's the responsibility of the exception handler to save and restore any general-purpose registers it uses. There is a separate stack pointer register at each exception level, so separate stacks can be set up at each level. When executing at EL1, EL2, or EL3, either the stack pointer at the current level or the stack pointer at EL0 can be used.

After the exception handler has restored any saved general-purpose registers, it uses the eret instruction to restore PSTATE to where it was and to return to the place where the exception occurred. PSTATE includes the 2-bit exception level in the currentel register, so this operation also returns the CPU to the exception level it came from.

Writing an exception handler is an advanced topic beyond the scope of this book, but in the next section you'll see how you can use an exception to call on the services of the operating system.

Supervisor Calls

The operating system, being privileged, acts as a supervisor over the resources of the computer. When an unprivileged application program needs to use privileged resources, it calls upon the operating system using a *supervisor call*.

In Listing 13-3 in Chapter 13, we used the write system call function to write Hello, World! on the screen one character at a time. The write function is a C wrapper for a supervisor call. The program in Listing 21-1 is called *freestanding* because it doesn't use any C library functions. Instead, we're using a supervisor call directly when we need the services of the operating system.

hello_world.s
```
// Write Hello, World! using a system call.
        .arch armv8-a
// Useful names
        .equ    NUL, 0
        .equ    STDOUT, 1
   ❶ .equ    WRITE, 0x40
        .equ    EXIT, 0x5d
// Stack frame
        .equ    save19, 16
        .equ    FRAME, 32
// Constant data
        .section  .rodata
```

```
message:
        .string "Hello, World!\n"
// Code
        .text
        .align  2
        .global my_hello
        .type   my_hello, %function
❷ my_hello:
        adr     x1, message     // Address of message
loop:
        ldrb    w3, [x1]        // Load character
        cmp     w3, NUL         // End of string?
        b.eq    done            // Yes
        mov     x2, 1           // No, one char
        mov     x0, STDOUT      // Write on screen
        mov     x8, WRITE
    ❸ svc     0               // Tell OS to do it
        add     x1, x1, 1       // Increment pointer
        b       loop            //   and continue
done:
        mov     w0, wzr         // Return value
    ❹ mov     x8, EXIT        // Terminate this process
        svc     0
```

Listing 21-1: The Hello, World! freestanding program

The gcc compiler assumes we are using the C hosted environment and requires that the first function be named main. Since we're not using the C libraries, we don't need to use the C hosted environment and can give our function any name we wish ❷. After assembling this function, we go directly to the loader and tell it where to start execution of the function with the -e option:

```
$ ld -e my_hello -o hello_world hello_world.o
```

When we need the operating system to output a character, we use the svc instruction ❸:

svc—Supervisor call

svc *imm* causes an exception to be taken from exception level EL0 to EL1. It stores 0x15 in bits 31 through 26 and *imm*, a 16-bit unsigned integer, in bits 15 through 0 of the esr register.

Exception level EL1 is handled in the operating system. The svc handler uses the integer in the x8 register to determine what action it should take. The number for the write operation is 0x40 ❶. The other arguments to the write operation in the operating system are the same as those to the C library write function. The argument to the svc instruction, *imm*, is not used in Linux.

Our `my_hello` function was launched directly by the operating system as a new process, not called from the C hosted environment. We terminate this process with another supervisor call ❹.

Notice that we do not need to create a stack frame or save any registers in this freestanding program. The exception handler for `svc` will restore the state of the general-purpose registers when it returns. Because this program doesn't return to the C hosted environment, we don't need to save the `sp` and `fp` registers.

The numbers for the operating system operations, the arguments to the operations, and the registers that these are all passed in are listed at *https:// www.chromium.org/chromium-os/developer-library/reference/linux-constants/ syscalls/*. There are four tables on this site: x86_64 (64-bit), arm (32-bit), arm64 (64-bit), and x86 (32-bit). Make sure you use the arm64 table with this book.

Table 21-5 lists some common `svc` codes.

Table 21-5: Some Register Contents for the svc Call

Operation	x8	x0	x1	x2
read	0x3f	File descriptor	Address of character(s)	Number of characters
write	0x40	File descriptor	Address of character(s)	Number of characters
exit	0x5d	Error code	—	—

For completeness, here are the instructions that cause an exception to be taken to the hypervisor, `hvc`, and to the secure monitor, `smc`:

hvc—Hypervisor call

`hvc` *imm* causes an exception to be taken from exception level EL1 to EL2. It stores `0x16` in bits 31 through 26 and *imm*, a 16-bit unsigned integer, in bits 15 through 0 of the `esr` register.

smc—Secure monitor call

`smc` *imm* causes an exception to be taken from exception level EL1 or EL2 to EL3. It stores `0x17` in bits 31 through 26 and *imm*, a 16-bit unsigned integer, in bits 15 through 0 of the `esr` register.

Further details of the exception processing mechanism in the AArch64 architecture are complex and beyond the scope of this book. A good next step is reading *Learn the Architecture–AArch64 Exception Model*, available at *https://developer.arm.com/documentation/102412/0103*.

YOUR TURN

21.1 Pick a program you've written in assembly language. Add the instruction `mrs x0, currentel` in a place where you know it will be executed. Your program should still assemble and link fine, but what happens when you run the program?

21.2 Modify the three functions write_char, write_str, and read_str in "Your Turn" exercise 14.4 on page 293 so that they use the svc instruction instead of calling the C write and read functions.

21.3 What is the supervisor call number for the mmap operation we used in Listing 20-2 in Chapter 20?

What You've Learned

Privilege levels   The operating system maintains its privilege over the hardware resources by tagging memory addresses and running applications with the CPU set at a lower exception level.

Exception levels   The CPU runs software at one of four exception levels: from least to most privileged, EL0, EL1, EL2, or EL3.

Exception   An interruption in the currently executing code stream that causes CPU control to be passed to software running at a privileged level (EL1–EL3).

Interrupt   Other hardware devices can interrupt the regular execution cycle of the CPU and trigger an exception.

svc   The instruction that causes an exception in AArch64.

Exception handler   A function in the operating system that gets called by the CPU when an exception or interrupt occurs.

Exception vector table   An array of exception handlers.

Freestanding program   A program that does not use the C library functions.

This has been a brief overview of exceptions and interrupts. The details are complex and require a thorough knowledge of the specific model of CPU you're working with.

This concludes my introduction to computer organization. I hope it has provided you with the tools you need to further pursue any of the topics that interest you.

INDEX

logic circuit, 107
    combinational, 107
    sequential, 107, 127
        designing, 140–149
logic instructions, 327
    immediate data in, 329
    shift register values in, 329
loop control variable, 246
looping, 246–255
Lospinoso, Josh, 387, 400

M

machine code, viewing, 228
machine instruction, xxi, 2
magnetic field, 93
main function, 26, 207
    in assembly language, 222–224
    minimum in C, 188
main memory, 153–154, 162
    organization, 153
man page, 5
mask, 324
mass storage, 152–153
    block size, 153
maxterm, 64
Mealy state machine, 128
mebibyte, 441
memory, 2, 151. *See also* cache memory;
        main memory
    access permission levels, 469
    addresses, 17
    addressing, 163
    addressing modes, 213–214
    cost, 152
    data storage in, 17–22
    hardware, 156–164
    hierarchy, 151
    layers, 152
    memory management, 440
    offline, 152
    page, 441
    page table, 441, 469
    physical, 441
    program characteristics in, 302–303
    random access, 17
        dynamic, 162–164
        static, 161
    read-only, 17
    read/write, 160–161

segments, 192
    speed, 152
    timing, 438
    virtual, 440
    volatile, 153
memory management unit. *See* MMU
metal-oxide-semiconductor field-effect
        transistor. *See* MOSFET
minterm, 63
MMU, 441
    page fault exception, 441
    TLB, 442
Moore state machine, 128, 130
MOSFET, 97–100
    channel, 97
    drain, 97
    gate, 97
    N-channel, 98
    P-channel, 99
    power consumption, 100
    source, 97
    switching time, 100
most significant digit, 13
multiplexer (MUX), 117–119, 160
multiplication, 340
    in assembly language, 344–348
    in C, 340–344
    by powers of two, 340
    using shift and add, 344
MUX (multiplexer), 117–119, 160

N

name decoration, 299, 392
name mangling, 299
negation, 46
newline character (\n), 21
nonvolatile memory (NVM), 17
not a number (NaN), 422
numerical accuracy, 434
nzcv register, 174

O

object, 387
    attribute, 387
    class, 388
    creating, 390–392
    instance, 387
    instantiation, 388, 390
    message, 387

V

variable
  automatic local, 192, 224, 279, 292–299
  declaration in C, 270
  definition in C, 27, 270
  global, 192, 271–276, 293–299
  local, 215–216, 270
  name scope in C, 270
  static local, 192, 293–302
very large scale integration (VLSI), 139
virtual memory, 440
  page, 441
volt, 86
von Neumann, John, 153
von Neumann architecture, 153
von Neumann bottleneck, 154

W

watt, 95
"What Every Computer Scientist Should Know About Floating-Point Arithmetic" (Goldberg), 434
while loop, 247–252
  compared to do-while and for, 254

Y

"Your Turn" exercises, how to use, xxv–xxvi

Z

zero register, 174

RESOURCES

Visit *https://nostarch.com/introcomputerorgforarm* for errata and more information.

More no-nonsense books from **NO STARCH PRESS**

INTRODUCTION TO COMPUTER ORGANIZATION

An Under the Hood Look at Hardware and x86-64 Assembly

BY ROBERT G. PLANTZ
502 PP., $59.99
ISBN 978-1-7185-0009-9

THE LINUX COMMAND LINE, 2ND EDITION

A Complete Introduction

BY WILLIAM SHOTTS
504 PP., $39.95
ISBN 978-1-59327-952-3

C++ CRASH COURSE

A Fast-Paced Introduction

BY JOSH LOSPINOSO
792 PP., $59.99
ISBN 978-1-59327-888-5

EFFECTIVE C, 2ND EDITION

An Introduction to Professional C Programming

BY ROBERT C. SEACORD
312 PP., $59.99
ISBN 978-1-7185-0412-7

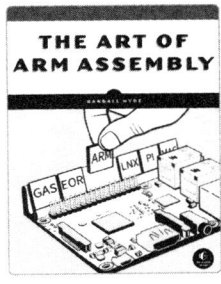

THE ART OF ARM ASSEMBLY

BY RANDALL HYDE
1,064 PP., $89.99
ISBN 978-1-7185-0282-6

COMPUTER ARCHITECTURE

From the Stone Age to the Quantum Age

BY CHARLES FOX
560 PP., $59.99
ISBN 978-1-7185-0286-4

PHONE:
800.420.7240 OR
415.863.9900

EMAIL:
SALES@NOSTARCH.COM

WEB:
WWW.NOSTARCH.COM

Never before has the world relied so heavily on the Internet to stay connected and informed. That makes the Electronic Frontier Foundation's mission—to ensure that technology supports freedom, justice, and innovation for all people—more urgent than ever.

For over 30 years, EFF has fought for tech users through activism, in the courts, and by developing software to overcome obstacles to your privacy, security, and free expression. This dedication empowers all of us through darkness. With your help we can navigate toward a brighter digital future.

ELECTRONIC FRONTIER FOUNDATION **EFF**